Conversations with Arthur Miller

Literary Conversations Series

Peggy Whitman Prenshaw
General Editor

Conversations
with Arthur Miller

Edited by
Matthew C. Roudané

University Press of Mississippi
Jackson and London

Copyright © 1987 by the University Press of Mississippi
All rights reserved
Manufactured in the United States of America
91 90 89 88   4 3 2 1

The paper in this book meets the guidelines for permanence and durability of the
Committee on Production Guidelines for Book Longevity of the Council on Library
Resources.

British Library Cataloguing-in-Publication Data is available.

Library of Congress Cataloging-in-Publication Data
Miller, Arthur, 1915-
    Conversations with Arthur Miller / edited by Matthew C. Roudané.
        p.   cm. — (Literary conversations series)
    Bibliography: p.
    Includes index.
    ISBN 0-87805-322-0 (alk. paper).   ISBN 0-87805-323-9 (pbk. : alk.
paper)
    1. Miller, Arthur, 1915-   —Interviews.   2. Dramatists.
American—20th century—Interviews.   I. Roudané, Matthew Charles.
1953-   II. Title.   III. Series.
PS3525.I5156Z463 1987
812'.52—dc19   87-17931
                                                                          CIP

Works by Arthur Miller

The Man Who Had All the Luck, in Edwin Seaver (ed.), *Cross-Section: A Collection of New American Writing* New York: Fischer, 1944.

Situation Normal New York: Reynal & Hitchcock, 1944.

Focus New York: Reynal & Hitchcock, 1945; Harmondsworth: Penguin, 1978.

All My Sons New York: Reynal & Hitchcock, 1947, and Viking: 1957; Harmondsworth: Penguin, 1961 [with *A View from the Bridge*].

Death of a Salesman New York: Viking, 1949, and Bantam, 1951; Harmondsworth: Penguin, 1961 and in Gerald Weales (ed.), Viking Critical Library Edition New York: Viking, 1967; Harmondsworth: Penguin, 1977.

An Enemy of the People, adaptation New York: Viking, 1951; Harmondsworth: Penguin, 1977.

The Crucible; New York: Viking, 1953; Harmondsworth: Penguin, 1968 and in Gerald Weales (ed.), Viking Critical Library Edition New York: Viking, 1971; Harmondsworth: Penguin, 1977.

A View from the Bridge, one-act version; New York: Viking, 1955 and in *Theatre Arts,* XL (Sep. 1956); two-act version; London: Cresset, 1957; New York: Compass, 1960 and Bantam, 1961; Harmondsworth: Penguin, 1961 [with *All My Sons*].

Memory of Two Mondays; New York: Viking, 1955 [with *A View from the Bridge*].

Arthur Miller's Collected Plays New York: Viking, 1957; London: Cresset, 1958, and Secker & Warburg, 1974. Contains an introduction by the author and *All My Sons, Death of a Salesman, The Crucible, A Memory of Two Mondays,* and *A View from the Bridge.*

The Misfits New York: Viking, 1961; Harmondsworth: Penguin, 1961.

After the Fall New York: Viking, 1964, and Bantam, 1965; Harmondsworth: Penguin, 1968; New York: Bantam, 1974 [television adaptation].

Incident at Vichy New York: Viking, 1965, and Bantam, 1967.

I Don't Need You Any More New York: Viking; London: Secker & Warburg; Harmondsworth: Penguin, 1967.

The Price New York: Viking, 1968; Harmondsworth: Penguin, 1970.

In Russia (with Inge Morath) New York: Viking, 1969.

The Portable Arthur Miller, Harold Clurman (ed.) New York: Viking, 1971.

The Creation of the World and Other Business; New York: Viking, 1973.

In the Country (with Inge Morath) New York: Viking, 1977.

The Theater Essays of Arthur Miller, Robert A. Martin (ed.) New York: Viking, 1978.

Chinese Encounters (with Inge Morath) New York: Farrar, Straus, Giroux, 1979.

Playing for Time; New York: Bantam, 1981.

Some Kind of Love Story; New York: Dramatists Play Service, 1982.

Elegy for a Lady; New York: Dramatists Play Service, 1982.

"Salesman" in Beijing; New York: Viking, 1983.

Danger: Memory! London: Methuen, 1986.

Contents

Introduction

Arthur Miller clearly enjoys militantly civil conversation. Perhaps the most remarkable feature of Miller in interview is his willingness to answer question after question with grace and substance, with a sense of social commitment and metaphysical curiosity. Although some interviewers ask the inane or the predictable—questions that seem geared toward evoking certain preconceived responses, questions that hardly break new ground in Miller scholarship, inquiries that the playwright has answered graciously for over forty years, comments that reveal the interviewer's lack of anything but the most superficial knowledge of the playwright's works—Miller still relishes good conversation.

Miller possesses an easygoing demeanor, an unpretentious manner that invites communication. Born in New York City in 1915, Miller stands 6′ 3″ and remains trim. He radiates understated confidence. Walking briskly down the New York City streets during our first meeting, he never stopped talking, using his long arms to emphasize ideas. Today Miller has a benevolent grandfatherly presence. Despite his outward graciousness, however, Miller presents strongly opinionated arguments. His remarks are often analytically rigorous, his observations carefully formulated with little wasted emotion. He usually carefully revises transcriptions of the interviews, clarifying, expanding his initial responses without the limitations of off-the-cuff remarks. One evening, I remember, my phone rang: it was Miller apologizing for taking so long to rework our interview; soon after a carefully revised—and enhanced—manuscript arrived, Miller's penciled in revisions noticeable throughout. As all skilled interviewers know, the process of revision is an indispensable step for elevating the conversation into a more adequate account of the author's views. If a degree of spontaneity is lost, the clarity and coherence the interview gains is measurable. The writer's voice comes into sharper focus.

Although not all the interviews in *Conversations with Arthur Miller* have been revised by Miller, one can identify those that have been: they tend to be more informative, more revealing of the psyche and devotion behind the writing.

Miller on Miller thus becomes much more than an informal talk within his home in Roxbury, Connecticut, or apartment in New York City. Miller's interviews complement the plays and his more formal and well-known theater essays (collected in Robert A. Martin's *The Theater Essays of Arthur Miller),* revealing his dramatic and aesthetic theories, his concern with language and structure, his awareness of the inner reality of his characters and how, when he is at his best, these concerns broaden to highlight universal social and metaphysical issues. Miller in conversation provides a unique insight into both the dramatic works and the man (and his *daemon)* behind those works.

Miller's first Broadway play, *The Man Who Had All the Luck* (1944), hardly sparked interest in the Miller interview.[1] " 'They [the reviewers] came down on me like a ton of bricks for that one," Miller remarked in 1947. "It was faulty, all right. It couldn't have succeeded because it was not a resolved play.' "[2] In 1972, responding to the question of what if his subsequent play, *All My Sons* (1947) had failed, Miller said, " 'I don't know. . . . I probably would have gone on anyway. But maybe not. . . .' "[3] The success of *All My Sons,* however, generated enough critical and popular interest to establish him as a significant new voice in the American theater. Of course, Miller would have to wait another two years before his name would become known on a global scale with a play that surely exceeded his own expectations. On 10 February 1949, the night *Death of a Salesman* made its epochal premiere at the Morosco Theatre in New York City, Miller suddenly became a major dramatist, a young writer whose work would eventually establish him, with Eugene O'Neill, Tennessee Williams, and Edward Albee, as one of the most influential American dramatists ever. After *Death of a Salesman,* the Miller interview has always received the attention of scholars, students, and the theatergoing public. Admittedly Miller's later plays—*The Creation of the World and Other Business* (1972), *The Archbishop's Ceiling* (1977), *The American Clock* (1980), *Elegy for a Lady* (1982), *Some Kind of Love Story* (1982)—do not match the resonance of the earlier works—from *All My Sons* and *After the Fall* (1964) to *The Price* (1968). Still, Miller commands a major national and international audience.

Undoubtedly his much-publicized marriage to Marilyn Monroe (from 1956-1960) only added to Miller's notoriety. Even today, as Miller enters what seems to be the twilight of his career, he deflects questions about his personal life. He particularly avoids discussion of Monroe, and disagrees with those who think that Maggie in *After the Fall* is modeled after Monroe, despite a script that invites the connection. But he welcomes discussion of his plays and the state of the theater. As the following interviews suggest, Miller's public reputation lies with the plays themselves, works that transcend local history and geographical place while exploring those very historical factors and national locales that are wedded to twentieth-century American culture. The private experience of the common person defines, for Miller, the public issues of a nation and, finally, of human existence itself. Audiences today discover new dimensions to a Miller play. The father-son relationship in *Death of a Salesman*, for example, especially since Dustin Hoffman played Willy in the 1983–84 Broadway revival, has evolved into a new psychodynamic: audiences today seem to focus more fully on Biff, Miller told me, whereas in the 1940s and 1950s the audience tended to focus much more on Willy. "No other American writer," C. W. E. Bigsby argues, "has so successfully touched a nerve of national consciousness. But Miller is claimed with equal avidity by the international community. *The Crucible* was seen by the Chinese as immediately relevant to a Cultural Revolution in which youth had exacted its revenge on an adult world. *Death of a Salesman* has been hailed in countries where the profession itself is unknown."[4]

The title of this book suggests its emphasis and purpose: to present what to my mind stand as the best Miller interviews since his emergence as a dramatist in the late 1940s. I have included several selections from such publications as *The New York Times* and *The Saturday Evening Post,* particularly selected early pieces filled with useful biographical sketches. On the other hand, I have largely avoided the hundreds of newspaper features on Miller; most provide little substantive information or only brief excerpts from Miller himself. I have devoted much of the book to those conversations that, through provocative questions asked by interviewers exhibiting a disinterested interest in the playwright's work, highlight Miller on Miller. Not surprisingly, the better conversations are those in which the playwright, not the questioner, takes over. All thirty-nine interviews within *Conversations with Arthur Miller* have been left unedited (except on one or two occasions wherein I have clearly noted any minor changes) and are arranged chronologically according to the dates they appeared in print.

Four decades of talk from the same writer inevitably begets repetition. As Charlie in *Death of a Salesman* might say, "it goes with the territory." In keeping with the editorial policies of the Literary Conversations series, I have made no attempt to omit interviews that seem to repeat preceding conversations. Yet such repetition provides readers with a fascinating chronicle of Miller's growth as an artist, from the early days as a struggling new writer to his status today as an elder statesman for the American theater. Above all Miller in conversation provides a clear record of his aesthetic preoccupations. Although each interview in the following pages contains its own unique set of responses, collectively they form patterns. Ever engaged with the personal and the public function of drama, Miller continually discusses the puckish role of tragedy and fate and their influence on what Miller calls "the common man." Miller outlines his firm belief in the talismanic powers of the theater to objectify the sweep and play of a culture thinking in front of itself. The interviews also suggest that, more than any of his American counterparts—Eugene O'Neill, Tennessee Williams, Lillian Hellman, Edward Albee, Sam Shepard, David Mamet—Miller demonstrates a sharp awareness of the history of the twentieth-century American stage. Other patterns discernible over forty years of conversation include his interest in the financial as well as cultural problems afflicting American theater; the myth of the American dream and the way in which objective reality, coupled with the individual's fallibility, too often subverts its alluring promise. Of compelling importance to Miller are his characters, the play's structure, in brief, the creative process itself. "In each of my plays the central creating force is the character . . ." says Miller. "I've paid probably an inordinate amount of attention to form because if it's not right, nothing works, no matter what. Form is literally the body that holds the soul of the play. And if that body doesn't maneuver and operate, you have an effusion of dialogue, a tickling of the piano keys, improvisation, perhaps, but you don't have music."[5] He also seems eager to tackle social issues, which perhaps emerges from Miller's own experiences as a young man living through the Depression and, in 1956, his having to endure questioning by the House Un-American Activities Committee.[6] Finally, certain interviews reveal a central thematic concern of Miller's, the exploration of what Robert A. Martin identifies as "the primal family unit."[7]

In the plays Miller gives artistic definition to the public issues of a nation and the private anxieties of its citizens. Through these interviews, similar concerns surface, but with one crucial difference: the actor/audience barrier is minimized, and the listener is left with the delightful prospect of engaging Miller, not through Willy Loman or Elizabeth Proctor or Kate Keller, or through critics interpreting the plays, but through the very person who reinvented so much of contemporary drama.

I gratefully acknowledge all the interviewers and publishers who have granted to reprint the material in this book. I wish to thank two individuals whose support has made it possible for me to complete this project: Virginia Spencer Carr, Chair, Department of English, and Clyde W. Faulkner, Dean, College of Arts and Sciences, Georgia State University. Both have provided professional support for my research. A Georgia State University Research Grant also enabled me to finish the book. Thanks to Thomas L. McHaney of Georgia State University, who first suggested I tackle this project on a Thanksgiving Day walk in 1984. Thanks to William J. Handy of the University of Oregon, whose insights were instrumental in my understanding of Miller's plays. Seetha Srinivasan, Peggy Whitman Prenshaw, and the staff of the University Press of Mississippi have been most helpful and understanding. Thanks to Leigh K. Pietschner, who proofed each page. I also want to thank Arthur Miller, who lent his full support to the book and who discussed frankly his work with me in 1983. Charles and Orient Roudané, again, know their influence. Above all, I am indebted to Susan Ashley, my wife, who took time from her career to be with Nickolas and to cover for me when I most needed the time.

MCR
March 1987

---

[1] For a useful account of Miller's earliest plays during his student days at the University of Michigan, see Kenneth Rowe, "Shadows Cast Before," in *Arthur Miller: New Perspectives*, ed.

Robert A. Martin (Englewood Cliffs, N.J.: Prentice-Hall, 1982): 13-32. See also C.W.E. Bigsby, *A Critical Introduction to Twentieth-Century American Drama* (New York: Cambridge University Press, 1984), II, 135-155. In addition to an account of Miller's early published and unpublished work, Bigsby intersperses his lengthy chapter on Miller with his own interview with the playwright. Since Bigsby's excellent interview is not presented as a "unified" conversation, I reluctantly omitted its inclusion here.

[2] John K. Hutchens, "Mr. Miller Has a Change of Luck," *New York Times,* February 23, 1947, Sec. II, p. 1.

[3] Josh Greenfeld, "Writing Plays Is Absolutely Senseless, Arthur Miller Says, 'But I Love It. I Just Love It,' " *New York Times Magazine,* February 13, 1972, p. 1.

[4] Bigsby, 248.

[5] Matthew C. Roudané, "An Interview with Arthur Miller," *Michigan Quarterly Review* 24 (1985): 378.

[6] See "The Testimony of Arthur Miller, accompanied by Counsel, Joseph L. Rauh, Jr." United States House of Representatives, Committee on Un-American Activities. *Investigation of the Unauthorized Use of United States Passports, 84th Congress,* Part 4, June 21, 1956. Washington: United States Government Printing Office, November 1956, pp. 4660-4690.

[7] Martin, "Introduction," 2.

Chronology

1915   Arthur Asher Miller born 17 October in Manhattan, New York, to Isadore and Augusta Miller.

1929   Family moves to Brooklyn. Family's business and savings damaged by the Depression.

1932   After graduating from high school in Brooklyn, works in a car parts warehouse.

1934   Enrolls in journalism at the University of Michigan.

1936   Composes *No Villain,* his first play, in six days during spring vacation; the play receives Hopwood Award in Drama, University of Michigan. Revises *No Villain* for the Theatre Guild's Bureau of New Plays Contest with new title, *They Too Arise.*

1937   Enrolls in Kenneth T. Rowe's playwriting class at Michigan. *They Too Arise* garners $1250 from Bureau of New Plays. *Honors at Dawn* wins a Hopwood Award in June. Starts writing *The Great Disobedience* for the 1938 Hopwood Contest.

1938   Revises *They Too Arise* with new title, *The Grass Still Grows. The Great Disobedience* does not win a Hopwood Award. Graduates in June with a B.A. in English from the University of Michigan. Joins Federal Theatre Project in New York City; composes radio plays, scripts, and stage plays for the Project, Columbia Workshop (CBS), and Calvalcade of America (NBC).

1940   Marries Mary Grace Slattery

1944   Visits army camps for background data for *The Story of G. I. Joe,* a screen play. Publishes *Situation Normal,* a journal of his army tour. *The Man Who Had All the Luck* produced on Broadway.

1945   *Focus,* a novel, published

1947   *All My Sons* produced and published; receives New York Drama Critics Circle Award.

1949   *Death of a Salesman* produced and published; receives Pulitzer Prize and other awards.

1950   *An Enemy of the People,* adaptation of Ibsen's play, produced and published in 1951.

1953   *The Crucible* is produced and published.

1954   Denied passport to visit Brussels by State Department.

1955   *A View from the Bridge* and *A Memory of Two Mondays* (one-act plays) produced and published. Possible Communist associations probed by New York City Youth Board. Divorces Grace Slattery.

1956   *A View from the Bridge* (two-act version) staged in London. Receives honorary doctorate from the University of Michigan. Testifies before House Un-American Activities Committee. Marries Marilyn Monroe.

1957   Found in contempt of Congress after trial in which he refused to identify persons seen at meetings organized by Communists. *Arthur Miller's Collected Plays* published.

1958   Contempt of Congress conviction reversed by U.S. Court of Appeals. Elected to the National Institute of Arts and Letters.

1959   Awarded Gold Medal for Drama, National Institute of Arts and Letters.

1960   Divorces Marilyn Monroe.

1961   *The Misfits* (film) is produced and published.

1962   Marries Inge Morath.
1964   *After the Fall* is produced and published. *Incident at Vichy* produced and, one year later, published.

1965   Elected president of P.E.N., international literary organization (term expired 1969).

1967   *I Don't Need You Anymore,* short stories, published.

1968   *The Price* is produced and published. Serves as delegate to Democratic National Convention in Chicago.

1969   *In Russia* (with photographs by Inge Morath), a travel journal, is published.

1972   *The Creation of the World and Other Business* is produced and published. Serves as delegate to Democratic National Convention in Miami.

1974   *Up From Paradise* (musical version of *Creation of the World*) is produced.

1977   *In the Country* (with photographs by Inge Morath), a journal, is published. *The Archbishop's Ceiling* in produced.

1978   *The Theater Essays of Arthur Miller* is published.

1979   *Chinese Encounters* (with photographs by Inge Morath), a journal, is published.

1980   *Playing for Time,* a film adapted from a book by Fania Fenelon, is produced for television and published. *The American Clock* is produced and published.

1981   *Arthur Miller's Collected Plays, Volume II* is published.

1982   *Some Kind of Love Story* and *Elegy for a Lady,* two short plays, produced and published.

1983   *Salesman in Beijing* published.

1984   *Death of a Salesman* filmed for television.

1986   *Danger: Memory!* is published.

1987   Writes "A New Candor at Issyk-Kul," a brief article concerning U.S.-Soviet cultural relations in *Newsweek. Clara* and *I Can't Remember Anything,* two one-act plays published as *Danger: Memory!,* produced.

Conversations with Arthur Miller

Mr. Miller Has a Change of Luck

John K. Hutchens/1947

From *The New York Times*, 23 Feb. 1947, sec. II, 1, 3. Reprinted
by permission.

It was a couple of years ago that Arthur Miller fell to talking with a
midwestern lady who told him a war profiteer whose daughter,
though she loved her father, exposed him and then ran away from
home.

"Where," the lady asked Mr. Miller only a couple of minutes later,
"do you get ideas for plays and stories?"

"I just pick them up," said Mr. Miller, "here and there."

He had, of course, just picked up the basic idea for *All My Sons*,
which came to town the other night, met with more hosannahs than
hoots, and has settled down to what promises to be a happy life on
the very boards where Mr. Miller's first Broadway play, *The Man Who
Had All the Luck*, perished of fiscal anemia two seasons ago.

His new drama's journey from that causal conversation to the
footlights was, naturally, less simple than it sounds else the paid-up
membership of the Dramatists' Guild would be translating stray
comments into gold on every corner of the Main Stem, and blocking
traffic. On the contrary, Mr. Miller—rendered wary by his previous
brush with the spotlights—spent two years, off and on, pulishing his
second Times Square entry; grew discouraged to the point of almost
abandoning it two months before he finished it; revised and rewrote
so extensively that, while the manuscript of his play runs to the
customary 110 pages, he has 700 other pages at home of trial heats
and exploratory drafts.

But when he completed it he had something in which he frankly
believes. For Mr. Miller, a lanky, easy talking young man who stands
something over six feet and possesses an engaging candor, believes
in himself, in his play and in the theatre, though he is perfectly aware
that the latter is a capricious business—"a sort of floating crap

game"—in which the artist succeeds or fails according to the first impression his play makes on a relatively few people. He doesn't care for that uncertainty.

"Along with this success," he said gravely, "there is the terrible realization that it might have been otherwise. This was going to be my last play if it didn't go."

However, that basic idea of All My Sons always did feel right to Mr. Miller, who reasoned that if the incident suggesting it could take place in the isolationist Midwest its appeal might be general. He was inclined, to be sure of it when he read the play to "five tough ex-GI's" who "were bowled over," and he was even more certain when, at the tryout in New Haven, it met the approval of former soldiers now at Yale under the GI Bill of Rights.

"According to the manager of the theatre up there," said Mr. Miller with justifiable pride, "it got the biggest ovation the house had heard since The Copperhead."

But what pleases him most is that the play's reception, including the mail he has received, bears out another notion he has had for some time—i.e., that the men coming back from this war would not be the bitter cynics their forebears were after World War I. He has felt this since he visited seventeen training camps and talked with thousands of men and women to get "atmosphere" for the film The Story of GI Joe.

"They're grateful I'm not a wise guy," said Mr. Miller. "They write that the play is about 'the things we feel but don't say for fear of being laughed at.' " He is happy about this because he is "an idealistic man" himself, even if he does frequently feel older than his thirty-one years.

Those thirty-one years began, for him, in uptown Manhattan, where he lived until he was 12, removing then to Brooklyn, where he went to Abraham Lincoln High School and proceeded in due course to the University of Michigan. He went to Michigan because he heard they gave a lot of literary prizes there, and, sure enough, he walked off with two of them—a pair of Avery Hopwood drama awards—in addition to a $1,250 Theatre Guild Prize. He must have been as startled as anyone, because up to that point he had seen only one stage play in his life and had read only a few and, before sitting down to write his first drama, in all innocence he asked a classmate how long an act was supposed to run.

However, said Mr. Miller, you will never see any of these plays on Broadway, nor a comedy he wrote for the Federal Theatre Project. A fellow of easier artistic conscience might be tempted to take these out of the trunk and touch them up a little, but not Mr. Miller, because "I don't believe in going back. I figure I've only got so many years to live."

Heaven and the box office willing, he will not go back to radio writing, either. He did a spell of it for the Columbia Workshop and other programs and because so adept that he could pound out a half-hour show in eight hours, from scratch. "I depise radio," said Mr. Miller flatly. "Every emotion in a radio script has to have a tag. It's like playing a scene in a dark closet." He winced a bit at the thought of it.

But a novel is something else again. It was a novel, *Focus,* which in 1945 established him as a writer of parts—an angry tale of bigotry and the makings of fascism in our midst, which achieved 90,000 copies. He will write another, an idea for which he is now weighing, though he might try the idea as a play. The choice does not bother him. Both forms—the theatre and the novel—satisfy him because they are free mediums for a writer who wants to speak his mind.

The theatre he especially likes, despite the fleeting life even of its better exhibits, despite the fact that "you have to be a little crazy to go on in it." Among his favorite modern American plays are Sidney Howard's *The Silver Cord* and Eugene O'Neill's *Anna Christie*—which, he said, "will give you an idea of the kind of theatre I believe in." He doesn't go to the theatre often, and he is as apt to attend a failure as a success, hoping to learn something there. Among the instructive failures was his own *The Man Who Had All the Luck.*

"They came down on me like a ton of bricks for that one," he said. "It was faulty, all right. It couldn't have succeeded because it was not a resolved play."

But, as noted, he doesn't believe in looking back. He still lives in Brooklyn, in an old brownstone house; and, talking with him, you get a definite idea that he is a young man on his way.

"It will take about a year to write another," he said.

Arthur Miller Grew in Brooklyn
Murray Schumach/1949

From *The New York Times*, 6 Feb. 1949, sec. II, 1, 3. Reprinted by permission

Last year after Arthur Miller's *All My Sons* had won the Critics Award, an acquaintance asked him why he had spurned lush writing offers from Hollywood. "If I put the same time into writing a good play," explained Mr. Miller, "I can make the same $2,000 a week and write what I want to write." So instead of the private swimming pool, Mr. Miller took a wheelbarrow and building tools to his Connecticut four acres.

There the lanky playwright toiled for six weeks on a sunrise-to-sunset schedule and erected a work shack. In the late spring the 33-year-old writer occupied his "five windows and a door." For the next six weeks his big-knuckled hands pounded from a typewriter *Death of a Salesman,* which moves into the Morosco on Thursday.

This desire for physical as well as mental labor is more than just a hobby. It is a conviction that emerges in his two-act tragedy when the doomed salesman says: "A man who can't handle tools is not a man." For Mr. Miller's approach to writing and living is that of a good carpenter to cabinet-making. He is interested primarily in the fundamentals of structure and function.

Mr. Miller builds plays more for durability than fashion and therefore chooses characters more for substance than manners. He strives more for utility than decoration and consequently is more concerned with the content of his dialogue than with its bon mots. The inevitable result is that Mr. Miller's dramas concentrate on what he calls "the significant commonplaces"—the relationships between father and son; between the individual and society.

Such a commonplace, Mr. Miller explained the other night at a hotel here, is the theme of *Death of a Salesman.* The motif is the growth of illusion until it destroys the individual and leaves the children to whom he transmitted it incapable of dealing with reality.

"Every man," said Mr. Miller, "has an image of himself which fails in one way or another to correspond with reality. It's the size of the discrepancy between illusion and reality that matters. The closer a man gets to knowing himself, the less likely he is to trip up on his own illusions."

Elaborating on this theme, he forgot temporarily the fatigue of rehearsal revisions and pre-opening tensions that had scooped deep hollows from his high cheekbones to jutting jaw. His New Yorkese became more pronounced with increasing enthusiasm.

Then, matter-of-factly, Mr. Miller turned to an analysis of the play's technique. The tragedy has two concurrent themes that are maneuvered by flashbacks until they collide in climax. Generally speaking, one theme delves into the past of the salesman, tracing his development and that of his family. The other theme handles the present.

"This was the play where I decided not to be hampered by the iron vise of plot," he said. "I've always been impatient with naturalism on the stage. But I knew I had to master naturalism before I tried anything else. *All My Sons* was in that category. The pattern I used for *Death of a Salesman* gives more more leeway for honest investigation and makes the people seem more lifelike. Of course, I think this play has more roundness of truth and handles a great many more aspects of people. I guess it has more pity and less judgment than there was in *All My Sons*."

Suddenly he stopped talking and his gaunt face became boyish as he grinned almost sheepishly. It is a slow, wide grin that usually accompanies his proud comments on his two children, his wife's mastery of the family exchequer or the behavior of his new convertible. He slid deep into his chair, stretched his long legs over another chair and closed his eyes.

"Dammit," he muttered wearily, "I hate living in hotels."

Mr. Miller dislikes living anywhere that cuts him off from the life of the average family. That is why his home is in Brooklyn and why each year he spends a few weeks working in a factory. "Anyone who doesn't know what it means to stand in one place eight hours a day," he said, "doesn't know what it's all about. It's the only way you can learn what makes men go into a gin mill after work and start fighting. You don't learn about those things in Sardi's."

Virtually everything Mr. Miller put into *Death of a Salesman* came from the writer's experiences or observations. The one-family house

Jo Mielziner used for a set is the model of countless such homes in Brooklyn where Mr. Miller grew up after moving to Flatbush from Harlem as a boy. The salesman was modeled on the fast-talking specimens he had seen so often because his father made coats. He knew how an adolescent can behave as a football hero because he played end at Abraham Lincoln High School in Brooklyn until his knees were banged up so badly he couldn't get into the Army.

Mr. Miller's acquaintances, who judge him by his intense face and writings, are surprised to learn he is not a born bookworm and that he spent his boyhood and most of his adolescence ignoring books for sports. The change came suddenly in his senior year at high school, when he read Dostoievsky's *The Idiot* and decided he had to be a writer. Thereafter, though he held tiring jobs as a truck-driver, waiter, crewman on a tanker, he used his spare time to read.

His first play, a three-acter, was writen at the University of Michigan in a week and won for him a $500 prize. That award, plus the confidence of a fellow-student, Mary Slattery, whom he later married, convinced him his writing should take the form of plays. He stuck to this idea fairly steadily, though there was years when his wife's salary as a secretary brought more income than his play scripts.

Only once did Mr. Miller lose faith. That was in 1944 after his first Broadway play, *The Man Who Had All the Luck,* flopped. He decided to try a novel and came up with *Focus.* While this taut study of domestic anti-Semitism and fascism was selling 90,000 copies Mr. Miller turned out *All My Sons,* a tale that had been kicking around in the back of his head.

Mr. Miller's pieces invariably fatten in his skull for a while before he begins writing. He is not of the notebook school of writing. Nor does he subscribe to the theory that a man should get behind a typewriter for a set number of hours every day, even if unaware of any ideas. In the case of *Death of a Salesman* the idea came one day "the way marble comes in a solid block if you hit it right." But once under way he works from 9 A.M. to 1 P.M. every day with a couple of more hours of production in the evening "that I usually throw away the next morning."

Regardless of Broadway's reception of his play, Mr. Miller is sure of two things. He'll head for his Connecticut retreat and relax in manual labor. And he'll continue to resist Hollywood. "I didn't go to Hollywood when I was poor," he says, "why should I do it now?"

Brooklyn Boy Makes Good
Robert Sylvester/1949

From *Saturday Evening Post,* 222 (July 16, 1949): 26-27, 97-98, 100. Reprinted by permission.

Considering the fact that he will probably earn more than $2,000,000 from a play which took him only six weeks to write, a thirty-three-year-old Brooklynite named Arthur Miller is showing a stubborn consistency about being a subway straphanger.

Five years ago, when Miller's first Broadway play was a disheartening failure, he rode the subway back to Brooklyn and holed in for a year to lick his creative wounds. Three years later, his second play won the coveted Drama Critics prize and considerable cash. Yet Miller took the subway again and used the cash to buy a Brooklyn home. When his *Death of a Salesman* opened this season to the wildest critical acclaim in a long time, became overnight the biggest box-office smash in years, and carried off the Pulitzer Prize together with another Drama Critics prize, Miller used his first royalties to furnish two rooms of his Brooklyn home. He is still a subwayite, still refers to his trips to Manhattan as "going into the city." Ownership of a partly furnished home convinces him that at last he really belongs to the wonderful borough of Brooklyn.

Arthur Miller is generally accepted as an authentic *Wunderkind,* the ablest writer of stage tragedies since Eugene O'Neill. More important, to the financially hardheaded show-business managers, his sad and bitter plays have an amazing popular appeal and are determinedly written so that production costs can be kept at a minimum. *Death of a Salesman* is called by most critics the outstanding dramatic success of many years, and can't miss making a fortune for everybody concerned. yet it cost less to stage than many a one-set failure. Beyond which, the play can be produced almost anywhere at practically no construction cost.

The man responsible for this solid milestone in theatrical history will be thirty-four years old next October seventeenth, is six feet, two and a half inches tall, weighs a meager 162 pounds, and until recently insisted that there was no truth to his friends' belief that he resembled a beardless Abraham Lincoln. Not long ago, his wife showed Jane Ellen Miller, age four and a half, a shiny new Lincoln penny. "Daddy on money," she said knowingly. Daddy sighed and accepted the inevitable.

A successful playwright who doesn't own a dinner jacket, is never nervous at his own *premières*, rarely attends his own plays after the first night, and who beat out the legendary Eugene O'Neill for the Critics prize with his second playwrighting effort, has enough to fascinate Broadway with these factors alone. Miller has other unusual qualities—such as being even prouder of the work he can do with his hands than of what he does with his head.

"A man who can't handle tools is not a man." says Willie Loman in the title role of *Death of a Salesman*. Willie speaks for his creator. Before *Salesman* was written, Miller built a house in which to write it. He owns some country property in Roxbury, Connecticut, and a year ago he dug a cellar, poured a concrete foundation, built a one-room shack with windows and door, installed workable plumbing and finally got the roof up. The roof gave him some trouble, working alone, but he devised a way to fit the rafters on the ground, get them on top of the house upside down, climb up on the beams and flip the rafter joists over and into place.

Then Miller sat down in front of a thirteen-year-old secondhand portable typewriter, bought ten years previously with part of a playwrighting prize, and started to write *Death of a Salesman*. Six weeks later, the play was completed. Produced with only the most minute changes, it may become the most profitable six weeks' work ever undertaken in the history of show business.

The Salesman, as it is known to the trade, is a cinch for virtually capacity business for two years and the producers expect a full three-year run on Broadway. Miller's royalties should be more than $150,000 a year from the original company. By fall there will be two, possibly three, touring companies, each returning a similar sum. Before the summer is over there will be at least twelve European productions, being played in varied translations, all paying—to the author. The published version of *Salesman* was a Book-of-the-Month-Club selection, which alone distributed 200,000 copies, and on direct sales the book has already set a record for printed plays. Also, The Salesman is the hottest title on the "secondary-rights" lists—stock, amateur, school and such productions. What secondary rights earn can be judged from the fact that the ancient *Charley's Aunt* still takes in more than $100,000 a year.

The value of the moving-picture rights hasn't even been considered as yet. A film sale now should bring at least $1,000,000, meaning $600,000 for the author under standard terms. But Miller and his associates are more ambitious; they intend to produce the movie themselves, with Miller as a full partner. . . . Miller, who has revolutionary convictions about what scenery should mean to a play, deliberately wrote The Salesman so that this remarkable scenic technique would be necessary. The saving of construction costs is a noteworthy result, and both artistically and economically Mielziner's treatment is certain to influence sharply scenic design in the future.

"I made up my mind with my first failure," Miller says, "that never again would anybody move scenery for a play of mine."

His first play was *The Man Who Had All the Luck*. Its luck consisted of six performances, in November of 1944, at a loss of $55,000. Miller still believes that if it had been produced as a tragedy instead of a folk comedy, it might have been a winner. He accepts part of the blame himself. *Luck* was a multiple-scene affair, and Miller saw his trend of dramatic thought lost among the shifting scenery of rehearsals.

"For the first four weeks," he says, "we rehearsed the stagehands. Then it was too late to rehearse the actors."

His *All My Sons*, three years later, was the story of a war profiteer who made defective parts for planes, and of the effect of his moral crimes on his family. *Sons* garnered a majority of critical endorsements, ran almost a year, brought a solid price from the movies, and won the coveted Drama Critics prize by nosing out Eugene O'Neill's *The Iceman Cometh*, the first work of that literary giant to reach the stage in twelve years. Pleased by this artistic and financial success, Miller still was not satisfied about scenery.

"Most scenery is too accurate," he contends. "Lots of plays would be better with no scenery at all. What I want is the kind of thing Jo Mielziner did for Salesman—suggestion scenery, just enough to help each person build his own scenery in his imagination."

With or without scenery, it is doubtful if any future Miller plays will be set in that cliché of playwrighting, the living room. Miller hates living-room scenes almost as much as he despises scenery itself. His own living room is still only partly furnished.

"Nobody spends his life in a living room any more," he contends. "Maybe they did in Ibsen's day. Where Ibsen wrote, it was too cold to go anywhere else."

The story of every overnight success in show business has its quota of anecdotes about early rebuff, failure and discouragement. Miller's story has a plethora of the first two, but none of the third. It is doubtful that he was ever seriously discouraged. He is so convinced that playwrighting is the only normal trade for a sensible man that he is inclined to dismiss from his own career what would be an important milestone in the career of any other professional writer.

With the failure of *The Man Who Had All the Luck* and Broadway's subsequent disinterest in his scripts, Miller had to figure out how to make a living. From his battered portable came a novel called *Focus,* published in 1945. *Focus* sold 90,000 copies, landing on the best-seller lists, and it may do better with its current reissue and the growing fame of its author. Yet Miller appears to have little interest in it.

"One person in a hundred can write a play," he explains. "At least eight in a hundred can write a novel."

For a man who always wanted to be a playwright, Miller was a laggard student. He was born on East 112th Street, Manhattan, the son of Mr. and Mrs. Isadore Miller. His father manufactured ladies' coats and was a successful shop owner through Arthur's younger years. Miller is the second of three children. His older brother, Kermit, is a salesman, and his sister, Joan, six years his junior, this year got her first real role as an actress in the hit melodrama *Detective Story.* Determined to succeed as her own, she uses the name Joan Copeland, never mentioning her famous brother to casting directors.

Miller's father lost his business just before the crash of 1929 and moved to Brooklyn, where Arthur spent a boyhood in what he calls "middle-class-poor" surroundings. The Millers lived on what was then Gravesend Avenue, near Coney Island, surrounded by a host of relatives. Miller claims that at least thirty uncles were in and out of his home, and that most of them were traveling salesmen. These breezy uncles made an impression which stood him in good stead some years later.

Miller struggled through high school with a record so bad that the University of Michigan refused to enroll him. On a subsequent plea, the university agreed to reconsider if he would get letters from four teachers indicating that in his last high-school year he had at least shown some maturing intelligence. Since one of his senior-year teachers had expelled him from class, another had flunked him three times in algebra, and most of the others considered him a doubtful intellectual bargain, the letters were unobtainable. So Miller tested out a few jobs.

He tried working for his father, and discovered that he hated the coat business, especially the way salesmen were maltreated by arrogant buyers. This so upset him that he laboriously typed out a short story called In Memoriam, a rather pointless character study of an aged drummer who might have posed for the window cards which now advertise The Salesman. He can't recall submitting the story anywhere; his mother recently dug it out of an old trunk.

Miller batted around at various jobs for three years. In those days everybody wanted to sing like Rudy Vallee and make the kind of money Vallee was making, and for several months Miller crooned over a small Brooklyn radio station. He might have pursued this career, except that suddenly he became addicted to heavy literature. He thinks his literary turn was inspired by his mother, a rapid and avid reader of almost all kinds of books. He also gives some credit to Dostoievsky, who convinced him that writing was worth anybody's time. He wrote the University of Michigan such a pleading letter that the institution surrendered and admitted him, three years after he graduated from high school.

"I told them I wanted to be a newspaperman," he remembers. "I was ashamed to admit that a numbskull like myself aspired to such a high plane as writing anything serious."

There were two features at the university which lastingly affected Miller—its awards to the best student playwright, founded by the talented writer of stage comedies, Avery Hopwood, and a girl from Ohio named Mary Slattery. The Hopwood awards consisted of $250 for the best sophomore play, $250 for the best script by a junior, and a dreamy $1250 for the best senior effort. Miller presently got busy on the sophomore project, and somewhere between Act 1 and Act 3 he met Miss Slattery.

"I met Arthur at a basement party," his wife recalls. "The first time

I saw him, he came toward me, ducking overhead heating pipes. I remember him from that night, but he doesn't remember me. He didn't even think of me until another party some time later."

Miller calls this a wifely libel, contending that he not only remembers his wife from the first meeting but that she was wearing a brown sports coat. "I always notice those things," he assures her. "After all, my old man was in the coat business."

But Mary goes right on with, "At that later party, when he did notice me, he asked for a date. I proposed a movie, but he didn't have any money. I treated to the movies, and afterwards to malted milks. Pretty soon Arthur borrowed my radio, and then everything was understood. We were married two years after graduation, in 1938." Mrs. Miller now presides over the Brooklyn household, which includes Jane Ellen, four and a half, and Robert, almost two.

Both Miller and Miss Slattery, the daughter of an insurance salesman, worked their way through Michigan. The Avery Hopwood awards helped Miller; he won the sophomore and junior competitions. He had a job tending hundreds of mice in a university laboratory. As a child, Miller had feared and hated mice, but these mice were special ones, sixty-third-generation mice with which the university scientists hoped to prove something or other. When one of them escaped, it had to be recaptured in good working order, with no damage to ears or tail. Miller caught so many loose rodents that he came to regard mice with some affection. He says, "The scientists wanted me to design a mouse trap which would nail strays without injury and I almost succeeded. If they had given me a postgraduate scholarship I would have licked the problem."

Miller counted on the rich $1250 senior Hopwood award, and thought his drama called *They, Too, Arise* was a sure winner. The judges, however, found it heavy and turgid. Miller suffered from this shock only until a year later, when the same script won the $1250 paid by the eminent Theatre Guild for the best work by an unknown playwright.

The Guild money went in part for the current Miller typewriter, and the machine was put to work hacking out plays which didn't get produced and radio scripts which sometimes did—at $100 each. Miller found radio writing depressing, and hopes never to attempt it again. "It's like writing on ice," he says. During the war, when he worked the swing shift in the Navy Yard at Brooklyn, he did scripts for bond drives, recruiting services and other patriotic causes. He thinks many of these scripts contained first-class material. "But the best ones were never done," he says now. "It just goes to show you what radio is like."

During his early years of radio and playwrighting, Miller toiled with a great waste of physical energy, pacing the floor, flinging his arms about and shouting sentences at the empty walls of his workroom. He thinks that he was afraid that if he stopped thinking and shouting for long, he would fall asleep. He can knock off for a short nap at any time. When he started to write The Salesman, he decided it was time for physical discipline.

"I found that I lost the sharpness of thoughts or construction in the time it took to dash to the typewriter and get seated. So I forced myself to sit still. The most I would permit was resting my hands once in a while on the typewriter table. The rest of the time I just pounded away. It proved a very sound method."

The Salesman came easily because, for one thing, it is an expression of Miller's own theories and beliefs in the rules of tragedy. In a rather schoolteacherish foreword to the printed version of his drama, he says: "From Orestes to Hamlet, Medea to Macbeth, the underlying struggle is that of the individual attempting to gain his 'rightful' place in society. Sometimes he is one who has been displaced from it, sometimes one who seeks to attain it for the first time, but the fateful wound from which the inevitable events spiral is the wound of indignity, and its dominant force is indignation. Tragedy, then, is the consequence of man's total compulsion to evaluate himself."

The worn-out salesman and bedeviled father who is Willie Loman in *Death of a Salesman* is the product of this theory. Everybody has met Willie Loman at some point in life.

"When we started rehearsals," Miller says, "Elia Kazan found an old book full of advice to salesmen. It had a long list of bright and tactful quips which could be used by a drummer to meet almost any situation. I had never seen the book before, but parts of it could have been lines from my play, almost word for word."

The Salesman was bought for production by Kermit Bloomgarden and Walter Fried almost at first glance. Both are young producers with successful records; Bloomgarden had sponsored three smash dramas and failed once with a small comedy. They were not only sure they had a hit but convinced that it was such a radical departure in stage technique that they refused many backers the traditional right to see the script and make production suggestions.

Like every hit play, The Salesman fooled some smart theater veterans. Leland Hayward, an eminent artists' agent as well as producer of *Mister Roberts* and other successes, cut his planned investment in half, once he was allowed to read the script. Joshua Logan, one of the most sought after of stage directors, said he couldn't understand the thing. Cheryl Crawford, a successful producer and investor, didn't like The Salesman a bit, and refused to join in the financing. There were others.

The production associates were confident enough, but the title of the play worried them. Bloomgarden feared it would drive away customers. Theater owners, ticket brokers, unpaid advisers and friends felt the same way. Robert Dowling, who owns the Morosco Theater, was so apprehensive that he wanted to keep the title off the marquee of his theater, which was to house Miller's play.

"I will pay for a research poll," Dowling offered desperately, "if you will change the title when the poll shows you how unattractive it is."

Miller, wavering himself, attended the final title conference almost convinced that the name was a dangerous mistake. He was about to announce his surrender when one of the associates produced a list of alternate titles. Miller canceled his surrender.

"Pure conceit," he admits cheerfully. "It annoyed me that anybody might think of a better title for my own play than I could. Also, I was furious that anybody else could come up with a whole list of titles, like a bunch of bananas."

The Philadelphia tryout allayed fears about everything, including the title, yet nerves were on edge when the curtain went up for the first Broadway performance last February 10th. A dozen things could have gone wrong with The Salesman and any one of them would have thrown the whole play out of gear. The drama has music which must integrate correctly, not too loudly and not too softly. It demands hairbreadth timing in costume changes, exits and entrances. The lighting and projected film patterns must be delicately adjusted or the illusion is ruined.

So everybody was nervous . . . except Miller. He went backstage and blessed the actors in Brooklynese and in double-talk. He greeted family and friends with composure. During the first act he was so satisfied that he left the back of the auditorium and walked out into the lobby, where he found producer Kermit Bloomgarden in a partial daze, a dead cigar splintered between his teeth.

"Stop smoking that cigar so loud," Miller told his producer. He then strolled up and down the street for a while.

Since *All My Sons* was an attack on war profiteers and *Death of a Salesman* is in a sense a criticism of the American way of life, Miller has been accused of communistic tendencies. He expect to be similarly accused following production of other plays he is planning, for they are variations on the same theme—man's need to examine himself and his relationship to society. Miller doesn't consider himself a communist, and he is angered by what he considers the unfair affixing of the communist label to many sincere liberals.

"I am a confirmed and deliberate radical," he says freely. Asked if he is affected by criticism of his ideology, he admits, "I am a very disturbed radical at the moment."

But he is not disturbed enough to equivocate or retreat from his position. He firmly believes that the stage is the last sounding board for an independent thinker, and he will use it that way.

"I wrote a play about a man who kills himself because he isn't liked," he says. "It would be a little silly for me to worry about who likes me and who doesn't."

The fantastic success of his drama gives Miller many little by-product pleasures. He is proud of the fact that despite the play's morbid undertone it is a prime favorite with salesmen at conventions and with the garment district wholesalers, who usually head their buyers to the girlie musical shows. Miller sometimes stands near the Morosco box office after a performance, on the infrequent occasions when he comes to Manhattan from Brooklyn, and beams when a patron who has just seen the show stops to buy—or try to buy—tickets for some future date. Most of all, however, he is proud of the record of the last-act bouquet of funeral flowers.

At the final curtain, Mildred Dunnock, as Willie Loman's widow, comes to the edge of the stage and steps down onto a lower platform a few inches from the first-row patrons. She makes her farewell speech to her suicide husband and lays a small, pitiful bouquet beside the imaginary grave. When she steps back and the curtain falls, the flowers remain outside, within easy reach of anyone who wishes to take them.

As this bouquet is a natural souvenir, the producers expected to lose a bunch of flowers with each performance. But The Salesman is still using its original bouquet. Nobody has ever touched it.

"I'm happy about that," says Miller, "It shows that the audience is still under the illusion, still thinking about poor Willie. It's a nice gesture of respect for the actors and the play."

There are no writers in either Miller's or his wife's family, but, as related, there are salesmen aplenty. Miller has at last convinced both his own family and his in-laws that he is something more than an artistic loafer. As a matter of fact, one of his salesman uncles was deeply interested as soon as Miller told him that his next play was about a salesman.

"Why, that's a good idea," said the uncle. "What line is he in?"

Now that the countryside has warmed up, Miller is back at Roxbury, Connecticut, where he is building a guest house on his property. Not until the other day, when he returned there to go to work, did he take note that his property is located at the junction of Goldmine Road and Tophit Road—an ideal address for a playwright.

Broadway Postscript: Arthur Miller and How He Went to the Devil

Henry Hewes/1953

From *The Saturday Review,* 31 January 1953, pp. 24-26. Reprinted by permission.

On the strength of two plays that sank deep into the heart of contemporary life, Arthur Miller has risen to the unchallenged position of being one of this generation's two foremost American dramatists, and there is no reason to doubt that he will continue to write about everyday situations with equal truth, equal power, and equal success. But, being something of a non-conformist, Mr. Miller has chosen to turn away from the modern arena, where he is demonstrably at home, to try his hand at writing a historical play that involves some fairly remote events that happened during the Salem witchcraft trials of 1692.

Visited during a rehearsal break at the Martin Beck, the tall mantis-figured playwright seemed tired and watchful as he sat with his legs dangling over the orchestra seat in front of him. But serious and concerned as he was, he appeared surprisingly untroubled about the increase in complexity that goes with staging a twenty-two character play set in another period, and putting into focus a tragedy of a whole society, not just the tragedy of an individual. "I've laid it out that way from the start," he said in a gently confident tone. The first scene is purely an overture in which we emphasize the inability of these Puritans to cope with the strange sickness of the minister's little girl, and the resultant turn to accusations of witchcraft. The strict beliefs under which they all lived were doubly responsible. Their tenets were filled with witches and the devil, and they gave them an authority-weighted reason for something they found hard otherwise to explain. In addition, the circle of children who made the accusations had grievances against the Puritan women they named, because these

women had made their lives and the lives of their husbands cold and
unpleasant. As Elizabeth Procter, one of the accused wives, says:
    It needs a cold wife to prompt
    Lechery, I counted myself so plain,
    so poorly-made, no honest love
    could come to me! Suspicion
    kissed you when I did; I never
    knew how I should say my love.
    It were a cold house I kept . . . !
    The thirty-seven-year-old writer maintains, however, that this
remorseless, unbending idealogy of the Puritans had constructive
uses in settling this country, as proved by the fact that the
Massachusetts colony succeeded against heavy odds, while the non-
ideological Virginia Colony failed despite an easier climate. "But, by
1692, the usefulness of the ideology had passed and it had become
an orthodoxy which had to destroy its opposition or be itself
destroyed. The tragedy of *The Crucible* is the everlasting conflict
between people so fanatically wedded to this orthodoxy that they
could not copy with the evidence of their senses."
    Also necessary to establish in the first scene is the atmosphere of
seventeenth-century Salem. "I used words like 'poppet' instead of
'doll,' and grammatical syntax like 'he have' instead of 'he has.' This
will remind audiences that *The Crucible* is taking place in another
time, but won't make it too difficult to understand, which it might if I
used all the old language with words like 'dafter' instead of
'daughter.' Also, I have varied some of the facts. Actually, the girls
were reported to be dancing in the woods and practising
abominations. I have them dancing *naked* in the woods, which
makes it easier for the audience to relate the Puritans' horror at such
a thing to their own."
    Mr. Miller has taken some other liberties with the historical facts, as
he read them in the Salem courthouse and in a book written by
Charles W. Upham in 1867. (Oddly enough, he is not familiar with
Tennessee Williams' short story "The Yellow Birds," issued recently
by Caedmon Records, which derives from the same incident.)
    For instance, from Abigail Williams, whose actual age was between
eleven and fourteen, plus the evidence that she tried to have Goody
Procter killed by incantations, he manufactured an eighteen-year-old
wench who had seduced Goody Procter's husband. Likewise there is

no specific evidence that Procter confessed and then recanted his confession as occurs in the play, although other accused persons did so. Says the author, "A playwright has no debt of literalness to history. Right now I couldn't tell you which details were taken from the records verbatim and which were invented. I think you can say that this play is as historically authentic as *Richard II,* which took place closer to Shakespeare's time than *The Crucible* did to ours."

After the overture of the first scene is over, the play more or less concentrates on the fate of one man, John Procter. "Any play is the story of how the birds came home to roost," says Miller. "Procter acts and has to face the consequences of his action. In so going he discovers who he is. He is a good man. Willy Loman in *Death of a Salesman* went through the same process, but, because he had lost Procter's sense of personal inviolability and had yielded completely to every pressure, he never found out who he was. That's what Procter meant near the end of the play when he talks of his 'name.' He is really speaking about his identity, which he cannot surrender."

Another character who interests Miller is Reverend Hale, who initiates the witchcraft investigation. "Hale," he says, "is a man who permits a beloved ideology to overwhelm the evidence of his senses past the point when the evidence of his senses should have led him to question and revise his ideology. His tragic failure along with certain other honest leaders of that community was a lack of a sense of proportion."

While the dramatist is willing to talk about themes within his play, he doesn't pretend to know exactly what his play means. "I never know until at least a year after I've written it. A complex play can have many themes, but I don't sit down to write a play with a specific theme worked out in my mind. What I do have in my mind is a general sense of the quality I want to have, much as you might try to present a picture of honesty or beauty by describing some honest or beautiful person you knew. Then I work on the script until it seems to have the aura of my original conception and at the same time I can see every moment of it as drama."

Although many people have seen Miller's previous plays as political or allegorical, the playwright is definite in his denial of any such simple intention. "I am not pressing an historical allegory here, and I have even eliminated certain striking similarities from *The Crucible* which may have started the audience to draw such an allegory. For instance, the Salemers believed that the surrounding Indians, who had never been converted to Christianity, were in alliance with the witches, who were writing as a Fifth Column for them within the town. It was even thought that the outbreak of witchcraft was the last attack by the Devil, who was being pressed into the wilderness by the expanding colony. Some might have equated the Indians with Russians and the local witches with Communists. My intent and interest is broader and I think deeper than this. After my first acquaintance with the story, I was struck hard by the breathing heroism of certain of the victims who display an almost frightening personal integrity. It seemed to me that the best part of this country was made of such stuff, and I had a burning desire to celebrate them and to raise them out of the historic dust."

Mr. Miller believes the reason his plays are thought to be so political is that the complete vacuousness of so many of our contemporary plays makes works of any substance seem political by comparison.

He points out that Girardoux's *Madwoman of Chaillot* was a really radical play, but that because it was set in Paris people here did not take it as such. As far as he is concerned in his own plays, Miller prefers to consider the area of literature and the area of politics to be separate.

"Literature is a weapon, but not in the sense that Marxists, Fascists, and our own 'Americanists' believe. It is possible to read a royalist-Catholic writer and draw sustenance for a leftwing position from him; it is possible to draw a conservative moral from an anti-conservative work. A work of art creates a complex world, and as the past hundred years have proved, the special 'truth' of one decade may turn out to be the reactionary falsehood of another. It is a poor weapon whose direction is so unstable as to serve one side at one moment and another side the next. The only sure and valid aim—speaking of art as a weapon—is the humanizing of man."

At this point we were interrupted by a deputation of actors who wanted the playwright to change a line or two in one of the scenes. Miller listened to them with a combination of Procter's sense of inviolability and the sense of proportion that Hale had lacked. Then he explained to the actors why this particular change should not be made.

"You know," he said after they had gone, "the most important thing for the playwright is to be able to make the right alterations during rehearsals. Each actor beings his own personality to his part and would—if you were not careful—tend to change the meaning of the play. The playwright must rewrite both in order to make the actor comfortable in the part and also to protect the meaning of the play from the intrusion of the actor's personal characteristics."

The Crucible is being directed by Jed Harris, who operates differently from most of the directors Miller is used to working with. "Jed works from the outside in, which I think is best for this kind of large-canvas play. He is a very serious man, with superb taste and perception. Sometimes there'll be hours of rehearsal when I get worried because nothing seems to be getting accomplished. But then suddenly he'll work very quickly and closely with the actors, and do in half an hour what some directors would take days to do. Above all he's a perfectionist."

Rehearsal was recommencing on stage, so I whispered a quick goodbye and tiptoed my way out, leaving Arthur Miller with his sense of proportion and his inviolability to Jed Harris's inviolate world.

Arthur Miller Discusses *The Crucible*
John and Alice Griffin/1953

From *Theatre Arts,* October 1953, pp. 33-34.

The Crucible, which opened at the Martin Beck Theatre in New York last January, has been described as a "powerful play," a "stirring melodrama," a "parable" and a work "chiefly concerned with what happened rather than why."

None of these interpretations, however, has been voiced by playwright Arthur Miller, who says that the idea of dramatizing the Salem witch trials had been in his mind for a considerable time, in fact, as far back as his student days at the University of Michigan in the thirties. "Salem," he explains, "is one of the few dramas in history with a beginning, a middle and an end. The drama is complete because the people saw the error of their ways quite soon after the tragedy occurred." He adds that he could not have written the play at any other time than the present.

The people of Salem appealed to Miller as characters for a drama because they were articulate. "I was dealing witih people very conscious of an ideology, of what they stood for . . . the revolution they had lived through was still in their minds . . . they were special people and could voice the things that were buried deep in them. Today's writers describe man's helplessness and eventual defeat. In Salem you have the story of a defeat because these people were destroyed, and this makes it real to us today because we believe in defeat. But they understood at the same time what was happening to them. They knew why they struggled . . . they knew how to struggle . . . they did not die helplessly. The moral size of these people drew me . . . they didn't whimper.

"We should be tired by now of merely documenting the defeat of man. This play is a step toward an assertion of a positive kind of value in contemporary plays. Since 1920 American drama has been a steady, year-by-year documentation of the frustration of man. I do not believe in this . . . that is not our fate. It is not enough to tell what is happening; the newspapers do that. In our drama the man with convictions has in the past been a comic figure. I believe he fits in our drama more now, though, and I am trying to find a way, a form, a method of depicting people who do think."

In discussing the historical basis of the play, Miller revealed that the plot and characters, except for Proctor and his wife, are historically accurate. He went on to indicate that his hero Proctor is a man who fights against the loss of his identity, a loss which he believes would result if he joined the group.

"There is a certain pride operating in him," the author pointed out. "Proctor could not go to his death as easily as Rebecca Nurse does. He believed in paradise but didn't want to go there so quickly. Besides, if you confessed you were a witch, you confessed to being a fraud; you were someone who pretended to be decent but who really was a liar."

Illustrating how the playwright has to make concessions when the play goes into production, Miller mentioned that the first scene, as the play was originally written, took place in a forest, but this had to be altered because of the expense involved in building this set.

Later in the run, six months after the New York première, Miller was able to include a forest scene, printed here for the first time. This new production, completely restaged by the author, did away with all scenery, and had the action take place against drapes and a light-flooded cyclorama. Favoring the change, the critics praised the new scene as providing additional motivation for Abigail, and they found the new version more fluid, forceful and poetic. This is the production which shortly is scheduled to begin a tour of major cities. Encouraged by the success of his initial attempt at directing, Miller has decided to direct his own plays in the future, as he is now convinced that he can achieve the dramatic effects he wants by working with the actors.

The Crucible earlier had received an Antoinette Perry award for "distinguished contribution to the current theatre season" and was runner-up in the New York Drama Critics Circle balloting to select the "best new American play" of the season. Miller won "Tonys" in 1947 for *All My Sons* and in 1949 for *Death of a Salesman. The Crucible* also shared the Donaldson Award with William Inge's *Picnic.*

The playwright was particularly interested in explaining whether

The Crucible was intended to be more, or less realistic than his earlier
Death of a Salesman. "In *Death of a Salesman,*" he said, "I tried to
give people a sense of reality in depth. I could have done this by
symbolic behavior, like impressionism, but felt that was an old
technique. I tried to show the facade-like surface realism of life in
realistic acting and at the same time melt this away and bring out the
half-conscious, subconscious life and combine both of these with the
social context in which the action was taking place. I had to have
these two working against each other.

"In *The Crucible,* as I said before, the characters were special
people who could give voice to the things that were inside them.
There is great danger in pathos, which can destroy any tragedy if you
let it go far enough. My weakness is that I can create pathos at will. It
is one of the easiest things to do. I feel that Willy Loman lacks
sufficient insight into this situation, which would have made him a
greater, more significant figure. These people knew what was
happening to them; they had insight in the sense that Hamlet has it.
A point has to arrive where man sees what has happened to him. I
think *The Crucible* is not more realistic but more theatrical than
Death of a Salesman."

A man who is always interested in cosmic themes, Miller appears
much concerned with what he terms "diabolism"—the fear and
hatred of opposites. "And when tensions exist," he explained, "this
fear is organized. In Salem these people regarded themselves as
holders of a light. If this light were extinguished, they believed, the
world would end. When you have an ideology which feels itself so
pure, it implies an extreme view of the world. Because they are white,
opposition is completely black."

Miller believes that the temptation toward diabolism has always
existed in mankind and exists today. "We have come to a time when
it seems there must be two sides, and we look back to the ideal state
of being, when there was no conflict. Our idea is that conflict can be
wiped out of the world.

"But until man arrives at a point where he realizes that conflict is
the essence of life, he will end up by knocking himself out."

Death of a Salesman: A Symposium

Arthur Miller, Gore Vidal, Richard Watts, John Beaufort, Martin Dworkin, David W. Thompson and Phillip Gelb (Moderator)/1958

From *Tulane Drama Review* 2 (1958): 63-69. Reprinted by permission.

Gelb: This series is concerned with "Ideas and the Theatre," and we feel Arthur Miller is qualified both as a thinker and as a dramatist. Actually, I think he also qualifies as a kind of prophet. He is a prophet in the sense that he warns us of the possible bitter harvest that may be reaped from our present limited ways; he calls attention to the moral and ethical decisions that must be made; and he dramatizes the problem and the need for individuality and will. These may well prove to be the ultimate meanings of hope. But why hope? *Death of a Salesman* is generally thought to be Mr. Miller's most important play; is it an affirming one? Let's refresh our memories.

Watts: The title, *Death of a Salesman*, has the virtues not only of being striking and provocative, but also of telling forthrightly what the drama is about. Mr. Miller is describing the last days of a man who is forced to face the terrible fact that he is a failure; that his vague ideal of success has crumbled; that his sons, on whose respect and success he has counted, have only contempt for him. With the utter collapse of Willy Loman's world, there is nothing for him to do but die. The story is as simple as that, and there is such truth in it that it is hard to see how any sensitive playgoer can fail to find something of himself in the mirror that it holds up to life. Only the most fatuous observer could think of *Death of a Salesman* as a propaganda play, and yet it manages to go so deeply into contemporary values that it becomes a valid and frightening social criticism. Mr. Miller looks upon the salesman ideal of success with an angry but discerning eye, and he sees its hollowness and treachery. Poor Willy Loman, who thought that for a successful salesman popularity and good fellowship were all

27

and tried to teach his sons what he believed was his wisdom, is a completely credible victim of a prevailing code as the encroachment of old age destroys its shabby plausibility. Set down with frank emotions (this) play is, I suspect, something to make strong men weep and think.

Gelb: Mr. Watts, that was an excerpt from your review of the play when it first opened in 1949; do you think the play still stands up?

Watts: Oh yes, I think so. The curious thing about this play is that it really was a tragedy for extroverts. The more extroverted people were that went to it, the more they seemed to be moved by it. Usually with a tragedy here, the wives drag their protesting husbands along and the husbands have an awful time and the wives cry. But I saw again and again that it would be the husband who would be moved by *Death of a Salesman*. He would see something of himself in it. He would get far more out of it usually than his wife did.

Gelb: If *Death of a Salesman* is so starkly pessimistic, what is so special about it?

Dworkin: The play is special and Miller's most meaningful work, because he really hit something deep in America when he made that play. The great American idea of the salesman goes back to the old Yankee trader of the Sam Slick type and exists today in the modern huckster who doesn't carry a suitcase or a sample-kit but sells, and in selling he has to take a part of what is human and make it marketable and put a price on it. I consider this Miller's greatest play because his own great skill, his dramatic sense, his artistry, gets beyond his argument so successfully. He has some severe criticisms to make of our society, and yet *Death of a Salesman* criticizes without being propaganda because the characters are so real. The play is an illustration of that paradoxical problem, that so often emerges when discussing works of art, in which the more valid the particularity gets, the more universal it is an exemplification. Willy Loman comes to represent a certain danger, a certain menace, a certain integral nature in salesmanship in general, because he is so much a particular Willy Loman and not simply a slogan out of the 1930's. He represents a condition where a man necessarily has to go out into space with nothing but a smile and a shoe shine and that packet of samples he is selling and get that order! This strange man, out in space, completely divorced from the fundamental productive processes which manufacture the merchandise that he is selling, not quite the friend and not quite the enemy and not quite the instrument of the people whom he is selling, somehow, this strange intermediary must sell himself in order to sell things.

Vidal: I disagree! I don't think the play is about salesmanship and money. Rather I think it is more concerned with a human being who tries to live by a certain set of standards to which he cannot measure up and what happens to him as he fails. I think money is a part of it, but it is much more simply keeping up with the Joneses, and bit by bit failing, and what happens. And Mr. Miller is quite beautifully saying that attention must be paid to this sort of failure in our society. I think Miller in a sense sentimentalizes it because I don't think the problem is all that great. I think people adjust to failure quite beautifully, since that is the lot of nearly all of us. It is not as tragic as that, even in this society at the level of a salesman on the Boston route. But except for a certain sentimentality in the handling of it, I think it showed a situation which nobody else had showed on the stage.

Beaufort: I am not sure I agree here. I do not believe Willy Loman is a tragic character. I think that he is a sad character. I think he is a vicious character. The trouble with Willy Loman, as a figure in dramatic tragedy, is that he never starts with any ideals to begin with. He is a man who, from the very beginning of the play, says it is a question of whether you're liked or whether you're well-liked. He encourages his sons to steal and cheat. He has no moral values at all.

Gelb: But what if one asks, isn't this Americana? Isn't this the common man?

Beaufort: It's one phase of Americana; but if Willy Loman truly represented the whole mass of American civilization of today, I think that the country would be in a terrible state, I just can't accept Willy Loman as the average American citizen. I can accept him as a specimen of a certain aspect of society. We all know that people like Willy Loman exist, and Miller has every right to write about him. I'm perfectly willing to accept him as a dramatic character on the stage; but I will not for a minute accept Willy Loman as the American "Everyman." I think that is nonsense.

Gelb: What reasons are there for people doing things in our mid-twentieth century other than to be liked or well-liked or to realize more material benefits? I suppose what I'm asking is how much of an influence, if any, do you think the moral and spiritual factors are in our time?

Beaufort: I think they're still very substantially influential. I'm not a social historian; I'm not a sociologist. All I'm willing to say is that I believe that for the most part the people in the United States are motivated by many such things or other and many finer things than Willy Loman was motivated by: love of country, religious principles, and ethical values . . . I mean you only have to consider in any situation the response of the American people to a disaster and the need for help to see that we are not an indifferent people. We are a concerned people. Oh, I don't mean to say that we never manifest indifference, we do; but all I'm trying to say is that you couldn't, at least I couldn't, accept Willy Loman as the reflection of the mean of American society in terms of the individual citizen. It just wouldn't be possible.

Gelb: Arthur Miller, how valid and pertinent are Mr. Beaufort's observations?

Miller: The trouble with Willy Loman is that he has tremendously powerful ideals. We're not accustomed to speaking of ideals in his terms; but, if Willy Loman, for instance, had not had a very profound sense that his life as lived had left him hollow, he would have died contentedly polishing his car on some Sunday afternoon at a ripe old age. The fact is he has values. The fact that they cannot be realized is what is driving him mad—just as, unfortunately, it's driving a lot of other people mad. The truly valueless man, a man without ideals, is always perfectly at home anywhere . . . because there cannot be a conflict between nothing and something. Whatever negative qualities there are in the society or in the environment don't bother him, because they are not in conflict with what positive sense one may have. I think Willy Loman, on the other hand, is seeking for a kind of ecstasy in life, which the machine-civilization deprives people of. He's looking for his selfhood, for his immortal soul, so to speak. People who don't know the intensity of that quest, possibly, think he's odd. Now an extraordinarily large number of salesmen particularly, who are in a line of work where a large measure of ingenuity and individualism are required, have a very intimate understanding of this problem. More so, I think, than literary critics who probably need strive less after a certain point. A salesman is a kind of creative person (it's possibly idiotic to say so on a literary program, but they are), they have to get up in the morning and conceive a plan of attack and use all kinds of ingenuity all day long, just the way a writer does.

Gelb: What about this, Mr. Miller? John Beaufort made the statement that if Willy Loman represented the whole mass of American civilization today, the country would be in a terrible state. He would not for a moment accept Willy Loman as an average American man.

Miller: Well, it's obvious that Willy Loman can't be an average American man, at least from one point of view; he kills himself. That's a rare thing in society, although it's more common than one could wish. But this "being average" is beside the point. As a matter of fact, the standard of averageness is hardly valid. It tells neither whether a character is a truthful character, as a character, nor a valid one. It's ridiculous. Hamlet isn't a typical Elizabethan either. Horatio probably is. What's the difference? It has no point unless we are not talking about literature but about patriotism. I did not write *Death of a Salesman* to announce a new American man, or an old American man. Willy Loman is, I think, a person who embodies in him some of the most terrible conflicts running through the streets of America today. A Gallup poll might not indicate that they are the majority conflicts; I think they are; but then what is the difference?

Gelb: Earlier, Martin Dworkin said that he feels the play makes a statement about the average American man because Willy Loman is such a particular Willy Loman. Do you feel that the best way to present a universal is in terms of a really specific story?

Miller: It is the best way! It is the hardest way, too! The ability to create the universal from the particular is not given to many authors, nor to any single author many times. You have to know the particular in your bones to do this. But it is the best way. As the few plays that are repeatedly done over generations and centuries show, they are generally, in our Western Culture anyway, those plays which are full of the most particular information about the people.

Gelb: What about this question of hope and hopelessness? I mean, is there a chance to make the positive value in drama dramatic? Or is drama, by its very nature, only an attack upon things?

Miller: Not only drama, but literature in general—and this goes back a long, long distance in history—posits the idea of value, of right and wrong, of good and bad, high and low, not so much by setting forth, but by showing so to speak, the wages of sin. In other words, when, for instance in *Death of a Salesman,* we are shown a man who dies for the want of some positive, viable human value, the play implies—and it could not have been written without the authors' consciousness that the audience did believe something different. In other words, by showing what happens where there are no values, I at least, assume that the audience will be compelled and propelled toward a more intense quest for the values that are missing. I am assuming always that we have a kind of civilized sharing of what we would like to see occur within us and within the world. I think that the drama, at least mine, is not so much an attack but an exposition of "the want." This kind of drama can be done only if the audience itself is constantly trying to supply what is missing.

Gelb: Although critic John Beaufort and playwright Arthur Miller seem to be in some disagreement over the character of Willy Loman, I think it is even more significant to note that Mr. Beaufort, in his earlier comments, came up with the very conclusion that Mr. Miller wanted from his play—the conclusion that there is a better way than Willy's way, that we can act on more meaningful values. In other words, John Beaufort supplies some of what Arthur Miller seems to be suggesting as the missing moral links between the *Death of a Salesman* and the Life of a Man. The day I first interviewed Arthur Miller was shortly after the Russians had launched the first satellite. This led me to ask Mr. Miller as to whether or not the various sciences, from nuclear physics to psychology, hadn't made the contemporary artist's job too difficult by giving him too many facts and views to consider. Under this deluge of knowledge, weren't apathy, anxiety and cynicism the natural results? Could any creative writer take even most of the available information and insights into consideration and still write creatively?

Miller: Well, whether it can be done remains for me or somebody else to prove. But let me put it this way: we're living, or I'm living anyway, with a great consciousness of the incredible force of objective thought. As we speak, there is an object flying around in the sky passing over this point every, I think it's one hundred and some minutes, which was put up there by thinking men who willed it to go up there. The implications of this are as enormous as any statement by or on the part of Zeus, or Moses, or Shakespeare, or any feeling man. Now, it may be a great bite to take, but I think the only thing worth doing (whether one can do it or not is an entirely different story, but aims are important) today in the theatre, from my point-of-view, is to synthesize the subjective drives of the human being with what is now demonstrably the case. Namely, that by acts of will he can and has changed the world. It is said that nothing is new under the sun. This is! It's right under the sun, and it's new! But it's only one of many things that are new. I've seen communities transformed by the act of a committee. I've seen the interior lives of people transformed by the decision of a company, or of a man, or of a school. In other words, it is old fashioned to simply go on asserting the helplessness of the individual.

Gelb: You're not in the large "artistic" camp then of those who write of, by, and for despair.

Miller: Well, for myself I can't write anything if I'm sufficiently unhappy. A lot of writers write best when they're most miserable. I suppose my sense of form comes from a positive need to organize life and not from a desire to demonstrate the inevitability of defeat and death.

Gelb: Do you think this becomes a kind of final analysis of many issues in life—social, political, economic, psychological? You made a statement putting you on the side of life against death. Aren't many "final answers" dependent upon whether this is or is not a basic commitment?

Miller: It is a commitment on my part. I don't see the point in proving again that we must be defeated. I didn't intend that in *Salesman.* I was trying in *Salesman,* in this respect to set forth what happens when a man does not have a grip on the forces of life and has no sense of values which will lead him to that kind of a grip; but the implication of it was that there must be such a grasp of those forces—or else we're doomed. I was not, in other words, Willy Loman. I was the writer, and Willy Loman is there because I could see beyond him.

Thompson: In summary then, "The curious thing" about Arthur Miller's *Death of a Salesman* is, as Mr. Watts said, that it really is "a tragedy for extroverts." In older drama, for example in Moliere, a bumbling, simple-minded hustler is always a figure of fun. He is the object of satiric criticism. Mr. Miller does criticize his salesman but earnestly, without a trace of the older comic view. And what is really curious is that the play, besides criticizing Willy Loman's dishonesty and vulgarity, asks that a great deal of sympathy and attention be paid to the failure himself. Willy is shown to be wrong in *every* respect of human decency but is still expected to be a great tragic figure. This asking for more sympathy than the facts seem to deserve is what gives, as Mr. Vidal said, "a certain sentimentality" to the play. As Mr. Beaufort put it, "I think that Willy Loman is not a tragic character. I think that he is a sad character. I think he is a vicious character. The trouble with Willy Loman, as a figure in dramatic tragedy, is that he never starts with any ideals to begin with . . . He has no moral values at all."

This word "values" set off the big controversy in today's program. In his reply to Mr. Beaufort's charge, Mr. Miller at first insisted that Willy Loman "has tremendously powerful ideals . . . The fact is that he has values . . . (he) is seeking for a kind of ecstasy in life." (One might note here in passing that the universal, primitive egotism of a child always leads to a generalized "seeking for a kind of ecstasy in life"—its worth depends entirely upon what specific values and forms mark that search, especially in adult life). Later, Mr. Miller seemed to contradict himself by saying that his play shows "what happens where there are no values," and that Willy Loman has "no sense of values" which will lead him to "a grip on the forces of life." This contradiction, of course, proves very little, except perhaps that Mr. Miller, fortunately for us, is a playwright and not a dramatic theorist.

There was, after all, general agreement among the participants as to Mr. Miller's important, even leading, position as a contemporary American dramatist. There was no denying that his *Death of a Salesman* is a powerful play giving a true-to-life portrayal of a certain type of American, who, as Mr. Dworkin said, is as old as the Sam Slick Yankee trader and as current as the modern huckster. If some of us, like Mr. Vidal, and Mr. Beaufort, feel the play is marred by a certain sentimentality in its demanding so much sympathy for Willy, this may only mean that we are neither salesmen or extroverts.

Perhaps in older, tougher days the subject of a foolish, childish salesman, plus Mr. Miller's keen sense of realistic detail, would have produced a biting social satire. Today, however, it is certainly not Mr. Miller's fault that his audience, composed mainly of hucksters, will accept criticism only in a sympathetic "tragedy for extroverts."

Morality and Modern Drama
Phillip Gelb/1958

From *Educational Theatre Journal*, 10 (1958): 190-202. Reprinted by permission.

Gelb: Mr. Miller, what about the apparent lack of moral values in modern drama?

Miller: Not only modern drama, but literature in general—and this goes back a long, long distance in history—posits the idea of value, of right and wrong, good and bad, high and low, not so much by setting forth these values as such, but by showing, so to speak, the wages of sin. In other words, when for instance, in *Death of a Salesman,* we are shown a man who dies for the want of some positive, viable human value, the play implies, and it could not have been written without the author's consciousness, that the audience did believe something different. In other words, by showing what happens when there are no values, I, at least, assume that the audience will be compelled and propelled toward a more intense quest for values that are missing. I am assuming always that we have a kind of civilized sharing of what we would like to see occur within us and in the world; and I think that the drama, at least mine, is not so much an attack but an exposition, so to speak, of the want of value, and you can only do this if the audience itself is constantly trying to supply what is missing. I don't say that's a new thing. The Greeks did the same thing. They may have had a chorus which overtly stated that this is what happens when Zeus' laws are abrogated or broken, but that isn't what made their plays great.

Gelb: Reverend John Bachman at the Union Theological Seminary said something similar. He said that the *Death of a Salesman* is moral to the extent that it is a negative witness. Now at the same time he felt that your play could not do any kind of a job in terms of presenting positive answers; this, of course, in his view, was the job of religion. Do you feel that that dichotomy actually—

Miller: It isn't always so. Ibsen used to present answers. Despite the fashion that claims he never presented answers, he of course did. In the *Doll's House* and even in *Hedda Gabler,* we will find—and in Chekhov, too—we will find speeches toward the ends of these plays which suggest, if they don't overtly state, what the alternative values are to those which misled the heroes or heroines of the action shown. The difference is that we are now a half century beyond that probably more hopeful time, and we've been through social revolution which these people hadn't witnessed yet. We have come to a kind of belated recognition that the great faith in social change as an amelioration or a transforming force of the human soul leaves something to be wanted. In other words, we originally, in the late nineteenth century, posed the idea that science would, so to speak, cure the soul of man by the eradication of poverty. We have eradicated poverty in large parts—well, in small parts of the world, but in significant parts of the world—and we're just as mean and ornery as we ever were. So that the social solution of the evil in man has failed—it seems so, anyway—and we are now left with a kind of bashful unwillingness to state that we still believe in life and that we still believe there is a conceivable standard of values. My feeling is, though, that we are in a transition stage between a mechanistic concept of man and an amalgam of both the rationalistic and what you could call the mystical or spiritualistic concept of him. I don't think either that man is without will or that society is impotent to change his deepest, most private self-conceptions. I think that the work of art, the great work of art, is going to be that work which finds space for the two forces to operate. So far, I will admit, the bulk of literature, not only on the stage but elsewhere, is an exposition of man's failure: his failure to assert his sense of civilized and moral life.

Gelb: A situation came up just the other day—I teach speech at Hunter College—in which somebody made a speech proclaiming the values of deceit: manipulative techniques, sophistry, and the rest. Most everybody went along with it to the extent that they felt that the use of techniques was automatically deceitful. Techniques were equated with trickery and the negative. I pointed out that integrity and honor, responsibility, rationality, logic—a lot of these things can be used as techniques, too.

Miller: That reminds me of a book by Thomas Mann about Moses, in which, with his tongue in his cheek probably, but certainly with high seriousness, he portrays Moses as being a man bedeviled by the barbaric backwardness of a stubborn people and trying to improve them and raise up their sights. He disappears into the wilderness, up on the mountain, and comes down after a considerable period of time with the Ten Commandments. Now the Ten Commandments, from the point of view that you've just been speaking about, is a technique. It is purely and simply a way of putting into capsule form what probably the most sensitive parts of the society were wishing could be stated so that people could memorize it and people could live by it. I am sure that there must have been a number of people that said it was a kind of deceit or dishonesty to try to pinpoint things that way, things that were otherwise amorphous and without form and which probably some old Jews felt were even irreligious to carve into stone—but it is a technique. The whole Bible is a technique; it has got a form. If you read the three Gospels of Matthew, Mark, and Luke you will see the tremendous effort being made to dramatize, to make vivid, an experience which probably none of them really saw—except possibly one. It was a job almost of spiritual propaganda. Why would they have to write this down? Why would they strive for the *mot juste*, for the perfect paragraph, for the most vivid image, which quite evidently they do? Technique is like anything else; it is deceitful only when it is used for deceitful purposes.

Gelb: Mr. John Beaufort, the critic for the *Christian Science Monitor,* attacked Willy Loman as a sad character, a vicious character, who couldn't figure in dramatic tragedy because he never starts with any ideals to begin with.

Miller: The trouble with Willy Loman is that he has tremendously powerful ideals. We are not accustomed to speaking of ideals in *his* terms, but if Willy Loman, for instance, had not had a very profound sense that his life as lived had left him hollow, he would have died contentedly polishing his car on some Sunday afternoon at a ripe old age. The fact is that he has values. The fact that they cannot be realized is what is driving him mad, just as, unfortunately, it is driving a lot of other people mad. The truly valueless man, the man without ideals, is always perfectly at home anywhere because there cannot be conflict between nothing and something. Whatever negative qualities there are in the society or in the environment don't bother him because they are not in conflict with any positive sense that he may have. I think Willy Loman is seeking for a kind of ecstasy in life which the machine civilization deprives people of. He is looking for his selfhood, for his immortal soul, so to speak, and people who don't know the intensity of that quest think he is odd, but a lot of salesmen, in a line of work where ingenuity and individualism are acquired by the nature of the work, have a very intimate understanding of his problem; more so, I think, than literary critics who probably need strive less, after a certain point. A salesman is a kind of creative person. It is possibly idiotic to say so in a literary program, but they are; they have to get up in the morning and conceive a plan of attack and use all kinds of ingenuity all day long just like a writer does.

Gelb: I think this idea of "a plan of attack" comes back to what we were talking about before, about techniques that become deceitful. The whole concept of present advertising is involved. By techniques the public is sold things they don't really need. Your plan of attack therefore becomes vicious; only the technique makes them buy.

Miller: Well, that's true. I see the point now. But compared to, let's say, the normal viciousness, if you want to use that term, of standard advertising techniques, Willy is a baby. I mean, Willy is naive enough to believe in the goodness of his mission. There are highly paid advertising people who are utterly cynical about this business, and probably a lot of people call Willy vicious who would think of themselves as simply the pillars of society. Willy is a victim; he didn't originate this thing. He believes that selling is the greatest thing anybody can do.

Gelb: This would seem to imply that Willy Loman, at least in terms of his problems and his anxieties, could be a lot of people. Now, Beaufort makes the statement, "If Willy Loman represented the whole mass of American civilization today, I think the country would be in a terrible state. I just can't accept Willy Loman as the average American citizen."

Miller: It is obvious that Willy *can't* be an average American man, at least from one point of view; he kills himself. That's a rare thing in society, although it is more common than one could wish, and it's beside the point. As a matter of fact, that standard of "averageness" is not valid. It neither tells whether the character is a truthful character as a character, or a valid one. I can't help adding that that is the standard of socialist realism—which of course wasn't invented by socialists. It is the idea that a character in a play or in a book cannot be taken seriously unless he reflects some statistical average, plus his ability to announce the official aims of the society; and it is ridiculous. Hamlet isn't a typical Elizabethan, either. Horatio probably is. What is the difference? It has no point unless you are talking about, not literature, but patriotism. I didn't write *Death of a Salesman* to announce some new American man, or an old American man. Willy Loman is, I think, a person who embodies in himself some of the most terrible conflicts running through the streets of America today. A Gallup Poll might indicate that they are not the majority conflicts; I think they are. But what's the difference?

Gelb: Maybe I should have read this statement first. This was made by the critic for *Progressive* magazine, Martin Dworkin, and he considers that *Death of a Salesman* makes a strong message for an average American man because "Willy Loman is such a particular Willy Loman. He is not simply a slogan out of the 1930s; he is not a banner to be waved to liberate people; he is not a criticism of society." And then Dworkin points out that because Willy is so particular, therefore he does these other universal things. What about the history of art and drama here that the best way to present a universal is in terms of a really specific story?

Miller: It is the best. It is the hardest way, too, and it isn't given to many authors or to any single author many times to be able to do it. Namely, to create the universal from the particular. You have to know the particular in your bones to do that. As the few plays that are repeatedly done over generations and centuries show, they are generally, in our western culture anyway, those plays which are full of the most particular information about people. We don't do many Greek plays any more, in my opinion not because they lack wonderful stories—they have wonderful stories—but in our terms, in terms of particularization of characters, they are deficient. It doesn't mean the Greeks were bad playwrights. It means their aims were different. But we do do *Hamlet*, we do do *Macbeth*, we do a number of more mediocre plays as well; but the ones that last are the ones that we recognize most immediately in terms of the details of real human behavior in specific situations.

Gelb: How do you apply that to T. S. Eliot and George Bernard Shaw? Do you feel that their people are very real or specific?

Miller: I don't think T. S. Eliot would even claim that he is creating characters, in the realistic sense of the word. It is a different aim. It doesn't mean that he can't do it; I don't think he can, but I don't think he is trying to do it. I think he is trying to dramatize quite simply a moral, a religious dilemma. The same is true of Bernard Shaw excepting for occasional characters, usually women, in his plays. They are more psychologically real than anything, of course, T. S. Eliot has done to my knowledge, excepting perhaps for *Murder in the Cathedral*. But the aim in these plays is not the aim of *Salesman* or most American work. It is the setting forth of an irony, a dilemma, more or less in its own terms. I think all the characters in Shaw can be reduced to two or three, really, and nobody would mind particularly. You always know that it's Shaw speaking no matter what side of the argument is being set forth, and that is part of the charm. I think his great success is due to the fact that he made no pretense to do otherwise; he was observing the issues in the dilemma of life rather than the psychology of human beings.

Gelb: I'd like to take issue with that and simply say that Shaw might be writing real people but they speak more eloquently, more intellectually than real people. Essentially, I am not sure that in *Pygmalion* the father isn't real. I don't think anybody would talk like that, but I think his motives are real. I think Higgins is a real person. I think Shaw simply is not happy with the inability of people to express themselves and so he says I will do it for them; but I never really felt that Shaw's people were not people.

Miller: I would put it this way. Shaw is impatient with the insignificance of most human speech, most human thought, and most human preconceptions. It's not that his characters are not people, it is that they aren't insignificant people the way people usually are. When you strip from the human being everything that is not of significance, you may get a valid moment out of him, a valid set of speeches, a valid set of attitudes, but in the normal, naturalistic concept, they aren't real because the bulk of reality is, of course, its utter boredom, and its insignificance, and its irrelevancy, and Shaw is absolutely uninterested in that. Consequently, if you just take the significant part of the character, it will be true but if this is lifted out of the rest of the character's psychology, you can no longer speak in terms of normal psychological writing. I happen to like this sort of thing; I am not criticizing it. I think it is a great thing to be able to do. But it isn't the tapestry work, let us say, of a *Hamlet* where you are carried through moment to moment, from one thought to the next, including the boredom, including the irrelevancy, including the contradictions within him which are not thematic. That is to say, they have very little to do with his conflict with the king or his mother, but they have much to do with creating a background for the major preconceptions of the play. Shaw is always eliminating the insignificant background, and it's possibly because he had so much to say and there was so little time to say it. But you mentioned one of the minor characters in *Pygmalion,* like the father. I think, in general, aside from the women, it *is* the minor characters who are most realistically drawn. The major characters are too completely obsessed with the issues that are being set forth. One of the signs of an abrogation of regular psychology is that people stay on the theme. You know and I know, even in this little interview, that it is very difficult, if not impossible, to spontaneously stay on the subject. You read Shaw's plays and see how rarely people get off the subject; and that's what I mean when I say that it isn't psychology he is following, it is the theme.

Gelb: Let's assume that Shaw is concerned with the intellectual or social significances and chooses his material accordingly. The statement has been made by anthropologist Solon Kimball that Tennessee Williams chooses materials by their psychological significance. Dr. Kimball says that while Williams' picture of a Southern community in part may be true, that this psychological orientation gives a distorted picture of the whole. Evidently even some truth to the community and to the psychology of characters is not enough. Do you feel that is true of Williams, or what do you think of the general idea?

Miller: Williams is a realistic writer; realistic in the sense that I was just referring to—that is to say, realistic in the way that Shaw is not. I think Williams is primarily interested in passion, in ecstasy, in creating a synthesis of his conflicting feelings. It is perfectly all right, of course, for an anthropologist to make an observation that Williams' picture of the South is unrepresentative. It probably is, but at the same time, the intensity with which he feels whatever he does feel is so deep, is so great, that we do end up with a glimpse of another kind of reality; that is, the reality in the spirit rather than in the society. I think, as I said before, that the truly great work is that work which will show at one and the same time the power and force of the human will working with and against the force of society upon it. Probably

Williams is less capable of delivering the second than he might be. Everybody has some blind spot. But, again, as with Willy Loman, I'm not ready to criticize a writer because he isn't delivering a typical picture. The most typical pictures of society I know are probably in *The Saturday Evening Post*, or on the soap operas. It is more likely to be typical of people to be humdrum and indifferent and without superb conflicts. When a writer sets out to create high climaxes, he automatically is going to depart from the typical, the ordinary, and the representative. The pity is, of course, that Williams works out of Southern material, I work out of big city material, so instantly our characters are compared in a journalistic sense to some statistical norm. Truly, I have no interest in the selling profession, and I am reasonably sure that Williams' interest in the sociology of the South is only from the point of view of a man who doesn't like to see brutality, unfairness, a kind of victory of the Philistine, etc. He is looking at it emotionally, and essentially I am, too. Inevitably, people are going to say that Willy Loman is not a typical salesman, or that Blanche Dubois is not a typical something else, but to tell you the truth, the writer himself couldn't be less interested.

Gelb: You point out Shaw as dealing with the intellectual, the social, the moral; Eliot with the moral, the religious; Williams with the psychological. Eric Bentley made the statement that he thought, perhaps, Arthur Miller was the one writer today who had the most possibility of combining all of these things, and yet he also thought that this was impossible. Can it be done?

Miller: Well, whether it can be done remains for me or somebody else to prove. But let me put it this way: we are living, or I'm living anyway, with a great consciousness of the incredible force of objective thought. As we speak, there is an object flying around in the sky, passing over this point, I think it is every hundred and some minutes, which was put there by thinking men who *willed* it to go up there. The implications of this are as enormous as any statement by or on the part of Zeus, or Moses, or Shakespeare, or any feeling man. Now it may be a great bite to take, but I think the only thing worth doing— whether one can do it or not is an entirely different story, but aims are important—the only thing worth doing today in the theater, from my point of view, is to synthesize the subjective drives of the human being with what is now demonstrably the case, namely, that by an act of will man can and has changed the world. Now it is said that

nothing is new under the sun; this is. It is right under the sun and it is
new. And it is only one of the things that are new. I have seen
communities transformed by the act of a committee. I have seen the
interior lives of people transformed by the decision of a company, or
of a man, or of a school. In other words, it is old fashioned, so to
speak, and it is not moot simply to go on asserting the helplessness of
man. This is true, I think, with variations: the great bulk of the weight
of evidence is that we are not in command. And we're not, I'm not
saying we are. But we surely have much more command than
anybody, including Macbeth's Witches, could ever dream of, and
somehow a form has to be devised which will account for this.
Otherwise the drama is doomed to repeating and repeating *ad
nauseam* the same pattern of striving, disillusion, and defeat. And I
don't think it is a modern day phenomenon.

Gelb: Gore Vidal made a statement similar to yours with almost
an exact opposite conclusion. His point was that he felt the only
influence he could be was in terms of man's ability to destroy and
despair, and so he wrote a play in which he is going to destroy the
world. He said this facetiously, but since he didn't present any
positive point of view, this led to the general topic of "the artist as the
enemy"—perhaps the thing behind it is that many artists like to see
the world destroyed. This isn't just a reporting; this is their own
feeling.

Miller: The enemy is the wrong word to me, although I would
concede it. The artist is the outcast; he always will be. He is an
outcast in the sense that he is to one side of the stream of life and
absorbs it and is, in some part of himself, reserved from its
implications; that is to say, a man like Vidal says we're out to destroy
everything. I think that you can't see a thing when you are in the
middle of it. To some extent, an artist has to step to one side of what
is happening, divorce himself from his role as a citizen, and in that
sense he becomes the enemy because he does not carry forth in
himself and believe what is being believed around him. He is the
enemy usually, I suppose, of the way things are, whatever way they
are.

Gelb: Does that mean, though, that he is always an inadequate
reporter, too, because he is not a part? Is the artist perhaps in the
least likely position to tell what might be true to most people?

Miller: The trouble with literature is that writers have to be the ones who write it. It's always partial; it's always partisan, and it's always incomplete. When I say that writers have to be the ones to write it, I mean that in order to generate the energy to create a big novel, a big play, an involved poem, one has to be a specie of fanatic. You have to think that that is really the only thing worth doing. Otherwise, you can't generate the intensity to do it well. And to that degree, by generating that intensity, you are blinding yourself to what does not fit into some preconceived pattern in your own mind. There's no doubt about that to me, and I think that probably lay behind Plato's prohibition of the artist in society. He was right in the sense that the artist doesn't know what he is doing, to some extent. That is, we pretend, or like to believe, that we are depicting the whole truth of some situation, when as a matter of fact, the whole truth is, by definition, made impossible by the fact that we are obsessed people. I don't know of a first class piece of work written by what I would call, or a psychologist would call, a balanced, adjusted fellow who could easily be, let us say, a good administrator for a complicated social mechanism of some sort. It doesn't work that way. We are not constituted that way; so consequently, to be sure, it will have to be partial. The impulse to do it is obsessive; it always is. One of the fairest, most just writers was Tolstoy, who was, to make it short, quite mad. I mean, you can't pretend that as a person he was judicious, balanced: he wasn't. Neither was Dostoevsky. Neither, certainly, was Ibsen. Probably the most generously balanced man I know of was Chekhov. And I suspect that half of his psychological life we will never know. He was very reticent, and in those days there were no interviews of this sort, and if he didn't choose to write some essays describing his methods and personal life, you'd just know nothing about him.

Gelb: I can get obsessive once or twice a year and maybe write a one-act play or something. The students have asked me this, "How do you take this obsessiveness and channel it into a discipline whereby you sit down and write regularly? Or is this always an individual problem?"

Miller: I don't know how to write regularly. I wish I did. It's not possible to me. I suppose if one were totally dependent upon one's writing for a living and one's writing was of a kind that could be sold, like Dostoevsky's was—he seems about the only big writer I know that wrote regularly, but he wrote regularly because he had to pay his gambling debts half the time and the sheriff was on his tail. I don't know what would have happened if he had been given a stipend of $10,000 a year. Well, he probably would have gambled it away and been in debt again, I guess. So he would have written regularly.

Gelb: Now you're very well established. You don't have to look for a theater, I imagine, just to see a play done. But do you feel that you might write more, or at least more regularly, if you were part of a group? I am thinking of the tradition of the writer as part of a theater group—as it was with Shakespeare, the Greeks, Molière, even Shaw usually worked for some kind of company.

Miller: I think that in the early life of a writer, in his beginning work—and this would go for Shaw, O'Neill, and anybody you wanted to mention—a connection with a group of actors could be very valuable. But I think you will find that as he grows older a playwright dreads the prospect of his play being produced. I mean that seriously. There are so many stupid things that happen which destroy the most valuable, the most sensitive parts of a manuscript that, truthfully, if I seriously contemplated the production of a play as I was writing it, I don't know that I could write it. It is too dreadful a risk, and I don't care how well established you are; it is always the same risk. Your work can go down the drain because you have happened to hire an actor who simply does not have the sensitivity for that role and you didn't know it until the night before you opened. Think of that when you put in two, or three, four years on a play, and you pick up a team of actors, so to speak, and put one guy in to pitch and another in to catch, and the catcher can't catch and the pitcher can't pitch, and there's your manuscript. And there's no critic alive who can tell the difference between a bad production and a bad script unless they are extremely bad in either direction. But where there is some reasonable excellence, nobody knows the difference. I have had plays that have failed in New York—*View from the Bridge* was one of them. I am sure that anybody who saw *View from the Bridge* in New York would not have recognized it in London. I had a great deal to do with the production there; it was a different mood, a different key, a different production, and I am sure anybody would have said it was a different play.

Gelb: In your case, your plays are going to be done for years and years, and you just can't be around, you don't know what kind of actors are going to do them. Any good playwright is at the mercy of a hundred and one different kinds of people, and personalities, and places. Why does one write for the theater then?

Miller: It is one of the minor curses of mankind, I suppose. I have a feeling that it is a way of seeing existence in terms of audible scenes. I was always a playwright. I was a playwright before I'd ever been in the theater. I wrote my first play, which was produced in various places and was a play, after having seen only two.

Gelb: From viewing current plays, one might conclude that maybe what makes most people write is antagonism, negative qualities: despair, getting even, spite.

Miller: For myself, I can't write anything if I am sufficiently unhappy. A lot of writers write best when they are most miserable. I suppose my sense of form comes from a positive need to organize life and not from a desire to demonstrate the inevitability of defeat and death. If I feel miserable enough, I can't work. A lot of writers, I am aware, then are spurred on to express their disillusion. All I know about that really comes down to this—that we are doomed to live, and I suppose one had better make the best of it. I imagine that Vidal shares that fate with me and will continue to. He is probably taking some perverse pleasure in positing the destruction of the world, but I suspect he wouldn't enjoy it as much as he says he would.

Gelb: You feel your need is to organize life and not to present the case for death and despair?

Miller: It is a basic commitment for me, sitting here now in America. For another writer who is, let's say, a French writer, an Italian writer, and who has been through a sufficiently profound social cataclysm, such as two world wars and a depression in-between in Europe, where he was faced with the ultimate disaster, it might seem foolish. My experience, though, is as valid as theirs. In other words, I can't pretend things are worse than they are, any more than they can pretend things are better. It is a commitment on my part that I don't see the point in proving again that we must be defeated. I didn't intend that—since you have mentioned *Salesman* so much in this interview—I didn't intend it in *Salesman*. I was trying in *Salesman*, in this respect, to set forth what happens when a man does not have a grip on the forces of life and has no sense of values which will lead him to that kind of a grip; but the implication was that there must be such a grasp of those forces, or else we're doomed. I was not, in other words, Willy Loman, I was the writer, and Willy Loman is there because I could see beyond him.

Gelb: Mr. Miller, in an interview I had with George Freedley of the New York Drama Critics Circle, Mr. Freedley stated that he thought some Broadway producers and investors shied away from your plays because they were too liberal, that perhaps some of your plays had difficulty in getting productions. Now has anything like that ever occurred?

Miller: Soon after *Salesman* I tried to do a new version of *An Enemy of the People,* which is a play by Ibsen, and which I had felt was never properly put on, and it was very difficult to raise the money. The reason was quite openly stated, at that time—this was back in 1951—that it was too evidently a counter-statement to McCarthy and at that time he was looking like he might be president of the United States and people were wary about supporting such a play. There's no question about that. It exists today. I have never had a play that was not produced for that reason, but I know that the pressure exists. I don't want to appear as somebody who is carrying the firebrand, but there's no question about it, the climate of opinion over the past ten years has been opposed to what we call an openly liberal approach. I suppose a demonstration could be made, however, that the bulk of the plays, rather than being reactionary, are liberal. There's a contradiction there, but it simply means that it is a small minority who do lead an attack on liberal things. The bulk of the people in the theater, and in my opinion, the bulk of the audience, are liberals. I think it is sad from many points of view to have to say that, because it means the enemy is almost non-existent, but that is the case, I think. I would be happier if there were more reactionary playwrights who were willing to put in the theater what they really feel about mankind and about the state of the world.

Gelb: It was Eric Bentley's statement that what he thought was lacking in Arthur Miller's plays was a character who could present the McCarthy point of view. Do you feel that it is the job of the playwright himself to introduce such a reasonable case?

Miller: I never attempted to do that because there was never any point in it, excepting in one play, and that is in *The Crucible* and through the judge who condemned the victims of the witch hunt. The trouble with doing that, though, was as follows: In all truth, the real backward, knuckleheaded reactionary is ridiculous. Now you can say this is merely Miller's viewpoint, but if I showed you the record of the Salem witch hunt and reproduced verbatim from the court record taken in 1692 in Salem, Massachusetts, what the judge said and what he did, you would simply not believe it. You would burst into laughter. I was charged, if not openly then by implication, with not giving the judge his due. The truth of the matter is that I was at my wit's end to give him some respectable viewpoint which one could listen to without simply throwing it out the window. I made a statement in the introduction to my play that we no longer believe in the positiveness of evil, that is to say that people will, with malice aforethought, go about creating bad situations for other people. It's a failure, perhaps, in our point of view, but it's true what Bentley says in that respect. That is to say, I wish there were a way of showing the conqueror, who is usually the bad one, in his own justifications. Think of writing a play about Hitler.

Gelb: I am sure the inquisitor in Shaw's *Saint Joan* is much more understanding and human than the real human.

Miller: We don't dare set forth evil in its full bloom in a person; we don't quite believe it. I go back again to *The Crucible*. Believe me, I think now my mistake in *The Crucible* was that I didn't make the judge evil enough. I think I should have gone the whole hog. I should have shown him conspiring with the witnesses to take evidence, which he did, still being a deeply religious man, a man who could quote any part of the Bible at will, who prayed at *every* opportunity, and met, as is known, with the girls who were hysterical and fed them cues as to what they should testify to an hour hence. He did that; there were others who did that. It was cooked up from their point of view. The hysteria, however, was not cooked up from the point of view of the average person in Salem. He believed it. And the judge was a great actor; he could get himself into a froth and a frenzy knowing, at the same time, that he had manufactured the whole thing. And one of the judges ended up drunk and insane as a result of the conflicts aroused in his mind by the behavior of this other judge and by his own behavior. I am trying to deal with that now, to tell you the truth. I am trying to deal with it because I can't see the problem of will evolving fruitfully unless the existence of evil is taken into account.

Gelb: So far you've been talking about this immensity of evil, its potential, within an individual. But something even worse and more immense occurs when this evil becomes social, when everybody says, "Well, I was obeying orders," or "I did what others did." Is this a problem that we should do nothing about; but simply mention that it exists, in terms of the theater? Well, I suppose what I am really asking is, can this kind of evil be understood dramatically in any way, the Nazi evil, for example?

Miller: It can be understood in one way. I'm not saying that this is *the* way to understand it, of course. A point arrives in the evolution of a society when a goodly number of people take a position knowingly in opposition to what we would call civilized values. I think it has been an old story with us. After all, Lincoln Steffens' autobiography is filled with the observation that the evildoers in his day, the early twentieth century, the political bosses in the big city, with absolute consciousness and awareness of what they were doing, faked elections, bought votes, engaged in every conceivable kind of corruption. And Steffens was probably one of the few reporters who ever confronted them with the facts of their deeds because he was philosophically interested in it. Their answer was that they were no more dishonest than the reformers who refused to understand what they were doing. The reformers had a stake in the graft and refused to see it; refused to see that, in many cases, reformers were professionals, or businessmen, or whatever, and their very professions and businesses were in some way dependent upon the favors that could be gotten from money.

Gelb: Think of *Major Barbara.*

Miller: Yes, it's Shaw's irony again, and so the admission of evil occurs. We blanked it out in this last generation, I think, as a result of the thirties. The depression taught us that we were all equally victims. Suddenly we were all the victims of something unseen and unknowable, and none of us was any worse than the other guy. We were all primarily in a situation; we were no longer individuals. And then along came psychology to tell us that we were again the victim of drives that we weren't even conscious of, so that the idea of a man being willfully good or willfully bad evaporated. We are nothing but what we were born and what we were taught to be up to the age of six, and we are essentially irresponsible. I think that's the situation we're in now.

Gelb: What about Germany?

Miller: Well, the Germans have been notoriously irresponsible since they formed the first states in Germany because of the fact that they never had a social revolution. The people of Germany never rose up, as the people of America did, and asserted a form of government; the form of government was always given them from above. They were essentially in the position of a servant; they were essentially in the position of a son, you might say, and consequently, the father idea, the idea of a strong leader, from Bismarck through Hitler, was a given quality. It was always there, and consequently they are irresponsible from that point of view. They tell the truth when they say they only did what they were told. They've always been doing what they were told. Every nation that does not establish its own government, by its own efforts, like France, like England, like America, creates that kind of irresponsibility below because the individual has had no say in the way things are.

Gelb: What are the possible alternatives? Is there a necessity of maintaining very consciously the importance of democratic institutions? I am thinking, for example, of people who object to Governor Faubus of Arkansas. Their reaction is, "Shut him up." It strikes me, "Let him hang himself," would be better. The one who is shut up, if I'm not mistaken, in the South today in the integrationist.

Miller: We have Faubus because the Civil War wasn't completed. Lincoln was shot about two years too early. The victory was given away in many respects, the victory of education that should have followed, and which undoubtedly would have followed, had Lincoln lived. In a sense, in a wider sense, it is good that Faubus exists because a lot of people will have to examine their own attitudes toward Negroes. People who disapprove of them in the North, for example, and are at heart, or in part of their hearts, not ready to give the Negro his rights, either. But of course, the field of action must be maintained: that is to say, the democratic situation, where this battle can be fought out through the educational process.

Gelb: I think that last statement's very important because I think you are implying here that the only alternative to the use of the democratic process is violence. Now maybe that's too extreme a conclusion; but, in addition to Little Rock forcing people to clarify in their own hearts how they feel about Negroes, maybe it might force some people to clarify how they feel about democratic institutions, and maybe it's the system that's continually being tested.

Miller: I suppose what the lesson is, if there is one, of the current struggle in the South is that an edict was given which reaffirmed the rights of all men to be equal and that for a very long time, not only in the South but in the North, all men have not been equal. What this has done creates no new situation, it simply is a firecracker under an old, old situation. I think it is being well worked out. I think that the suffering involved there is less than would be the case if this were being treated in a dictatorial way. It isn't being treated in a dictatorial way. The use of troops down there was the enforcement of a law, democratically arrived at, and democratically asserted in a normal democratic way. The reaction to it, in my opinion, is the dictatorial reaction. That is, there's no question any more that the threat of violence came not from the United States government but from probably a small minority of people who are fanatically interested in the subject. I'm not in Arkansas, but from up here it would seem that the solution to a deficiency in democracy is—I think Lord Bryce said it—is more democracy. I think that struggle, the struggle to raise up men, is part of the given situation of man. It will never end.

A Conversation with Arthur Miller

Kenneth Allsop/1959

From *Encounter*, 13 (1959): 58-60. Reprinted by permission.

The aspect of Arthur Miller's East 57th Street apartment is unexpectedly MGMish: white sofas and spreading ice-cap expanses of white fitted carpet. There is, in fact, a sharp division when you enter Mr. Miller's work-room, and after Miss Marilyn Monroe, like a twirl of spun sugar in matador pants and fisherman's jersey, has mixed drinks, curled up to discuss Russia for a few minutes, and returned to the snowy gorgeousness beyond the door, you are left in an isolated pocket of workmanlike maleness, the stokehole below the first-class lounge.

With one window high above New York's roar, the small room is crowded with desk, bookshelves, day-couch, and a writer's litter. On the desk is an afternoon paper. Its front page carries stories about eleven teenage Puerto Ricans robbing a shopkeeper and stabbing him to death, about the trial of seven colored youths for murdering a crippled boy, and about a fifteen-year-old highschool boy who had taken a sawn-off shotgun into the washroom and blown off the head of a classmate. Mr. Miller, in opennecked white tennis shirt and heavy Abraham Lincoln, lights a big black pipe and talks intently about present-day metropolitan society and the theatre that that society produces.

"New York—America—hasn't got any worse in this respect," he says, poking his pipe at the newspaper. "I was brought up in Harlem. It was always a rough neighborhood. Nothing that happens now is any worse than what I saw when I went to school. But at that time there was no such alarm because society was then much more confident. Nor is there anything new about the Beat Generation. I knew beats in the 'thirties and 'forties. Delinquents of a kind. But the context was different then, so that they didn't seem of all that significance. The context now is such that if someone gets out of line, he is thought to threaten the State. Before, there was no fear of that sort. I would evaluate the Beat Generation as a recurrence of a kind of bohemianism which before the Korean War never had a dominant place in the average citizen's mind. Now it has gained a greater meaning. These people, the beats, are regarded as a serious reproach. Before they were an aberration; now society is beginning to wonder if they may be partially right in rejecting all our technological easy-living. . . .

"A change of attitudes is certainly perceptible. I am working on a novel—the first since *Focus* in 1944—which is concerned with the intimate relationship between people and nature, our responsibility towards natural things, animal life, that does exist however deep it may be buried, and which must be reasserted. I am writing this as a novel (it will be called *The Misfits*) because I don't know how to do it on the stage.

"I started a play many years ago and I hope it will soon be ready. It is about the present day, about people who lived through the events of the 'thirties and 'forties, and are now face to face with their lives in a world they never made. I am trying to define what a human being should be, how he can survive in today's society without having to appear to be a different person from what he basically is.

"I don't feel any community of understanding with the kind of drama we are getting in America today. Many of the plays appear to be plays of protest, but they are not genuine. We have no satire. There is something decadent in the protest. It is not protest in the name of the future. It is anti-dramatic drama. They are terribly sentimental. There is something terribly evasive about it. The hero is saying: 'Look at this—it reflects a world where the results of the action are difficult to find.' But the flaw is that they themselves are involved in organization and bigness—they are part of it. I once wrote a definition of how birds come home to roost. A man has to dredge up from within his nature the strength to deal with them and in the process he is made more complete, but in our drama nowadays the birds just keep hovering about, and society can't admit their reality. That is what makes me suspect that a good deal of this writing is special pleading. It does not examine the concept of justice. One of the problems of the delinquent is that he has no regard for consequences or he can't conceive them. . . .

"I think the point has come where a cliche about personal
difficulties has developed into a general principle, one which I was
not even aware of years ago, and which goes through a lot of plays. A
kind of shorthand has been unconsciously developed between
authors and audiences. A lot of these plays deal with inability of
people to communicate with each other; those I have in mind have to
do with the conflict between extremely neurotic younger people and
older people, but they are fundamentally falsified. There is something
being left out. There is something specious about the theme. It is
being portrayed purely in its own terms. The point of view in the
plays is limited to that of the oppressed younger person. While
sympathy may be shown for the older generation, there is no
wisdom, because there is no basis of identification with the older
generation. One explanation may be that there has been a collapse of
a basic sense of authority in every field—and yet at the same time
Authority takes on greater and greater pretensions for itself. My
quarrel is that this is such a constricted viewpoint. . . .

"The question must be asked as to who is going to be responsible
for running the world and are the complaints expressed by our young
and successful writers serious or are they complaints of the immature?
We have a serious play such as *Hamlet* which has the viewpoint of a
man who is a son, and in that play there is the sense that the first
thing that is being contested is whether *Hamlet* is capable of
administrating. But the contemporary play attempting to examine the
same problem becomes *Hamlet* with everything ripped out that has
to do with kingship and his aims as a mature man, with only his
conflict with his mother left.

"I have become, I must confess, rather jaded with the whole
attitude. I am not criticising the art with which these plays are
rendered, but their limitations are becoming aesthetically ugly.

"The world and the power which controls our existence are not
visible on the stage. Our theatre is dealing with a group of people
who are not so much disillusioned as congenitally lonely. It has
become a private kind of drama. We have arrived at one of the times
when everything is predictable. A pattern was set at the beginning of
the Korean War, with the great boom that the Korean War started.
We were in a state of recession before that. Then one did not know
whether to look back to the New Deal or forward to some kind of
new form of that. What happened was that the mood of that time

developed into conformism, fear, and an atrophy of spontaneity in
this country, the super organization of life. In the arts there was an
almost complete mistrust of almost anything that reflected the idea of
progress except material progress. We were really in that rat race,
going round in circles . . .

"Now there is change for numerous reasons. One is boredom. The
American people have a very volcanic emotional life—which is
sometimes a good thing and sometimes a bad thing. There is
boredom now even with what eight or nine years ago was a
shockingly revolutionary sexuality in the movies. Before the second
World War millions of people lived beyond their means—but they felt
guilty about it. Now it has become normal and accepted to live on
credit. Hedonism has dulled our sense of social responsibility. We
have lost friction with the future. America was always in a state of
becoming. Now we've got there and we were uncertain whether it
was the right destination. For a while we were happy because in a
business sense we were the last word. Then Sputnik happened, and
the doubts really took hold. We relapsed into caution, into a
vegetable state, not only in the arts but also in business—they can't
any longer find the old romantic breed of salesmen who invented the
need for material profusion. Now American business is working on
echoes. The only way they know how to fight Recession is to whip
people into buying more and more. Exactly this happened in '32 and
'33. The theory then was that the way to beat Depression was to
manufacture fads. The newspapers had spotted in every column *Buy
Now*. . . . This is my second time round. This is an old story. The
pattern has got to be disorganized before the new one can develop.
There is a lull now. Recession is the worm in the apple. But I believe
that it will make life more social again. It seemed to many of us for a
long time that the big machine was beyond the reach of young man's
determination to change it. Now it can be seen to be vulnerable. . . .

"In our big car civilization we still clutch to our breasts those
chromium-plated iron hulks in the hope that they are salvation. We
want salvation, but how is it to be found? By following a personal
conviction of necessity."

The State of the Theater
Henry Brandon/1960

From *Harper's*, 221 (Nov. 1960): 63-69. Reprinted by permission.

Brandon: What stimulates you into writing a play?

Miller: If I knew, I could probably control the inception of it better. I'm at the mercy of it; I don't really know. I cannot write anything that I understand too well. If I know what something means to me, if I have already come to the end of it as an experience, I can't write it because it seems like a twice-told tale. I have to astonish myself, and that's of course a very costly way of going about things, because you can go up a dead end and discover that it's beyond your capacity to discover some organism underneath your feeling, and you're left simply with a formless feeling which is not itself art. It's inexpressible and one must leave it until it is hardened and becomes something that has form and has some possibility of being communicated. It might take a year or two or three or four to emerge.

Brandon: So you really don't know how your play is going to end when you start it.

Miller: I don't. I have a rough notion . . . for instance, if a play has a hero in it who will die, I know that. And I must know the core of irony involved. But little else in terms of the progression of the story. The shape and, so to speak, the tempo of the development are created within the play itself.

Brandon: When you, for instance, wrote your new film script, *The Misfits,* did you write it with your wife in mind for a part in it?

Miller: I was of two minds about that, because I happen to believe that she can do anything on the screen. But it's impossible for me to write for a person, inasmuch as my vision is concentrated on something quite different, on some evolving paradox. The question of an actress, an actor, is the furthest thing from my mind at that time. Only toward the end of *The Misfits* did I become thankfully aware that this would be wonderful for Marilyn.

56

A play is made by sensing how the forces in life simulate ignorance—you set free the concealed irony, the deadly joke.

Brandon: So it's really a rather tortuous birth, isn't it?

Miller: I can write very quickly, but that's simply the last stage of the process. By that time, I have found the walls of life and I can feel them, and I can fill that room now and I can proceed. It's when there is no inner evolution that I am lost.

Brandon: Do you think that American drama has been an authentic expression of life in this country?

Miller: It depends on the level on which you're thinking of American life. Any people has a conventional idea of what they're like. Americans fancy themselves, for instance, to be openhanded, on the side of justice, a little bit careless about what they buy, wasteful, but essentially good guys, optimistic. But under that level of awareness there is another one, which gets expressed in very few movies and very few plays, but in more plays in proportion than in the movies: the level which confronts our bewilderment, our lonely naïveté, our hunger for purpose.

Brandon: Some critics think that the Angry Young Men in England were influenced by American writing on that deeper level.

Miller: I think that there is an American note in their writing. I don't mean that a play like John Osborne's *Look Back in Anger* could not have been done without the American influence, but there's a certain straightforward, even brash, thrust to these works which in tone is very American, and which to my mind does not typify modern English letters—which are much more oblique and remote. I found myself very much at home with the writing. Osborne's attitudes were always those of the plain fellow kicking through the conventional class lines in all directions—something that has become commonplace in this country since even Mark Twain.

The American play is pre-eminently active, relatively unreflective as such. It deals with nothing it cannot act out. It rarely comments on itself; like the people, it always pretends it does not know what it is doing. It must *be* something rather than be *about* something. But when a play does both at once it is most highly prized. It is a hard school to go to, but in my opinion the best one at the present time.

Brandon: Do you see anything as "indigenous" in the American theater as is the Westerner in films?

Miller: Literally speaking, the Westerner as he appears in Westerns is the last "indigenous" person in the United States today.

The number of people involved, let's say, in cattle raising, in being cowboys, is very small. The number of people in the West, however, who are involved in trade and industry is much greater. What the Westerner in the Western is, of course, is a folk hero, but he doesn't typify anything any more except escape and a memory of what people like to believe the past was like. I think the salesman is much more typical of American life, both in viewpoint and numbers. God knows, for every cowboy there are one million salesmen.

Brandon: To switch for a moment to a more modern character: As one who had a brush with McCarthyism, do you think that this phenomenon is now dead in America?

Miller: As such it is. Two things happened: one was that the Army defeated him, not—I'm sad to say—liberals or the Left—not the people who knew what he was about. It was another conservative authority that knocked him down. I don't think one can push an attack on the integrity of the United States government itself to the lengths that he did and get away with it. However, the legacy of McCarthy is still with us. But it doesn't have the mass backing that it could call up at any juncture a few years ago.

Brandon: You mean he was defeated for the wrong reasons.

Miller: Yes. He gained the antagonism of people who essentially didn't disagree with him very much—not all of them, but a good many of them. My own opinion is that he may have been demented toward the end; he misjudged his position and his power.

Brandon: Well, do you mean to imply, then, that you think it could recur?

Miller: If an international crisis sufficiently intense gripped us, I think something like it could happen again, yes.

Brandon: Still he stands basically in most American eyes exposed as a bad influence.

Miller: He does, but what he did doesn't. Guilt-by-association, for instance—I would say quite as many people believe that as believed it before. I don't think they'd recognize it as McCarthyism, if it were presented in another form. When you don't defeat somebody on the basis of principle, he is only personally defeated, but that's all.

Brandon: Not long ago I discussed with Peter Ustinov a complaint of yours that American playwrights write important social plays, but that they fail to grasp the total social problem. Peter felt that there was a lack of sensitivity involved in what you said, that you could say the same thing about Chekhov—that he was only dealing with a cross section of weary landlords on the point of bankruptcy, but as soon as the revolution broke out these things were accepted as very valid criticism. After all, Peter said, the writer's job is to stimulate—to ask questions, not to provide solutions.

Miller: Ustinov is wrong about Chekhov and he is wrong about me. I have never been able to understand why one is insensitive because one looks beyond the individual to society for certain causations and certain hopes. It seems quite the reverse to me. I never had the illusion that Chekhov was only writing about some weary landlords. Bolsheviks, indeed, accused him of this, and defensive conservatives hoped it was true, but if it were he would be known now merely as a genre painter, a curio. It is an almost international mistake, even now, to see him as a writer satisfied to reveal life's absurdities, even as a celebrant of futility. But, in fact, Chekhov was tortured by his inability to settle on solutions—he accused himself of deceiving his public because he could not tell them what they must do. The plays are great, for one thing, not because they do not give answers but because they strive so mightily to discover them, and in the process draw into view a world that is historical.

It is not right to confuse Chekhov's modesty with his accomplishments. In *The Cherry Orchard* when the real-estate developer destroys with his axe the lovely but unproductive basis of the characters' lives, Chekhov was not merely describing a picturesque piquancy, but the crude thrust of materialism taking command of an age. His plays are full of speeches about having to go to work and somehow to become part of productive society. He was seeking some reconciliation for these much-loved people and the forces displacing them. A playwright provides answers by the questions he chooses to ask, by the exact conflicts in which he places his people. Chekhov wrote: "A conscious life without a definite philosophy is no life, rather a burden and nightmare." A writer who has not spent his life trying to find and articulate "answers" could not have written this.

I am not calling for more ideology, as Ustinov implies. I am simply asking for a theater in which an adult who wants to live can find plays that will heighten his awareness of what living in our time involves. I am tired of a theater of sensation, that's all. I am tired of seeing man as merely a bundle of nerves. That way lies pathology, and we have pretty well arrived.

Brandon: Talking about ideology, how does the religious drama of Graham Greene impress you?

Miller: I must confess that as a dramatist I find his work faintly formularized. His philosophic dilemma is real, but it seems to end in a bald assertion. He's caught between two needs. On the one hand, he has to keep his works on a lay level, because that's his style as well as the level on which life is lived in this age. On the other hand, he has to broach a spiritual solution, which has no embodiment in the course of the play. God escapes realism. I find them to be good plays until they have approached the point where what is most important to him enters into them—the leap to another form of consciousness. I don't see how that leap is possible within his realistic form. To make it you would have to create an inspired world from the beginning; I could believe in that. I don't think I could explain it, but I could believe in it. I admire the quality of his conviction, even of his dilemma, but he has forced it into a geometry at the end. I have to look at his experience from the standpoint of the daylight world because Greene is presenting his vision as, so to speak, a daylight vision.

Brandon: The American theater has no religious content; do you have an explanation?

Miller: There's one possible clue in this schizophrenia of the American mind in that respect. We're probably the most church-going nation in history. But there is a sharp line drawn between going to church and thinking that way. In daily economic life, there is no more materialistic or efficient population. However, on Sunday it's quite the other way. Life is lived, so to speak, without reference to a religious ideology, excepting the weekly nodding toward the sky.

Now I suppose our theater naturally reflects this. I think the big change for the American theater came when it was no longer possible to contain the increasingly absurd contradictions of existence within the formula of a play which simply presented a more or less evil influence, and a more or less good influence, and batted it out between them. The evil influences had become so pervasive and so ill-defined that we were left with, I think a hero whose enemies were invisible: the victim *as* victim came to the fore. The story of almost every important American play is how the main character got his corners knocked off.

So, I would say, our main tradition from O'Neill to the present revolves around the question of integrity—not moral integrity alone, but the integrity of the personality. The difficulty is to locate the forces of disintegration. I have to believe they exist and can be unveiled.

I wrote *The Crucible* in this frame of mind. It happened that it was written at the time of McCarthyism so that a kind of personification of disintegration existed among us again. But it was an attempt to create the old ethical and dramaturgic order again, to say that one couldn't passively sit back and watch his world being destroyed under him, even if he did share the general guilt. In effect, I was calling for an act of will. I was trying to say that injustice has features, that the amorphousness of our world is so in part because we have feared through guilt to unmask its ethical outlines.

The plays of the forties, which began as an attempt to analyze the self in the world, are ending as a device to exclude the world. Thus self-pity and sentimentality rush in, and sexual sensationalism. It is an anti-dramatic drama, and it reflects the viewpoint of a great many people who seem to feel that's the way life is today. To me it's a challenge to define what is creating these effects among us.

Brandon: American drama is really still very young. How do you see its evolution?

Miller: We had a very slight indigenous American drama until the first world war. By that I mean a direct reflection of American manners, American life, barely existed on the stage. The plays were melodramas, for the most part, with a very few exceptions. It's after the first world war that real attempts were made to create a modern drama that reflects the life of the people at the moment. And I think O'Neill has to be set aside from the main stream because his preoccupation was not so much with the journalistic reportage of what was going on—which is, I think, true of most of the other writers in the twenties and thirties—but with the quest for the relationship between an individual, and for want of a better word, fate. At bottom their world was rational, his a mystery.

Brandon: Which writers are you thinking of?

Miller: Well, you take the plays like Anderson and Stallings' *What Price Glory?* and Hecht and MacArthur's *The Front Page,* which were great influences, I think, and Elmer Rice's *Street Scene.* For the first time, for instance, profanity was used in the way that it's used commonly in the United States. The old hokum of sentimental idealism was destroyed. The war was viewed without the usual ballyhoo of past plays, which made a glorification of it. It was now looked at as a dirty business. A new, brash iconoclasm entered, the contemporaneous cynicism and the gaiety.

I think a great influence was probably David Belasco, who was a naturalist, what we would think of as corny because his plots were frightful. There were scenes in his plays such as the one where the hero is about to be executed and the heroine runs onto the stage with the American flag and throws it over him—and the United States Army could not fire through the flag, naturally.

However, in the making of the productions he was enormously inventive in naturalistic terms. He created volcanoes on the stage—and Child's Restaurant down to the flies on the mince pie. Stanislavsky saw his work and thought Belasco was a very great director. He seized on a tool which the American theater is still using and to much better effect—the naturalistic actor. What was added subsequently was the story whose proportions were closer to the reality as the audience knew it. Robert Sherwood, Maxwell Anderson, S. N. Behrman, Philip Barry, Elmer Rice, George Kelly, Sidney Howard—all began or had their roots in the thirties. They brought it of age.

Brandon: How does their work strike you now?

Miller: Today a lot of their work seems mild, a bit too play-conscious and even innocent, despite their efforts to break with the older tradition of pose and stage sham. Some of their work is very fine—the workmanship is good, perhaps too good for our current taste. But some of O'Neill seems more valid now, perhaps because we share his neuroticism. O'Neill spoke like a minority man, like us; the others were more public speakers. We prize the subjective now; they prized craft, wit, comment on manners, iconoclasm.

Some of the best work of these men was done in the thirties, but that epoch was characterized for many people by the minority voices, mainly Clifford Odets and Lillian Hellman. The social playwrights were still trying to be craftsmen, still spoke publicly, but in Odets and Hellman the inner voice broke through in that they personally felt the public anguish of the Fascist years. In Odets a new lyricism; a prose larger than life. In Hellman a remorseless rising line of action in beautifully articulated plays. Both these writers expressed personality—their works identified them. But the symbols were often so tuned to the particulars of the thirties that when that brief cataclysm passed into wartime, their world seemed out of date. It remains to be seen whether this is really so. I am not the one to judge this because I was deeply moved by these plays and remember them with love.

One ought to remember that it was by no means only the "Left" writers who wrote social plays. Maxwell Anderson, Sherwood, Rice, Sidney Howard, even Behrman and Barry were involved with the themes of social and economic disaster, Communism and Fascism. But Odets and Hellman made these themes personal to themselves. They matured with the depression; the others before.

Brandon: And what followed then?

Miller: Since the forties, the line of development has been toward more and more intimacy of statement by playwrights and less attention to the older idea of craft, of stage logic. In this sense O'Neill remains the leader. His work is just as full of ill-digested Freudianism as the others, just as absorbed with questions like Socialism, the Negro problem, social justice, etc., and as weighted down as any other with out-of-date slang and mawkish devices and melodrama. But he could not for long be drowned in his moment—we hear his inner voice, we respond to many of its tones. His self-pity, his tortured questing, his relentless doubts, overwhelm his often stagy solutions; the other writers too often were sealed up in their plays.

The fifties became an era of gauze. Tennessee Williams is responsible for this in the main. One of my own feet stands in this stream. It is a cruel, romantic neuroticism, a translation of current life into the war within the self. All conflict tends to be transformed into sexual conflict. The sets have therefore become less and less defined in realistic terms, for the society is more and more implied, or altogether blotted out. Its virtue is its ability to intensify the sensual—using that word to mean the senses, feeling.

It has all moved now to a dangerous extreme of triviality. It is a theater with the blues. The genuine original cry has become a rehearsed scream of a self-conscious whimper. The drama will have to find its way back into the daylight world without losing its inner life. I sometimes long to see a set with a ceiling again. The drama will have to re-address itself to the world beyond the skin, to fate.

Brandon: Did you see Samuel Beckett's *Waiting for Godot?*

Miller: I've read it. I never got to see it. I admire that play for the rebellion in it. It is an intimate statement—a very hard thing to do on the stage, and at the same time an abstract of the time. It has feeling and it has a brain. I find it necessary, however, to ask what are its limits—its viability for the future. It enforces upon us a sense of the desolate—which is just what it is designed to do. But I do not think it flexible enough to embrace other moods, so to speak. A criticism of it would be that it is addressed, I think, exclusively to its own cultural level. That is legitimate and proper. But, for myself anyway, the challenge is still the Elizabethan one, the public address on the street corner.

Brandon: I think that you and Sartre are the two most powerful dramatists today. The difference between you and him, it seems to me, is that his writings are dominated by ideas. . . .

Miller: There is a great difference between us. For one, I'm writing in a culture that does not truck with ideas; it resists knowing what it is doing. This goes for an ordinary individual and a gigantic corporation.

In France—to a much greater degree—the people are aware that if they don't know what they're doing, it is possible to characterize it objectively anyway; that is, they will concede that *somebody* knows what they're doing, and that this is a legitimate kind of work, so to speak. Here, this sort of approach is a luxury, which a few cloistered people may indulge in, but it's of no consequence. What the hell is the difference if you do know? We believe in necessity here; we're loyal slaves of it. The necessary, here in America, is mistaken for the right. But sometimes men must interfere with the inevitable.

Brandon: Is this partly due to a certain anti-intellectualism?

Miller: I would like to make clear my attitude toward the charge of anti-intellectualism in this country. I believe some of this feeling among Europeans and Englishmen is based on a distortion.

My own feeling is that foreigners are overly impressed with the fact that we have no sense here of an intellectual *class*.

I am not at all sure, for instance, that there are more people in other countries who understand what an intellectual *does*. There are more people abroad who have learned to tip their hats to the idea of an intellectual. It reminds me of a barber I used to go to. He'd been cutting my hair for years and never said more than Hello and Thank you until my picture got into the *Daily News* when I won some prize or other. Then he asked me if I had heard of D'Annunzio. (He was an

old Italian who could barely speak any English at all.) I said I knew
his work. From this time the barber's eyes lit up whenever I came into
the shop, and when I sat in his chair, he would give me a warm,
rather intimate smile, nod his head, and say, "D'Annunzio." He knew
nothing, really, of D'Annunzio's work, but had attached to
"D'Annunzio" a feeling of national pride and accomplishment.
"D'Annunzio" made a barber feel more valuable.

Brandon: You had become an intellectual in the eyes of your
barber because you knew D'Annunzio.

Miller: Writers here have no such connotation for the masses as
D'Annunzio had for the Italians. Nor would any writer regard
himself—as Russian writers have and many French—as spokesman
for the national spirit or something of the kind. In a word, we have no
status excepting that we are makers of entertainment, or heavy
thinkers, or earners of big money.

In the profoundest sense, of course, this is an anti-intellectual
attitude, but it is neither hateful nor contemptuous for the most part.
The truth is that no other occupation is regarded symbolically as a
national adornment, so to speak, excepting, possibly, that of the
soldier in wartime. Nor do we have a consciousness of an "American
Culture" in the way the French have, and other European nations.
But it does not mean we do not value our plays, movies, paintings,
music. It is simply that they are enjoyed without being called
manifestations of the national spirit.

This has both good and bad consequences. Most obviously, it
makes the country appear from outside like a nest of peddlers. Denial
of public recognition makes some intellectuals take on an unnatural
defensiveness toward themselves, an inferior feeling which breeds
isolation and hopelessness and weakness. Perhaps the worst effect is
that when, as during the McCarthy period, it is necessary for basic
principles of human existence to be upheld, the natural upholders—
the intellectuals—are face to face with a population that is unused to
listening to their advice.

In a word, we are not so much persecuted as ignored. But
everybody else is ignored too. I doubt there is a single professional
class in this country which feels it gets due public thanks or
recognition. This even includes businessmen who are always
revealing a sense of occupational inferiority, and who envy and resent
how artists are all the time being publicly acclaimed!

The benefits, if one may call them that, are not inconsiderable. Art here is irrelevant to life, in the minds of most, so it is free to do what it will with life.

Brandon: Doesn't that depress an artist?

Miller: Yes. The artist is hard put to reassure himself that his occupation is anything but trivial. And this, I think, is the biggest wound the American attitude inflicts. To survive it, an artist has to cling to his dignity with his teeth sometimes, often at the very moment he is being acclaimed, for it is a rare thing to be acclaimed excepting for irrelevant reasons. But will a public cult of intellectualism really result in a higher understanding of art's relevance to life? If Europe is an example, I wonder. . . . I have heard, in my very limited experience, some of the loudest avowals of pro-intellectualism from some of the most corrupt and unphilosophical people.

The single important advantage of the attitude, I think, is that it presses the artist the more to overcome it. You have to hit the public when it is not looking, so to speak; you have to make it real to them the way the subway is real. You can't depend on their embracing your work because it is art, but only because it somehow reached into the part of them that is still alive and questing. This kind of challenge can almost destroy a delicate art like poetry, but for the drama and the novel it can muscularize them. It can also make them musclebound, and strident, and screaming, and sensational. But all I want to make clear at the moment is that the thing is not a dead loss by any means.

Brandon: Where, do you think, are we moving?

Miller: One thing the theater will not stand for too long—at least not in this country—is boredom. The blue play is now becoming predictable in mood. We expect a pathetic defeat in the play and the documentation of alienated loneliness. I think they're quite suddenly going to become old hat.

Perhaps it is only my feeling; but I think life is now perhaps less impossible than it was, say, even two years ago. And this is as much a political and social fact as it is a theatrical fact. I mean to say that the possibility of the survival of the human race now appears to be a reasonable hope for a person to take hold of. Certain steps have been taken that would indicate that a rapprochement of some sort can be made between two civilizations.

The theater as yet has not got the reach, the breadth of vision to see much more than the center of the web in which we struggle. But I think there are indications that we may have a right to state once again that all is not lost. And as soon as that really happens, the black air surrounding many plays may appear unjustified; it will not long seem the way things are; and the style itself will seem willful and self-conscious.

Arthur Miller Ad-Libs on Elia Kazan
Show/1964

From *Show,* (Jan. 1964): 55-56, 97-98.

With this article, *Show* introduces a person-to-person form of communication in which literary roadblocks like the Q and A device are eliminated. We feel it is time to give Q the hook and get him out of the act. A *Show* editor asked Arthur Miller some questions about his new play, *After the Fall,* opening in New York January 23 as the first Lincoln Center Repertory Production—and especially about Elia Kazan, who is directing the play. Mr. Miller's off-the-cuff answers were tape-recorded and then placed in continuity sequence, with the questions and the "and . . . ers" swept out of your way. Finally, Mr. Miller went over the manuscript to pencil in a few clarifications. The result, we think, is a direct connection between artist and reader. Without interference from interviewer's bias or formal literary maneuvers.

Ready? Curtain up. The scene is wherever you are. Arthur Miller speaks:

There was no opportunity for Kazan to read my play, *After the Fall,* before deciding to direct it, because the play at that time was not far enough along. I said I was excited about it, and I guess he felt that if I wanted to put a play on, a repertory theater of this kind should do it. And besides, in a lot of ways Lincoln Center Rep is one of the biggest and most serious crap-shooting operations that has ever taken place on the face of the earth. I hope it stays that way. Robert Whitehead came by about two years ago and told me he was the producer of Lincoln Center, about which I'd heard only that there was a Philharmonic Orchestra. He described the repertory concept, which is very exciting to me—always was. At that time I'd been working on various versions of the basic concept of *After the Fall*. But I didn't have the present script, I had an immense amount of work behind me but nothing you could call a play. So I said, well—I have no play, but I have an idea, and I want to do it.

Whitehead came back a couple of weeks later to say that Kazan was going to be the director of Lincoln Center. How would I feel about him directing my play? I said that to my mind Gadg Kazan would be, without question, the best director for the play, no doubt about it.

Before I explain why, let me tell you something about *After the Fall*. I've been in a hole by myself for the last two years, discovering it. This play is remarkable not only because it really was discovered as it was written, and was designed to be that way, but also because you'll sense that as you watch it. It's an open evolution of a concept on a stage, an attempt to give form to life before your eyes.

I couldn't very well tell Gadg the way it was going to end, because the ending was discovered while I was writing it, discovered in what had developed under me. I will have 180 pages of manuscript played on the stage. To get that 180 pages, I have written around 5,000 pages. It was a long and laborious and very chancy operation, because it could possibly never come off. It's the biggest sweep of embrace that I've ever taken. I don't know of any bigger one. It involves a new form.

The play is a continuous stream of meaning. It's not built on what happens next in terms of the usual continuity of a tale—but upon what naked meaning grows out of the one before. And the movement expands from meaning to meaning, openly, without any bulling around. The way a mind would go in quest of a meaning, the way a new river cuts its bed, seeking the path to contain its force. And sometimes it stumbles and loses its way, only to find its way back. But all of it in the open, before your eyes, creating its own form.

The thing at issue in *After the Fall* is an elusive point of rest or clarity which the leading character, Quentin, is seeking. He's carrying his sense of reality into his life in pursuit of that moment—a moment which he thinks he once had, and which he knows he *must* find again, the moment when his life, and presumably life itself, cohered in a form.

If I were writing this play for Broadway, I would be spiritually discouraged. I would write it anyway, because I was working on it and toward it for years before Lincoln Center ever started. But I would feel a sort of wasteful defensiveness—that I was writing it against a torrent running the other way. The idea behind Lincoln Center has reduced the sense of friction against that torrent.

Now, this play requires two opposing qualities of direction at the same time, and I don't know any director except Kazan who has the possibility of both. One is his approach to character—he gets an intensity into acting that you don't find in the work of other directors. From time to time—maybe in the Tennessee Williams plays—it's a little too intense and a little too hectic. I think Gadg knows that, and I think he intends not to press that hard. It is analogous to a playwright over-writing.

But, personally, I prefer this intensity to lethargy. I prefer it to not exploring as far as you can go in a character. I prefer it to what happens more often, which is letting well enough alone. I enjoy art more that is nearly wrong. Some directors see the thing working, and they stop too far short of error. Ask a few sharp questions about what the actor's really doing up there, and there's a whole world the actor never entered into. The acting in Kazan plays is always well motivated, even if at times it has pressed its motivations into the abstract and the general.

This particular play offers Gadg a challenge as well as continuation of his previous development. The challenge is to match the style of acting to the writing. The play is about the real world, both in and outside the head. It's about real people, all kinds of people from highly educated to very uneducated. People of a relatively high class in society, and people of a lower class. There are elements of love story and elements of great social conflict. It requires everybody to do what I did, which is to stretch inwardly and outwardly toward an image larger than life. From one moment to another, actors are going to have to assume an entirely different attitude toward their own actions. I haven't delivered a neat little package which actors can step into. They're going to have to act realistically at one moment—and at the next adopt a perspective on their own behavior, until the abstract and the real are one. This play is a life-process literally in-being.

The second—and in some ways opposing—quality of direction required by this play is Gadg's organic sense of the connection between any individual moment and the thematic statement of a

play. I've never been able to indulge myself in the theater. In my
plays, people say and do what is forced out of them. Whatever else is
said about them, they are inevitable. This play's fantasy makes a
steadily lengthening, hardening shadow. The aim of Gadg's kind of
direction at its best, is dialectic inevitability. That is, he always tries to
make a whole of opposites. He will question an actor who is doing
anything unthematic, anything that has no real inner connection with
the rest of the play; to remind him of the negative to his positive
feeling, and vice versa.

In some plays the organic connection is tenuous. Mine are built
around connections made between seemingly disconnected things.
These hidden things all accrue, finally, in a climax. A director may be
a wonderful visual stylist on the stage, he may be a wonderful
director of actors, but unless he has this organic dialectic sense he is
not a good director of a play of mine.

Gadg *is* a showman—he should be, but all his plays and movies
have attempted either superficially or in depth an exposition of a
theme of some importance. He has tried to find society in a gesture.
Pure showmanship would simply defeat this whole purpose. It's when
he fails that it is showmanship.

If you don't *believe* in a serious play, you might as well go home,
it's bad showmanship. I've never seen him exploit a sensation at the
expense of the play. If the Rev. Mr. Jones were directing Tennessee
Williams, you would get certain effects because they're written into
the plays. They're what the plays are about. In many cases Tennessee
writes about sexual conflicts or homosexual conflicts with an alien
world and there's no way to deal with that except to deal with it. My
plays don't lend themselves to such effects, but I don't think Gadg
has exploited them in the Williams works either, and I mean out of
their proportion in the scripts. I think *A Streetcar Named Desire* was a
beautiful movie—Gadg's best, in my opinion.

Gadg would make no attempt to influence me in the last two years
while I was writing *After the Fall.* Quite simply because this play is
making its own rules. Good or bad, it is obviously a quest so
individual that all anyone outside can say is perhaps that he doesn't
understand some passage or line. And that I want to hear, although I
can't always do better.

Sometimes Gadg would come up with Bob Whitehead and I'd
read sections because we needed to begin casting—actors like Jason

Robards and others we might end up wanting are sometimes booked for two years in advance. Secondly, for my own benefit, I wanted to see whether some of the strange connections I was making could be followed by anyone else. That turned out to be less of a problem than I had feared. As a matter of fact, that is one of the reasons why I made cuts in the play—because the connections turned out to be much more common among people than I expected—at least so far.

The first time Gadg ever heard the script as a whole was that first day of rehearsals in October when I read it to the cast. It had a second act he had never heard. And I'll tell you about that reading.

I decided from the start that I would *use* this repertory theater, not as a theoretical anticommercial freedom, but as a positive thing, a real theater. Gadg and Bob asked me to read this play for the purpose of giving the actors—the first time they heard this dialogue—a vision of the whole area of development before they fell into the minutiae of their own roles. And I wanted to try certain things myself on this audience—I'm very sensitive to an audience—because this is a highly experimental work. I can always leave things better when I read aloud, read to convince. And I seem to be getting younger as I'm getting older; I have more energy for rewriting.

I would never have done this kind of experimenting on Broadway. The whole impulse on Broadway is, you've got two and a half weeks to go before you run smack up in front of an invited audience. In three and a half weeks you're opening to critics in Boston or someplace else. I wouldn't take up a day of that short rehearsal period with *my* reading. I would use that day to let the actors read it.

And on Broadway I'd never think of coming in with a script which I still felt ready to uproot, if necessary, for one simple reason: the relation between the author, director and producer on one side of the fence and the actors on the other is one of authority over the proletariat, you see? You've got to keep the whip hand, there's a whole mythology about that. There's so little time, there can't be any real questioning of anything. The actors are being paid reasonably well, it's a great opportunity, so keep your mouth shut and go. That's the attitude, really. It's larded over with all kinds of "dears" and "darlings" and all that stuff, but that's what it's about.

In Lincoln Center Repertory, we've got three months to rehearse, minus two weeks when Gadg will take time out to start rehearsing S.N. Behrman's *But Whom for Charlie* with some of these same actors. A few days before the reading, I got a wonderful new view about a certain crucial area in the middle of the second act. Instead of coming in with the version that was perfectly finished, I did what I wanted to do. I brought in this unfinished second act. When I came to the point where I hadn't had time to complete the area involved, I described roughly what was going to happen and then went on. I told the actors, "I rely on you people, we're in this together. You'll be in on the growth of this thing. But from time to time I might want to come up to you and say, look, it's a great scene, and you've done it beautifully, but I'm just going to throw it out. Because I've just thought of something better." I may not have that feeling on another play, but I do on this. It is the opposite of improvisation, a refusal to quit before one's soul has.

I've always wanted to work this way. So has Gadg—he was brought up in the Group Theater where they always wanted to do this, but they never really had the time or the money to mature the idea. I really can't speak for others, but, as far as I know, Gadg's relations with the playwright have always been very friendly. He puts a stamp on his productions, sure, but I have no reason to say at the playwright's expense. He's directed my plays, and Tennessee's and Robert Anderson's. Does anyone confuse Tennessee's or Bob's plays with mine because of his stamp? Hardly.

I don't believe in the possibility of a director's taking off with a play. Not a rooted play, something with its own face and form. He can squelch the material, or fail to get the values of a scene. That can happen. It was partly my fault that it happened in *The Crucible*. We got off on the wrong foot. We were operating in a Broadway situation; once you start, it's an express train and cannot be allowed to stop. I was acting as a kind of mediator between Jed Harris and the actors, quite foolishly, because I didn't want the production to fall to pieces. Jed Harris directed it into a kind of Dutch painting, "classic," ballet-type fix where the intensity and the passion in it were simply gone. When Word Baker directed *The Crucible* again off Broadway with the simple human warmth and feeling that I wrote into the script, it ran two years. I don't write classics, I write plays.

It's scientifically impossible for anyone seeing a play to make an exact judgment of the director's contribution. Nobody can do it. Absolutely he can't. For one thing, except for absurd cases of bungling, you'd have to read the play before it was acted, to lay the blame precisely. But when I see a play whose dialogue is fine but cluttered with unnecessary words, I have the impulse to get up and crush out the impeding elements. My reaction is, it would have been so damn subservient to the playwright. Equally, when actors rush past critical moments and dwell on the unimportant, I damn the director. But "production" is subtler than that.

It's certainly a director's duty to point out whatever flaws he sees in the script, no matter whose script it is. Take Shakespeare—he wrote a four-hour *Hamlet,* didn't he? When is *Hamlet* played in four hours? Suppose Shakespeare is a contemporary writer and his poor play is cut by an hour and a half? Whose duty is it to make the decision that *Hamlet* is more endurable in two and a half or three hours, except on special occasions?

If a director is going to do his job, he must be as constructive as he knows how to be—but he must know how to stop at the point where the author says he doesn't feel this is the way it ought to be. Stopping takes as much talent as going. Those two tensions should be maintained. Gadg and I have had many collisions. We have them every day. But they really amount to trying to see different visions of the same thing. When I think he's got a wonderful notion, I'd be an idiot not to reach for it, especially if it leads toward lucidity. If I think it's without foundation, oversimplified, alien, I'll say no. With *All My Sons,* Gadg pressed me to cut out a beautiful scene at the end of the first act. It was a nice piece of color, an extension of a minor character, but essentially beside the point of the action, and that play depended heavily on its action. I'm still doubtful, but I wouldn't say it was any crime to pull it out. With *Death of a Salesman* he pointed out a little cutting: I tend to make sure that I'm getting an effect, so I kind of overdo it from time to time. At one point in *Death of a Salesman*, if I recall, Gadg had the idea of eliminating some or most of Willie Loman's memory scenes. We tussled for a couple of days and then gave that idea up. I'm sure that if I'd said nothing Gadge would probably have fooled around with this and then arrived at the same conclusion to leave the memory scenes untouched.

Gadg wrote the script for his new movie *America America* himself, and I think this experience has possibly increased his respect for the writer and for writing. He knows even more concretely now, as you know only when you've tried to do something, how excruciatingly difficult it is to do it well. He's never been cavalier toward writing, mine in any case, but now he seems to be leaning over backwards not to make any suggestions at all. I think it's because he knows how tough it is to carry them out. I will listen to anything that leads toward lucidity, to nothing that only simplifies.

Gadg puts a definite stamp on his work. A great deal of it comes from his casting and handling of actors. He handles actors better than anybody I know. He's an actor himself, and he literally put himself in the actor's position, too much so at times; but most of the time I think it's the play that finally wins. He's careful not to act out the parts, because nobody wants an actor imitating somebody else. Now and then he has an impulse to mimic a sound or a gesture, but mostly he directs by analyzing words into feelings, fears and hopes. I think he tries most of all to liberate the actor to become his role, rather than make a puppet out of him. Occasionally there is an actor who *is* a puppet and that's that.

Gadg and I both believe in type-casting to the spirit of a role. There's a certain music a person makes. One person makes a very timid, frightened music. I suppose a fine actor with that kind of personality can conceivably play a splashy, heroic part. I'll admit it's theoretically possible, but I've never seen it happen. You see, especially in a good play—and especially with good direction—all the actor's weaknesses come out. They'd better be the right weaknesses.

Let's say you need a braggart, but he must look completely competent and not at all a braggart. I'm just picking this out of the air, it doesn't happen in my play, although there was such a guy in the earliest conception of the play. Well, you can find people who are obvious braggarts—very uninteresting. If you find someone who doesn't have that hollowness at all in him, who basically is not tuned to that kind of agony, he's gonna have to make it up out of whole cloth. And you're gonna *know* he made it up out of whole cloth. Or I will, anyway.

You must find someone who has the braggart in him but is perhaps not aware of it himself. That's the best kind of casting. You've got the cover of the element and you've got the element itself. It's a chancy business, though, because you don't know whether or not you're right until you've worked with somebody a long time. But very great actors can make even *untruth* interesting.

I've never seen Gadg get rough with an actor. He's as gentle a director as I've ever seen work. I'm more likely to break an actor down than he is, and you know how I do it? I do it inadvertently, because I certainly don't want to hurt any actor. I get intellectualized and drive them out of their minds. I tell them what something means instead of how to do it. You can't act what something means. You act what something is.

We had two girls come in several times separately and unknown to each other for the same part in *After the Fall*. It was hard to make up our minds; they are both extremely good actresses. After the fourth reading, I told one of them, "Now, could you possibly do it as though the character were . . . " I gave her a whole different vantage point. She simply broke into tears. Burst into tears right there and refused to do anything more. The following day the competition girl came in. I did the same thing and she broke down too. The simple truth, though, is that I couldn't hear the right music from them.

Gadg knows actors much better than I do, but he knows he can't make them what they aren't. If an actor isn't getting over the essential quality of the character, Gadg will keep at him until the guy loses his grip on the false image. But the guy must be capable of the true one. And he never intends to "break them down." There's no point to that, really, because what overpowers the audience is confidence. You sense immediately when an actor is shaking in his boots, when he's uncertain or without force. No director wants that.

Gadg tries to give the actor this confidence; any good director has to. But he makes actors feel that their work means a great deal to him, that their aims are the same—presumable the actor wants to be good, too. Yes, there's canniness involved; sometimes you have to use ruses and devices to bring the actor unknowingly to a certain point of sincerity. Gadg is aware at every moment that he's dealing with very uncertain people—I'm not talking of them as citizens, but as people trying to create a role—they are desperately uncertain, and it's right that they should be uncertain, because they open themselves up that way. If a guy comes out and says "That's the way I'm gonna do it, period," you just let him go because he's not going to be any good, it will be for him a twice-told tale, expertly retold, perhaps, but not discovered.

Gadg is discovering the script in rehearsals just the way I discovered it in the first place. A good director recapitualates in shorter time the author's original process of discovery. And the actors are discovering it. I sit beside him everyday and give my own information about a character, because I am ahead of them, I have already gone through what they are beginning. If a man or a woman onstage should take an attitude that seems theatrically cogent but is characteristically false, I would immediately tell Gadg why. He would understand immediately that something wrong had happened. And stop it. If I'm not sure I say I'm not sure.

Or else I'll suggest a thing they could try. Well, sometimes Gadg can make it happen and sometimes it's impossible and he'll say so. Sometimes it's an idea which interferes with the tempo of a scene—psychologically true but not theatrically true. Sometimes I end still believing it's possible.

I've found over the years that our working together is not wasting itself on the wrong kind of struggle. I don't suggest things capriciously, and neither does he. We're both referring to the same objective plan, and the theme as we mutually understand it, which again assumes Gadg's organic sense. If I see something I think is unthematic, I'll say so, knowing this is decisively important to him as it is to me. And if he sees something in the script which he thinks is less connected than it needs to be, he'll say so. The objective element, the play and its theme, is standing right in front of us. All in all I'd say we both believe in serving it. The faults he has, he has, but not the fault of looking at a play and directing it because it reminds him of something else.

Question: 'Am I My Brother's Keeper?'

Barbara Gelb/1964

From *The New York Times*, 29 Nov. 1964, Sec. II, 1,3. Reprinted by permission.

Last winter while traveling in Europe, Arthur Miller attended the Nazi murder trials in Frankfurt. "I had never seen a real live Nazi, and I was curious," he said the other day. His tone of humorous detachment told nothing of the emotional pang it had obviously cost him to satisfy his curosity.

His immediate reaction to the trials was to write an impassioned article attempting, in his words, to "reinstate an understanding in the public mind of the dynamics of Fascism." His thoughts then turned to writing the play, *Incident at Vichy*, which dramatizes the same subject and which will open on Thursday at the ANTA Washington Square Theater.

While the episode on which *Incident at Vichy* is based had been in Miller's mind since 1950, the trials sharpened his viewpoint about guilt and responsibility—the leitmotif of the play—and he was able to turn out a final draft in three weeks last May. Only 20 lines have been altered since then.

"I suddenly saw the play whole," Miller said. "It happens like that sometimes."

This may startle some Miller fans who, recalling the nine-year hiatus between *A View From the Bridge* in 1955 and last season's *After the Fall,* regard him as an inordinately slow writer. But the fact is that during that period, in addition to spending a year and a half writing the screenplay of *The Misfits,* Miller worked on five plays, none of which he considered satisfactory.

As the mainstay of the Lincoln Center Repertory Theater's current repertory, with *Incident at Vichy* scheduled to alternate with *After the Fall,* Miller appears to have entered a new phase of productivity.

He is itching to start work on his next play. "It's only an image now," he said. "I live for the time I'm working." And his life, anything but private during the years of his marriage to Marilyn Monroe, seems to have settled down into soothing domesticity since his marriage in 1961 to the Austrian-born photographer, Inge Morath.

At 49, Miller is an ascetically thin, intimidatingly tall, gaunt-faced, bespectacled man with a receding hairline. His conversation is thoughtful and incisive and his manner is relaxed. On a recent morning in town, where he is confined until the opening of his new play, he talked expansively of his present and future and reservedly of his past.

His headquarters in Manhattan is the old Chelsea Hotel, celebrated as the one-time home of O. Henry, Thomas Wolfe and Dylan Thomas. His suite there is pleasantly shabby and cluttered.

"It's not really set up for housekeeping," Miller said, explaining that his wife and two-year-old daughter, who were out on an errand, made the best of it in order to be with him during the weeks of rehearsals and previews.

Miller, wearing rumpled slacks and a red flannel shirt, arranged his lanky frame on a sofa and smoked, in measured succession, two pipes, three cigarettes and a cigar.

"I'm not concerned anymore with the public reaction to my plays," he said, referring to what he regards as "the nimbus of myth and hysteria" that greeted *After the Fall*. There was more speculation, he feels, as to whether the play was literally about Marilyn Monroe, than there was discussion about its intrinsic artistic merits. "It is certainly not a literal play," he said. But he acknowledges, somewhat defensively, that he might have been partly responsible for this "irrelevant" speculation. He maintains that he failed to notice in time that the actress who plays the role identified by many playgoers with Marilyn Monroe could so obviously be identified.

"Barbara Loden doesn't look or act anything like her, really," he said. "It honestly never occurred to me that anyone was trying for a literal resemblance, or that the audience would see one, because I didn't see one."

Miller declared that his only concern now was whether a play satisfied his own artistic standards. "No matter what the reception of *Incident at Vichy* is, for instance, I'm satisfied that the play exists," he added. "It has a shape, a form, a truth. It very successfully does what I want it to do."

Incident at Vichy is Miller's ninth play to produced since he first started writing for the theatre in 1944. It is somewhat shorter than the standard Broadway product and will be played without intermissions. It has an all-male cast of 17, is set in a detention room in Vichy in 1942 and deals with a Nazi roundup of French Jews.

Unlike *After the Fall*, its form is straightforward narrative, employing no flashbacks or soliloquies. These are the dry facts. As for the play's philosophical content, Miller, who dislikes analyzing a play of his own before production, said:

"The occasion of the play is the occupation of France, but it's about today. It concerns the question of insight—of seeing in oneself the capacity for collaboration with the evil one condemns.It's a question that exists for all of us—what, for example, is the responsibility of each of us for allowing the slums of Harlem to exist? Some perfectly exemplary citizens, considerate of their families and friends, contributing to charities and so forth, are indirectly profiting from conditions like that."

Miller went on to illustrate his point with the example of a real-estate developer, dedicated "with the logic of his own calling" to "clearing" a scenically wooded area, in order to build a parking lot.

"It's the real estate man's business to develop," Miller said, "and that's the only logic that applies for him. Whether the development has a damaging effect on esthetics of the countryside, whether it will inconvenience as many people as it is theoretically designed to convenience, does not concern him. This is true of every other pursuit and profession, each dominated by its own logic totally unconcerned with any overall judgment of values, any sense of complicity or willingness to assume responsibility."

"I don't know if the problem is soluble. But I feel I must try to at least create an awareness that the problem exists." In *Incident at Vichy* Miller closes in on the crucial question of guilt and responsibility in a dialogue between a Jewish doctor and an Austrian prince detained by mistake, who believes himself to be a moral man. The doctor wrings from the prince an admission that he has, "somewhere hidden in his mind, a hatred for the Jews," and that "each man has his Jews"—including the Jews.

"The characters in the play are flesh-and-blood people, each with a subterranean life of his own." Miller said, "but they are also symbolic in the bearing they have on ourselves and our time."

Incident at Vichy, Miller believes, is linked in theme and development to *After the Fall,* just as *After the Fall* is linked to his earlier works. All examine aspects of personal guilt: *Incident at Vichy* deals somewhat more abstractly with man's guilt toward his fellow man. Miller is once more affirming the answer to the question: Am I my brother's keeper?"

"Any body of work is a voyage with ports of call," he observed. "Each of my plays has carried through some element of an earlier play."

The reason Miller's artistic voyage was interrupted for nine years, he explained, was a temporary disillusionment with the theater.

"The production of *A View From the Bridge* clinched a growing feeling that the work I was doing was regarded as unimportant," he said. "I felt I was a kind of entertainer, succeeding in drawing a tear or a laugh, but it seemed to me that what was behind my plays remained a secret. I think every artist gets to this stage.

"I decided that either the audience was out of step or I was. There seemed to be no resolution and yet I felt that there must be one. I began writing more for myself. In the five unproduced plays I worked on before *After the Fall,* I was attempting to develop a viewpoint toward the world and myself. The plays were searching, but came to no dramatic conclusions that satisfied me. Then in 1959, I had the idea of doing *After the Fall,* a play that presented the search itself."

Miller's narrative was interrupted at this point by the arrival of his wife with their daughter, Rebecca. Both were dressed in red, and both were bubbling with accounts of their outing. Rebecca was hugged and kissed by her father, then whisked off to the kitchen for lunch by her mother.

The Miller domesticity is palpable. Mrs. Miller is selective about her brief, out-of-town photography assignments, and does her printing at home in a large darkroom built by her husband. Home is a house in Roxbury, Conn., where Miller prefers to spend most of his time. He works in a small detached studio at a desk he constructed from an oversized door. He starts work at eight in the morning.

"I can never sleep later than 7" he said. He works until lunchtime, naps after lunch and sometimes returns to his desk when things are going well. He uses a typewriter. "I can type as fast as I think, and I can't think without a typewriter; besides my handwriting is so bad I can't read it myself." He paces the grounds outside his studio ("I

have to walk while I'm working.") And during arid stretches he
pursues his hobby of carpentry or fishes for trout in a pond he has
stocked himself. ("I raised them from puppies, my wife cooks them.")

Describing his routine in the country appeared to remind Miller of
his forced stay in the city. "It's impossible for me to write here," he
said, glancing out of the window. "There are too many interesting
things going on in the street."

Stubbing out his cigar, he speculated about the tenancy of O.
Henry, Wolfe and Thomas.

"I wonder what they were doing here," he mused. "Surely they
weren't writing."

Miller in London to See *Crucible*
James Feron/1965

From *The New York Times,* 24 Jan. 1965, 82. Reprinted by permission.

LONDON, Jan. 22—Arthur Miller paid a fleeting visit here today to see one of his old plays, *The Crucible,* and to arrange the production of a new one, *Incident at Vichy.*

Looking lean but relaxed, the playwright stopped long enough to discuss these works and the difficult decade between when he found himself unable to write effectively.

He spoke in the makeshift South Bank offices of the National Theater, whose production of the 1953 drama of Salem, Mass., witch trials has received the most enthusiastic notices of the season.

"*The Crucible* is only done by college and university groups in the United States these days," Mr. Miller said, "although it had a very successful revival in 1959 off Broadway."

He smiled and said, "I was congratulated then for revising the play so that it was 'warmer,' although he added, "it was the same play that had appeared during the McCarthy era."

On whether the play had retained its topicality, Mr. Miller said, "Not now. There's no such movement with that kind of power, but there always is that movement." He said it had not been the first period of witchhunting and would not be the last.

"I saw the McCarthy thing, but I was writing underneath it, trying to express some universal element in man. Often the historical element is mistaken for the theme."

On whether this misapplication was true of *After the Fall,* which has been supposed to be about the life of the playwright's former wife, the late Marilyn Monroe, he said:

"It wasn't really about . . . " and he paused, "what people said it was about. Possibly some day *After the Fall* will be seen in this light."

But if it was not about Miss Monroe, why avoid mentioning her name? Was there any reluctance to confront the situation?

"The avoidance is so obvious," he said softly, that "it is virtually a confrontation."

Mr. Miller, who arrived with his wife, Inge, from Paris, where *After the Fall* opened this week, said he was eager to see his plays performed here although what he called language difficulties were often worse than problems of translations.

"You can't change the language here," he said. "It's so close yet the distance is lunar." The only thing that can be done, he said, is to change the idiom.

The playwright said that he had written nothing for eight years before he completed *After the Fall*. "I was fed up with theater. I couldn't formulate my thinking. I wrote more than ever before during the period, but it just didn't work."

"I couldn't formulate what I wanted to say satisfactorily. It's difficult to orient one's way in the snake pit we're living in."

He said he was working on something now but had not developed the theme. He said he was largely concerned with "Shakespearean technique, the juxtaposition of people, with no transitions. Though the structure I like best is the Greek as condensed and short as it can get."

Mr. Miller said he looked forward to an English cast's approach to *The Crucible.*

"American actors sometimes tend to psychoanalyze the parts too much—the nature of the acting can often be decisive." He added that the Paris version of *After the Fall* seemed to be "closer to the emotional truth" than the New York production at the Lincoln Center for the Performing Arts.

He spoke bitterly of the Lincoln Center turmoil. "It's in a state of flux. They've canned Robert Whitehead, and I suspect the Center will end up booking special attractions, sort of an elevated Shubert system. It's a disaster, Whitehead had finally learned what had to be done, and when he learned, they fired him. They fired 23 totally unrelated actors of whom 13 were students. The hope was that these young people would develop into professionals in that time. This was just plain nonsense."

Mr. Miller said he would continue to work with Mr. Whitehead, in whom he had confidence.

The Art of the Theatre II: Arthur Miller, an Interview

Olga Carlisle and Rose Styron/1966

From *Paris Review* 10 (1966): 61-98. Reprinted by permission.

Arthur Miller's white farmhouse is set high on the border of
the roller-coaster hills of Roxbury and Woodbury, in Connecticut's Litchfield County. The author, brought up in
Brooklyn and Harlem, is now a country man. His house is
surrounded by the trees he has raised—native dogwood,
exotic katsura, Chinese scholar, tulip and locust. Most of
them were flowering as we approached his house for our
interview last spring. The only sound was a rhythmic
hammering echoing from the other side of the hill. We
walked to its source, a stately red barn, and there found the
playwright, hammer in hand, standing in dim light amid
lumber, tools, and plumbing equipment. He welcomed us,
a tall, rangy, good-looking man with a weathered face and
sudden smile, a scholar-farmer in horn-rimmed glasses
and high work shoes. He invited us in to judge his prowess:
he was turning the barn into a guest house (partitions here,
cedar closets there, shower over there . . .). Carpentry, he
said, was his oldest hobby—he had started at the age of
five.

We walked back past the banked iris, past the ham-
mock, and entered the house by way of the terrace, which
was guarded by a suspicious basset named Hugo. Mr.
Miller explained as we went in that the house was silent
because his wife, photographer Inge Morath, had driven to
Vermont to do a portrait of Bernard Malamud, and that
their three-year-old daughter Rebecca was napping. The
living room, glassed-in from the terrace, was eclectic,
charming: white walls patterned with a Steinberg sketch, a
splashy painting by neighbor Alexander Calder, posters of
early Miller plays, photographs by Mrs. Miller. It held
colorful modern rugs and sofas, an antique rocker, oversized black Eames chair, glass coffee table supporting a

bright mobile, small peasant figurines—souvenirs of a recent trip to Russia—unique Mexican candlesticks and
strange pottery animals atop a very old carved Spanish
table, these last from their Paris apartment; and plants,
plants everywhere.

The author's study was in total contrast. We walked up a
green knoll to a spare single-roomed structure with small
louvered windows. The electric light was on—he could not
work by daylight, he confided. The room harbors a plain
slab desk fashioned by the playwright, his chair, a rumpled
gray day bed, another webbed chair from the thirties, and
a bookshelf with half a dozen jacketless books. This is all,
except for a snapshot of Inge and Rebecca, thumbtacked
to the wall. Mr. Miller adjusted a microphone he had hung
crookedly from the arm of his desk lamp. Then, quite
casually, he picked up a rifle from the day bed and took a
shot through the open louvers at a woodchuck who,
scared but reprieved, scurried across the far slope. We
were startled—he smiled at our lack of composure. He
said that his study was also an excellent duck blind.

The interview began. His tone and expression were
serious, interested. Often a secret grin surfaced, as he
reminisced. He is a storyteller, a man with a marvelous
memory, a simple man with a capacity for wonder, concerned with people and ideas. We listened at our ease as
he responded to questions.

Interviewer: Vosnessensky, the Russian poet, said when he was
here that the landscape in this part of the country reminded him of
his Sigulda*—that it was a "good microclimate" for writing. Do you
agree?

Miller: Well, I enjoy it. It's not such a vast landscape that you're
lost in it, and it's not so suburban a place that you feel you might as
well be in a city. The distances—internal and external—are exactly
correct, I think. There's a *foreground* here, no matter which way you
look.

Interviewer: After reading your short stories, especially "The
Prophecy" and "I Don't Need You Any More," which have not only
the dramatic power of your plays but also the description of place, the

*A resort in Lithuania.

foreground, the intimacy of thought hard to achieve in a play, I wonder: is the stage much more compelling for you?

Miller: It is only very rarely that I can feel in a short story that I'm right on top of something, as I feel when I write for the stage. I am then in the ultimate place of vision—you can't back me up any further. Everything is inevitable, down to the last comma. In a short story, or any kind of prose, I still can't escape the feeling of a certain arbitrary quality. Mistakes go by—people consent to them more— more than mistakes do on the stage. This may be my illusion. But there's another matter; the whole business of my own role in my own mind. To me the great thing is to write a good play, and when I'm writing a short story it's as though I'm saying to myself, "Well, I'm only doing this because I'm not writing a play at the moment." There's guilt connected with it. Naturally I do enjoy writing a short story, it is a form that has a certain strictness. I think I reserve for plays those things which take a kind of excruciating effort. What comes easier goes into a short story.

Interviewer: Would you tell us a little about the beginning of your writing career?

Miller: The first play I wrote was in Michigan in 1935. It was written on a spring vacation in six days. I was so young that I dared do such things, begin it and finish it in a week. I'd seen about two plays in my life, so I didn't know how long an act was supposed to be, but across the hall there was a fellow who did the costumes for the University theater and he said, "Well, it's roughly forty minutes." I had written an enormous amount of material and I got an alarm clock. It was all a lark to me, and not to be taken too seriously . . . that's what I told myself. As it turned out, the acts were longer than that, but the sense of the timing was in me even from the beginning, and the play had a form right from the start.

Being a playwright was always the maximum idea. I'd always felt that the theater was the most exciting and the most demanding form one could try to master. When I began to write, one assumed inevitably that one was in the mainstream that began with Aeschylus, and went through about 2500 years of playwriting. There are so few masterpieces in the theater, as opposed to the other arts, that one can pretty well encompass all of them by the age of nineteen. Today, I don't think playwrights care about history. I think they feel that it has no relevance.

Interviewer: Is it just the young playwrights who feel this?

Miller: I think the young playwrights I've had any chance to talk to are either ignorant of the past or they feel the old forms are too square, or too cohesive. I may be wrong, but I don't see that the whole tragic arch of the drama has had any effect on them.

Interviewer: Which playwrights did you most admire when you were young?

Miller: Well, first the Greeks, for their magnificent form, the symmetry. Half the time I couldn't really repeat the story because the characters in the mythology were completely blank to me. I had no background at that time to know really what was involved in these plays, but the architecture was clear. One looks at some building of the past whose use one is ignorant of, and yet it has a modernity. It had its own specific gravity. That form has never left me; I suppose it just got burned in.

Interviewer: You were particularly drawn to tragedy, then?

Miller: It seemed to me the only form there was. The rest of it was all either attempts at it, or escapes from it. But tragedy was the basic pillar.

Interviewer: When *Death of a Salesman* opened, you said to *The New York Times* in an interview that the tragic feeling is evoked in us when we're in the presence of a character who is ready to lay down his life, if need be, to secure one thing—his sense of personal dignity. Do you consider your plays modern tragedies?

Miller: I changed my mind about it several times. I think that to make a direct or arithmetical comparison between any contemporary work and the classic tragedies is impossible because of the question of religion and power, which was taken for granted and is an *a priori* consideration in any classic tragedy. Like a religious ceremony, where they finally reached the objective by the sacrifice. It has to do with the community sacrificing some man whom they both adore and despise in order to reach its basic and fundamental laws and, therefore, justify its existence and feel safe.

Interviewer: In *After The Fall*, although Maggie was "sacrificed" the central character Quentin survives. Did you see him as tragic or in any degree potentially tragic?

Miller: I can't answer that, because I can't, quite frankly, separate in my mind tragedy from death. In some people's minds I know there's no reason to put them together. I can't break it—for one reason, and that is, to coin a phrase: there's nothing like death. Dying isn't like it, you know. There's no substitute for the impact on the mind of the spectacle of death. And there is no possibility, it seems to me, of speaking of tragedy without it. Because if the total demise of the person we watch for two or three hours doesn't occur, if he just walks away, no matter how damaged, no matter how much he suffers . . .

Interviewer: What were those two plays you had seen before you began to write?

Miller: When I was about 12, I think it was, my mother took me to a theater one afternoon. We lived in Harlem and in Harlem there were two or three theaters that ran all the time and many women would drop in for all or part of the afternoon performances. All I remember was that there were people in the hold of a ship, the stage was rocking—they actually rocked the stage—and some cannibal on the ship had a time bomb. And they were all looking for the cannibal: it was thrilling. The other one was a morality play about taking dope. Evidently there was much excitement in New York then about the Chinese and dope. The Chinese were kidnapping beautiful, blond, blue-eyed girls who, people thought, had lost their bearings morally; they were flappers who drank gin and ran around with boys. And they inevitably ended up in some basement in Chinatown where they were inevitably lost by virtue of eating opium or smoking some pot. Those were the two masterpieces I had seen. I'd read some others, of course, by the time I started writing. I'd read Shakespeare and Ibsen, a little, not much. I never connected playwrighting with our theater, even from the beginning.

Interviewer: Did your first play have any bearing on *All My Sons,* or *Death of a Salesman?*

Miller: It did. It was a play about a father owning a business in 1935, a business that was being struck, and a son being torn between his father's interests and his sense of justice. But it turned into a near comic play. At that stage of my life I was removed somewhat. I was not Clifford Odets: he took it head-on.

Interviewer: Many of your plays have that father-son relationship as the dominant theme. Were you very close to your father?

Miller: I was. I still am, but I think, actually, that my plays don't reflect directly my relationship to him. It's a very primitive thing in my plays. That is, the father was really a figure who incorporated both power and some kind of a moral law which he had either broken or had fallen prey to. He figures as an immense shadow . . . I didn't expect that of my own father, literally, but of his position, apparently I did. The reason that I was able to write about the relationship, I think now, was because it had a mythical quality to me. If I had ever thought that I was writing about my father, I suppose I never could have done it. My father is, literally, a much more realistic guy than Willy Loman, and much more successful as a personality. And he'd be the last man in the world to ever commit suicide. Willy is based on an individual whom I knew very little, who was a salesman; it was years later that I realized I had only seen that man about a total of four hours in 20 years. He gave one of those impressions that is basic, evidently. When I thought of him, he would simply be a mute man: he said no more than 200 words to me. I was a kid. Later on, I had another of that kind of a contact, with a man whose fantasy was always overreaching his real outline. I've always been aware of that kind of agony, of someone who has some driving, implacable wish in him which never goes away, which he can never block out. And it broods over him, it makes him happy sometimes or it makes him suicidal, but it never leaves him. Any hero, whom we even begin to think of as tragic, is obsessed, whether it's Lear or Hamlet or the women in the Greek plays.

Interviewer: Do any of the younger playwrights create heroes—in your opinion?

Miller: I tell you, I may be working on a different wave-length but I don't think they are looking at character any more, at the documentation of facts about people. All experience is looked at now from a schematic point of view. These playwrights won't let the characters escape for a moment from their preconceived scheme of how dreadful the world is. It is very much like the old strike plays. The scheme then was that someone began a play with a bourgeois ideology and got involved in some area of experience which had a connection to the labor movement—either it was actually a strike or, in a larger sense, it was the collapse of capitalism—and he ended the play with some new positioning vis-à-vis that collapse. He started without an enlightenment and he ended with some kind of enlightenment. And you could predict that in the first five minutes. Very few of those plays could be done anymore, because they're absurd now. I've found over the years that a similar thing has happened with the so-called absurd theater. Predictable.

Interviewer: In other words, the notion of tragedy about which you were talking earlier is absent from this preconceived view of the world.

Miller: Absolutely. The tragic hero was supposed to join the scheme of things by sacrifice. It's a religious thing, I've always thought. He threw some sharp light upon the hidden scheme of existence, either by breaking one of its profoundest laws, as Oedipus breaks a taboo, and therefore proves the existence of the taboo, or by proving a moral world at the cost of his own life. And that's the victory. We need him, as the vanguard of the race. We need his crime. That crime is a civilizing crime. Well, *now* the view is that it's an inconsolable universe. Nothing is proved by a crime excepting that some people are freer to produce crime than others, and usually they are more honest than the others. There is no final reassertion of a community at all. There isn't the kind of communication that a child demands. The best you could say is that it is intelligent.

Interviewer: Then it's aware . . .

Miller: It's aware, but it will not admit into itself any moral universe at all. Another thing that's missing is the positioning of the author in relation to power. I always assumed that underlying any story is the question of who should wield power. See, in *Death of a Salesman* you have two viewpoints. They show what would happen if we all took Willy's viewpoint toward the world, or if we all took Biff's. And took it seriously, as almost a political fact. I'm debating really which way the world ought to be run; I'm speaking of psychology and the spirit, too. For example, a play that isn't usually linked with this kind of problem is Tennessee Williams' *Cat on a Hot Tin Roof*. It struck me sharply that what is at stake there is the father's great power. He's the owner, literally, of an empire of land and farms. And he wants to immortalize that power, he wants to hand it on, because he's dying. The son has a much finer appreciation of justice and human relations than the father. The father is rougher, more Philistine; he's cruder, and when we speak of the fineness of emotions, we would probably say the son has them and the father lacks them. When I saw the play I thought, this is going to be simply marvelous because the person with the sensitivity will be presented with power and what is he going to do about it? But it never gets to that. It gets deflected onto a question of personal neurosis. It comes to a dead end. If we're talking about tragedy, the Greeks would have done something miraculous with that idea. They would have stuck the son with the powers, and faced him with the wracking conflicts of the sensitive man having to rule. And then you would throw light on what the tragedy of power is.

Interviewer: Which is what you were getting at in *Incident at Vichy* . . .

Miller: That's exactly what I was after. But I feel today's stage turns away from any consideration of power, which always lies at the heart of tragedy. I use Williams' play as an example because he's that excellent that his problems are symptomatic of the time—*Cat* ultimately came down to the mendacity of human relations. It was a most accurate personalization but it bypasses the issue which the play seems to me to raise, namely the mendacity, in social relations. I still believe that when a play questions, even threatens, our social arrangement, that is when it really shakes us profoundly and dangerously, and that is when you've got to be great; good isn't enough.

Interviewer: Do you think that people in general now rationalize so, and have so many euphemisms for death, that they can't face tragedy?

Miller: I wonder whether there isn't a certain—I'm speaking now of all classes of people—you could call it a softness, or else a genuine inability to face the tough decisions and the dreadful results of error. I say that only because when *Death of a Salesman* went on again recently, I sensed in some of the reaction that it was simply too threatening. Now there were probably a lot of people in the Forties, when it first opened, who felt the same way. Maybe I just didn't hear those people as much as I heard other people—maybe it has to do with my own reaction. You need a certain amount of confidence to watch tragedy. If you yourself are about to die, you're not going to see that play. I've always thought that the Americans had, almost inborn, a primordial fear of falling, being declassed—you get it with your driver's license, if not earlier.

Interviewer: What about Europeans?

Miller: Well, the play opened in Paris again only last September; it opened in Paris ten years earlier, too, with very little effect. It wasn't a very good production, I understand. But now suddenly they discovered this play. And I sensed that their reaction was quite an American reaction. Maybe it comes with having—having the guilt of wealth; it would be interesting if the Russians ever got to feel that way!

Interviewer: *Death of a Salesman* has been done in Russia, hasn't it?

Miller: Oh, many times.

Interviewer: When you were in Russia recently did you form any opinion about the Russian theater public?

Miller: First of all, there's a wonderful naïveté that they have; they're not bored to death. They're not coming in out of the rain, so to speak, with nothing better to do. When they go to the theater, it has great weight with them. They come to see something that'll change their lives. Ninety percent of the time, of course, there's nothing there, but they're open to a grand experience. This is not the way we go to the theater.

Interviewer: What about the plays themselves?

Miller: I think they do things on the stage which are exciting and deft and they have marvelous actors, but the drama itself is not adventurous. The plays are basically a species of naturalism; it's not even realism. They're violently opposed to the theater of the absurd because they see it as a fragmenting of the community into perverse individuals who will no longer be under any mutual obligation at all, and I can see some point in their fear. Of course, these things should be done if only so one can rebut them. I know that I was very moved in many ways by German expressionism when I was in school: yet there too something was perverse in it to me. It was the end of man, there are no people in it any more; that was especially true of the real German stuff: it's the bitter end of the world where man is a voice of his class function, and that's it. Brecht has a lot of that in him, but he's too much of a poet to be enslaved by it. And yet, at the same time, I learned a great deal from it. I used elements of it that were fused into *Death of a Salesman*. For instance, I purposefully would not give Ben any character, because for Willy he *has* no character—which is, psychologically, expressionist because so many memories come back with a simple tag on them: somebody represents a threat to you, or a promise.

Interviewer: Speaking of different cultures, what is your feeling about the French Théâtre National Populaire?

Miller: I thought a play I saw by Corneille, *L'Allusion Comique*, one of the most exciting things I've ever seen. We saw something I never thought I could enjoy—my French is not all that good. But I had just gotten over being sick, and we were about to leave France, and I wanted to see what they did with it. It was just superb. It is one of Corneille's lesser works, about a magician who takes people into the nether regions. What a marvelous mixture of satire, and broad comedy, and characterizations! And the acting was simply out of this world. Of course one of the best parts about the whole thing was the audience. Because they're mostly under 30, it looked to me; they pay very little to get in; and I would guess there are between 2500 and 3000 seats in that place. And the vitality of the audience is breathtaking. Of course the actors' ability to speak that language so beautifully is just in itself a joy. From that vast stage, to talk quietly, and make you *feel* the voice just wafting all over the house . . .

Interviewer: Why do you think we haven't been able to do such a thing here? Why has Whitehead's Lincoln Center Repertory Theater failed as such?

Miller: Well, that is a phenomenon worthy of a sociological study. When I got into it, *After the Fall* was about two-thirds written. Whitehead came to me and said, "I hear you're writing a play. Can we use it to start the Lincoln Center Repertory Company?" For one reason or another I said I would do it. I expected to take a financial beating (I could hope to earn maybe twenty percent of what I normally earn with a play, but I assumed that people would say, "Well, it's a stupid but not idiotic action.") What developed, before any play opened at all, was a hostility which completely dumbfounded me. I don't think it was directed against anybody in particular. For actors who want to develop their art, there's no better place to do it than in a permanent repertory company where you play different parts and you have opportunities you've never had in a lifetime on Broadway. But the actor seemed to be affronted by the whole thing. I couldn't dig it! I could understand the enmity of commercial producers who, after all, thought they were threatened by it. But the professional people of every kind greeted it as though it were some kind of an insult. The only conclusion I can come to is that an actor was now threatened with having to put up or shut up. He had always been able to walk around on Broadway where conditions were dreadful and say, "I'm a great actor but I'm unappreciated," but in the back of his mind he could figure, "Well, one of these days I'll get a starring role and I'll go to Hollywood and get rich." This he couldn't do in a repertory theater where he signed up for several years. So the whole idea of that kind of quick success was renounced. He didn't want to face an opportunity which threatened him in this way. It makes me wonder whether there is such a profound alienation among artists that any organized attempt to create something that is not based upon commerce, that has sponsorship, automatically sets people against it. I think that's an interesting facet. I also spoke to a group of young playwrights. Now, if it had been me, I would have been knocking at the door, demanding that they read my play, as I did unsuccessfully when the Group Theatre was around. Then *every* playwright was banging on the door and furious and wanted the art theater to do what *he* thought they should do. We could do that because it belonged to us all—you know—we thought of the Group Theatre as a public enterprise. Well, that wasn't true at all here. Everyone thought the Lincoln Theatre was the property of the directors, of Miller and Whitehead and Kazan and one or two other people. Of course, what also made it fail was, as Lawrence Olivier suggested, that it takes years to do anything. But he also made the point that with his English repertory theater he got encouragement from the beginning. There were people who pooh-poohed the whole thing, and said it was ridiculous, but basically the artistic community was in favor of it.

Interviewer: How about the actors themselves? Did Lee Strasberg influence them?

Miller: I think Strasberg is a symptom, really. He's a great force, and (in my unique opinion, evidently) a force which is not for the good in the theater. He makes actors secret people and he makes acting secret, and it's the most communicative art known to man; I mean, that's what the actor's *supposed* to be doing. But I wouldn't blame the Repertory Theater failures on him, because the people in there were not Actors Studio people at all; so he is not responsible for that. But the Method is in the air: the actor is defending himself from the Philistine, vulgar public. I had a girl in my play I couldn't hear, and the acoustics in that little theater we were using were simply magnificent. I said to her, "I can't hear you," and I kept on saying, "I can't hear you." She finally got furious and said to me, in effect, that she was acting the truth, and that she was not going to prostitute herself to the audience. That was the living end! It reminded me of Walter Hampden's comment—because we had a similar problem in *The Crucible* with some actors—he said they play a cello with the most perfect bowing and the fingering is magnificent but there are no strings on the instrument. The problem is that the actor is now working out his private fate through his role, and the idea of communicating the meaning of the play is the last thing that occurs to him. In the Actors Studio, despite denials, the actor is told that the text is really the framework for his emotions; I've heard actors change the order of lines in my work and tell me that the lines are only, so to speak, the libretto for the music—that the actor is the main force that the audience is watching and that the playwright is his servant. They are told that the analysis of the text, and the rhythm of the text, the verbal texture, is of no importance whatever. This is Method, as they are teaching it, which is, of course, a perversion of it, if you go back to the beginning. But there was always a tendency in that direction. Chekhov, himself, said that Stanislavsky had perverted *The Seagull*.

Interviewer: What about Method acting in the movies?

Miller: Well, in the movies, curiously enough, the Method works better. Because the camera can come right up to an actor's nostrils and suck out of him a communicative gesture; a look in the eye, a wrinkle of his grin, and so on, which registers nothing on the stage. The stage is, after all, a verbal medium. You've got to make large gestures if they're going to be seen at all. In other words, you've got to be unnatural. You've got to say, "I am out to move into that audience; that's my job." In a movie you don't do that; as a matter of fact, that's bad movie-acting, it's overacting. Movies are wonderful for private acting.

Interviewer: Do you think the movies helped bring about this private acting in the theater?

Miller: Well, it's a perversion of the Chekhovian play and of the Stanislavsky technique. What Chekhov was doing was eliminating the histrionics of his actors by incorporating them in the writing: the internal life was what he was writing about. And Stanislavsky's direction was also internal: for the first time he was trying to motivate every move from within instead of imitating an action; which is what acting should be. When you eliminate the vital element of the actor in the community and simply make a psychiatric figure on the stage who is thinking profound thoughts which he doesn't let anyone know about, then it's a perversion.

Interviewer: How does the success of Peter Weiss' *Marat/Sade* play fit into this?

Miller: Well, I would emphasize its production and direction. Peter Brook has been trying for years, especially through productions of

Shakespeare, to make the bridge between psychological acting and theater, between the private personality, perhaps, and its public demonstration. *Marat/Sade* is more an oratorio than a play; the characters are basically thematic relationships rather than human entities, so the action exemplified rather than characterized.

Interviewer: Do you think the popularity of the movies has had any influence on playwrighting itself?

Miller: Yes. Its form has been changed by the movies. I think certain techniques, such as the jumping from place to place, although it's as old as Shakespeare, came to us not through Shakespeare, but through the movies, a telegraphic, dream-constructed way of seeing life.

Interviewer: How important is the screenwriter in motion pictures?

Miller: Well, you'd be hard put to remember the dialogue in some of the great pictures that you've seen. That's why pictures are so international. You don't have to hear the style of the dialogue in an Italian movie or a French movie. We're watching the film so that the vehicle is not the ear or the word, it's the eye. The director of a play is nailed to words. He can interpret them a little differently, but he has limits: you can only inflect a sentence in two or three different ways, but you can inflect an image on the screen in an infinite number of ways. You can make one character practically fall out of the frame; you can shoot it where you don't even see his face. Two people can be talking, and the man talking cannot be seen, so the emphasis is on the reaction to the speech rather than on the speech itself.

Interviewer: What about television as a medium for drama?

Miller: I don't think there is anything that approaches the theater. The sheer presence of a living person is always stronger than his image. But there's no reason why TV shouldn't be a terrific medium. The problem is that the audience watching TV shows is always separated. My feeling is that people in a group, *en masse*, watching something, react differently, and perhaps more profoundly, than they do when they're alone in their living rooms. Yet it's not a hurdle that couldn't be jumped by the right kind of material. Simply, it's hard to get good movies, it's hard to get good novels, it's hard to get good poetry—it's *impossible* to get good television because in addition to the indigenous difficulties there's the whole question of it being a medium that's controlled by big business. It took TV seventeen years

to do *Death of a Salesman* here. It's been done on TV in every
country in the world at least once, but it's critical of the business
world and the content is downbeat.

Interviewer: A long time ago, you used to write radio scripts. Did
you learn much about technique from that experience?

Miller: I did. We had twenty-eight and a half minutes to tell a
whole story in a radio play and you had to concentrate on the words
because you couldn't see anything. You were playing in a dark closet,
in fact. So the economy of words in a good radio play was
everything. It drove you more and more to realize what the power of
a good sentence was, and the right phrase could save you a page
you would otherwise be wasting. I was always sorry radio didn't last
long enough for contemporary poetic movements to take advantage
of it, because it's a natural medium for poets. It's pure voice, pure
words. Words and silence; a marvelous medium. I've often thought,
even recently, that I would like to write another radio play, and just
give it to someone and let them do it on WBAI. The English do radio
plays still, very good ones.

Interviewer: You used to write verse drama too, didn't you?

Miller: Oh yes, I was up to my neck in it.

Interviewer: Would you ever do it again?

Miller: I might. I often write speeches in verse, and then break
them down. Much of *Death of a Salesman* was originally written in
verse, the *The Crucible* was all written in verse, but I broke it up. I
was frightened that the actors would take an attitude toward the
material that would destroy its vitality. I didn't want anyone standing
up there making speeches. You see, we have no tradition of verse,
and as soon as an American actor sees something printed like verse,
he immediately puts one foot in front of the other—or else he
mutters. Then you can't hear it at all.

Interviewer: Which of your own plays do you feel closest to now?

Miller: I don't know if I feel closer to one than another. I suppose
The Crucible in some ways. I think there's a lot of myself in it. There
are a lot of layers in there that I know about that nobody else
does . . .

Interviewer: More so than in *After the Fall* . . . ?

Miller: Yes, because although *After the Fall* is more psychological
it's less developed as an artifice. You see, in *The Crucible* I was
completely freed by the period I was writing about—over three

centuries ago. It was a different diction, a different age. I had great joy writing that, more than with almost any other play I've written. I learned about how writers felt in the past when they were dealing almost constantly with historical material. A dramatist writing history could finish a play Monday and start another Wednesday, and go right on. Because the *stories* are all prepared for him. Inventing the story is what takes all the time. It takes a year to invent the story. The historical dramatist doesn't have to invent anything, except his language, and his characterizations. Oh, of course, there's the terrific problem of condensing history, a lot of reshuffling and bringing in characters who never lived, or who died a hundred years apart—but basically if you've got the story, you're a year ahead.

Interviewer: It must also be tempting to use a historical figure whose epoch was one of faith.

Miller: It is. With all the modern psychology and psychiatry and the level of literacy higher than it ever was, we get less perspective on ourselves than at almost any time I know about. I have never been so aware of clique ideas overtaking people—fashions, for example—and sweeping them away, as though the last day of the world had come. One can sometimes point to a week or month in which things changed abruptly. It's like women's clothing in a certain issue of *Vogue* magazine. There is such a wish to be part of that enormous minority that likes to create new minorities. Yet people are desperately afraid of being alone.

Interviewer: Has our insight into psychology affected this?

Miller: It has simply helped people rationalize their situation, rather than get out of it, or break through it. In other words—you've heard it a hundred times—"Well, I am this type of person, and this type doesn't do anything but what I'm doing . . ."

Interviewer: Do you think the push toward personal success dominates American life now more than it used to?

Miller: I think it's far more powerful today than when I wrote *Death of a Salesman.* I think it's closer to a madness today than it was then. Now there's no perspective on it at all.

Interviewer: Would you say that the girl in *After the Fall* is a symbol of that obsession?

Miller: Yes, she is consumed by what she does, and instead of it being a means of release, it's a jail. A prison which defines her, finally. She can't break through. In other words, success instead of giving freedom of choice, becomes a way of life. There's no country I've been to where people, when you come into a room and sit down with them, so often ask you, "What do you do?" And, being American, many's the time I've almost asked that question, then realized it's good for my soul not to know. For a while! Just to let the evening wear on and see what I think of this person without knowing what he does and how successful he is, or what a failure. We're *ranking* everybody every minute of the day.

Interviewer: Will you write about American success again?

Miller: I might, but you see, as a thing in itself success is self-satirizing; it's self-elucidating, in a way. That's why it's so difficult to write about. Because the very people who are being swallowed up by this ethos nod in agreement when you tell them, "You are being swallowed up by this thing." To really wrench them and find them another feasible perspective is therefore extremely difficult.

Interviewer: In your story "The Prophecy," the protagonist says this is a time of the supremacy of personal relations, that there are no larger aims in our lives. Is this your view too?

Miller: Well, that story was written under the pall of the Fifties, but I think there's been a terrific politicalization of the people these past four or five years. Not in the old sense, but in the sense that it is no longer *gauche* or stupid to be interested in the fate of society and in injustice and in race problems and the rest of it. It now becomes esthetic material once again. In the Fifties it was *out* to mention this. It meant you were really not an artist. That prejudice seems to have gone. The Negroes broke it up, thank God! But it has been an era of personal relations—and now it's being synthesized in a good way. That is, the closer you get to any kind of political action among young people, the more they demand that the action have a certain fidelity to human nature, and that pomposity, and posing, and role-taking not be allowed to strip the movement of its veracity. What they suspect most is gesturing, you know, just making gestures, which are either futile, or self-serving, or merely conscientious. The intense personal-relations concentration of the Fifties seem now to have been joined to a political consciousness, which is terrific.

Interviewer: Do you feel politics in any way to be an invasion of your privacy?

Miller: No, I always drew a lot of inspiration from politics, from one or another kind of national struggle. You live in the world even though you only vote once in a while. It determines the extensions of your personality. I lived through the McCarthy time, when one saw personalities shifting and changing before one's eyes, as a direct, obvious result of a political situation. And had it gone on, we would have gotten a whole new American personality—which in part we have. It's ten years since McCarthy died, and it's only now that powerful Senators dare to suggest that it might be wise to learn a little Chinese, to talk to some Chinese. I mean it took ten years, and even those guys who are thought to be quite brave and courageous just now dare to make these suggestions. Such a pall of fright was laid upon us that it truly deflected the American mind. It's part of a paranoia which we haven't escaped yet. Good God, people still give their lives for it; look what we're doing in the Pacific.

Interviewer: Yet so much of the theater these last few years has had nothing to do with public life.

Miller: Yes, it's got so we've lost the technique of grappling with the world that Homer had, that Aeschylus had, that Euripides had. And Shakespeare. How amazing it is that people who adore the Greek drama fail to see that these great works are works of a man confronting his society, the illusions of the society, the faiths of the society. They're social documents, not little piddling private conversations. We just got educated into thinking this is all "a story," a myth for its own sake.

Interviewer: Do you think there'll be a return to social drama now?

Miller: I think there will be, if theater is to survive. Look at Molière. You can't conceive of him except as a social playwright. He's a social critic. Bathes up to his neck in what's going on around him.

Interviewer: Could the strict forms utilized by Molière appear again?

Miller: I don't think one can repeat old forms as such, because they express most densely a moment of time. For example I couldn't write a play like *Death of a Salesman* any more. I couldn't really write any of my plays now. Each is different, spaced sometimes two years apart, because each moment called for a different vocabulary and a different organization of the material. However, when you speak of a strict form, I believe in it for the theater. Otherwise you end up with anecdotes, not with plays. We're in an era of anecdotes, in my opinion, which is going to pass any minute. The audience has been trained to eschew the organized climax because it's corny, or because it violates the chaos which we all revere. But I think that's going to disappear with the first play of a new kind which will once again pound the boards and shake people out of their seats with a deeply, intensely, organized climax. It can only come from a strict form: you can't get it except as the culmination of two hours of development. You can't get it by raising your voice and yelling, suddenly—because it's getting time to get on the train for Yonkers.

Interviewer: Have you any conception of what your own evolution has been? In terms of form and themes?

Miller: I keep going. Both forwards and backwards. Hopefully more forwards than backwards. That is to say, before I wrote my first *successful* play, I wrote, oh I don't know, maybe fourteen or fifteen other full-length plays and maybe thirty radio plays. The majority of them were non-realistic plays. They were metaphorical plays, or symbolistic plays; some of them were in verse, or in one case— writing about Montezuma—I turned out a grand historical tragedy, partly in verse, rather Elizabethan in form. Then I began to be known really by virtue of the single play I had ever tried to do in completely realistic Ibsen-like form, which was *All My Sons.* The fortunes of a writer! The others, like *Salesman,* which are a compound of expressionism and realism, or even *A View From the Bridge,* which is realism of a sort (though it's broken up severely), are more typical of the bulk of the work I've done. *After the Fall* is really down the middle, it's more like most of the work I've done than any other play . . . excepting that what has *surfaced* has been more realistic than in the others. It's really an impressionistic kind of a work. I was trying to create a total by throwing many small pieces at the spectator.

Interviewer: What productions of *After the Fall* do you think did it the most justice?

Miller: I saw one production which I thought was quite marvelous. That was the one Zefferelli did in Italy. He understood that this was a play which reflected the world as one man saw it. Through the play the mounting awareness of this man was the issue, and as it approached agony the audience was to be enlarged in its consciousness of what was happening. The other productions that I've seen have all been really *realistic* in the worst sense. That is to say, they simply played the scenes without any attempt to allow the main character to develop this widened awareness. He has different reactions on page ten than he does on page one, but it takes an actor with a certain amount of brains to see that evolution. It isn't enough to feel them. And as a director Zefferelli had an absolutely organic viewpoint toward it. The play is about someone desperately striving to obtain a viewpoint.

Interviewer: Do you feel in the New York production that the girl allegedly based on Marilyn Monroe was out of proportion, entirely separate from Quentin?

Miller: Yes, although I failed to foresee it myself. In the Italian production this never happened; it was always in proportion. I suppose, too, that by the time Zefferelli did the play the publicity shock had been absorbed, so that one could watch Quentin's evolution without being distracted.

Interviewer: What do you think happened in New York?

Miller: Something I never thought could happen. The play was never judged as a play at all. Good or bad, I would never know what it was from what I read about it, only what it was supposed to have been.

Interviewer: Because they all reacted as if it were simply a segment of your personal life?

Miller: Yes.

Interviewer: Do you think contemporary American critics tend to regard the theater in terms of literature rather than theater?

Miller: Yes, for years theatrical criticism was carried on mainly by reporters. Reporters who by and large had no reference in the esthetic theories of the drama, except in the most rudimentary way. And off in a corner, somewhere, the professors, with no relation whatsoever to the newspaper critics, were regarding the drama from a so-called academic viewpoint. With its relentless standards of tragedy, and so forth. What the reporters had very often was a simple, primitive love of a good show. And if nothing else, you could tell whether that level of mind was genuinely interested, or not. There was a certain naïveté in the reportage. They could destroy plays which dealt on a level of sensibility that was beyond them. But by and large you got a playback on what you put in. They knew how to laugh, cry, at least a native kind of reaction, stamp their feet—they loved the theater. Since then, the reporter-critics have been largely displaced by academic critics or graduates of that school. Quite frankly, two-thirds of the time I don't know what they really feel about the play. They seem to feel that the theater is an intrusion on literature. The theater as theater—as a place where people go to be swept up in some new experience—seems to antagonize them. I don't think we can really do away with *joy*: the joy of being distracted altogether in the service of some esthetic. That seems to be the general drift, but it won't work: sooner or later the theater outwits everybody. Someone comes in who just loves to write, or to act, and who'll sweep the audience, and the critics, with him.

Interviewer: Do you think these critics influence playwrights?

Miller: Everything influences playwrights. A playwright who isn't influenced is never of any use. He's the litmus paper of the arts. He's got to be, because if he isn't working on the same wave length as the audience, no one would know what in hell he was talking about. He is a kind of psychic journalist, even when he's great; consequently, for him the total atmosphere is more important in this art than it is probably in any other.

Interviewer: What do you think of a certain critic's statement that the success of a really contemporary play, like *Marat/Sade*, makes Tennessee Williams and his genre obsolete?

Miller: Ridiculous. No more than that Tennessee's remarkable success made obsolete the past before him. There are some biological laws in the theater which can't be violated. It should not be made into an activated chess game. You can't have a theater based upon anything other than a mass audience if it's going to succeed. The larger the better. It's the law of the theater. In the Greek audience fourteen thousand people sat down at the same time, to see a play. Fourteen thousand people! And nobody can tell me that those people were all readers of *The New York Review of Books!* Even Shakespeare was smashed around in his time by university people. I think for much the same reasons—because he was reaching for those parts of man's makeup which respond to melodrama, broad comedy, violence, dirty words, and blood. Plenty of blood, murder, and not very well motivated at that.

Interviewer: What is your feeling about Eugene O'Neill as a playwright?

Miller: O'Neill never meant much to me when I was starting. In the Thirties, and for the most part in the Forties, you would have said that he was a finished figure. He was not a force any more. *The Iceman Cometh* and *The Long Day's Journey into Night*, so popular a few years ago, would not have been successful when they were written. Which is another example of the psychic journalism of the stage. A great deal depends upon when a play is produced. That's why playwrighting is such a fatal profession to take up. You can have everything, but if you don't have that sense of timing, nothing happens. One thing I always respected about O'Neill was his insistence on his vision. That is, even when he was twisting materials to distortion and really ruining his work, there was an image behind it of a possessed individual, who, for good or ill, was himself. I don't think there is anything in it for a young man to learn technically; that was probably why I wasn't interested in it. He had one virtue which is not technical, it's what I call "drumming;" he repeats something up to and past the point where you say "I know this, I've heard this ninety-three different ways," and suddenly you realize you are being swept up in something that you thought you understood and he has drummed you over the horizon into a new perception. He doesn't care if he's repeating. It's part of his insensitivity. He's a very insensitive writer. There's no finesse at all: he's the Dreiser of the stage. He writes with heavy pencils. His virtue is that he insists on his climax, and not the one you would want to put there. His failing is that so many of his plays are so distorted that one no longer knows on what level to receive them. His people are not symbolic; his lines are certainly not verse; the prose is not realistic—his is the never-never land of a quasi-Strindberg writer. But where he's wonderful, it's superb. The last play is really a masterpiece. But, to give you an example of timing: *The Iceman Cometh* opened, it happened, the same year that *All My Sons* opened. It's an interesting sociological phenomenon. That was in forty-seven, soon after the war. There was still in the air a certain hopefulness about the organization of the world. There was no depression in the United States. McCarthyism had not yet started. There was a kind of . . . one could almost speak of it as an atmosphere of good will, if such a term can be used in the twentieth century. Then a play comes along which posits a world *really* filled with disasters of one kind or another. A *cul de sac* is described, a bag with no way out. At that time it didn't corroborate what people had experienced. It corroborated what they were *going* to experience, and pretty soon after, it became very timely. We moved into the bag that he had gotten into first! But at the time it opened, nobody went to see *Iceman*. In a big way, nobody went.

Even after it was cut, the thing took four or five hours to play. The production was simply dreadful. But nobody made any note that it was dreadful. Nobody perceived what this play was. It was described simply as the work of a sick old man of whom everybody said, "Isn't it wonderful that he can still spell?" When I went to see that play not long after it opened, there must have been thirty people in the audience. I think there were a dozen people left by the end of the play. It was quite obviously a great piece of work which was being mangled on the stage. It was obvious to me. And to a certain number of directors who saw it. Not all of them. Not all directors can tell the difference between the production and the play. I can't do it all the time, either, though *Iceman* was one where I could. But as for the critics I don't think there is anybody alive today, with the possible exception of Harold Clurman, who I would trust to know the difference between production and play. Harold can do it—not always, but a lot of the time—because he has directed a good deal.

Interviewer: Could this question of timing have affected the reaction here to *After the Fall?*

Miller: Look, *After the Fall* would have been altogether different if by some means the hero was killed, or shot himself. Then we would have been in business. I knew it at the time. As I was saying before . . . there's nothing like death. Still, I just wasn't going to do it. The ironical thing to me was that I heard cries of indignation from various people, who had in the lifetime of Marilyn Monroe either exploited her unmercifully, in a way that would have subjected them to peonage laws, or mocked her viciously, or refused to take any of her pretensions seriously. So consequently, it was impossible to credit their sincerity.

Interviewer: They were letting you get them off the hook.

Miller: That's right. That's exactly right.

Interviewer: And they didn't want Quentin to compromise . . .

Miller: I think Günter Grass recently has said that art is uncompromising and life is full of compromises. To bring them together is a near-impossibility, and that is what I was trying to do. I was trying to make it as much like life as it could possibly be and as excruciating—so the relief that we want would not be there: I denied the audience the relief. And of course all these hard realists betrayed their basic romanticism by their reaction.

Interviewer: Do you think if you had done it in poetry that would have removed the threat more?

Miller: Yes, I suppose so. But I didn't want to remove it. It would have seduced people in a way I didn't want to. Look, I know how to make 'em go with me . . . it's the first instinct of a writer who succeeds in the theater at all. I mean by the time you've written your third play or so you know which buttons to push; if you want an easy success there's no problem that way once you've gotten a story. People are pretty primitive—they really want the thing to turn out all right. After all, for a century and a half *King Lear* was played in England with a happy ending. I wrote a radio play about the boy who wrote that version—William Ireland—who forged Shakespeare's plays, and edited *King Lear* so that it conformed to a middle-class view of life. They thought, including all but Malone, who was the first good critic, that this was the real Shakespeare. He was an expert forger. He fixed up several of the other plays, but this one he really rewrote. He was seventeen years old. And they produced it—it was a big success—and Boswell thought it was the greatest thing he'd ever seen, and so did all the others. The only one was Malone, who on the basis of textual impossibilities—aside from the fact that he sensed it was a bowdlerization—proved that it couldn't have been Shakespeare. It's what I was talking about before: the litmus paper of the playwright: you see Ireland sensed quite correctly what these people really wanted from *King Lear*, and he gave it to them. He sentimentalized it; took out any noxious references.

Interviewer: And did it end with a happy family reunion?

Miller: Yes, kind of like a Jewish melodrama. A family play.

Interviewer: To go back to *After the Fall*. Did the style in which this play was presented in New York affect its reception?

Miller: Well, you've hit it right on the head. You see, what happened in Italy with Zefferelli was—I can describe it very simply: there was a stage made up of steel frames; it is as though one were looking into the back of a bellows camera—you know, concentric oblong steel frames were covered, just like a camera is, but the actors could enter through openings in these covers. They could appear or disappear on the stage at any depth. Furthermore, pneumatic lifts silently and invisibly raised the actors up, so that they could appear for ten seconds—then disappear. Or a table would be raised or a whole group of furniture, which the actors would then use. So that the whole image of all this happening inside a man's head was there from the first second, and remained right through the play. In New York the difficulty was partly due to the stage which was open, rounded. Such a stage has virtues for certain kinds of plays, but it is stiff—there is no place to hide at all. If an actor has to *appear* stage center, he makes his appearance twenty feet off the left or right. The laborious nature of these entrances and exits is insuperable. What is supposed to "appear" doesn't appear, but lumbers on stage toward you.

Interviewer: Did that Italian production have a concentration camp in the background? I remember a piece by Jonathan Miller complaining of your use of the concentration camp in New York.

Miller: Oh yes. You see in Italy the steel frame itself *became* the concentration camp, so that the whole play in effect was taking place in the ambiance of that enclosure. This steel turned into a jail, into a prison, into a camp, into a constricted mechanical environment. You could light those girders in such a way that they were forbidding—it was a great scenic idea.

Interviewer: Why did you choose to use a concentration camp in the first place?

Miller: Well, I have always felt that concentration camps, though they're a phenomenon of totalitarian states, are also the logical conclusion of contemporary life. If you complain of people being shot down in the streets, of the absence of communication or social responsibility, of the rise of everyday violence which people have become accustomed to, and the dehumanization of feelings, then the ultimate development on an organized social level is the concentration camp. Camps didn't happen in Africa where people had no connection with the basic development of western civilization. They happened in the heart of Europe, in a country, for example, which was probably less anti-Semitic than other countries, like France. The Dreyfus case did not happen in Germany. In this play the question is, what is there between people that is indestructible? The concentration camp is the final expression of human separateness and its ultimate consequence. It is organized abandonment . . . one of the prime themes of *After The Fall.*

Even in *Salesman* what's driving Willy nuts is that he's trying to establish a connection, in his case, with the world of power; he is trying to say that if you behave in a certain way, you'll end up in the cat-bird seat. That's your connection; then life is no longer dangerous, you see. You are safe from abandonment.

Interviewer: What is the genesis of *The Crucible?*

Miller: I thought of it first when I was at Michigan. I read a lot about the Salem witch trials at that time. Then when the McCarthy era came along, I remembered these stories and I used to tell them to people when it started. I had no idea that it was going to go as far as it went. I used to say, you know, McCarthy is actually saying certain lines that I recall the witch-hunters saying in Salem. So I started to go back, not with the idea of writing a play, but to refresh my own mind because it was getting eerie. For example, his holding up his hand with cards in it, saying, "I have in my hand the names of so-and so." Well, this was a standard tactic of seventeenth-century prosecutors confronting a witness who was reluctant or confused, or an audience in a church which was not quite convinced that this particular individual might be guilty. He wouldn't say, "I have in my hand a list . . . , " he'd say, "We possess the names of all these people who are guilty. But the time has not come yet to release them." He had nothing at all—he simply wanted to secure in the town's mind the idea that he saw everything, that everyone was transparent to him. It was a way of inflicting guilt on everybody, and many people responded genuinely out of guilt; some would come and tell him some fantasy, or something that they had done or thought that was evil in their minds. I had in my play, for example, the old man who comes and reports that when his wife reads certain books, *he* can't pray. He figures that the prosecutors would know the reason, that they can see through what to him was an opaque glass. Of course, he ends up in a disaster because they prosecuted his wife. Many times completely naïve testimony resulted in somebody being hanged. And it was because they originally said, "We really know what's going on."

Interviewer: Was it the play, *The Crucible* itself, do you think, or was it perhaps that piece you did in *The Nation*—"A Modest Proposal"—that focused the Un-American Activities Committee on you?

Miller: Well, I had made a lot of statements and I had signed a great many petitions. I'd been involved in organizations, you know, putting my name down for 15 years before that. But I don't think they ever would have bothered me if I hadn't married Marilyn. Had they been interested they would have called me earlier. And in fact I was told on good authority that the then Chairman, Francis Walter, said that if Marilyn would take a photograph with him, shaking his hand, he would call off the whole thing. It's as simple as that. Marilyn would get them on the front pages right away. They had been on the front pages for years, but the issue was starting to lose its punch. They ended up in the back of the paper or on the inside pages, and here they would get right up front again. These men would time hearings to meet a certain day's newspaper. In other words, if they figured the astronauts were going up, let's say, they wouldn't have a hearing that week; they'd wait until they'd returned and things had quieted down.

Interviewer: What happened at the committee hearing?

Miller: Well, I was indicted for contempt for having refused to give or confirm the name of a writer, whether I had seen him in a meeting of Communist writers I had attended some eight or ten years earlier. My legal defense was not on any of the Constitutional Amendments but on the contention that Congress couldn't drag people in and question them about anything on the Congressman's mind; they had to show that the witness was likely to have information relevant to some legislation then at issue. The Committee had put on a show of interest in passport legislation. I had been denied a passport a couple of years earlier. Ergo, I fitted into their vise. A year later I was convicted after a week's trial. Then about a year after that the Court of Appeals threw out the whole thing. A short while later the Committee's Chief Counsel, who had been my interrogator, was shown to be on the payroll of a racist foundation and was retired to private life. It was all a dreadful waste of time and money and anger, but I suffered very little, really, compared to others who were driven out of their professions and never got back, or who did get back after eight or ten years of blacklisting. I wasn't in TV or movies so I could still function.

Interviewer: Have your political views changed much since then?

Miller: Nowadays I'm certainly not ready to advocate a tightly organized planned economy. I think it has its virtues, but I'm in deadly fear of people with too much power. I don't trust people that much anymore. I used to think that if people had the right idea they could make things move accordingly. Now it's a day to day fight to stop dreadful things from happening. In the Thirties it was, for me, inconceivable that a socialist government could be really anti-Semitic. It just could not happen because their whole protest in the beginning was against anti-Semitism, against racism, against this kind of inhumanity; that's why I was drawn to it. It was accounted to Hitler; it was accounted to blind capitalism. I'm much more pragmatic about such things now, and I want to know those I'm against and who it is that I'm backing and what he is like.

Interviewer: Do you feel whatever Jewish tradition you were brought up in has influenced you at all?

Miller: I never used to, but I think now that while I hadn't taken over an ideology I did absorb a certain viewpoint. That there is tragedy in the world but that the world must continue: one is a condition for the other. Jews can't afford to revel too much in the tragic because it might overwhelm them. Consequently, in most Jewish writing there's always the caution, "Don't push it too far toward the abyss, because you're liable to fall in." I think it's part of that psychology and it's part of me, too. I have, so to speak, a psychic investment in the continuity of life. I couldn't ever write a totally nihilistic work.

Interviewer: Would you care to say anything about what you're working on now?

Miller: I'd better not. I do have about five things started—short stories, a screen play, etc. I'm in the process of collecting my short stories. But I tell myself, "What am I doing." I should be doing a play. I have a calendar in my head. You see, the theater season starts in September, and I have always written plays in the summertime. Almost always—I did write *View From the Bridge* in the winter. So, quite frankly, I can't say. I have some interesting beginnings but I can't see the end of any of them. It's usually that way, I plan something for weeks or months and suddenly begin writing dialogue which begins in relation to what I had planned and veers off into something I hadn't even thought about. I'm drawing down the lightning, I suppose. Somewhere in the blood you have a play, and you wait until it passes behind the eyes. I'm further along than that, but I'd rather leave it at that for now.

The Contemporary Theater
Arthur Miller/1967

Michigan Quarterly Review, 6 (1967): 153-163. Reprinted by permission.

Miller's informal remarks in this piece were made before a large audience at The University of Michigan on February 28, 1967.

I thought I might talk about the situation of the theater these days, rather than about plays and about the art of the theater, because there won't be any art of the theater if the situation doesn't change. It's an easy subject to talk about, the American theater is, because we hardly have any. And this has been a rhetorical statement for many years which is rapidly becoming a fact. We have shows in this country—I've been boring people with this for years—and I'll bore you with it now because it is boring but it is the truth. We have shows in New York, but we don't have any theater in New York.

As you know, in every country the theater is, for numerous reasons, usually the creation of a city. It is concentrated in the city, whether it be Paris or London or Moscow, and when it dies in the main city or diminishes, it generally diminishes in the whole country. Whatever was wrong with the Broadway set-up for many years since, let's say, the First World War, it also provided the plays of our time. It is just now over the edge, in my opinion, in being unable to even do that.

Specifically, I strongly doubt as of this year, whether a serious play—by that I mean a serious comedy or serious drama—but one which is something more than trivial, whether such a play with terrific reviews—or I should say a terrific review, there being only one morning critic left in New York—could survive for a season. In other words, the old chestnut that a good play will always come through, is now, in my opinion, on the verge of not being the case. A good play

with good reviews will not survive in New York today. That's almost
the case. It may well be the case. There have been examples in the
last two years of plays with pretty decent reviews, plays with some
value, I'm told—I didn't see all of them—which simply could not find
an audience any more. This shouldn't have surprised anybody, and
indeed it hasn't, excepting the people most intimately involved.

There is no more irresponsible group of people I think in this
country than people who are engaged in making theater. They are
universally, almost, committed to the idea that while the general
situation may be dreadful, there's still a place for a good one. And it
has become a den of gamblers, so to speak, who think that they're
going to crack through that sound barrier and beat the system. And
of course occasionally they do. And gradually the system degenerates
and finally all that we have left now are a handful of showplaces,
show houses in New York City.

The audience for any real theater in New York stays home because
the student, the teacher, the serious person of any kind, or the joker
who likes to see a good play but hasn't got thirty dollars to spend to
go out at night with his wife or girl friend, can't come any more to
this arena of the arts, and we are left with the expense-account
people, who don't pay for their seats, whose companies give them a
certain allowance for playing, and who are, of course, not in the
mood, generally speaking, for anything but a musical or a quick
laugh. And as Carl Sandburg once said, "Great poets need great
audiences"—we don't have the audience, and we certainly don't
have the poets.

So as students and as people presumably interested in this nearly
lost art, it might behoove you to think about some of the perspectives
which are now nearly totally lost, which the art requires if it is to
survive, to say nothing of flourishing. Where there is no vision, as I
think Thomas Jefferson may have said, the people perish. The same
is true of the theater or anything else. We have gone as far as the
real-estate business can carry us. There is nowhere else to go. What is
the solution? It is easy to say that we need a government-subsidized
theater. We do. In all likelihood, if there is a future, that will be it—
some kind of national or state subsidy for repertory theater scattered
through the country and in New York.

A long time ago that sounded simple and sufficient. However, one
lives and learns, and the solution has to be looked at with a certain

amount of skepticism but at the same time with an insistence upon its positive aspects. I'll tell you what's wrong with it. We aren't mature enough in this country, in my humble opinion, to give away money to a bunch of lunatics, such as artists generally are, without some important kind of political interference. We had a publicly subsidized theater in the thirties, the WPA Theater, which was, of course, basically an attempt to alleviate the unemployment situation. But, nevertheless, it did create many theaters in many cities in the United States, and, in half a dozen instances, the government stepped in to stop particular productions because they were too left-wing, or something of that sort. And finally the thing was abandoned as the economic situation improved, and there was nothing left of it. But I'm just pointing that out as one kind of danger.

Worse yet is that a government theater tends to subsidize also a great many people who are hanging on who really aren't artists. They wouldn't be artists, excepting that there was a government payroll to call them artists. There's all that that goes on when a tremendous bureaucracy starts to move in. It's our curse. We will never be able to get rid of it. I see no hope of ever getting rid of it. But, with all that, it would still provide for that one man in a hundred, or maybe it's a thousand, who has a vision, an aesthetic vision, who wants to make theater because he is a theatrical man—a writer or director or an actor—and out of this morass of mediocrity can come something worthwhile. Out of the mass of mediocrity now something worthwhile can't come, for the simple reason that we have to face facts: the American public, only a minority of it, is ready to pay for the quality the drama can give. I think it could grow and be made to grow, but at the moment it's simply not there.

The public for that kind of theater isn't there. It has to be developed and can be developed. So that in a competitive situation such as exists on Broadway, the bad money drives out the good money. An investor facing the choice of investing in a trivial play, which he believes has a large audience, or in something different that has a small audience, the same dollar will generally go into the trivial play. In a subsidized theater, the principle involved is such, and it is hallowed enough in its usage, to require that something more than triviality be presented. People come into such a theater with a different attitude; they expect to be cultivated; they expect to be exalted; they don't expect merely to be tickled and entertained, and consequently there is the chance for something better.

We've had experience in New York with the Lincoln Center, which was such an attempt, and is such an attempt, and I find a few things about it which I'd like to speak about. I discovered to my astonishment, when the Lincoln Center was being organized—that is, before it had opened any plays or indeed had even selected any plays—that there was a quite unbelievable hostility to it, not on the part of the Philistines necessarily—that is, the Broadway producers naturally were very unhappy because they mistakenly assumed it was going to be a great success, and they thought, "Here go all the playwrights, and all the actors will be sucked in to this stupid artistic stuff, and we won't be able to get any good plays any more." They proved to be wrong. But the hostility also came from actors, from writers, from a good part of the public. I can't say that I understand it altogether, even now, but I have some clues, which we might as well face.

There is no prestige in this country at the moment in any kind of activity that doesn't earn the label of "commercial." The big prestige goes to where the money is. I had thought originally that when I had agreed to give a new play to this unproved theater, that the reaction of the people whom I knew and the people in the theater would be: "What a fool he is to give up a lot of money, which that entailed, to take a risk of this sort"—which it certainly was. I thought I would be blamed rather for an excess of idealism, which it certainly wasn't, I think. But, on the contrary, what that action generated was simply hostility, as though somehow one had turned one's back upon a valuable idealistic community of some sort, namely Broadway, for something quite unworthy. In other words, it all kind of . . . turned itself up on its head. And I talked to people at length about it and finally discovered a little about what their hostility came to.

I still don't know altogether, but I think what was involved there was that a great many people have made a spiritual living, so to speak, on complaining about the state of the arts. They live on these complaints. And when you say to some of them, let us say, a writer, "Where is the play that has not been produced because of the terrible situation?" And he says, "Well, I can't get myself to write it, it's so discouraging." I'm exaggerating a little but, unfortunately, not much. Or the actor who can't get himself to speak up so that peple in the back row can hear him. You say, "Well why don't you speak better?" And he says, "Well, they didn't build these theaters for actors, they built them for the real-estate people," meaning that the seats are too close together, the ceiling is too low, or something of the sort, so that whole aesthetic systems begin to develop as a result of the hostile attitude of the actor toward his environment, or the writer toward his environment.

Here suddenly comes a theater which threatens to eliminate the source of the irritation. In other words, here threatens to be a theater where no longer would the writer be at the mercy of tomorrow's reviews altogether, because, being a repertory theater, it would continue putting his plays on more or less independently of how they were critically received, within limits. In other words, you couldn't close him up altogether in a few days. He would have a chance with his play to go on for months at intervals during the season and maybe his play would make its effect later on. Here is a chance for an actor to play not just himself on the stage, which is the way actors are usually cast, for what they are rather than what they can do. He could be thirty years old and play Shylock, or he could play Romeo, or he could play some realistic role in a contemporary play in the same week or the same month. So it's a terrific opportunity, one would imagine.

But it wasn't looked at that way. It was looked at vaguely as some sort of a plot. A threat against the complaint. And the appreciation of what an art-theater might be—let's forget art-theater—repertory theater was, and I'm ashamed to say, still is, nearly nil. For example: I don't think you could get together twenty-five people in the New York theater to agree on whether a subsidized repertory theater should do new plays, whether any of those new plays should be plays that could have been done on Broadway, namely plays with a mass appeal, whether they should only do plays, which are difficult to comprehend so that one could say no Broadway producer would do them, or plays which have a smaller amplitude of effect so that only a smaller audience would be—a more intellectualized audience so to speak—would be interested in them, or whether that theater should be devoting itself to classics only, or whether it should revive old American plays.

There would be no agreement primarily because we have been brainwashed to a degree unimaginable to me, before I went through this experience, by the commercial theater. We are as commercialized as what has been attacked all these years. And, of course, it has to be so because you can't live in an environment . . . you can't put a fish in salty water and not have him absorb the salt, and you can't exist in a visionless community without losing some of your visions.

At the moment, it's a curious thing, I thought that this perhaps was only a question of New York, but just last week I was approached by another theater, which is in New Haven, Connecticut, a smaller city, which is subsidized by local businessmen and the same thing has exploded. Namely, there is no audience-comprehension, let alone that of the board of directors, as to what such a theater is and should be. And I think, at this stage, that we've got to stop pretending that we know answers and get very primitive and fundamental about this, or we're going to lose whatever remains of an artistic community of actors, writers, and directors. I think we will have some movies left and perhaps an occasional production that will be exciting, but nothing more.

There isn't much time for me to do this today, but I would just throw certain guidelines out and say, from any point of view, it has to be a theater that loses money because a repertory theater, the more successful it is, the more money it loses. The reason for that is simple: you don't expand the number of seats at all, but the more successful you are the more productions you do, which means the more sets you have to build, the more stage hands you have to have, and the more actors you have to have. As you're failing, it gets less expensive. As you're succeeding, it costs more. This is a deficit business. A hospital that's doing very well financially is usually on the rocks medically. A hospital that is expanding all the time, and always needs money because its services are improving, is in debt. The same thing is true with the theater. That's number one.

Number two is: what is its attitude toward the public? It must without question take the public unto itself. It has to educate people. We are extremely primitive in relation to this whole institution. We really don't know what to ask of the theater, and the theater doesn't know what to give us back. If the Lincoln Center continued, I wanted to have several weeks where there was no theater but simply the public coming in, and we'd have discussions as to what they expected from the theater. What they wanted from it. Was it simply that somebody had told them it was cultivated to go to the theater?— what they really thought about the avant-garde; how much of it they understood; how much of it mystified them; did it move anybody?— etc., etc.

There is no communication, as Saroyan said in a wise and foolish little play he wrote once, "There's no foundation all the way down the line." And there's no communication all the way down the line. There's a big shadow-play going on, with immensely expensive constructions going on all over this country—more to come—big mausoleums where . . . You see we have no spirit moving yet, and until we do, it comes down to a few people, perhaps like myself, who go on with this because we love it, because we figure one day somehow, somewhere there will be a theater that can really do these plays the way one imagines they exist, and you wait for the desert to bloom.

But I'm here today in part because I wanted to make you see that as ignorant as you are, you are as ignorant as we are, that you have to ask yourself fundamental questions as to why there should be a theater. Maybe there shouldn't be. Maybe it's a dead art. Maybe it ought to be dead. Maybe what we want is a sculpture of the automobile, which sometimes isn't bad, and the jazz that we have, which is sometimes wonderful, and the popular arts that we really take to, that take no effort on our parts to enjoy. I always dislike the idea of people having to go to these damned things, to the theater. It's like people wanting to be better. They shouldn't want to be better; they should need this thing the way they need food. And I'm not sure we do. Maybe there's something farcical and unreal about it all that we're trying to prop up with new buildings.

Well, that ought to depress you enough. I would only add a most important thing, which is that it can't die. It can't die because we must have, in order to live at all, some kind of symbolization of our lives. The theater is not like life. Life is like the theater. We have to have, whether it be in some deserted basement or in a great building, an art which expresses, more fully than any individual can, the collective consciousness of people, what they share with each other, and where they're different. So that we can become individuals again we have to become a spiritual unity again. That's what it can do, and the need for it will always be there. So I'm not ultimately pessimistic but simply trying to warn us all that we have not got the solution now, but it's worth thought if one cares about it at all. I'll take some questions, if there are any.

An inaudible question from the front row.

He asked if I liked *The Time of Your Life,* which I called foolish. It wasn't foolish, it was moving.

"Why do you say there is only one critic on Broadway?"

Well, I give him the distinction because there's only one morning newspaper. We used to have several, because there were several newspapers, and, as you know, a play runs or closes in New York by the verdict of these critics, and gradually the attrition of the newspaper business has been such that only *The New York Times* is left, so we have one critic which is equivalent, if you can imagine such a thing, to all the books in the United States—history books, economics books, fiction, poetry, drama—being approved of or disapproved of by one man.

He is supposed to be the world's greatest expert on musical comedy, the avant-garde theater, classical theater, even ballet, and we're supposed to believe that. That's the way it is though. A few weeks ago I complained that this was perhaps not the most rational way to go about things, and *The New York Times* agreed that it wasn't. And in fact Mr. Kerr [Walter F. Kerr, dramatic critic, *The New York Times*] independently had expressed some worry about this situation, which was none of his doings, of course. He did not destroy the other newspapers. But they asked me if I would like the job of being the other critic on the newspaper. That's how desperate things are. What I suggested was that they have at least two critics per night, and they thought that would compromise the unified opinion of the newspaper. As though anybody thought that something called *The New York Times* wrote these reviews. And they wouldn't do that, but they did think that they could ultimately find two men to do Sunday pieces. By which time, of course, the play which has been destroyed on Monday isn't there any more. It's a holocaust, it is a major disaster. And this only demonstrated, or should have, that it *is* so. That it is a disaster.

An inaudible question from somewhere down front.

Well, I wish that were so. The curious thing is that the spirit of which I speak, and which I don't have to label because I think we understand what it is, is more likely to exist in provincial theaters (I don't use that word with any condescension, I mean theaters outside New York). That's really a European expression. It doesn't mean anything lower. It just means that generally speaking, and in our case it's certainly true, I couldn't take a new play of mine and hope to cast

it in Chicago, with the available actors, with the degree of excellence
that I could in New York. I couldn't cast in Los Angeles. I could there,
possibly, because many of the actors work also in movies and
television, most of which is done in California. But that's sort of a
branch of New York. You can't get set designers for the most part.
There are some in some university theaters that are pretty damned
good. The level of performance, because our audience is perhaps
more demanding, is higher. There are exceptions to this. I may seem
to be contradicting myself, but I'm not, because when I say that much
of it is not good, but enough of it is—I'm speaking now of
performance—is beyond what any other city in this country could
manage.

Another inaudible question.

I suppose it does, but my only demurrer there would be . . . you
see, I believe, as of tomorrow morning, that if I had a theater (in New
York, I am speaking, I don't know the other cities as well) where I
could have a hundred actors, and be able to charge, due to subsidy,
a maximum of three dollars a seat, that I wouldn't have an empty
seat for as long as I wanted to play. That to me is the problem. I
avoid going to the theater for a very simple reason. If I go to the
theater, I'm paying enough to buy a pair of shoes. That's what it
comes to, you know. If you park your car and you go to the theater
and so on—many people tell me it's fifty dollars. Well, they have to
have dinner somewhere in that area, and it's very expensive. Now
how are you going to run any kind of an art form with the toll on
people of fifty dollars? It's ridiculous. You're already weeding out
probably something on the order of eighty-five percent of the
American people. And who's left? The people who are left are the
guys who are half asleep from having drunk too much. You can't find
anybody who's still what I call young—I mean I'm just fifty. They're
all blasted in there—they don't know what show they've seen.

A question about subsidized theater.

I think the British example is the most applicable to this country
because they also don't believe in political interference with any art,
and, as a matter of fact, they've sought to guard against that by
having a kind of buffer committee between the government's treasury
and the acting companies. So that you don't get a government
minister actually handing the money over to an actor. He hands it
over to a neutral committee, which is in between both of them. And

that committee is made up of people who could be lawyers, they could be educators, they could be businessmen, or—a couple of writers are on it too—called the Arts Council, and those people have the confidence of the government and the confidence of the theaters. And they give out these subsidies in various amounts. I think we could end up with such a system to our advantage. The problem with us, of course, is that everything costs about ten to twenty times what it does in England. An actor in England will work for thirty pounds a week. That's less than eighty dollars, I guess. And I don't see anybody here working for eighty dollars a week. Not that he should. But I mean that their problem is that much less, but of course they have much less to hand around too.

"Mr. Miller, what do you think the purpose, the ultimate purpose, of the theater is, really?"

I couldn't even speak in those terms because it's like asking, "What is the ultimate purpose of the Universe?" To me the theater is not a disconnected entertainment, which it usually is to most people here. It's the sound and the ring of the spirit of the people at any one time. It is where a collective mass of people, through the genius of some author, is able to project its terrors and its hopes and to symbolize them. Now how that's done—there are thousands of ways to do it of course . . . I personally feel that the theater has to confront the basic themes always. And the faces change from generation to generation, but their roots are generally the same, and that is a question of man's increasing awareness of himself and his environment, his quest for justice and for the right to be human. That's a big order, but I don't know where else excepting at a playhouse, where there's reasonable freedom, one should hope to see that.

"Why do you think the theater is so important?"

I could give you a lot of reasons but I suppose the basic thing is that I'm a playwright. I suppose I hoped in some way to prove that, and also it's a way of changing my world.

"Mr. Miller, could you comment on the power of the critic in molding taste?"

The power of a critic is in direct proportion to the—in my opinion this is—his power is greater where there is more cliquism in the theater, where the audience is less generalized, where the audience comes from a small class of people. But if there were a big audience in New York and outside New York, there would be a greater sense of proportion as to the critic's value and what his importance is. People would not be overwhelmed by this. You see, if you have to pay seven, eight, or ten dollars for a ticket you want to be pretty sure you're going to get your money's worth. If it costs a dollar, two dollars, three dollars, well—you may be told that this is not a masterpiece, but you say, "Well, maybe it's interesting." I confess, three dollars is something interesting. You see, I may not get a masterpiece every week. It turns out that those masterpieces aren't masterpieces anyway, it's just that he felt good that night, and he got excited.

"Why don't we have a theatrical community in this country?"

We do have a theatrical community in this country. It's spread out over the United States to some degree but especially in New York. There are people who have a strong idea about what is valuable in the theater, and they have a strong idea as to how it should be done, but there isn't the money to do it. It takes years to create a company, for example, that one could call a company, which could show what a repertory company could do, etc. The danger from the whole thing is that you sometimes ensconce mediocrity in such a thing, and it has to be blasted out, but that's the problem of living, anyway. You've got to do that in a university, you've got to do it in the Standard Oil Company, you've got to do it anywhere. Now we have no problems at all; there simply is no situation here.

"What is the value of the Off-Broadway movement, plays like America Hurrah, *for instance?"*

What is their value? Well, I didn't see that play, I couldn't get in, thank God. I mean, I'm glad it was so crowded. It was early on in the run, maybe it's not as crowded now. I've only heard about it, *America Hurrah*. But I'd just like to make one comment about what I think you think. And that is that I'm very much in favor of any kind of experimentation provided that ultimately, sooner rather than later, it gets past the early incubation stages of self-expression and starts to deal with feelings and concepts in an organic fashion. There's a tendency in the Off-Off-Broadway theater to simply blow off steam, to write anecdotes that are half finished, and to shock the bourgeoisie by the most infantile procedures. But I think that's rather inevitable as a starting point. I don't think they should be judged by any other standard than that they're fooling around. They *should* fool around, after all the word *play* means you play. And it should be playing. I wish there were more places where they could play. I assume there must be something fascinating about that play, or they wouldn't have gotten the kind of audiences they're getting, and I hope for everybody's sake that it's very good, but I don't know.

"What about the good run of Marat-Sade?*"*

It didn't have a good run. That play was put on for a limited engagement by David Merrick at government expense. In other words, this is a Foundation, so if they lose all the money, it's simply a tax deduction. Which is not to underestimate the idea he has of using tax money in this way. But it was a limited engagement. In other words, to make your money back in a commercial theater, that play would have to run, probably with that cast, paid on American standards, I would roughly judge two and a half years, to really make a pile of it, which is what they would require of it. That play was begun by the Royal Shakespeare Company, I believe, in England, which has a subsidized theater. So he can spread out about thirty-five or forty actors on his stage. Thirty-five to forty actors in New York City at two hundred and fifty dollars a man is quite expensive, and, believe me, if it had been produced in New York to start with, it would have ended up with about a dozen lunatics spread out over the stage. It would have gotten more insane.

"Do you think there is a credibility gap between the audience and modern playwrights? What do you think of Robert Brustein, for instance?"

I have found that in general Robert Brustein tends to take adamant postures against the obvious, as though we were about to hear a tremendous thought falling, and you look around and there's cornflakes on the floor. There's nothing there. I haven't read everything he's written by a long shot, but I just remember an article or two I've recently read. For example, he announced the Theater of Joy—you know—since we don't have any theater, we have slogans. There's a Theater of Cruelty, the Absurd Theater, there's a commercial theater, there's a Pious Theater, and now suddenly you have the Theater of Joy. He was the master of the revels, and out comes *Viet Rock*, which is just nothing but a lousy play. And then the next job was another one he discovered at the Yale Drama School, which is a sketch of some sort, but you don't make theater by making slogans. You have, it seems to me, to create organic plays. And these plays are not organic. They are effusions of one sort or another, usually in bad taste, in which dirty words are said to shock us all to death and somebody's against Viet Nam and that's supposed to be terrifically adventurous. Your questions was whether there was a gap—you see, it's a meaningless question, but I can see where you got it, because he puts things that way.

A question about Robert Brustein's criticism of Edward Albee.

Yes, but why does he have to knock Edward Albee to do that? It depends on who's got ahead that year. I have to warn you that this is all journalism. This is not criticism. I could be very critical of Albee, I'm not defending him here, I'm just attacking a method. So that happens to be there that year, and it casts a long shadow over everybody because there are so few plays and here's one that holds together and people come in droves, so he's got to say that it is not funny enough. Well, he's not trying to be funny. He was trying to be Albee. Sure there's room for something else. But I don't see the point of having to destroy one thing in order to raise up something else. Especially if it's of some value. This is just to show how superior he is to the whole thing, and I'm happy about one development in our theaters: that several critics have become theatrical producers and ringmasters of one kind or another, and without exception they have produced the most vapid stuff of the times. And, of course, it's one thing to be a critic—it's an honorable profession—but there is a tendency to edge criticism in and the artist out. And it's totally unnecessary. I don't think it's part of the game at all. I think all he desires is to have a stage in a theater and not to be blasted because he's not funny. He may be over-pious, that's possible, but it's not supposed to be funny.

"Why does New York have a monopoly on the theater?"

We've got probably about ninety-five percent unemployment among the New York actors. So it's not a monopoly of any kind. It's in desperate straits. I don't care where it springs up. I have no vested interest in New York, I don't live there any more. It's all the same to me. But that's where the talent is collected, and if it doesn't happen there, generally it doesn't happen anywhere else. I wish it would happen in Ann Arbor, when you get a new theater.

Inaudible question.

The Lincoln Center problem is simple at this moment. They have solved it by—gradually they will be—turning the theater into a booking house. They won't admit it but—I'll tell you a secret—which

probably won't get back to New York, but, when the original
company was still playing, when there was no question that it was
going to continue, it was filling the theater eighty-five percent of
capacity all the time, which is more than almost any Broadway show
could do. I discovered by the grapevine that the new building, the
Vivian Beaumont Theater, which was still—at that time—incomplete,
was to be completed the next year, that they were negotiating with a
great star and a private producer to open this theater with a revival of
a Shakespeare play, completely unconnected from the repertory
company, the Lincoln Center company. It was a purely commercial
operation. At which point I said that if that would turn out to be true,
I was going to quit now and withdraw all my plays at once, so they
stopped it. But I'm not there any more, of course, and now they've
announced that they have forwarded the cause of repertory by letting
out the theater to, again, a completely private production, and how
this advances repertory nobody has explained. It is a complete
abandonment of the idea, but they're not prepared yet to admit it.
This is going to be little by little. They're not prepared to announce it
yet.

   Inaudible question about Robert Whitehead.

   I think he's embittered about it. Anyone would be. He really did
organize the whole business and was on the verge—well, I'll give you
a quick statistic—you see he had money enough to hire 22 actors.
The British National Theatre has 145, the Moscow Art Theater has
about 175, the Munich Theater has about two hundred and
something, etc. Since we understand numbers quicker, that will give
you an idea as to what the financial backing of this thing was. It was
smaller backing than you would get, let's say, at Erfurt in Germany—
some small town—you know with a hundred thousand population.
Well, he naturally couldn't get all the people he wanted the first year,
but as a result of the operation of a year and a half, every decent
actor in New York was on line trying to become a member of this
company. And within, I would guess, six months of the time that he
was bounced, we would have started to have a really first-class
theater. There's no doubt about it.

   *"Did you run into more trouble at Lincoln Center than you
expected?"*

   No, but I knew what I was in for. It was starting. You can't begin an
automobile factory and hope to manufacture your first car without

bugs. It was difficult. I think that that break-in period was necessary, and what they did was they scrapped it just as they were learning.

"Don't you think there is some value in musical comedy?"

The musical comedy is obviously the one American invention, or—I wouldn't call it an invention, but an adaptation of European operetta—which is indigenous to us and has a terrific life and a viability, and there should certainly be a place for it. It is a real art and a good one. And there's no contradiction between that and any other kind of theater. I would hope that a repertory theater one day would be able to do terrific musicals. They should be able to do anything.

"Why do you find repertory theater so important?"

Even in the short experience that has been had at Lincoln Center, it gradually dawned on people—I'll give you a concrete example— there's a fellow named Hal Halbrook who does the Mark Twain impersonations. He was in our original company and he played in *After the Fall, Incident at Vichy,* and he played in *Tartuffe.* There were three different roles. I thought he was marvelous, but his publicity image hadn't been created. Then we broke up, and Hal went and did his act, which he's been doing for years all over the United States. He opened on Broadway with it and became a sensation. Now the repertory theater at that time—before it broke up—was about to ask Hal, and Hal would have agreed, to do his one-character job, which is fantastic, on certain evenings during the repertory year. Imagine what it does to you as an audience, to see Hal Holbrook standing there as Mark Twain, absolutely believable and quite marvelous, and then the next night he's playing a German officer in 1942, who is going out of his mind with an agonizing conflict; the third night he's playing Quentin in *After the Fall;* and and the fourth night he's playing a part in *Tartuffe.* Now there's just one actor. You see what happens is that the audience begins to get involved in the transformations of these people. And the very changes from evening to evening throw perspectives on what the play is about that they're doing now—because you know it's Hal Halbrook, ex-Mark Twain, and now he's a Nazi officer. The changes from night to night are part of the theater. The changes from night to night add an immense perspective to any one of those shows. I think that what happens is that an audience begins to participate in the creation of that art in a way that is not quite possible if you've got a play running for two years and the same guy does the same thing every night. You have no relationship to the thing excepting that of a customer. I know that process began to happen, and of course it was aborted, but it will come back again, it'll start again. That's just one element of the audience relation to such a theater. And that's what repertory does.

Arthur Miller Talks Again

Michigan Quarterly Review/1967

From *Michigan Quarterly Review* 6 (1967): 178-184. Reprinted
by permission

A chat with a class in stage directing, in a practice room—
an arena theater—in the Frieze Building, The University of
Michigan, March 1, 1967.

Q:"Is it a general rule in the New York professional theater that a
playwright has the pick of his director?"

Mr. Miller: Of course, legally, we do—a contract has it that we
can—that a producer can't do anything, can't pick an actor even,
without the playwright's consent. But the way it works, really, it
depends upon the personality of the playwright a great deal and the
degree to which he is established at the time that particular
production goes on. In other words, a new playwright, more or less, I
suppose, would rely on the judgment of the producer, or on
happenstance. A lot of times a director—he happens to give his play
to a guy who says he's a director, or wants to be a director, or has
directed something in school and has an opportunity to get some
backing. As you grow older, though, you get to know what directors
are like. I would say that by the time a man has written a couple of
plays for the professional theater, at least he would be decisive in
selecting. Some playwrights rely on the judgment of others, on the
judgment of the producer, I suppose.

Q: "Would you say that Quentin's problem in *After the Fall* is the
same as Hamlet's or Othello's?"

Mr. Miller: *Hamlet* and *Othello* are different plays. I don't like
these analogies because there's too much that's different. Hamlet's
problem really isn't the problem of whether or not to assert a value to

128

life, which is what Quentin is trying to do, faced with the fact that it seems that everybody betrays everybody else. His problem is really—one of them—is to discover within himself a conviction by which he can act against this injustice. It's just superficially that they're the same in the sense that in all of them there are long monologues and a multiplicity of scenes. There are many many scenes in Hamlet. I've never counted them, but I'm sure there are more individual scenes than in almost any Shakespearean play.

Q: "What do you think is the best way to train directors? Is it through universities?"

Mr. Miller: Well, of course, the best way to do anything is to do it. And in the university, I presume, you would have more chance to work than you would if you were pitched out into the society where it's pretty difficult to find a work situation. Less is involved; it's not a question of money involved here directly, I mean you don't have to make your success in the sense that the play will run for years or something. You can be more experimental. You can relax and discover yourself better, so I would suspect that a university was an admirable situation for a director to start in. There is no substitute for it in our country, because there is no theater. Part of the real theater's job, for example, would be to offer part of its cast to people who want to direct that cast in an experimental production of some sort, or even a non-experimental production, just to show that he can do this. But we don't have such things. So you have the closest aproximation in the university.

Q: "One of the most recurrent criticisms of the modern theater seems to be that in original productions the director dictates more of the final script than the playwright. Is it true in your experience?"

Mr. Miller: I've never had that experience. I suppose it goes on, but I think—let's put it this way—in all the arts now, but especially the theater, the element that has come to the fore is everything but the art-work. What's come to the fore is the critic. For example, in a recent review in *The New York Times* by one of the former editors or current editors—I'm not sure which—of *The Tulane Drama Review*, he said that it's much harder to write a good review than a good play. This is what it comes to, you see, it finally got so where there was a work of art involved it's simply a platform from which he can aggrandize his own career. And that's because we're in an age of journalism and publicity. A critic has access to publicity and journalism much more frequently than an artist does. It takes a year, two years, or whatever, to write a book or a play. It takes ten minutes to write a good quip. So that they use the art to advance themselves. And that's how, I think, we're at a low point of life in that respect.

Similarly, the directors, in many cases, are using plays to show what they can do with the play rather than what that play is. They use a play to draw attention to the direction. This is especially true in terms of the direction of older plays where there is a conventional viewpoint towards the play and the director then redoes the play according to some new scheme. All that is so, yes, but it's so in part because the playwrights, to a degree that's unfortunate, have given up, or never arrived, at some sort of an organic sense of their plays.

We're in an age where anything that's in dialogue is a play. And that may turn out to be the case. I don't believe it; I do think there's more to it than that. So that if that is the case, and it's really an elongated anecdote rather than an organic conflict of some sort, which has a beginning and a middle and an end, well, then you can hardly blame the director who asserts another arbitrary thing. Since the whole thing's arbitrary, to start with, why not add another fillip here and there and make it even better?

You see, it's only in an organic piece of work that you can't cut lines out of very easily, whose lines you can't change very easily, because suddenly the whole fabric starts to fall to pieces. But if there's no fabric, anyway, well, then you can throw in this line instead of that line. It's all a surface stuck together with lights, and attitudes of actors, and stylistic invention, and so forth. It falls to the ground as soon as you take away these props. Well, he might as well do the best he can to keep your interest going, keep you from getting bored. I blame it a lot on the playwrights.

Q: "What do you think is the essential function of the director as opposed to the playwright or actor? What do you look for the director to do that you can't do as a writer?"

Mr. Miller: He's an interpreter, really. As we know, if you take one actor and put him in a role—take a classic role, for example—you'll get one sort of tonality out of it. It will be, let us say, supposing it were Hamlet, and you put in a guy who's twenty years old. Well, you get the youthfulness of Hamlet. You'd get his idealism. You wouldn't get his exhaustion. Well, you put in a man who's forty. You would tend to find it hard to see his idealism as much and you would see more of his exhaustion. He would be world-weary, rather than nerved-up, and tired from hearing the same thing over and over again in his life. These decisions as to how the same text is to be emphasized are directorial in the sense that no two actors are alike—so that the director is presented with a script, which he casts, having made up his mind, if he's a good director, what the salient key of that script is going to be in this production.

Q: "Don't you think that the director can bring something more, something different to a play?"

Mr. Miller: I've made some remarkable discoveries in that respect. I think that actors add more than any director ever adds. I know that this is a directing class, but this has been my experience, and maybe I was—it's different. You see, you can't make a silk purse out of a sow's ear. If you've got dead actors, you've got a dead production. If you've got actors who are alive to this situation, who are relaxed, by whatever means they get to be relaxed, invention starts to come. The best inventions I have seen in my plays were invented by the actors, in that respect, in terms of behavior. The director is vital in the sense that he can free-up actors, if he's a good director, so that they can invent. And the best directors know this. They don't say it in interviews, but they know damned well that they are at the mercy of these actors. And it's the actor's invention, really, that you're watching in terms of performance. And a director can, or fail to, liberate the actor to invent and to come alive. But what he's inventing, the best things I've seen, the most memorable things, came out of that actor's mind, or his heart, in the course of the production. I have great love for actors, but they do make me very impatient, but the great inventions, and they are inventions as far as behavior is concerned, the director can—you've heard about a director making a great star out of a lump. I've never seen it.

Q: "What is the playwright's working relationship with the director?—say your own relationship with Kazan?"

Mr. Miller: Well, it was a very good one. I've always worked well with Kazan. At least with me, he's always tried to serve—he knows that I don't write arbitrarily—that if it's there, there's some reason. It may not be a good one, but it isn't there by accident. So we have a kind of collaboration, when it comes to the actor. He might have an actor, and he sometimes does, overdo something, do it too broadly, too loudly, too fast, because he's a little bit afraid that he's going to lose the audience. And, for example, say that it's just a—you lost the reality there. Maybe you woke up the audience, but nobody's going to believe what they see. And then he'll recognize, or argue about it, saying "Now you're looking at it the way it would be in life, but we're on the stage now." Well, we kick it around, try it in front of an audience and see whether it does get unreal. Many times the playwright would tend to make too many naturalistic pauses, because he loves his lines, when in fact they should be run on, even though, realistically speaking, people wouldn't be running on that way. There is such a thing as tempo, which has nothing to do with anything but the theater itself. It does not represent reality. There are certain ideas in a play which don't take very long to understand for the audience. They shouldn't take as long to say as those ideas or relationships which are a little more difficult to get. It has nothing to do with the way it would be said in life. The playwright too often would tend to relate the play to life rather than to the theater. So your relationship is—he's the theater man. He's relying on me to keep him alive, you see. To bring him back. I sense where my climaxes are. He might go right past one—and very often does, because he sees a climax two pages on. Well, sometimes I'll say, "The climax is right here; this is the nub of it, and you went right through the whole damned thing." And he'll say, "Well, gee, that's true. I hadn't seen that." Lots of times I'll say, "This is another one, but we're going to save it for the next one, because we have four climaxes in three pages." It's that kind of tugging and hauling, but with most directors I've worked with, it works out that we can manage together.

Q: "Do you do all your communicating through the director, or do you ever come into contact with the actors yourself?"

Mr. Miller: Lots of times I act it for them. I get up there and do it. Overdo it, I might add.

Q: "Is this at the invitation of the director?"

Mr. Miller: Well, by that time, we're not that formal.

Q: "Why was scene one cut from Act Two in the original production of *The Crucible*?"

Mr. Miller: The reason for that was—see, I like the scene. That scene actually wasn't in the script as we went into rehearsal. I added that later. I added it because I thought it would expand our awareness of Abigail.

I'm of two minds about whether it belongs in there or not. For instance, the British National Theater does the play now. Olivier directed it, and—this was a year and a half ago now—he asked me what I wanted to do with that scene, and I said, "As a matter of fact, I want to rewrite it, because I have a better idea." And I rewrote it, and he went crazy about it—it was wonderful. Of course, I know exactly now what that scene should do. And he staged it. And then he dropped it. And I said, "Why?" And he said, "You know, really, you don't need it. It's nice, when you read the play. You get an expanded view of it. But it destroyed that certain marching tempo that starts to get into that play to that place. There's a drumbeat underneath, which begins somewhere—I don't know exactly where—but in a good production it starts to beat, and this scene stops the beat." So you've got to sacrifice one thing for another. It's like doing *Hamlet* in the uncut version—I don't know if you've ever seen it—it goes on for four hours and fifteen minutes. Well, when you come away from that, you know a hell of a lot more about it than you would in a cut version, but you also are pretty damned tired. It depends on what mood you want.

Q: "Didn't you originally have a direct confrontation between Abigail and Proctor in the original version?"

Mr. Miller: I did some rewriting on the stage because at a certain point—I believe it was in the second half—it suddenly appeared as though there were too many—put it this way, you see the fates of all these people—of the people other than Proctor and Rebecca Nurse and Elizabeth Proctor—were repetitious, one of the other. You know, so one guy was arrested for this or that, but they were all falsely accused of something because we know there's no witchcraft. I had cluttered one scene in the last half, and I cleaned it out so you have what you have now. It represents all the people like Giles Corey's wife, the old peasant's wife. I had her in there for a while. But it wasn't necessary. You just refer to her. You see, a play like that, involving so many people, it's almost inevitable that once you get it up there, you're going to start combing it out. Because you see that some of this detail is repetitious—you don't need it. You symbolize it in speech.

Q: "Why was Tituba hanged?"

Mr. Miller: Was she hanged? No. Tituba isn't hanged. She wasn't hanged, she was put in jail. You see you were hanged if you didn't confess, once they had accused you. Where you did confess, in some cases, but not all, you went to jail for having been involved with the devil. So you didn't get hanged for that. You were only hanged if you refused to incriminate others. That meant that you hadn't broken your pact with the fiend, that you were still a part of the plot.

Q: "How does adverse criticism affect you, now that you're a successful playwright?"

Mr. Miller: The way I feel now, I just go on doing as I do because I figure that what I'm doing is going to last longer than what they're doing. Really, what bothers me about it, you see, is the mis-education of the young that goes on. There's a lot of so-called criticism that's nothing but self-puffery. These guys try to find some angle here which can be identified with themselves. One of them will discover a new theater, it's the Theater of Joy. It has no meaning whatsoever, and you'll say, "Well, which plays are you talking about?" Well, they don't exist, they never existed, never will exist.

All theater is joy. If you go to the theater and it's wonderful, it's joy. He wants—this is Brustein—the old theater is not joy. His theater is joy. It's a slogan—it's like advertising—like saying, "Luckies are better," or you "Go to Marlboro Country." You know what I mean? It's a slogan. The thing has no substance whatsoever. To one guy it's a Theater of Joy, and to another guy, it's—there's another slogan that's going around, the Theater of Cruelty. They discovered people are cruel to each other. This is all to identify themselves with that slogan. They say, "This is the man that discovered that." What? Those three words. That's what he discovered. It's the way publicists go about things. You see, you've got to make an image for this thing even if there's no *thing* there, as long as there's an image. You've got something to sell. It's impossible. Because we are flooded now—as never before in history—with publicity. It can be publicity on a so-called elevated level like in the *Tulane Drama Review*. You see publicity in *Life* magazine, on television.

But to really discuss what is integral in a work, what that work implies, to the writer, to humanity—nobody's bothering with that stuff—it's too hard. You've really got to really work at it if it's worth doing at all. I don't know. That's what criticism used to think was worth doing—but now it's just: "He's better than him, but I'm better than all of them." That's the implication. "Really, if I chose to write a play," is implied here, "I could really slaughter them all." In a few cases where these guys have tried to do something in the theater, like Blau—he's a very nice man—he discovered the theater of—the

Impossible Theater he discovered. And he made it, too. Because if he discovered the Impossible Theater and all we've got is the possible theater, we want what he's got. So they went and brought him all the way from San Francisco (where he had a fairly good, but not, by any means, a great, repertory theater—I think the one here is probably better—because he had publicized himself in his book. It had nothing to do with the work. He had discovered this angle, and they said, "Well, what is that? That sounds terrific!" It's incredible. It's just unbelieveable sometimes. They float in on a slogan and float out again. But when you try to do something, you see, make it happen on a stage, that's another story.

Q: "Do you think we are going to get a theater in the future that approaches the broad comprehensive view of man that is in Shakespeare's plays?"

Mr. Miller: It's fruitless to try to even envisage a reproduction of a historical period. Because Shakespeare—I think there is very little question but that, as massive a genius as he was, he had to have come at the right time. Just imagine, suppose he had been born fifteen years later; he would have run head-on into a reaction where they wouldn't tolerate the theater. As a matter of fact, his plays—they wouldn't do them. They were too dirty, too irreverent, they were too revolutionary in terms of a fixed society. Furthermore, he arrived at a time when the language was in a state of development. It wasn't fixed the way it later became, so that the manipulation of the language was probably at its freest in relation to what went before and what came after. So I can't imagine those circumstances recurring as such.

I don't know where it's going now. I know where it is, more or less. It's in a state which is reflecting the nihilistic side of contemporary consciousness, which is the easiest thing to do. In other words, I could prove to you now probably that we haven't got a prayer. There are strong forces that indicate that. The country is losing its age-old localism, the small unit, the town, even the city is giving way in its authority and its vitality to the Pentagon, to enormous structures of business, the army, and—none of this is fictitious. It's there. We have fewer newspapers than we ever had, more of them are the same than they ever were, the canned entertainment is put out by a robot, you're in a university where it would be a miracle if you could go for a walk with a professor. You can't talk to anybody. If he's got a half an hour, it's a great day.

Well, when I was in school here, I could go for a walk with a professor, talk to him on a street corner. It was not a problem. So you could make a hell of a case for the mechanization of the human psyche, of its spirit, for example, and make a hell of a play out of it like, let's say, Mr. Zero, you know, Elmer Rice's play, whatever it's called, *The Adding Machine*. The only trouble with it is that it leaves out the thing that is not easy to do. It leaves out the fact that I can say what I've just said and you understand what I'm saying. In other words, you're not accepting all of this quite, you don't know what to do about it naturally, but you know that it isn't right—I don't mean morally right—I mean that there's something death-like about it. There's something that's anti-life about it. As long as that's true, I've got to put that into the play. That's tough. That tragic balance, so to speak, is what isn't in the theater today. The play is either indifferent to those problems altogether and takes a trivial viewpoint toward them and doesn't confront them, or else in confronting them, it leaves out the inexorable demand of mankind that it be human and makes trouble for those cataclysmic processes.

Q: Another question about the present state of the theater, and its future.

Mr. Miller: We're going through, I suppose, what you would call neurasthenic strike-plays. You know, right off, that nothing good can come of this. The boy can't warm up to that girl because it's against the rules. And he can't really keep his illusions about her, and the mother can't be any good. The father's got to be an idiot, and you're in business. Well, pretty soon you're going to dissemble whatever life they have, whatever vitality they might have had will shortly become cutouts, and you'll simply be bored with the whole prospect, that's all. You say, "Well, I know that already."

And then somebody's going to have to find some new observations to make. What that will be, I don't know. It may become a more pictorial theater, more dance-like, maybe more militant again. I can see where a writer could write a hell of a stirring, wonderful play about, say, the Viet Nam situation. It could happen. I am inclined to doubt anymore that you're going to get a single unified development of any kind, because this country's too complex, the country's too variegated. I think that probably you'll have many kinds of styles going at the same time.

Arthur Miller
Walter Wager/1967

From *The Playwrights Speak,* ed. Walter Wager (New York: Delta, 1967): 1-24. Reprinted by permission.

This interview was tape-recorded in Mr. Miller's suite in the Chelsea Hotel, New York City, on November 10, 1964. The questioner was the editor of *Playbill* and of this volume. Arthur Miller, a lanky, bespectacled, earnest and good-humored man, had come down from his home in Connecticut for the final rehearsals before the Lincoln Center Repertory Theater production of *Incident at Vichy.*

Arthur Miller was born on 112th Street (Manhattan) in New York City on October 17, 1915. A good friend and working colleague of the playwright, director-critic Harold Clurman, has described the dramatist's parents as "unequivocally middle-class and Jewish." Miller has often commented that while he did not become a devout practicing Jew he did absorb "a certain viewpoint—a commitment to the continuity of life and the need to go on even though there is tragedy in the world." Miller's mother was born in the United States. His father, Isidore, whom the playwright has described as "a much more realistic guy than Willy Loman"—the tragic protagonist of *Death of a Salesman*—was a clothing manufacturer who migrated to the United States from Austria-Hungary at the turn of the twentieth century.

The dramatist completed elementary school in Harlem, and then achieved a mediocre academic record at a Brooklyn high school. He wanted to go to the University of Michigan because he was attracted by its theatre program. Teen-aged Arthur Miller was a baseball fan who had seen only two plays in his life, both potboiler melodramas, but he had read enough Ibsen and Shakespeare and other playwrights to know what theatre could be. But by the time Arthur Miller was ready for college, business reverses made it impossible for his father to pay the tuition, so the young man worked a year in a warehouse to earn the tuition. He persuaded Michigan that his talents surpassed his high-school grades, was admitted and at Michigan wrote several plays which won Hopwood prizes. It was also at Ann Arbor that he met his first wife, Mary Grace Slattery, whom he wed in 1940.

He wrote his first play in six days in 1935, during a school vacation, but worked harder on another drama which won him a $1,250 prize in a Theatre Guild competition. After his graduation in 1938, the prize money and $22.77 a week from the Federal Theatre Project permitted Miller to exist in Patchogue, Long Island, while he continued to write. Although a number of his early works were submitted to the Group Theatre and other producing units, none was staged. To help support his wife and two children, he wrote several radio dramas.

In an excellent interview with Olga Carlyle and Rose Styron published in the Summer 1966 issue of *The Paris Review,* Miller recalled that "We had twenty-eight and a half minutes to tell a whole story in a radio play, and you had to concentrate on the words because you couldn't see anything. You were playing in a dark closet, in fact. So the economy of words in a good radio play was everything. It drove you more and more to realize what the power of a good sentence was, and the right phrase could save you a page you could otherwise be wasting. I was always sorry radio didn't last long enough for contemporary poetic movements to take advantage of it, because it's a natural medium for poets."

Miller himself was writing a good deal of verse in his early plays, and later the initial draft of *The Crucible* was done in verse, as was much of *Death of a Salesman.* He "broke it up" because he ws afraid of the effect of verse upon American actors. In these early years Arthur Miller also wrote two books—*Situation Normal,* a diary of his work on a film about Ernie Pyle, and *Focus,* a novel about anti-Semitism that was published in 1945.

It was in 1944 that Miller saw the first professional production of one of his theatre works. *The Man Who Had All the Luck,* a drama about a conflict between a socially conscious son and a father whose business was facing a strike, ran for four performances on Broadway. One critic, Burton Rascoe, saw Miller's powerful promise, and several producers asked to see his next script. That work, which opened on January 29, 1947, to critical acclaim, was *All My Sons.* The Clurman-Kazan-Fried production was honored as Best Play of the Season by the Drama Critics' Circle and brought Miller his first national recognition.

It also brought him the first substantial and steady income of his life, for *All My Sons* was a popular success that ran 328 performances. In 1949 *Death of a Salesman* started a run that was to last 742 performances and bring Miller both the Pulitzer Prize and another Drama Critics' Circle award. Years later the playwright was to reflect that the haunted fantasy-ridden central figure, the agonized father who pursued the seductive but unreal "bitch goddesses" of popularity and success, was based on a salesman whom he had known rather slightly and briefly. This was a play that touched many people, disturbed quite a few others. Some oddly viewed the protagonist's work as the key issue, and one Japanese theatregoer is reported to have commented that "If a salesman fails to make sales, he deserves to lose face."

Death of a Salesman, like the two preceding Miller plays, involved a father in conflict with his son on a moral issue. "Miller is a moralist," Harold Clurman wrote in Volume One of *Theatre,* the annual of the Repertory Theater of Lincoln Center. "A moralist is a man who believes he possesses the truth and aims to convince others of it. In Miller this moralistic trait stems from a strong family feeling. In this context, the father as prime authority and guide is central. From *The Man Who Had All the Luck* through *Death of a Salesman,* the father stands for virtue and value; to his sons he is the personification of Right and Truth. . . . The shock which shatters Miller's dramatic cosmos always begins with the father's inability to enact the role of moral authority the son assigns to him and which the father willy-nilly assumes. . . . Both may be innocent, but both suffer guilt. . . . Woman in Miller's plays is usually the prop of the male principle without whom man falters, loses his way."

Miller's focus on father and family began to become somewhat less prominent in the dramas that he wrote after *Salesman.* The next play was *The Crucible,* the 1953 work on Puritan era witch-hunting that was admittedly based on the then current Red-hunting of Senator Joseph McCarthy and his allies. Miller has twice said that *The Crucible* may be his favorite among his own works, and that is understandable in light of the political and professional ordeal that he himself endured. Arthur Miller, who had been so conservative as a youth that he had favored Hoover over Roosevelt in the 1932 election, was known to be somewhere left of center and to be an articulate critic of what has come to be called McCarthyism. It may well be that *The Crucible* was not among the favorite plays of right-of-center Congressmen, and it is possible that some of Miller's essays and public comments angered those legislators most committed to purging America of Communists. In 1956—the year that he divorced Mary Miller to wed Marilyn Monroe—Miller was found guilty of contempt of Congress for refusing to tell the House Un-American Activities Committee the names of individuals who had attended a meeting of Communist writers eight years earlier. The playwright has publicly suggested that he was being punished for the refusal of the famous second Mrs. Miller to pose for a photograph with the Committee's publicity-hungry chairman.

Whatever the facts about this grotesque incident, Miller was cleared of the charge by the U.S. Court of Appeals in 1958. Shortly before his trouble with Congressman Walter, Miller's *A View from the Bridge* had been produced in 1955 and it was not then a success in New York. Subsequently it has fared better both abroad and in Off-Broadway staging. During the nine years that followed *A View from the Bridge*, Miller—beset by personal problems and troubled by the effects of McCarthyism on many "friends"—wrote his unsuccessful drama titled *A Memory of Two Mondays* (1955) and then *The Misfits* as a novel and film. His second marriage ended, and in 1962 he wed Austrian photographer Inge Morath. This marriage produced a daughter and also helped move Miller back toward work that he himself regarded as acceptable. *After the Fall,* which the dramatist insists is not entirely autobiographical despite the bitter protests of friends of the late Miss Monroe, was staged in 1963. In 1964 *Incident at Vichy* followed.

Miller is writing again, and he has recently stated his goal quite succinctly. "Günter Grass has said that art is uncompromising and life is full of compromises," Arthur Miller said in the spring of 1966. "To bring them together is a near impossibility, and that is what I am trying to do."

Wager: I have been reading your collected plays which Viking put out, and I notice one play, *The Man Who Had All the Luck*, is not included. Why?

Miller: I never felt I really have finished it; I had written it when I was very young, and I thought I was writing a perfectly realistic play.

It turned out that it really wasn't altogether that. It was a kind of a myth, and when it was produced it was produced as a completely realistic play, and it made very little sense that way. It has one foot in both camps; it has a foot in each camp. And I think it should be rewritten to take on a consistency which it doesn't quite have now and as a result, can't come to a true climax.

Wager: Do you ever go back to a play that's finished and rewrite it?

Miller: I could with that, because I know the solution to it, but the subject doesn't interest me anymore.

Wager: That was what I had in mind; you seem to move on to new subjects. But the introduction to your collected plays has one recurring reference that intrigues me. That's the question of reality and realism. This is a major occupation of yours.

Miller: It always has been, yes. My aim is to deliver up the symbolic meaning of what I see, what I feel, and I've never been able to do it through a naturalistic technique. And yet I don't think that the solution is a completely symbolic drama. In other words, I am trying to account as best I can for the realistic surface of life as well as Man's intense need to symbolize the meaning of what he experiences. There are numerous methods of trying to accomplish that, and I think from one play to another of mine there have been different attacks on the same problem of delivering up the meaning of what the experience is.

Wager: When you go to write a play, do you determine in advance what your technique is going to be? Have you soberly evaluated what sort of style you want, what would fit the subject best?

Miller: In the most general way, yes. Actually, any play I finish and produce has had a tendency to create its own laws. I can attack some material with a firm plan in mind, but generally speaking, after five or six minutes of playing it lays down its own form.

Wager: It has its own natural inner structure?

Miller: Yes, that's right.

Wager: Yes, I would suspect that this would be true, because going back to the introduction to this most interesting book, you make frequent reference to the need for passion in play-writing, which means that these are not soberly planned plays as, say, certain types of modern musicians might write almost mathematical music.

Miller: I plan as far as it is possible to plan—that is, I plan up to the point where the plan is there in order to open the way to the passion. It's not there for its own sake. I have no special admiration for any formalism in itself. I can write in numerous ways, but there's no point in doing that. And I'm seeking for the key to whatever material is at hand.

Wager: You have mentioned that some people have felt your work was negative or nihilistic, and yet it seems quite clear that those are not your views at all. You say life has meaning. You refer to the fundamentals of life and man's relation with man and with God. Are most people aware of the fact that you are concerned with God?

Miller: I think most people aren't aware of anything. We have trained the audience in America to go to the theatre. It's a convention that they go to the theatre to have, so to speak, the glands of emotion exercised, and what the play's really about, aside from its story, is taken to be an embarrassing excrescence implanted by the author. The fact that a whole structure, all the emotion and all the observations in it, are to throw light on a certain mystery is rather beside the point. These elements are rarely, if ever, discussed by anybody.

Wager: As I walked out of *The Deputy*, which is obviously less than a perfect play, I was astounded and quietly infuriated to find people strolling out as if they'd seen *Hello, Dolly!* They're saying, "Hello, Gertrude, where're we going to eat, where'd Charlie park the car?" They had not participated in the play. They had seen it, but it had not really reached them.

Miller: Well, I think that's partly because of the training this audience has to regard the theatre as the most superficial kind of entertainment in the way that, oh, the circus or a Western is, is always thrown into one pot.

Wager: Where's the responsibility for that? How has that happened?

Miller: Well, in general the Anglo-Saxon mind flees from any objectivity about what it's looking at. It's more French, Middle European to ask the question of "What is this really about? What lies behind this? What symbol of meaning is the author attempting to throw light on?" With the English and with us, there is a terrific resistance to any knowing what you are doing in an objective way.

Wager: And that would create a problem in regard to another comment you made—the goal of drama is the creation of a higher consciousness. That would make a dramatist face a rather difficult problem with our Anglo-Saxon audience.

Miller: Oh, it is difficult. Very, very tough. But it has its compensations only in one respect, and that is that it forces our drama into concreteness—which is a good thing. It makes the American writer prove with immense evidence, concrete evidence, what he's driving at. However, it is defeated finally by the unwillingness and the inability of this audience to consider what he's driving at, over and beyond the overt story. After all, most reviews of most plays are retelling the story of the play, the overt story of the play.

Wager: Is that why you took your most recent plays from Broadway to the Lincoln Center Repertory group?

Miller: Well, one reason is that I had hoped, and I still believe, that the first order of business in this theatre is to open the theatre to a wider audience, an audience of students, of people who are not totally oriented to the most vacant kind of entertainment. After all, the audience is half of the production, and I think that one way or another that audience must be broadened, and it must be given a new environment in which to be an audience. I think over the years, whether it be Lincoln Center or it and other such companies, a new kind of attitude will develop toward plays, an attitude which does take into consideration and is in fact basically interested in what underlies this structure that they're looking at. It is an audience, finally, not of strangers. You see, this audience today is totally strange to the aims and the preoccupations of the artists.

Wager: This is an audience that's seeking a social experience, to a large degree.

Miller: I don't think they're seeking an experience so much as an escape from experience, and they're at odds with serious writing so much of the time. And I think that's the problem.

Wager: Speaking of serious writing, one question that must be asked of any playwright or creative writer many times is exactly how do you write? Quite literally, where do you write, and how do you write?

Miller: At home, in Connecticut, where I've lived for many years now. I've always worked in the country, even twenty years ago when I had to rent a house for $75 a year. I can't write in this city, possibly because I was born here. And I work generally in the morning. On good days I can work all day. On most days three or four or five hours, on the typewriter. And the writing is a series of thrusts and sharpening of those thrusts and discarding of false issues and a purification of the image that originally impelled the play to seem like a play. Consequently, there's normally either literally on paper or for years before in the mind a series of revisions taking place. I have written plays in a matter of two weeks, six weeks, five weeks.

Wager: Since you became a recognized playwright?

Miller: Oh, sure.

Wager: What plays did you write in five or six weeks?

Miller: *Death of a Salesman.*

Wager: Really?

Miller: But by the time such a thing gets written, it has been in effect written and rewritten a thousand times in the head. There are other ways of doing it. *The Crucible* was seven months; *All My Sons* was two years; *A View from the Bridge* was three weeks.

Wager: Speaking of *The Crucible* and *A View from the Bridge,* those were made as foreign films?

Miller: Right, French. For a long time I was *persona non grata* here in the movie industry. They wouldn't do anything of mine after *Death of a Salesman* because I had left-wing connections and was in effect blacklisted. That's the main reason.

Wager: That seems incredible today, looking back on it. Of course, that whole period seems almost just as incredible as the subject matter of *The Crucible.*

Miller: Well, it's not incredible to me.

Wager: No, that's a real experience that you will not ever leave.

Miller: It's a fact, and that's the only reason why that happened.

Wager: I see. Now your newest play, *Incident at Vichy.* What brought you to that subject matter?

Miller: Well, I have always felt—and as the years go by I feel even more strongly—that the period of the Nazi occupation of Europe was the turning point of this age. I think as time goes by we'll be seeing more and more it is that. Not only in the political sense, but in the whole attitude of Man toward himself. For example, we discovered after the war—seemingly independently—that there was an immense social pressure to conform, a chilling of the soul by the technological apparatus, the destruction of the individual's capacity for choosing, an erosion of what used to be thought of as an autonomous personality—all this was carried to its logical extremes by the Nazi regime, which ended up by controlling not only Man as a social animal in his job and on the assembly line or in his office or in the Army but in his bed, in his relationships to his children, who were taught to carry any expression of opinion by him to the authorities as a patriotic act, until you had created a nation of people who could be said to have lost or given up or been robbed of what for two thousand years was supposed to have been the—their human nature. They now existed to carry through a social program. In my opinion we have inherited this. Whatever else it was, it was a total development of industrial psychology. We are struggling with the same incubus. But we, by virtue of different tradition—I hope by virtue of having learned something from the past, although I doubt it—we are struggling against that and still trying to keep an efficient technological machine going. There is unquestionably a contradiction between an efficient technological machine and the flowering of human nature, of the human personality. It's for that reason that I'm interested in the Nazi machine, the Nazi mechanism.

Wager: Is that why you went to the war-crimes trials in Germany?

Miller: When I went there I had no idea why I was going there. I happened to have been in Austria, and I read in the paper that these trials were going on in Frankfurt. They had been going on for a long time, and I had been vaguely aware of them because certain small articles had been published in the press here. But I had never seen a Nazi. Simple as that. And I had certainly never seen a mass murderer, and I was near enough to go, and without too much difficulty. And when I went there, I discovered that these trials had been going on for nearly a year, that some of the Nazis had been in jail as long as three or four years, and that, as an avid newspaper reader, I had noticed hardly anything about it. And so when I got there the newspapermen who were covering this for the wire services—there were four or five of them—asked me to write something about it in order to draw public attention to it, because it was of immense importance not only to Germany but to the whole world. And I did. I'm glad to say that, as a result of that, the amount of space given this trial increased immensely from that time. It became an interesting story finally. But in going there and traveling in Germany a good deal, I became reminded again of what I had been thinking about that time for twenty years. I know a good deal more about it than I ever did then, before this last few years. The basic story of *Incident at Vichy* I had known at least ten years ago, but I hadn't really known how to make a play out of it.

Wager: You had heard of a factual event or incident which, with the playwright's art, you have developed and expanded into a statement of the nature of Man?

Miller: That's right, yes. It usually needs only some turn of a phrase sometimes. Sometimes it's one action that can set off, that can trigger a play.

Wager: You must catch your passion before you can communicate the passion.

Miller: Yes. I can't manufacture a play just because it's a good idea. There are numerous great stories that I know that I could never make into a play because they don't match some personal preoccupation of my own.

Wager: Now there was a period of a number of years, as the press has pointed out rather repeatedly, in which you did not write. Or is it that you didn't write anything that you wanted to produce?

Miller: That's it. I wrote as much if not more than I had before, but I have an immense respect for the dramatic form, and if I can see holes through something I can't go on with it. And if I can't account for the action I'm putting on the stage, I don't expect anybody else is going to be able to, and it just didn't seem dramatically whole or true enough for me to produce what I had written.

Wager: Then we were misinformed, in fact. What Arthur Miller wrote was not up to Arthur Miller's standards.

Miller: It just wasn't capable of being completed satisfactorily. That's all.

Wager: Do you think you might go back to that, or are you moving on to new projects?

Miller: I can never go back. It's impossible. I've never been able to do it. I wouldn't go back.

Wager: A play such as *Incident at Vichy* presents certain fundamental problems about mankind even though it's set twenty years ago.

Miller: Well, that play applies. Put it this way—the occasion of the play is something that happened twenty years ago. The play is about tomorrow morning. There's a difference between the occasion of a play and what it is about.

Wager: I'd like to quote from something you wrote, which is a very treacherous thing to do, but I'll play the theatregoer's David Susskind, if I may. "A play cannot be equated with a political philosophy, at least not in the way a smaller number of multiplication can be assimilated into a larger. I do not believe that any work of art can help but be diminished by its adherence at any cost to a political program, including its author's, and not for any other reason than there is no political program—any more than there is a theory of tragedy—which can encompass the complexities of real life." Now that I have made this elaborate preamble, the question of politics as such is not really one that concerns you nearly as much as the question of Man and his nature. Is that right?

Miller: It concerns me as a citizen because politics is the way we regulate our destructive instincts. Without politics we would be at each other's throats more than we are. But as a dramatist, politics is one very important expression of the human dilemma, and it's the human dilemma which I'm interested in. I don't think a great many people know who ran for Vice President eight years ago when everybody might have been excited about one man or another, but the impulses that create political conflicts are my business. They are the human impulses, the human contradictions. And those are the ones that I think a drama has to deal with.

Wager: You have said that drama and its production is an expression of profound social needs. What needs do you have in mind?

Miller: Well, there are many. One—drama is one of the things that makes possible a solution to the problem of socializing people. In other words, we are born private, and we die private, but we live of necessity in direct relation to other people, even if we live alone. And dramatic conflict of significance always verges on and deals with the way men live together. And this is incomprehensible to Man as a private person. He is always trying to find out where he stands in his society, whether he uses those terms or not. He always wants to know whether his life has a meaning, and that meaning is always in relation to others. It is always in relation to his society, it's always in relation to his choices, to the absence of his coices, which are dominated by other people. I think that when we speak of dramatic significance we're really talking about, either openly or unknowingly, about the dilemma of living together, of living a social existence, and the conflict is endless between Man and his fellows and between his own instincts and the social necessity.

Wager: That was, I think, expressed quite vigorously in *After the Fall.*

Miller: Yeah, sure.

Wager: Which seems to me to be one of the more profoundly misunderstood plays of our time, by the critics anyway.

Miller: Well, in this country. But in Europe it isn't. It has opened in twenty-three different theatres in about eleven countries, and the reviews I've gotten so far deal with it as a play. In that sense, it fared no differently than almost anything else I have written. *Death of a Salesman* was taken to be a play about an old salesman. *A View from the Bridge* was taken to be a play about an incestuous longshoreman. What underlies these plays is not discussed, but, as I say, it's part of a long tradition that they wouldn't be discussed that way.

Wager: Then you would say our critics are more reportorial than analytical or critical?

Miller: For the most part that's true. I don't see how it can be much different when you have to write a review in twenty minutes or half an hour. You are bound to be driven back to retelling the story and saying whether or not you were affected by it. I don't know how you would reach any further in that given time, but again I say that, as things stand now, the bulk of the Broadway audience is not interested in any more than that. And I think they will someday be made to be interested when they find that it is interesting. It's a process of maturation, that one should ask not only what is the story or what happened, but what it signifies.

Wager: One could say there are only one or two critics in New York who could understand what anything signifies.

Miller: Well, that may be so. I don't really know.

Wager: Or who really care, go that deeply into the question.

Miller: That may be so.

Wager: The style of the most recent play, *Incident at Vichy,* would you call that a realistic style?

Miller: No, but I don't have a ready label for it. The style of that play is commanded, so to speak, by the situation; it is dealing with the literal situation as well as the moral and ethical situation. It deals with a group of people who are faced with the need to respond to total destruction, and when that is the situation, you are not in what can normally be called a realistic situation.

Wager: They're facing death?

Miller: Yes. Or the possibility of death. And totally senseless death. Death with no reason. And when that happens, you can't imagine people behaving as they would in any other circumstance so that the intensification of all reactions creates a kind of symbolization of people, just when one faces a sudden emergency you act in ways you never dreamed you could act. And those actions go to imprint themselves on others who observe you—a personality which is quite possibly strange to your ordinary personality so that you automatically adopt when you could call a style of behavior. It's that style that this play is written in.

Wager: Survival style?

Miller: Well, you could call it that.

Wager: Now before, when you spoke about the failings or lack of maturity of Broadway audiences, is that something you think is limited to the Broadway audience, or is it common with theatrical audiences throughout the country?

Miller: I find it's less so outside New York. Principally because outside New York the theatre would attract those culturally starved people, the schoolteacher, the doctor, even the trade-union man who finds that there's nothing much interesting in his environment and wants to see something which might perhaps throw some light on his earthly career. My own experience with those out-of-town audiences in general is that they tend to try to dig deeper. A larger proportion of them regard the theatre as not merely a way of wasting two or three hours.

Wager: Or as entertainment.

Miller: Yeah. Well, of course, the most entertaining thing I can imagine is the most interesting thing, and I think one of the most interesting things we can consider is embodied in one word—"why," not "what."

Wager: That is the clue to your definition of reality, too.

Miller: Sure.

Wager: A play which has realism is why people do it, not merely the account of what happens.

Miller: That's right. A play's an interpretation. It is not a report. And that is the beginning of its poetry because, in order to interpret, you have to convince, you have to distort toward a symbolic construction of what happened, and as that distortion takes place, you begin to leave out and over-emphasize and consequently deliver up life as a unity rather than as a chaos, and any such attempt, the more intense it is, the more poetic it becomes.

Wager: You are aware that there is poetry in your plays?

Miller: Well, to be precise, there is poetry, and there is verse. I'm not a poet in the sense of being a versifier. That is something else entirely.

Miller: No, but there are great bursts of lyricism, which are as specifically identifiable of you as a hatband which says "Arthur Miller."

Miller: Well, yes.

Wager: That pleases you.

Miller: Well, it pleases me if it's anything that tends to forcefully set forth the vision behind the play. And it could be a silence, it could be a gesture, it could be one character handing to another a cigarette case, and it can be a speech, or a series of speeches. The metaphor is everything, the symbolized action, the action which is much greater than itself and is yet concrete is what we're after, I think. I think the structure of a play should be its essential poem—what it leaves out and what it follows to a real climax. Before there can be the other poetry, there must be that.

Wager: Do you go the theatre very much yourself?

Miller: I go very rarely. I read plays more than I see them. I go mostly when I'm about to cast a play to see the actors that are working and to refresh myself with the fact of the theatre. But not ordinarily.

Wager: I didn't realize that you took an active role in the casting and the actual production.

Miller: I do as far as is possible for somebody who is not aware of everybody who's working and who is around. I wish I knew more about them, and from time to time I make sporadic attempts to find out. But to really cast well you should obviously know who is around and what they can do. I find I have to rely on others too often.

Wager: Now in the course of a production, is there likely to be some rewriting before opening night?

Miller: It depends. Some plays I hardly touch at all. Others I do some work with.

Wager: This is an intimate association with the director, right? Well, do you have any comments on the general state of our playwriting, compared to, say, the British playwrights? Do you feel they're moving in different directions?

Miller: I don't see a direction, to tell you the truth. That's not a

statement of criticism; it may be just as well. We don't have enough
new plays of any significance produced to speak of any direction.
Since I've been around, there's been a group of individuals who
work at the same time in many different directions, and I suppose the
most obvious trend is what's called "theatre of the absurd," which is a
meaningless category because you can't put Albee in the same box
with Beckett, who, of course, is not an American. Albee is essentially
much more concrete in terms of behavior and is much more realistic
and is much closer to the realistic tradition in this country. I don't see
a trend. As a matter of fact, I never have. We often talked about
trends in the Thirites, when plays so often had some open social
protest involved with them. But there again you couldn't put Odets
and Lillian Hellman in the same box because one was much more
involved with lyricism than the other, and one was closer to Ibsen, the
other possibly to Chekhov, who are very opposite poles, and yet they
were all thrown together because they were both interested in social
protest. I wouldn't have any over-all comment to make about it. I
don't see one unity.

Wager: Let me ask you one final question. In addition to your
plays, you have written two films, one for the Army during the war,
right?

Miller: Well, I wrote the original screenplay for *Story of G.I. Joe,*
which was never used.

Wager: I see.

Miller: It was the basis of the final picture.

Wager: And you did one novel.

Miller: Yes.

Wager: Which I think I read before I ever saw any of your plays.

Miller: *Focus.*

Wager: Yes.

Miller: I've written about fifteen short stories, which will be
collected soon, and a number of essays.

Wager: But do you think you may ever go back to novels or are
plays your business?

Miller: I would doubt it very much. I have too many plays to
write, and I'm more at home in the medium, I love it more, and I can
do it better.

The Writer and Society
Richard I. Evans/1969

From Richard I. Evans, *Psychology and Arthur Miller* (New York: E.P. Dutton. 1969), 85-116; reprinted as *Dialogue with Arthur Miller* (New York: Praeger, 1981). Reprinted by permission.

Evans: We might continue our discussion with a problem that I think is a very difficult one for the average psychology student. It centers around this problem: can we develop a true science of psychology? We have one point of view, behaviorism, which contends that there is no truly scientific way to deal with what's "under the skin" in the human organism—what the individual experiences. This should lead us to focus on predicting and controlling man's responses, since the responses man makes are observable physical units just like the matter which is examined in physics and chemistry. By manipulating the environmental contingencies which evoke these responses, we can learn to predict and control man's behavior. As we mentioned earlier, another view proposes a more humanistic emphasis which, although recognizing the difficulties of engaging in the scientific study of man while maintaining a humanistic stance, would argue that a humanistic position which includes the study of man's subjective experience is an indispensable part of understanding the individual. It brings up the question of whether or not the behaviorists should attempt to control or predict human behavior without fully understanding it. In your earlier remarks concerning your experience at the American Psychological Association meeting, you were already reacting negatively to the mechanistic view of the behaviorists and expressed fears concerning a psychology which teaches us to scientifically search for means of controlling man but fails to reflect a humanistic compassion for man. Would you care now to expand on your views of this problem?

Miller: I admit that it raises a certain alarm in me, and lot of doubt.

For example, in my opinion, the problem of living today is not so much one of control is it is one of decontrol. It would seem to me that if you want to control people, I should imagine that history shows various ways of doing it pretty well. You can do it by terrifying them, or you can do it by punishing them. The Nazis did that, and they did it fairly well. If you did anything that was outside the rules, you got your head knocked off. The Communists have done it in various places from time to time. It can be done. The question is the value of the person that come out of these various attempts: How human he ends up being, how human he thinks he is, how human you think he is. From my point of view, there's no point asking what the efficaciousness of a technique is but what it is you're after. I have no opinions about those techniques. I don't know the easiest way to control people, or to make them do what you think they ought to do, or what we might think they ought to do. I do have views about what human behavior consists in, in the best sense of the word, and what inhuman behavior or ahuman behavior consists in. I must say in advance, the possibilities of really shaping people by scientific means, I think, are ultimately doomed. And I say that only because every child is born primitive; he is a threat to injustice because biologically he wants his share. You've got to start from scratch with every generation, and there are too many unforeseen possibilities. I think that the possibilities are infinite and that they're going to get away from you, finally. I have trouble myself if I try to figure out why I do what I do; it would be pretty hard, and I know a lot more about myself than a lot of people know about themselves.

Evans: Let me play the devil's advocate for a moment. Some psychologists would argue this way: they'd say, "Well, we try to predict and/or control behavior employing maximum scientific objectivity, rigor, and exactness, so that our conclusions are valid. If you allow a humanistic dimension in the value system of the researcher to influence the study of man, you are building up 'noise' in the hopefully objective, experimental system that can't be controlled. Thus, one can't conduct research which yields reliable data." In other words, for all practical purposes then, you're eliminating psychology as a scientific discipline. Are you saying that we should do that?

Miller: I sense that an attempt is being made despite everything to find *the* system or a system from which human behavior cannot escape, so to speak. It sends chills up my back, to tell you the truth. I would much rather that people spent their time asking: what does it consist of to be human? How can science advance man toward that goal? Of course, I don't think that this approach obliterates the scientific approach. I think it makes science more difficult, but I wouldn't say that it obliterated it. The "noise" in these systems may simply be humanity trying to get out of them.

Evans: Well, let me be a little bit more specific. In your characterizations, you've shown us what you think makes a human being human, and your views are based not on scientific discourse but on a complex intuitive perceptiveness and ability to understand and integrate what you observe. If you were going to tell a psychology student what you think makes a person human, what would you say?

Miller: I don't quite know how I would state that in a syllogistic way; maybe it can be done. I don't think you can differentiate human behavior, though, in pure terms of drives. Sex, hunger, fear, and so on are shared by other species. Even the capacity to build is not ours alone, and some animals are even monogamous, evidently. I think you have to reach out beyond such drives to social and even ethical impulses to find the differences. Some will define man as the animal most likely to destroy his own kind, and on the record this is hard to knock down. But there is also a countervailing impulse, an impulse toward changing his environment in order to enhance life, and doing so in a conscious way. This also differentiates us. Perhaps a possible definition is that what makes a person human is the conflict in him between the forces of life and death. And since we've been referring back to my plays here, I might add that for me as for most writers there is a perpetual mystery cloaking man, this very same question as to what in him so to speak drives him to death-dealing acts and attitudes toward himself, and what decrees his stumbling search for what is life-giving. I often think that is basically what I am writing about, and what my morality consists in—I mean, of course, the moral element in my plays. Incidentally, we spoke earlier of masks. Masks are always to some degree frightening. Because they speak of the dead, of death. They cover what is alive and thus create a fundamental tension, *the* fundamental tension. And in our time, as in others in the past, the tension comes from the uncertainty as to whether we are, in fact, nothing but the mask, the representative of

an interest, of a concealed or open social necessity, mere switchboxes
with turbine illusions. And there is undoubtedly a general fear,
conscious or not, that man as a unique thing is disappearing or has
already, but I don't think it comes from nowhere, this fear. It is an
inevitable part of the contradiction that on the one hand we are trying
to make society rational, efficient, wasteless, and on the other we
extoll the individual. Progress, after all, means ordering, at least as we
commonly think of it, while "man" in the best sense implies acts of
private judgment and will, self-expression, the personal and
individuated reaction to reality. Something has to give. Up to this
recent time it has been the individual who has given, but now the
reaction has set in. The system of ordering itself is under attack. But
the strongest single idea that has come out of it is a worship of the
irrational, as though in this is the protection of the individual. It is not,
however, a promising attitude. If only because the hippie, for
example, does depend on everybody else going to work on time, the
subways continuing to run, the food being raised in an orderly
fashion. A viable viewpoint, in other words, has to include one's
unspoken reliance on the garbage being removed regularly. It must
also include, and have at its center, really, the fact that man deprived
of the habit of making real decisions is lessened and can, as we know,
effectively vanish.

Evans: In this regard, you might find the actions of one early
behaviorist rather amusing. When John B. Watson first began
attacking the study of human experience because it wasn't scientific,
he used to challenge his detractors by the statement, "Prove that
you're conscious."

Miller: Well, I can't prove that either. I'll speak about what I know
instead of about psychiatry, and maybe it'll throw some light on
psychology. I think that the basic impulse of any writer is that,
through the process of writing, he speaks his own uniqueness. By
that I mean he deals with what he has discovered himself. That
means that nobody else has discovered them, and that but for him,
there wouldn't exist this vision, this particular kind of style, this
particular kind of relationship he's talking about, if not the particular
kind of moral he draws from the story. And that reflects his own
uniqueness. Now, what this has to do with psychological work or
science, I have no idea. All I know is that the history of literature is so
long and evidently so fascinating to so many generations of peoples

of all cultures that there must be some validity in that quest. Possibly a way to understand the human being is to try to understand his own concept of his uniqueness and his fear of its disappearing.

Evans: Then what you are saying is that creativity is a form of the ultimate expression of uniqueness. Therefore, by definition, this creative effort becomes data that presumably will explain something about what it is to be human.

Miller: It is a kind of data. You see, I think we tend to attack these problems at the later stages rather than the earlier ones. I know a young man who is about eighteen; I was talking to him a few weeks ago, and the main questions were whether or not he should go to college and what he should do, the usual crises that people of that age go through, as all of us more or less went through it. At one point he made a very revealing remark. I said, "Why?" Tell me why do you feel negative about pursuing any defined line in life, whatever it might be." And he couldn't answer right away, but later he said, "You know, I feel that everything has been done." He is by no means an incompetent person in any way, either with girls or studies or anything else. Well, that's a hard one to answer. Finally the thought went through my mind, and I said to him, "You are you. There was never another guy like you. There will never be another guy like you again. You're like most people in most respects, but in some one respect you aren't; in some small way what you think and see is unique. There can only be one of you." Well, it seemed to make a dent in him; how deep a dent I don't know, but he seemed pleasantly shocked. To me, the striking thing was that he'd gone through the American educational system for eighteen years. He's been in school for thirteen years. He's been reading and going to movies and the rest of it. Now his thinking is an ideology, you see. It's what he believes to be true about himself and the world, and it's operating on him. It's the ideology, it seems to me, of a kind of spiritual leveling or canceling-out which has been equated with realism. He has been put into a position where he is trying, quite against his own will, to fit in so much that finally he can't see what will be left of him if he does fit in. And he creates a kind of pause to live in. Incidentally, he went not to a public school, but to a private school that places special emphasis on psychological insights; the teachers are in many cases analyzed people or people highly conscious of psychology and psychiatry. I think that what has happened with it all is that we are "nothing-but" people. That is, whatever you feel is "nothing-but" this or that kind of unconscious conflict, and the whole system reduces feelings to nullifying, devaluating constructions. It started out as a good idea. That is to say, you were relieving the guilt or the anxiety of the people by saying, "Well, everybody does this or feels this." Finally this kind of psychology ended up I think by saying, "You are absolutely no different from anybody else." So what the hell is the use of living?

Evans: Yes. You are touching on something here which is important. Many writers and individuals in the social sciences are expressing concern at the possibility that we are creating a culture of overconformity. Your example in terms of what was happening to this young man, his loss of identity in the morass of shaping forces, would seem to suggest your concern with this. As you know, of course, in recent years David Riesman dealt with this problem in his book, *The Lonely Crowd,* as did William White in *The Organization Man.* Erich Fromm, Otto Rank, and many other important thinkers in psychology in the last forty or fifty years have also been particularly concerned with this idea that man is being siphoned off. You have dealt with this theme in your work. Are there any particular characters in your plays, as you recall, who you think personify man caught up in this social shaping process and losing his identity and his individuality?

Miller: I think that from that point of view you could find people in every play of mine who would come under that umbrella. If you start with *All My Sons,* the son, by overlooking his father's crime, is offered the chance to live a peaceful life without conflict. To be sure, there would be no justice. He would not have participated in a moral decision of some kind, but at the same time, he would have left that vision behind—that anger, that remorse, that pathos that he felt. He would have negated it by deadening it and himself. There is an instant where he was immediately connected to a social or moral or transcendent issue, namely the question of his own emotional attachment to the men he had led in the war, and it meant dying to that degree. The way it happens to him is unique. And that uniqueness would have been gone if he had chosen, if he had been able, to turn himself away from what he conceived was necessary to do. There is another example of this uniqueness from the opposite direction, and that is in Willy Loman. His individuality has nothing to

do with such an overt case of a wrong or social injustice in the legal
or even in the moral sense of the word. I think what happens and
what I was getting at in *Salesman,* or what got me when I was writing
the work, was an implied simplicity, which is to be sure nostalgic and
romantic. Willy's father went across the country in a covered wagon,
and he made flutes. He wasn't anybody's employee nor anybody's
boss; he was a free man. He had a certain colorful character as
opposed to Willy, who stuck in Brooklyn and worked for a company
that was gradually trying to tell him that he wasn't needed any more.
His one claim to existence was that he could sell, that the people on
the road knew him, that he was celebrated by the people on the
road, that he could park his car anywhere in New England and cops
would treat it like their own and that the firm needed him. And
suddenly this uniqueness is revealed as merely his economic
function. It turns out a mirage. In the meantime, he has foregone in
his life what he loved to do and what he was able to do. In his case it
happened to be working in concrete and painting the house and such
things, all of which have no social status whatsoever. His uniqueness
was bypassed in favor of his total obedience to social stimuli, and he
ends up as he does in the play, believing in what he is forced to rebel
against. Similarly, there is in *The Crucible* a man who is confronted
with the opportunity, the possibility of negating himself, of calling true
what he knows is half-truth. He's being asked to give way to his guilt,
a guilt that arises because he has broken moral laws. By sinning that
way, he's being asked by the court to condemn himself to a spiritual
death. He can't finally do it. He dies a physical death, but he gains
his soul, so to speak, he becomes his rebellion. In one way or
another, I suppose, it is in all the plays. In *A View from the Bridge*, it
takes place in still another context. A man has betrayed other people
and then the desolation he feels inspires him to want to be destroyed.
So what I'm positing in all this work, I suppose, is the secret existence
of what used to be called an immortal soul, though I never thoughjt
of it in so many words. I would call it a unique identity of a moral
kind. I admit that it's possible that it is simply a question of a
consensus that over the ages, mainly through religion, the conception
of a unique identity was instilled in man. We haven't the religion any
more, so all we've got left is the arbitrary conception, which I admit is
withering away at a great rate, but once it's given up, I think the game
is up. Science will really be a game, a word game. It won't matter

anymore because the subject will no longer be definable or visible; it will simply be a relationship of certain fairly obvious forces, and the human will simply be the adaptable.

Evans: Erich Fromm uses the term "automaton-conformist" to describe the condition that you're describing here; when man becomes an automaton-conformist, he loses his identity and for all practical purposes, he's like a kind of instrument that's controlled by various forces.

Miller: I often feel that man himself, the concept, is an act of will, an invention. It may have no natural existence and can be wiped out as man thought of himself in the past. It is an act of will which has to be engaged in by the intellectual class of the country because they are the heirs of it through their literature and through science itself, but they have to posit it not because it's provable but because it's necessary. Now that's on one level an unscientific statement, I suppose, but it's no more so than a physicist trying to measure something that is invisible and is engaged in mathematical calculations that would posit the existence of something. Well, up to that point it's an act of will. He's asserting something for which there is no conceivable proof, and then he blows up a bomb and they say, "Well, you see it was always there." However, conceivably the bomb wouldn't blow up, or it wouldn't have for three hundred years. I've come to believe that positing man is as important as discovering him, and that's what I find missing, by the way, not only in psychology but in a lot of writing. The assumption is that one describes events, and that is scientific. Well, I don't believe anybody can be that above it all and remain open to human suffering, and truth itself. I would believe it if there were a class of gods who had no vested interest in man, but a scientist has that interest and if he hasn't, he's got an illusion to say the least.

Evans: The underlying philosophical questions that you are raising concerning free will and determinism are regarded by many philosophers as being too abstract and circular to deal with meaningfully.

Miller: I don't think it can be considered separately or abstractly, either. That's where this would be difficult to talk about. I think this way as a writer and probably I write plays because it is the only way I can really express this thought. I couldn't construct a play that would be persuasive or seem related to human life on the basis of free will,

despite what I've just been saying. I believe that my concept of free
will is a conditioned concept. Nevertheless, I didn't invent this. It
came out of conflict and struggle. It is as if to say that if there weren't
this element in us, the conception of what is not yet, I would not be
interested in living. So therefore, it must be natural. Having an
existence is as important as my blood supply. I think that in various
situations where it is no longer really possible for people to conceive
of something which is not yet, they become zombies. This is a
common concentration camp syndrome. There were some
individuals in the concentration camp who simply could no longer
conceive of another situation. Would it be scientific to simply report
this condition if it took over the world—and even to call it human
nature?

Evans: In this same vein, moving I think through Willy, in *Death of
a Salesman,* you share with us brilliantly the existential problems of
aging. It might be interesting to relate your insights to the experiences
of many psychotherapists. When asked, "Why are you seeking
psychotherapy?" some aging patients will say, "Well, I don't know
what I'm living for. I don't know what the purpose of all this is. I'm
not even sure who I am." This question is not generally asked by the
individual until he actually sees himself as aging, but is otherwise well
established in life. However, perhaps ninety percent of the population
is still concerned with satisfying needs more primitive than those of
self-actualization; they apparently do not, at least overtly, face
existential dilemmas. They never come to grips with the question.
According to your definition, then, these people do not exist.

Miller: The old, like the unskilled, are unnecessary to the
production apparatus. I've never come across a study of the
similarities in the viewpoints of both these classes, but I'd bet there
are many. But the unskilled unemployed don't get into the hands of
psychotherapists. I wouldn't be surprised, though, if they asked the
same existential questions as they aged. I know that back in the
Depression it was a common thing to hear an unemployed man
conjuring up what in better hands would be called fundamental
questions of the meaning of existence. A sense of futility can have
many roots and aging is only the most obvious, and probably the
most pathetic. Actually, though, Willy doesn't quite fit into this
category, at least in my eyes. He discovers he is unneeded anymore,
but what he is reaching for is something like a token of immortality, a

sign that he lived. You might call it some affirmation by others of the values for which he struggled. This demand is not confined to the old, they merely illuminate by the desperation of the Last Days, so to speak, what is eating people of any age group. I want to say something contradictory, though. Obviously I see people as being intensely conditioned by what society does to them. But the interior geography of man doesn't change very much, I think, from one period to another. Different virtues are prized at different times, of course—the emphasis differs as to what makes a man valuable, evil, worthy, and so on. But if you read through the testimony of the Salem Witchcraft Trials, for instance, you will come on the common sexual fantasies, repressions, symbolizations, and so forth that we are so aware of today. In other words, the sociological attack is very limited if you are looking for some way of understanding what goes into making a man. Something quite permanent and unchanging persists in him through all the systems that have sought to control him. There is a continuity in us which goes back into Egypt, into the beginnings. My point is that there is such a thing as Man, or at least a matrix that conditioning cannot wholly surround and quench. This would demand a certain humility in the use of any analytic technique. In recent years we've seen the resistance of this creature in the Eastern countries, for example, and now through the rebellions of youth and the Negro in our own country. The creature is not wholly malleable after all. I'd even go so far as to say that perhaps part of his difficulty in changing—even for the better—is his instinct to protect his repetitious human definition.

Evans: Earlier, Jung's notion of archetypes was introduced into our discussion. As you recall, Jung developed the concept to suggest that there were pervasive behavior potentials in man that cut through time and various cultures, and to understand these potentials, you must go back to man's early beginning. In a sense, you're again pointing to the validity of Jung's notion of archetypes.

Miller: I think that the proof is that you can read literature from older cultures that are absolutely divorced from ours and have nothing in common with it, and you see a parade of individuals who with the slightest superficial changes are people who are walking around today. Now that kind of information is irreproachable because the man putting it down had no interest in proving anything of the kind that we're talking about.

Evans: Yes, it is quite fascinating. But let me just take another approach to what you're saying. Jung and many other scholars with historical perspective have tried to look at the problems as you do. But yet modern cultural anthropologists, who emphasize cultural determinism, believe that we are what we are as a function of the specific culture in which we develop and that cultural influence can be modified. For example, Margaret Mead has done a very interesting study of how an entire culture in New Guinea changed almost overnight when Americans brought their values into the culture. You may be familiar with this work.

Miller: Yes, I am.

Evans: What is your opinion of it? Do you think that these changes might actually be superficial?

Miller: Let me say this, and don't laugh. Superficial changes can be decisive, in the sense that I could see where a superficial change in a culture would increase the supply of people to that culture; for example, a superficial change like the introduction of penicillin or teaching a midwife to wash her hands just before she's going to deliver a baby. That doesn't take much changing, just a bar of soap. But it can make an island overpopulated and even start wars, which in turn demand character changes in people, military rather than peacetime virtues, a paranoid fearfulness rather than trust and confidence. What I'm driving at, I suppose, is a synthetic approach to man, that is to say, the virtue that I finally see in literature and its value apart from the literary or esthetic value is that to me it's the one way a man has found to synthesize all his insides in a dynamic fashion, so that it defends us against doing what so many psychological systems fall into doing, and that is to partition people. That makes it much more difficult, I admit, to draw conclusions about what makes people tick. But I still say that you have to keep your eye on your source material, namely man and his most immediate refection that I know about, his art, his literature. Given Freud or anybody else, it is still the best picture, the best and most analytical, if you will, source of insight and wisdom into men because it is the only one that attempts to synthesize the various aspects of human life; the greater the literature, the greater variety of the forces it brings into play. Now, Shakespeare was a great writer not only becaue he was a poet, which is part of what I'm about to say, but because a character in his play is the product of his past, his present, his individual nature, his immediate conflict, and numerous other forces. And that dynamic quality is the reality. I'm worried, in effect, by some of the attempts that I hear about from time to time to pick out of this complex group of forces one or two or three or four which it is said will control man. I'm worried not only because it isn't true, but it might distract people dangerously for a time. That is to say, men are very impressionable, and if they think something is true, they act accordingly. They'll even take on a neurosis suggested to them, and one has to be very responsible toward people when one suggests certain things about them, and says this is why people act. When I was a kid, I remember there was a thing called the inferiority complex to which I believe you referred in another context earlier in our discussion. I knew nothing about anything but I clearly recall that everybody suddenly discovered that he had an inferiority complex and that was the basis of both his success and his failure; of course, you can make a great case out of it. I think one of the reasons we even have this conversation is that culture in terms of the deep and steady use of literature is so sparse in this country. I think in a way psychology is trying to fill a gap. We're creating a psychological culture in the sense that other countries have created a literary or artistic culture.

Evans: In this respect, I think you have raised a very interesting point: you're proposing that this ego, this will, or whatever makes man at least partially self-determined is a very fragile thing, and psychologists might be perfectly capable of destroying this in the individual through some systematically applied behavioral shaping or controling techniques of the sort we discussed earlier.

Miller: I think it is possible, at least for a time. Sometimes it can have more than academic or even literary ramifications, such as the problem of juvenile delinquency in this country. I spent a few months in the streets of New York in 1957, thinking I would someday write about juvenile delinquency, and I went through the usual sources. I always like to know what anybody else knows about something before I decide what I know about it or before I decide that I know anything about it. In this case I had never been a juvenile delinquent, but I had been brought up in Harlem and I knew a little about them just from my childhood experience. I had a head start there, but that was all. I talked with sociologists and psychiatrists and psychologists, many of whom were working on this problem directly for the city in one respect or another, mostly formal projects but some simply out of personal interest. Now, if you talk to the cultural anthropologist from Columbia, you've got one picture of why they were delinquent and what had to be done about it. If you talked to psychologists, you got another picture. If you talked to psychiatrists, you got still another one, and if you talked to a sociologist, you got a fourth or fifth one. Finally, I realized that my view was probably as good or as bad but certainly no worse than theirs. All I knew was that one element was missing from the whole business. These kids had been conceived as having entered some new area of human behavior. A new world had been created from which nondelinquents were barred. They were in a special category now. They were juvenile delinquents, and they were being observed that way. At one point, out of desperation, we had a meeting to which I called about ten people, and they attended it because they really, at bottom, were desperate. After all their personality theories had been stated, they really were getting nowhere becaue they could not change the society. You couldn't psychoanalyze all the jokers in that neighborhood, but if you could, would you want to?—to make them learn to tolerate the intolerable? That is, I think, a good example of the synthetic approach or the want of it; by "synthetic" I mean a way of thinking that brings all the elements of a situation together, as opposed to an analysis that pulls things apart and leaves them in pieces.

Evans: Who was in the group that you called together?

Miller: Well, they represented various disciplines. By this time they were all humble if not humiliated by their failure to affect anything except individuals here and there among the delinquent kids. The idea was that they were about to set up Mobilization for Youth, which was, as you know, an attempt in New York City not only to do something but to measure the results of what they were doing. And as I've told you, I know nothing about sociological procedures or the rest of it, and all I knew was what I observed by sticking around and trying to write about it; I emphasize trying to write about it, because by just observing it, you don't arrive at that high attention of really trying to symbolize the meaning of something. It seemed to me that what was really missing in the kids was not only a sense that they could join society which is a general way of putting it, but that it was possible to give them the responsibility for themselves in society right now, not someday when they were cured or when they would grow up and be nice fellows and keep their noses clean and go to college and become lawyers. I said, "Suppose they live in bad housing and go around in gangs of fifty or sixty, why not give up telling them not to break the windows in the housing project, or not to do this or not to do that or offering them examples of a good father in terms of the social worker, or any of those methods? Instead, why not give them the idea of protesting so that they really get in trouble with the authorities, not as patients, not as an exercise, but as a social movement." Because it had occurred to me that I was brought up during the Depression where I wandered around with a lot of guys who broke windows and stole things. And one of the big things that happened that I thought might have reduced what we call delinquent acts in these kids was that they got a sense that they could protest their condition through a social movement, through some combined action. That made them social beings, curiously enough, because their point of view was directed toward society instead of the opposite direction. Well, Mobilization for Youth did this. Or it attempted to do this in a faltering and rather frightened way. They opened their premises to people who had started a rent strike because of the abysmal conditions in which they were living; they refused to pay any more rent. They allowed them to use their mimeograph machine. They didn't supply actual leadership because they were prohibited from doing so by their charter, but they inevitably had to provide some if the people wanted to protest. And they did not regard it as a delinquent action. The result was just as I must say I predicted in the beginning. I'd said, "If you're really doing well, you're going to get in trouble with the police department and the mayor and everybody else. If you're not accomplishing anything, everybody's going to say you're great." And sure enough as soon as the protest became serious, Mobilization for Youth was striped of autonomy and forced to conform. Now the alternative to this was what? All the psychiatrists had said that we'd need six thousand analysts for this neighborhood alone. It would presumably take at least two years to analyze each kid. Well, I'll stop right there because obviously, you can't do that. So we get back to my original propostion, which was that in order to proceed even scientifically in this respect, one had to knowingly inject a judgment of the value of certain ideas as opposed to others. In my view, which was not a separated and completely esthetic or judicial judgment, there was a value, a human value, in opening up the road to protest. I think protesting is a healing mechanism, and I think people who have lost it or have been prohibited from using it are losing some of their identity. Now in those few cases where the people accomplished something, their pride returned, their sense of being citizens of the city of New York returned. Suddenly power that had completely overwhelmed them before to the point where they had contempt for it was something they too could now participate in and even manipulate, even cause it to recognize their existence. And they began to exist as unique human beings, in the most primitive way imaginable, of course, but this was never carried through, and God knows what would have happened if it had. But in other words, I think that there is a humanistic premise that I believe science cannot set aside; if it does, it will truly cease to be science either.

Evans: I think your example of delinquency is an excellent one because to some degree, this becomes the battleground for these value systems. Perhaps naïvely applied theories of significant social thinkers such as Durkheim and Marx have had a tremendous effect on social welfare agencies and resulted in a strong commitment to social determinism; that is, if you can change social conditions and relieve the physical and economic plight of the individual, you also change him in the process. In a delinquency project similar to Mobilization for Youth in which we were involved, we concluded that one of the dangers in some well-meaning social welfare activity predicated on a naïve social determinism is that instead of necessarily solving a person's problem over the long run, imposed social change may merely breed greater dependency in him. The alternative is investing some repsonsibility in the individual, or as you put it, at least begin with some sense of the capacity to protest. As the direction of the recent protest movements has indicated, there is a very fine balance however, isn't there? That is, it's a risky thing.

Miller: That's another point, by the way. I sense in some of these approaches a fear of risk, a fear of risking freedom. What right have you got to tell kids that they have any less right to protest their condition than people who live in a good neighborhood, who certainly are not going to sit there and do nothing when their conditions become dreadful. Why do you say that others have the right and these kids don't? You see, these differentials communicate themselves. In other words, I believe that a delinquent has learned to be a delinquent. Somebody has taught him to be a delinquent. Delinquents are not born; they're made. And I hate to use that dreadful word, society, but I mean by that us and what we think is the way out, not just the gangsters and real estate owners who don't take care of their property. Those kids were given a certain message over many years by social workers: they were told they were delinquent. This is not to be discounted because the slums are full of social workers; they are the delinquent's sole contact with the so-called respectable world.

Evans: Your point reminds me of a scene in *West Side Story* which satirizes this notion of shifting responsibility away from the self. The juvenile delinquents are with Police Officer Krupke. They taunt him in song that they aren't responsible for their delinquent behavior but social conditions are. It would be interesting to see the kind of play that you would create from your experience. Had you begun speculating in terms of characterization in a play about this problem?

Miller: Yes. I started out to do a screenplay. You see, I was approached by people from the New York City Youth Board, which was a city-financed attempt to develop methods of dealing with what was then the big problem, gang fighting. It has since become dope, which is the opposite of gang fighting; it's complete acquiescence. Dope addiction is the total victory of conformism. The object at that time, in the middle fifties, was to stop the warfare. I got interested in it only because I knew nothing about it, and I thought that I would be interested in seeing what was happening right under my nose, but also hoped that a movie could be developed out of it. But what happened over a period of months was that I began to see the obvious, namely that the people who were operating the project were at sea. It wasn't as though I was confronted with a solution and could show its operation among delinquents and how they were saved. I felt finally that the savers needed saving as much as the kids did. I started the script on the first basis and broke off because I realized I had nothing to say in this respect, nor did anybody else, and consequently, I spent four months in the street trying to find out what it was clear nobody could tell me. Nobody knew. And I came up with the solution I just told you. It isn't a solution, but at least it was a way in which to approach the whole problem. It was finally tried to a degree, and was slugged to death by the city administration. In the process, I got involved personally in a minor side drama which helped to abort that particular project at the time; the emissaries of the House Un-American Activities Committee went down to the city of New York secretly and told them that if they had anything to do with me, they would be sorry, so that I was offered the project provided my name didn't appear on it, which I somehow connected with the whole question of juvenile delinquency, except that this was adult delinquency. I refused to adopt anonymity or pledge allegiance and got into a big fight with the city. The end of it was that I got out of the project. But someday I might do something about the problem again. I don't know.

Evans: We've been talking about significant problems, but an even greater threat to man is nuclear war. On one occasion during a conference I attended, Sir Julian Huxley drew a very large thermometer. He drew a high boiling point on this thermometer and said that it represented the technological growth and development which lead to the nuclear war potential that would enable man to destroy himself. Then he checked a very low below freezing point on the thermometer and said that it indicated the progress men have made in understanding one another. He said the gap is so great that we may have little hope of overcoming it. But this gap between social psychological communication and understanding and technological development must be closed if man is not to be destroyed. In the discussions I've had as part of our National Science Foundation project with the world's notable contributors to psychology, these men have generally responded to this question of this gap by suggesting that if we look at this problem in a purely detached and rational manner, we certainly will have to conclude that man will probably destroy himself. Yet they generally go on to maintain that this very cynical belief might lead to a self-fulfilling prophecy. So faith and hope must be maintained, that this gap between a potentially destructive technology and man's capability for coping with it will be overcome. How do you feel about this problem?

Miller: First of all, I have no doubt that we are capable of dropping another atom bomb, this time on Vietnam. There is a species of thinking which regards the bomb as merely an intensification of TNT. We could do this because we are politically in bankruptcy in Vietnam; we have put into power and linked our prestige to a junta which obviously has no significant popular following. We have done the same thing for a century in Central America, Cuba, and Hawaii, the Philippines, and other places. The difference this time is that we arrived late—after a nationalist movement had matured in Vietnam which is not having any of this. The problem is that our military is having to admit that it has not won a war; our aircraft and armaments technologists and industrial experts are having to admit that all their destructiveness has not broken the will of naked peasants. Politically, our geopoliticians are having to admit the limits of American power. Internally, we are having to admit that the beneficence of our salvationism is brutal underneath. But all of this has come about contingent on one fact—that if we drop a bomb the world itself may end. Science, therefore, challenges us to a new—and very old—vision. The vision of man humiliated in his pride, humiliated and made more wise by the oncoming, stubborn, immortal nature of man himself, of man and his limits. I, no more than anyone else, am by any means sure we won't "solve" the problem by the ultimate refusal to recognize those limits and that barren pride, solve the problem by splattering the planet into the heavens. But I knowingly engage in an act of will, that's all. It is an act based on biological imperatives but willful nevertheless because I could also choose to believe that we will never destroy the world, only Vietnam, and go about my business perhaps somewhat depressed, but hoping that someday we will be allowed to rehabilitate that poor country, or some guilt-offering of the sort. I believe that man is indeed capable of the ultimate in destruction; therefore, I can only will that it not come to pass. What basis is there for such willfulness? For one thing, the refusal of the Vietnamese to give up under our immense superiority in arms, before our myth. If they can stand up to it on the battlefield, we can and must stand up to it here, where it is far less dangerous. But it is also that in all our stupidity, our mendaciousness, our self-generated illusions about what we do, there is a powerful desire to help, to live in peace and so forth. It is not a question of being optimistic but of recognizing the dialectic and of choosing which side of it one will lend one's strength to. I am perfectly aware that a point arrives where people are incapable of resisting irrational aggressive behavior, total destruction. It is not despite but because of that that I feel as I do—because the resistance to it is also a fact, a possibility equally real.

Evans: What you're saying is quite consistent with the work of Neal Miller and John Dollard in their theory of frustration-aggression. They proposed the theory that all frustration leads to aggression. Thus the very act of stifling aggression produces more frustration which leads to more aggression. Police action against rioters has illustrated this. You're suggesting this same idea, more or less.

Miller: My point here is that anyone who really and truly wants peace has got to beware of the threshold beyond which it is dialectically impossible any longer to stop short of total war. I think we are drawing very close to that point in Vietnam, where with the best will in the world, the wisest politicians might still be saying that it is to our interest not to fight a total war, but they would be incapacitated by the public feeling in relation to this thing which they themselves have inflamed.

Evans: Now, in a way, the characters in your plays illustrate the plight of man and his responsibility and guilt, but here you feel that the mechanism has already been set in motion so that by rational analysis, you think we will probably have a nuclear war before too many years.

Miller: I would say yes, I think so. And yet I think it need not be if certain lessons are learned objectively and learned now. I see no alternative but to try to teach those lessons and for people to try to learn them. And that is that we are very fragile beings. We are not in control of ourselves beyond a certain threshold. I know people right now who know as much as I do about Vietnam who feel that it is a fruitless war and something that will not ultimately rebound to our profit, and yet they say, "Well, we're in it, and therefore we must go on with it." And you say, "Why?" Well, then you get into an area of irrationality. It's quite obvious it's irrational. Why should it not be true that the greatness and honor of the United States would not be enhanced by the President's saying, "Look, we have despite everything been drawn into a dreadful error. And this country is great enough to say that we will not compound the error at the sacrifice of the lives of millions of people." It seems to me that's a new definition of what man is, of what honor is, but at the same time people would understand, even welcome it.

Evans: Yes, I think that you're raising the question of circularity. Of course, various psychological research findings suggest that attitudes are not really based on information or fact but are basically irrational. In fact, it is very difficult to find any support for the presence of truly rational belief systems, attitudes, and values in most people. So how can you ask rationality of man, who may be in the final analysis an irrational creature?

Miller: That gets to a thing that I wanted to talk about, and that is, we think about everything except what is happening. The fact that underlies my feeling in this respect is that a large number of people who are neither Communist, capitalist, or anything else but just people are being destroyed here, and that includes our own men. I'm sure if we took a poll of the dead, their political opinions for the most part would be unrelated to this whole so-called issue, except for the cadres of leadership of the Viet Cong, who I'm sure are in the minority in Vietnam as they are in every country. Most people are not politically inspired. Now as a playwright, my first question is, "What is happening?" I've used different terminology in the past; I've said that people have masks and that the purpose of drama is to tear away those masks, but perhaps a better way of putting it is that we all have illusions about what we are doing, what the other person is doing, what the nature of the conflict is. The drama works best when I present what I call in the first act the "visible reality." The audience nods to itself and says, "Yes, that's the way it is." And then gradually, I turn the scene around until I show them that maybe that is not the way it is, that what it appears to be is sometimes directly contradictory to what it is. And what we need is a Grand Dramatist in this world who would possibly be able to do that. Unfortunately, the cast of characters is too big.

Evans: Well, Mr. Miller, we had an opportunity to discuss some of your masterful works from a psychological perspective and hopefully have given psychologists and nonpsychologists alike a great deal to think about. May I ask, where do you go from here?

Miller: Well, it's hard to describe; I'll be able to tell you better when I've done them. I can't answer that question rationally or schematically. In general, I find myself trying to make human relations felt between individuals and the larger structure of the world. This kind of relationship is particularly invisible to me, particularly difficult to touch or to formulate, and yet I think it can be. By the larger world I mean the political world, the social world, the world of war and peace. The humanities are falteringly trying to create an irreducible image of what it means to be human. You see, there is either a concentration on psychological behavior or depersonalized social metaphors, and frankly, I am not any longer preoccupied with that kind of partitioning. The totality is always the great challenge. To me the problem is man as a creature in a universe which he knows somewhere in his head is moving him, which he can't seem to reach even as he is altering it as never before. I think the world has to strive toward an opening of consciousness of man as the center, a way to reach beyond conditioning so that after all decisions are made, and necessity has its hour, we will go on to ask ourselves, "What happens to people here?" Even necessity is only what we believe it to be. It ends up basically an esthetic problem to me, a question of unity, of form. You see, my mind goes back to Elizabethan drama where the lines of connection between the state, the polity, the habits of the king, and what went on with the gravedigger were strong lines. We have no structure for his kind of connection. We have to synthesize or formulate one. We have to invest on the stage the connections that finally make the whole. For they exist, however concealed they may be.

Evans: Maybe so, Mr. Miller, but in our discussion you certainly have formulated many fascinating connections—both positive and negative—between your ideas and those of psychology. You have given me very forthright and honest reactions to some very complicated questions, and have not shirked any of them. Thank you very much.

Arthur Miller—Tragedy and Commitment
Robert A. Martin/1969

From *Michigan Quarterly Review,* 8 (1969): 176-178. Reprinted by permission.

R.M.: When a playwright is writing a play, is he always aware of a character as a total person other than what we learn about him in the dialogue? For example, I think you once mentioned that when you were writing *Death of a Salesman* you laughed as you wrote it because all of a sudden everything fell into place. Did everything fall into place with Quentin as you were working on *After the Fall,* so that you could see what was finally going to happen to him?

A.M. Well, only vaguely. I tried, as a matter of fact, to hold off any fixed conclusion for it because—and this is something that is so hard to act in the play, although it sometimes gets done the way I wanted it—I wanted to hold off any fixed conclusion as though to say to myself, "Well, this could end where he all but shoots his brains out," and to leave it suspended in air until the forces worked themselves out into this balance. What I tried to do in the play was to have him say, "Well, yes I see that it has all been a series of betrayals from beginning to end." Some of them for questions of interest; the interests of one party diverged from the other, and he is betrayed on that basis. In another instance, it is a betrayal because people fall out of love despite themselves, so that's a kind of betrayal. It's not a willed one, it just happens that way. There's no question of financial interest involved or of political interest. On any level, therefore, we are inconstant and there is no guarantee. What is required then? It's not to be afraid. It is to say, "Yes, I am fully aware of the impermanence of all arrangements and I choose to commit myself, nevertheless."

R.M. Do you see Quentin as an extension of Chris Keller or Biff Loman? Both those characters are very nearly the same person.

A.M. I hadn't thought of that.

R.M. For example, at the end of *All My Sons,* Kate, the mother asks, "What more can we be?" and Chris says, "there's a universe of people outside and you're responsible to it." In *Death of a Salesman,* Biff, on the other hand, finally recognizes that Willy is Willy, and there are to be no more prizes. But Quentin goes one step beyond that and says in effect, "Well, there is something more there. I may not find it, but I'm going to look for it." And Reverend Hale in *The Crucible* is, in this sense, also much the same person. He also sees finally that it's necessary to face life with a great amount of personal courage.

A.M. These plays are attempting to reflect what I take to be a fact of existence. We're all very discouraged; it's almost the fashion to be despairing. But the birth rate goes up all the time. I mean this is an irony—it's breathtaking. In the most despairing time in civilization, maybe, people go about giving birth to more babies than they ever did before. Now a lot of it, of course, in certain countries like India, is simply a question of scientific inability to institute birth control. But in Western societies, where this is not the problem, having a family, for most people, is an act of faith. They have to believe in the survival, at least over the next generation, of the human race. And the fashion is to believe that it can't survive, that it won't, and the logic of the whole bombs-race and the rest of it is that we're going down the drain at a terrific rate. The easiest thing that I can imagine is to make a case that is hopeless.

R.M. You mean where there's no way out?

A.M. That's the work to me of an afternoon. I can do it on a political level, I can do it on an economic level, etc. Or, I come to the University here, and it's certainly worse than it was the last time I was here, and the last time it was worse than the previous time. And what's my reaction to it? I look at these kids and from the institutional point of view if somebody said, "Well on what basis can you have any hope that you're ever going to reconstitute an atmosphere of learning, an atmosphere of a group of individuals sharing conceptions and thoughts on a human basis? How can you ever hope such a thing will ever happen again?" I couldn't answer that! As far as I can see, it's going to get worse; there'll be 75,000 people here in five years for all I know. They keep getting born, and they have to go someplace. The only thing that I have to counter it all with is when you talk to a kid—not all of them but enough of them—in effect he's saying to you, "I can't stand this." Now if I were the only one that saw that this was the problem, that this was inhuman, then I would say, "Well, look friends, it's all over. Forget the whole thing. Turn all these guys into accountants, put them in the slot and forget the whole idea of education in the old humanistic sense of the word. It's gone." But then you talk to the people who are involved in the whole thing—to some of them—whether it's on the faculty or in the student body, and you see that the dream doesn't die. So what's the answer? The answer is if it doesn't die under these circumstances, there's a terrific validity to it! Because it's getting no support from anywhere. It must be indiginous to the human race that something else is natural; that this is not natural.

So if I were to write a play, let's say, about a university, I would have to document what is the case—that it's grinding itself into a mechanical atmosphere with no human content. And I could say "Well that's it." Then what do I do about my own observation of the people who stand there saying, "It's intolerable?" What does it mean when they say it's intolerable? It means that something in the human heart is being violated by this whole thing. I can't call that hope, but at least I have to lay it on the scale of the balances. I have to project a human nature, in other words, implicitly in the play, which this current situation contradicts, and there's the basic tension. It could be even a tragic tension. I can see somebody finally, in an extreme situation, coming to a bad end because of this kind of conflict.

R.M. Could you write a tragedy about a college professor or a student on the same level that you could write a tragedy about a John Proctor or a Willy Loman?

A.M. Provided that the freight, so to speak, of the events engaged the question of the survival of the civilization in one way or another. If it was tea and sympathy, no. This is a question of a neurosis. It's a question of someone who's afraid of girls, and that, to be sure, is a real problem for some people. But it was always a problem for some people, it's always going to be a problem for some people, and whether he makes it or doesn't make it is not going to change the way we live, or save or destroy the values of a civilization. But if it involved, in the student's or the faculty member's conflict, the refraction of a very important and profound question, yes. Just spitballing it for the moment, what does it involve? It involves the question of how a human being is to regard himself. Is he to settle for his mechanization?" Is he to say, "Well, I will find within this iron box a warm corner." Then you see what happens to him when he finds his warm corner. You see whether it kills his life or expands it. So we're talking again about a potential. I have to throw up on the back screen there some consciousness, some awareness. I have to reflect the audience's awareness that this can't be the fate of man; it's intolerable! I haven't made that up. You wouldn't be able to understand what I was talking about if I'd made it up. You would only react to it by saying, "Yes, I see now that we can't accept it." I think in a tragedy, some way or another, there has to be the question of the survival of that society.

R.M. Or of the individual in the society?

A.M. Yes, but I'm going further.

R.M. Suppose the individual goes under, but the society doesn't? Does that alter your concept of tragedy?

A.M. As I think I've said, we're not dealing with characters on a stage as though they were real people. It looks like they're real people, but the truth of the matter is that they are basically relationships of forces. By the time a play is half an hour old, you may not be consciously aware of it (I'm talking now about a tragic play or a play that is aspiring in that direction), but he is sucking into himself the question of the value of certain posited credos of the society.

R.M. But Willy Loman didn't. He took all the wrong ones.

A.M. Well, we say wrong. He took the common ones. He carried in his pocket the coinage of our day.

R.M. And that destroyed him.

A.M. And that killed him.

R.M. But it can't destroy Quentin.

A.M. No, because he's got his heels dug in. His illusions are not of that sort. He knows better than that.

R.M. John Kennedy once described himself as "an idealist without illusions." Is that the only way that man can survive today?

A.M. I would call Quentin that at the end of the play, or as close as you can get to it. I think Kennedy, by the way, since you mention him, seemed so contemporary to people because of the fact that he never covered up the difficulties of existence with a lot of rhetoric. But he never let go! He represented a kind of balance, or the potential of a balance. You got the feeling that the guy was not illusioned. He was a hard-headed, tough character, but at the same time he was insisting that things need not be this way. And that, I think, was a very accurate reflection of the real contemporary feeling.

The Creative Experience of Arthur Miller: An Interview
Robert A. Martin/1969

From *Educational Theatre Journal,* 21 (1969): 310-317. Reprinted by permission

Martin: What do you think in particular has most influenced you in your work? Some critics have said that Ibsen played an important part. I can see it in *All My Sons,* but in nothing after that.

   Miller: I tell you the truth. I misled people inadvertently at the beginning of my life because of the fact of *All My Sons,* which was a sport. I had written, I don't know, a dozen or more plays earlier which hadn't been produced. I wrote a verse, or near verse, tragedy of Montezuma and Cortez, for example, which had no relation whatsoever to any Ibsenesque theatre. I wrote a rather expressionist play about two brothers in the University when I was a student. It's true I wrote a very realistic play, my first play, a family play.[1] I wrote two or three attempts at purely symbolistic drama, and, when it came time to write *All My Sons,* I was nearing thirty. I had had no success whatsoever with any of these things. That wasn't what bothered me. What bothered me was that I didn't believe in any of these plays that I had written. I couldn't go in front of an audience, or in front of another person, and say that I had been mistreated by the American theater. And why? Because I had not spoken clearly. And so I said to myself, "I am not going to waste my life as I have seen others do." I knew writers who were then in their 40's and older, who went on and one writing things which they lamented nobody would do. And I read them and said, "Well, I wouldn't do them either. If I had the money, I wouldn't put it in this play. I see the intent is very high, but the god damn play doesn't work." And I said to myself, "Well, do something which is first of all clear." And I worked two years on hammering that thing out. Now, inevitably it reflected the Ibsen kind of narration, but I never cottoned to him in the way that is thought, not really.

Martin: Are you saying then that most of the plays you've written from *All My Sons* through *The Price* are really expressions of what you, at another point, called, "what's in the air?"

Miller: Yes. In the air in that I never thought of the theater as journalism in the sense of what's in the air. You know, "this is what people will be interested in," because I don't know that. I have no way of knowing that. I'm always surprised at what people are doing, and I'm always surprised at what they're interested in. I know what interests me. When I do know it I write a play, and when I don't know it I go for a long time without writing a play.

Martin: So most of your plays have been about things that are immediate?

Miller: Well, I suppose they seem immediate because they're immediate to me. I make them immediate, in other words, or in some cases I don't. For instance, *Incident at Vichy* is for a large number of people simply "old hat." It's something that happened 25 years ago and who the hell wants to talk about that?

Martin: You mentioned earlier that the ideas for some of your work came from stories told to you by someone. Is that true also of your plays?

Miller: No. It is true of, for example, *All My Sons*. That play was based on a real incident. There wasn't a son involved but the daughter of a manufacturer in the United States who turned him in during the war. I never knew the people involved, and it turned out that it wasn't a daughter, but a son in my play. All I knew was just what I told you, that this had happened in the MIddle West. I never saw it in the paper or anything. But that was, I would say, the only play.

Martin: And *Incident at Vichy?*

Miller: And *Incident at Vichy* was based, yes, upon an incident that was told to me.[2]

Martin: That brings me to another question. Yesterday we were talking about contemporary themes in a play, and if you look at all of your plays, on a historical basis at least, you can see that *Death of a Salesman* was about something that was current. *The Crucible* was also about something that was current in a slightly different way.

Miller: Except, think of it this way. Suppose I hadn't written *The Crucible,* suppose it didn't exist. Do you realize that there was no play on the American stage at all, good, bad, or indifferent, about this subject? The point I'm making is that the American writer did not respond to this subject. I don't know this, but I can't off-hand recall a novel about it. I'm sure there must have been something written, but I couldn't tell you what it was.

Martin: Are you talking now about the witchcraft trials or the McCarthy hearings?

Miller: No, the McCarthy affair or anything to do with it. In effect, if I hadn't written *The Crucible* that period would be unregistered in our literature, on any popular level. That is, on a level outside of scholars writing about it or articles. But as far as literature is concerned, it didn't exist. So, therefore, when one says "It was in the air," I *made* it in the air, and here's a good example of it. Now look at *Death of a Salesman.* I don't know of another play which dealt with the question of what one could call the ordinary man's strangulation by the system of values that was going on. You can say, "That was in the air." Well, it congealed in my head, so to speak, and I nailed it to the historical wall. Therefore, it isn't a question of reporting something, you see, it's a question of creating a synthesis that has never existed before out of common materials that are otherwise chaotic and unrelated.

Martin: If we move then from the background of *The Crucible* toward your writing *After the Fall,* let me ask this. If you take what you feel is in the air and "make it in the air," is it correct to say that the issues raised in *After the Fall* are concerned thematically with an idea that's been in your plays for a long time?

Miller: Right.

Martin: But isn't *After the Fall* a quite different play from any of your previous ones? There is a rather definite critical tendency to see *After the Fall* as being more autobiographical. That is, it is about, according to certain critics, Arthur Miller and Marilyn Monroe. Can you actually separate the man who writes a play about Salem in 1692 (which happens to have many parallels with McCarthyism) from the man who writes a play about two marriages that failed and a Congressional hearing? I think the autobiographical intrudes in *After the Fall* more directly than in any of your plays, and consequently leads critics to an autobiographical conclusion on the internal evidence of the play itself.

Miller: Yes, that's right. The only thing is, let's suppose you pick up a novel by anybody—Thackeray, Meredith, Jane Austen,

Dickens—and you're not a scholar in that period. Of course, this is a
long time since they've written it, but even if you went back 25 years
we could say the same thing I'm about to say. Unquestionably in
Meredith's time, when he was alive, and in Dickens' time, when he
was alive, when it came to light that Dickens, indeed, had been
obsessed with prisons, for personal reasons, what did this do to the
work? Well, what the hell is the difference? I'm not reading Dickens
now, if I do read him, because he was obsessed with prisons. I'm
reading him because the work itself has some truth in it—for me,
some generalized truth. Now if he had never been anywhere near a
prison, would that make it any less or more true, or more valuable as
a work of art? It wouldn't. It's only, it seems to me, an easy way out
for people who will not or cannot examine the work at hand. So what
they do is examine the author.

Martin: Would you say then, in spite of the resemblances in *After
the Fall* to your own life, such as two marriages, being called before a
Congressional committee, etc., that although they came from certain
experiences in your life, they have no direct relevance to the play? I
think there is, perhaps, a case to be made that the play represents
some part of your own life. But let's assume that it's a foundation, an
experience. When it all goes into the play do you consciously exclude
part of it? Would you say, for example, that nothing in the play is
based on any conversation or any experience that you actually had?

Miller: No. You see, the thing to me that is of interest, that is at
stake, so to speak, is the synthesis made of the material, rather than
whether this is or is not actually a fact in the person's life. I've had
people tell me that they knew some character in one of my plays (not
After the Fall), and I'd say, "Really, who and where is he?" Well, it
turns out that I'd never been in the place where they were talking
about. I'd never heard of these people. I take it as a species of
compliment, really, that it was so real that they could see this
character and say, "That must have been the fellow."

Ibsen wrote *Hedda Gabler* for example. In the first performance
somebody in the audience detected that the age he had given Hedda
was chronologically impossible. I've forgotten how it worked exactly
with the mathematics involved, but it's as though he had said that she
was 24 years old and an experience that she refers to is an historical
event in Norway that happened 40 years ago. So she would have
had to be 60 years old in order to have shared it. Do you see what I
mean? Well, why did that happen? It happened because he slipped,

you see. He was talking about the real woman. Now, who the hell cares? That play is either a play that's integral to itself or it isn't. It has no value, or isn't devalued, because it was about this woman or it wasn't about the woman. Look at *When We Dead Awaken* or *The Master Builder.* Ibsen himself happened to have been involved with a young girl.

Martin: So it makes no difference whether the playwright is in the play or not, if the play has a universal truth?

Miller: Of course not. It's an absurdity because that's looking at it like a first-person narrative the other way. Now consider the tortures of Tolstoy in relation to his own wife; it wouldn't take a genius to see them in *Anna Karenina.* You can see his whole inability to settle on what a woman was or his own sensuality, which was what drove him finally near madness.

Martin: In an article you published in *Life* (February 7, 1964) you wrote of *After the Fall* that "the play is neither an apology nor the arraignment of others,—quite simply, overtly, and clearly, it is a statement of commitment to one's own actions." In the context you're talking about Quentin, but I was wondering if you had any sense of a personal commitment to one's actions that was intended as a reply to some of the criticism of *After the Fall?*

Miller: Yes. I wanted there to direct attention to what the play was dealing with in order to arrive at some judgment as to what I'd written as opposed to what was attributed to me personally. Because otherwise there is no way to say anything at all about the play. It's a circular argument. In other words, what do you say to Stephen Crane who writes *The Red Badge of Courage.* Supposing he'd done that last week and you say, "What division were you in?" He says, "I wasn't in any division." "Well, where did you find out about the Army?" He says, "I never did." "You didn't do any research?" "No." "Well, then this can't be true." "Well, I don't know," Crane says, "does it seem true?" That's the only answer.

Martin: Yes, and I think that's the right one.

Miller: What other answer can there be? See, we're living in an age of such journalism. We're flooded with publicity and reportage in a way that is obvious no other civilization ever was. Between the television, and the movie magazines, and the newspapers, we've lost any respect for the imagination of man or any sense of what it means to synthesize experience.

Martin: Is this all related to why it's so hard to write a tragedy? If we have lost our ability to synthesize, then what can you as a playwright say abut the individual human condition in a society that to many people seems to be flying apart?

Miller: Well, a worship of fact—by fact I mean in the crudest sense—is always an obstruction if one is looking for the truth. There's a difference between the facts and the truth; the truth is a synthesis of facts. We now see the reflection of a technological age where facts are king. That is to say, the president doesn't make a speech until he finds out through polls what people are thinking, then he addresses that poll. He's not addressing people any more. The idea of asserting a synthesized meaning any more from experience is suspect. And that's why, I think, we've gotten to the point where someone could write in the *New York Times,* as one critic did in reviewing a book by Harold Clurman, that it's much harder to write a good review than a good play. It's come to that. You see, the critics now, by virtue of their frequency in the press and their command of the publicity apparatus, as opposed to the rarity with which a playwright can possibly produce a play, have come to the point where they are the center of the situation. They're no longer waiting upon the work of art; the work of art is simply an excuse for them to write a criticism, to express *themselves*, because that criticism verges more closely upon what we call fact. It's more objective; it isn't this suspect subjective thrust. It is an objective thing. We respect that much more, believe in it much more. Maybe it is all a fear of feeling; the equal validity of felt knowledge.

Martin: I wanted to ask you about a remark by Leslie Fiedler. He says that you and Paddy Chayefsky "create crypto-Jewish characters; characters who are in habit, speech, and condition of life typically Jewish-American, but who are presented as something else—general-American say, as in *Death of a Salesman,* or Italo-American, as in *Marty.*" Fiedler calls this "a loss of artistic faith, a failure to remember that the inhabitants of Dante's Hell or Joyce's Dublin are more universal as they are more Florentine or Irish."[3] And other critics have suggested that Willy Loman is really a Jewish character. Do you have any particular point of view about being Jewish yourself? Have you ever thought of a play about a Jewish family that is clearly Jewish?

Miller: My first play, written at The University of Michigan in 1934, I think, was about a Jewish family. It was produced by the Hillel Foundation and got me three awards. I've written about twenty full-length plays and maybe fifteen one-acters and can't go through them all now, but I imagine two or three of those were about Jews as Jews. This is Fiedler's problem, not mine. Where the theme seems to me to require a Jew to act somehow in terms of his Jewishness, he does so. Where it seems to me irrelevant what the religious or cultural background of character may be, it is treated as such. In *A View From the Bridge* they are Sicilians because the social code which kills Eddie Carbone is made in Sicily and it must be localized before it can be extended to all people. I see nothing in *Salesman, All My Sons, After the Fall,* or *The Crucible* which is of that nature. *Incident at Vichy* deals directly with the anti-Semitic problem so there are Jewish characters. Similarly, Gregory Solomon in *The Price* has to be Jewish, for one thing because the theme of survival, of a kind of acceptance of life, seemed to me to point directly to the Jewish experience through centuries of oppression. For me it is the theme that rules these choices. Fiedler's opinions in this instance seem to me irrational. He reminds me of the time somebody in *Commentary* magazine accused me of changing my name from some other name.

Martin: You mean your own name rather than a character in a play?

Miller: Yes, Miller. This kind of thing can get pretty vile, you know. My family's name has been Miller as far back as I know anything about. My mother thought one side was named Mahler in Europe, but she wasn't sure. Miller happens to be a fairly common name for Jews and others in Europe. It is all part of the same parochialism which is expressed now in sophisticated terms. The Jews in Fiedler's novels—or novel—I only read one, were not Jews to me so much as figments; they are outside my experience, which may be my lack. But their being Jewish certainly doesn't help their universality.

Martin: So then a Jewish writer couldn't write another *Ulysses* . . . ?

Miller: Neither could a Gentile, could he? I understand what this kind of critic is saying; that a Jewish writer cannot obtain any universality unless he writes about Jewish people as such. But I write about what reflects *my* experience. I come from people who rarely, if ever, spoke Yiddish. I had no doubt I was Jewish, but I simply wasn't brought up the way Fiedler evidently thinks I should have been.

By the way, since Joyce has come up—in order to universalize the Irish he used a Jewish hero. Now that's odd, isn't it?

Martin: Then all the names for your characters, Loman, Keller . . .

Miller: Well, they're as Jewish as Miller.

Martin: But they're not intentionally a neutralization?

Miller: No, but there's another thing too. You see, I don't believe and never did, because of the peculiarity of my own experience, in the uniqueness of the Jew in terms of his relationship to society. There are differences, but I would have to labor—belabor—a play, put it that way. I would have to really work at it, provided we're talking about anything fundamental.

Martin: Anything in your plays, then, that reflects a Jewish characteristic is only incidental?

Miller: Not incidental—organic, as Jewishness is in me. Why don't they say that John Proctor is "really" Jewish? Well, you see, I could answer that. I could say that John Proctor *is* Jewish. I could make a whole thesis about the Jewishness of the Puritan ideology, which, after all, is based not on the New Testament but on the Old. The names did not come from the New Testament, they came from the Old Testament. For all I know this very well may have helped to attract me to the period. But I fail to understand what this has to do with *The Crucible's* value as a play.

Martin: Then what you are intentionally trying to do in a play is to write about man in the universal sense and not in any particular sense.

Miller: I am trying to write about man as I see him. I've written short stories, for instance, about Jewish people. In a book of short stories I've had published, *I Don't Need You Anymore,* the lead story is about a little Jewish boy.

Martin: As you said that I was just thinking of Newman in *Focus* who looks Jewish but who isn't.

Miller: Yes, I take all this as an accusation that somehow I'm "passing" for non-Jewish. Well, I happen to have written the first book about anti-Semitism in this country in this recent time.[4] I've written numerous stories about Jews as Jews. In this book of nine short stories (and some of these stories go back fifteen years) four of the nine stories are about Jewish people who are obviously Jewish people. And this is no new discovery on my part. In other words, some of these stories were written, as I say, in 1951 and 1952, which is roughly when I started publishing stories.

Martin: It occurred to me when I read Fiedler's comment that anyone who tried to write plays reflecting *only* his particular ethnic and cultural background probably wouldn't have much to say that would be dramatically relevant.

Miller: No, I don't think so either. But it's different in different cultures and with different writers. In this country, I would have to be belaboring something. I'm talking now from my experience, from what I know. To me it's simply an aspect of the narrowed vision. They were probably brought up with people who were in a different position vis-à-vis the immigration in this country, and they can't conceive that anybody would have been brought up any differently. My mother was born in this country. My father came over when he was five years old. He grew up to be six feet two inches tall with blue eyes and red hair and everybody thought he was an Irishman. So, consequently, I didn't get exactly that kind of an identification.

Martin: Would you say then that being Jewish isn't important to you as a playwright?

Miller: It gets important to me as I try to decide the genesis of some of my ideas and feelings historically. For instance, the persistence in my work and in myself of a refusal to adopt a nihilistic attitude. I realize that a non-Jewish writer could have the same aversion, and obviously some do, but there would be possibly different reasons for it. My feeling is that when you sell nihilism, so to speak, you are creating the grounds for nihilistic destruction, and the first one to get it is the Jew. It even happens in the most strange situations. You see, the Jew is always the one, or most of the time, who stands at the crack of the civilization, in geology it's the shearing point. For instance, in Harlem, the militant Negroes have adopted a terrific anti-Semitism. Why? Because there are a lot of Jewish storekeepers in Harlem. They are the face of the white society; it's what they see there. Now these Jewish storekeepers, in terms of the whole bourgeoisie, are in fact the most powerless part of the bourgeoisie because nobody would have a store in Harlem if he could help it. It's not exactly the most gracious life you could imagine. A Jew who could develop a business in a neighborhood with less social stress and strain, who wouldn't be afraid to go to work in the morning and go home at night, I'm sure would do it if he could manage it.

I think, therefore, that part of my struggle with nihilism may well express my Jewishness. For example, much of this struggle in *After the Fall,* comes from some very old and imbedded sense that nihilism ends up with a club in its hand. That's one of the arguments that I have with a lot of the contemporary celebration of nihilism and I would love to say to some of these guys, "Watch out now, this is liable to get real." The roots of my aversion may well be Jewish, but my concern is for the country as a whole.

[1]*The Man Who Had All the Luck* (1944).

[2]Miller has also attributed the origins of two other plays to stories that were told to him. In the "Introduction" to his *Collected Plays* (1957), he says of *The Man Who Had All the Luck* (1944): "I had heard the story of a young man in a midwestern town" (p. 14). In discussing *A View from the Bridge* (1955), he states: "I had heard its story years before, quite as it appears in the play" (p. 47).

[3]Leslie Fiedler, *Waiting for the End* (New York, 1965), p. 91.

[4]*Focus*, (1945).

Interview
Ronald Hayman/1970

From *Arthur Miller* (London: Heinemann 1970). pp.1-14. Reprinted by permission

Ronald Hayman: I wanted to ask you about the Willy Lomans we saw in England, Frederick March in the film and Paul Muni on stage as compared with Lee J. Cobb. Who gave you most of what you wanted?

Arthur Miller: Lee Cobb did it the best from my viewpoint. I felt that—that to take the movie first—Freddie March played him as though he were insane. It was a psycho-drama of some sort, and it was not at all his fault; Freddie's a very good actor—he could easily have done it. It was the fault of the director and the screen-writer, who saw the play in totally psychiatric terms—in part I think because they were afraid of the subject matter at that time—the play was very doubtful about American mores and the American system. Actually when they did that play into a movie, Columbia Pictures manufactured a trailer—a short movie on their own to precede the showing of *Death of a Salesman* in all the theatres and that movie was an attempt to extol the trade of salesmanship and to show that in reality and contrary to the movie you were about to see, it was one of the most rewarding professions that a man could follow in this country. It was cultural MacCarthyism and it occurred just about the time the play was being attacked in this country as a time bomb set by Communists to blow up the country. I forbade the showing of the short or trailer and they never showed it. But part of the reason for making Willy seem mad was to take the pressure off what he was talking about.

Paul Muni played it in London and he didn't do it right in the sense that he had come to a time in his career when he was listening to his own voice—he was a very good actor but his style had been superseded twenty years earlier really. The style was too studied, too technical. There was too little real inner life in his performance.

Cobb was the best. As often happens, the man who creates the role originally has the advantage of discovering it all new. And when you discover something in that way you invest yourself in it; you don't protect yourself from it quite the way later people do from the performances that preceded them, to do something else even though it may be wrong just to individuate themselves. Cobb was in it, and he of course is personally that way anyway. His nature is superbly fitted for that role.

Ronald Hayman: In some ways *The Price* seems to be closer to *All My Sons* and *Death of a Salesman* than any of the intervening plays in the sense that it goes back in a way to the father and two sons' relationship even though the father is dead.

Arthur Miller: From my point of view, the whole son-father thing is a dried husk in that play. You see it isn't really operative in the way it was in the others. Basically what I was interested in in *The Price* was what it takes to be a person who refuses to be swept away and seduced to the values of the society. It is in one sense the price of integrity. In other words the policeman has refused to adopt the sex and success motives of the society. He has walled himself up against them and he has kept a certain kind of perverse integrity as a result of that but you see what he pays for that. Still, he is saner than Walter, with a hold on reality. So basically what is involved in the forefront of the play is the question of what it takes—the deformations that both viewpoints take in this society. The deformations that are taken on by people who are able somehow to block themselves off from the sweep of opportunity and the never-never land that society promises. The father-son thing is a superficial part of this play, its occasion rather than its subject.

Ronald Hayman: But doesn't the guilt of the father play quite a large part in the pre-history of the play as it does in *All My Sons?*

Arthur Miller: Yes, but hopefully, you see I wish another writer would have written it, I mean a writer who'd never written of fathers and sons. I purposely leave the father uncharacterized except the misunderstood past, the dead matrix from which the others have sprung. He himself no longer makes any demands, but the sons are struggling with his values in themselves. He is simply there as a shadow really—in fact they neither forgive him nor remember him. He is finally absolved by the others. But it's all now.

Ronald Hayman: But Victor is trapped in something that, had he resisted the father more, he could have—

Arthur Miller: But that is of course so long ago. And he even sees through it himself. The father had diminished in his size—he only has the last laugh, to be sure, as the dead always do because they made us, because they are in us even as we reject them.

Ronald Hayman: I read some critic who said you considered yourself dramaturgically a descendant of Ibsen.

Arthur Miller: It all comes from one essay I wrote. What I was saying was that you can no more dismiss Ibsen than you can dismiss some kind of architecture that has given birth to other kinds of architecture. He was a strong influence on my early youth but I have no debt to him in the sense that one is insisting upon recreating him all the time. What he gave me in the beginning was a sense of the past and a sense of the rootedness of everything that happens.

Ronald Hayman: How do you feel though about these plays like Pinter's, which almost reject the past altogether in the sense that you never get to know the character's history?

Arthur Miller: I think of them quite frankly as a kind of naturalism, and by that I mean that in ordinary contact in life you don't ever get very much of somebody's past. You infer and impute things to people but what they're doing is of course in the present. I like his work very much. I can't help wishing, though, that such forcefully built trees would form more tangible fruit.

Ronald Hayman: But a lot of your plays like *The Price* could be interpreted in a Freudian way. You can see Victor as conditioned by his father.

Arthur Miller: Oh certainly. You see I'm not trying to give an impression of life. I'm trying to analyse something and therefore the past is something you must take into acount—it's simply impossible to individuate people in my opinion without it and I don't think we want any past any more in any way. Solomon in *The Price* says it better than I could say it. Nobody wants that kind of furniture because it *implies* a past and it implies that the past can't be broken. They want to go shopping. You see they want a new lease on life, they want to feel they have infinite options, limitless choices. He says there's no more possibilities when you've got furniture like this. You're limited by the past—and of course you are. And it's delusory to think otherwise. I think it's an escape and a romantic one into the bargain. But I'm in a small minority. Most of the art we have is assuming the past isn't there. But I don't think they're dealing most of the time with people, they're dealing with constructs of attitudes to an existence, openly and unabashed. But the past, looked at bravely, can liberate as well as imprison you in repetitions of its illusion.

Ronald Hayman: How important do you think the element of mimicry is in playwriting?

Arthur Miller: I am a good mimic. I can speak in any dialect I've ever heard. It's very important to me, to know accents and the way people talk, especially in this country where speech and speech mannerisms and habits of language are so deeply connected with attitudes. We have so many different kinds of immigrants, from the Negro to the Swede to the Jew to the Italian. A playwright writes with his ears.

Ronald Hayman: When did you move out of New York?

Arthur Miller: Not until I went to college, when I was nineteen. Then I went to the Middle West, to Michigan, but up to then I was in New York all the time. I was born in Harlem. I went to grammar school there, and I was part of the time in Brooklyn. But it's the same kind of people basically, except that there were no Negroes in Brooklyn at that time but the other groups were all there. So it's always been part of my life. I was born and brought up in New York City and what somebody was was always connected with what his ethnic background was. I couldn't think except in terms of the differentiation of speech.

Ronald Hayman: I believe you enjoyed writing *The Crucible* more than you enjoyed writing any of the other plays. I wonder why you've never gone back to a historical play.

Arthur Miller: I might do that again. It was fun because of the fact that I needn't make up the whole story. I didn't do it again I suppose because I never thought of another period that was so relevant to ours and maybe there isn't any. It was a lot of joy—you can just work on the writing. It takes me a year to invent a story. It required an immense amount of sheer editing, you might say. In fact there were hundreds of people involved in this thing as there always are in historical events. I've got five judges in the one judge.

Ronald Hayman: Does it take you longer to invent a story now than it did when you started, because I believe you wrote fourteen or fifteen full length plays before *All My Sons*.

Arthur Miller: No I don't think it takes any longer. It took two years for me to write *All My Sons* which has got a very involved story. I don't think that anything has taken me that long to write since.

Ronald Hayman: You used to write in verse—I wonder whether you still do—and then rewrite in prose.

Arthur Miller: I've done that. I didn't do it on *The Price* because it had no relevancy to that. I've been writing verse for years, but primarily as an exercise, to contract and squeeze the language and clear the mind. So I was never interested in becoming a professional poet. I still do it. But I don't want an audience thinking they're listening to verse because it's beside the point now but I do want them to feel that they're getting a packed, a dense speech without their taking note of the fact that it's at all odd. Maybe I've succeeded too well in fact, because it is one of the criticisms of my work from time to time that it lacks poetry. My attempt has been to make it simply dense, just to advance the action that much more quickly and it's also more pleasurable. I think it's more beautiful that way. Basically what I'm after is the compression of the psychological and social into forward-moving speech with the requisite consciousness. The theatre has to this day never caught up with the consciousness ordinary people have of their social situation. Anyone who goes into a factory and listens to the way people talk, they're way ahead of the theatre, they're so often quite aware that they're right snugly inside a real cul-de-sac in relation to society. You can't talk five minutes with anybody without talking sociology, be he a plumber or a carpenter or anything else. But it is done from his vantage point, with his ignorance and his stupidity and his knowledge. And the compression is purely and simply the compression of his personality and the social attitudes he has without violating his lack of awareness or underrating it.

A good example is Solomon. The ellipses that go into those speeches, the packing of his . . . Now of course everybody thinks that it's a great Yiddish accent but in truth the involution of those speeches in which he is relating his own desperation at the age of ninety, trying to decide whether to live or die in effect and the social milieu in which he finds himself—you see it's all webbed together. It is compressed. And I try to do that in everything I can.

Ronald Hayman: Did you find it a problem in *A View from the Bridge* moving from the poetic speech of Alfieri to the plain speech of the others?

Arthur Miller: Yes I did. You see that story is—to anybody who knows plain Sicilians or Calabrian people—that story is age-old. I didn't know it when I heard it the first time, but just telling it around a few times to people who lived on the waterfront where I used to live, it was quite obvious that—in its details it was a little different but basically the orphan girl or the niece who is not quite a blood relation living in the house is a stick of dynamite which always ends badly and the betrayal by an individual in a passion—his betrayal of some group is part of it, generally. It had myth-like resonance for me. I didn't feel I was making anything up, but rather recording something old and marvellous. I might add that Raf Vallone has toured Italy three times with it and especially in the small southern towns the people, he tells me, react to it almost as a rite.

Ronald Hayman: So in that sense it was a historical play too?

Arthur Miller: It was. Yeah. I did know a lawyer who worked down on the waterfront—he had nothing to do with this story actually—he'd come from a Neapolitan family and he used to laughingly say 'They're just going through all the Greek myths down here'. Every week somebody comes and has done or has thought of doing one of the great tragic stories. I sensed a feeling of powerlessness in him; I mean that he'd got to feel that he knew what was going to happen before it happened. And there he was standing just picking up the pieces, and that was the feeling I wanted to get over. So I wanted to lift the language above mere everyday language without giving him too stiff a quality or he couldn't have related to these people. In fact, in life, he did elevate his language with them as he strove for some authority over their passions.

Ronald Hayman: How did you feel about the way it was done in London?

Arthur Miller: The problem there again for me—you see they couldn't approximate the dialect. There was just no way to do that, so they made up a dialect of their own but I could never feel at home with it, though the average English audience didn't know the difference. It's probably the way we do a British lord—if you heard it your hair would stand up. But I thought Peter Brook had managed the staging beautifully. His set was quite apt, useful and kind of inevitable. And Quayle did get a sense of the sheer brute gigantic quality of the guy, which is what he'd have to have. And the fellow who played Marco, this Scottish actor—

Ronald Hayman: Ian Bannen

Arthur Miller: Ian Bannen was terrific in it but it was more related to Scotland basically than it was to Brooklyn. But I think they should do that. They'd have to make a false and tenuous relation to Brooklyn if they made a relation to wherever they came from and whatever they came out of.

Ronald Hayman: But could the production have done more to integrate Alfieri into the action?

Arthur Miller: Alfieri shouldn't be all that integrated. He is objective, after all. In life, I mean. But perhaps you're right. It was done very simply off-Broadway here—the mixture of contact with Eddie and distance. There was no possibility to disintegrate the relationship because the theatre was only as big as a living-room. When you get up on a big stage it's a question of connecting people; when you're on a small stage it's a question of separating them.

Ronald Hayman: I was very interested to see there was a page of typescript of yours in that *Paris Review* interview you gave . . .

Arthur Miller: That was a weird thing you know. I had been interviewed three or four months earlier than the moment I'm about to tell you of and suddenly they called me up and said, 'Give us anything, something preferably with your handwriting on it.' So I reached in a cabinet where there's a whole pile of undifferentiated paper, perhaps five thousand sheets that go back for twenty years. Maybe five pages of a play I never went on with or twenty pages or it could be two and a half acts that I'd forgotten completely I'd written, and I picked up this lump and there was what seemed to be a fairly amusing page—that is to say one got some feeling out of it. I had no more idea of writing a play with Solomon in it at that time than of writing a play about the Empire State Building, and it was only after the play was opened that somebody mentioned this. It was total accident. I must have started fifty plays in my life that are in that stage.

Ronald Hayman: I took it to be an earlier draft.

Arthur Miller: Well evidently it was but you see it was a very primitive attempt—I was just sort of playing around on a keyboard with that. I was fooling around with his speech on that page, with the unexpectedness of his speech. Every time he opens his mouth he says not quite what you expected him to say. He's himself, you see, He can't be led anywhere. He appears to be going the way you're going but it turns out he never is. It was a weird coincidence—then a short time after I started to work on *The Price* with that character. I must have been ready to have made that selection but I didn't know it.

Ronald Hayman: How much did you get out of that playwriting course you did at Michigan?

Arthur Miller: I got probably one most valuable thing—you see when I started out there was no off-Broadway. There was absolutely no place to produce a play except in the commercial theatre, which even then we knew was dying. So one needed an audience and it provided that.

Ronald Hayman: But do you think that playwriting is something that can be taught beyond giving useful criticism of scripts?

Arthur Miller: It's taught anyway. Nobody who has never been in a theatre or never seen a television show or never seen a movie starts writing plays. It's a conventional form. I don't think you can ever teach anybody to be a playwright who isn't a playwright. Out of that class in Michigan I don't know of another playwright. So that's the answer. But their viewpoint was correct: they said 'It'll make them better audiences.'

Ronald Hayman: Do you think of the size of an audience that you're communicating with?

Arthur Miller: I don't think of it as such but I can't imagine obliterating the whole thought. I mean the play is so manifestly a communicating mechanism.

Ronald Hayman: But when you were writing *The Misfits* and thinking of what must be a mass audience for a film you didn't have to simplify beyond what you would in writing for the stage.

Arthur Miller: The reason I'm not a good movie writer and not at home in it is just that. It is wrong of me to do that but I do find myself simplifying. I'm not sure it's that I think the audience is dumber. There's something cruder about the mechanism of the movie—it makes everything—even the so-called philosophical films are strangely banal finally. I suppose it's the fact that words are very much the product of a specific culture and they have ambiguities that are much more subtle than anything you see, it seems to me. Maybe that's why it's so difficult to arrive at a satisfactory dramatic form now, because society is so contradictory that the vocabulary can't socialize experience any more. And images—you believe in it because it's there but that sort of truth is, by itself, rather superficial after all.

Ronald Hayman: Would this be tied up with the reason that you're more interested—as you put it yesterday—in analysing rather than in giving an impersonation of life?

Arthur Miller: I've always done the same thing really in one way or another—and that is to show the process. It's the way my mind works—to ask how something came to be what it is, rather than to play along the apparent surfaces of things to give a sense of what they are . . .

Ronald Hayman: Or to show them in the process of becoming what they are—we see Victor as he has become, we hear about how he has become it.

Arthur Miller: The same thing with Willy Loman or anyone else in my plays. And that's a foregone or a foresworn aim now, it appears to me. It's probably because so many theories of how one becomes anything are so exploded now. But it's also I think that nobody really wants to be positioned as being responsible for what he's doing and if you invoke that idea it's very dubious to people if only because it implies that they must and can make choices and exercise will.

Ronald Hayman: Are you interested in this Hippy movement as a playwright? You use a policeman who is a drop-out from society but you haven't handled any young characters in the recent plays.

Arthur Miller: Actually I've been fooling with an original film script in which the leading character might be called hip.

Ronald Hayman: You made a remark about a playwright needing special knowledge of a subject.

Arthur Miller: Yeah, I think that in the little area in which he works he ought to be or to feel he is the expert. I think he should have special knowledge. Otherwise it becomes derivative—I think that's the problem now. A lot of these people there are deriving their impressions from the other person: there's a great mythology now as to what—for example you mentioned the Hippies—as to what they are, what they're about and who they are. And there's a curious thing about it—you can never really find one, they're always referring to somebody else. One almost believes it's a figment of advertising, a lot of people chasing a mode. If you approach somebody as a hippy you are going to get nowhere, because after all he is a citizen and a person, far less certain than the mode would have him, far more susceptible of pain. That's why I think even in all the years that have gone by since the Hippy thing started and with all the writers who are involved in it, no Hippy qua Hippy has popped up in a work in a convincing way as a human being. It's a strange thing. You would think that somebody would have come along with the Willy Loman of the Hippies, the archetype. And I have a feeling that it's because so much of the attitude that is called Hippy is so outer-related—it's so much a self-conscious thing that it has no reverberations, it has no depth—they are never seen as private people, always as examples.

Ronald Hayman: But there's a sort of movement of fashion now isn't there against the idea of the possibility of being wholly known—you use that phrase about Eddie Carbone. In a sense all your central characters need to become wholly known.

Arthur Miller: It's quite the opposite now—the need now is to become a more or less distinct possibility but by no means become wholly known because it must be false—it would contradict the unpredictability of life. The whole idea of process is out of the window—it is gone—it's unstylish, it's unfashionable because nothing has happened as it should have, supposedly. And my reaction to it is that it simply means that the capacity for sensing reality has been defective and one must develop better sensory apparatus to find out what's going on, rather than relapsing into a kind of self-satisfied feeling that since everything is unpredictable, to hell with it and live for tomorrow morning and so on. That kind of demoralization was always present, though; it simply lacked a triumphant stylishness.

Ronald Hayman: Would I be right in thinking that for you the process of writing *After the Fall* was some such experience of thinking your way through a patch of experience in which you had to put yourself into a play in a different way from which you ever did before?

Arthur Miller: Yeah, well it's an attempt to find some viable synthesis of the experience instead of simply roaming around in the experience, which leaves the experience where it was you know, to try to render the chaos and at the same time to seek out whatever structure it has. *The Price* goes in the other direction more—it emphasizes the structuring of experience because it is a play about the impact of the past but there are endless possibilities which I don't think I've reached yet in the direction of doing two things at the same time. I suppose by structure I always mean the same thing which is a paradox—that's the existence of fate, or high probability, which means that when a man starts out to do what he intends to do, he creates forces which he never bargained for, but whose contradictions nevertheless spring dialectically from the force of his thrust. I think this is true of almost every play. And then he's got to relate himself to what the results of his actions were. It's true of Eddie Carbone, it's true of Willy Loman, it's true of John Proctor. What I find myself trying to face more and more openly is the existence of human will as an ultimate category. I tried to do it in *After the Fall*—I mean at the end of the play he has to decide that it is at least equally real that when he wakes up in the morning, he feels like a boy, he feels wonderful in spite of all this and that that sense of life and promise is also possibly valid. . . . In other words to choose to use that energy which is the energy towards life as opposed to simply giving way to the desolation of what he knows to be the result of experience. For the latter is a cancelling-out of the life force that he knows he feels alongside of despair. A decision has to be made. And in *The Price* a man is faced with the fact that he participated in his own alienation from himself and in so doing discovers himself in what he did. In short, a far higher consciousness of our own powers over life still awaits us as a breed. I might add that in this lies a real revolution. Victor Franz refuses to merely rediscover the love he put into the house and finally persists in seeing it as a value, whatever others made of it.

Ronald Hayman: But doesn't the play in a sense act as his accomplice in exculpating him—I mean the guilt of the father, from the way it's brought in in the second act, does seem to be an explanation of what's happened, as though Dad is responsible?

Arthur Miller: Except that ultimately as it turns out he knew that the old man had something. So it's split. I can't say—I don't think anybody can—that it was all him or all so to speak the society or the past. But there's a point comes where one has to move, with insufficient evidence, always.

Ronald Hayman: But does this work for you as completely as you'd like it to? I think it succeeds in large measure but what I can't a hundred per cent accept is the relationship which you establish very forcibly at the beginning of the play about the impossibility of living according to the ideal and then the narrowing of the focus to these personal relationships in which the family doesn't seem to be entirely effective as an incarnation of Society for the play's purposes.

Arthur Miller: It works to this degree and that is that ultimately the mystery remains as to where the decisive spring is, and I like that about it. It's open. I've tried as far as I could to set forth the balance of evidence and I don't know how else you can set forth an organism otherwise—excepting in some extreme situations which by their extremity are not interesting. I guess the impulse I had was more to open up a life and its process than to lay judgement, in the sense that the two forces were laid bare to the point where the man could recognize himself in his own actions. When this play starts he says, 'I can't find myself in what I've done'—until he discovers again that he did love the old man; it's the recrudescence of that feeling that illuminates for him how he got into this—so that his experience becomes his own then rather than some imposed unreality. That is the story structure of the thing to me—the web of social and individual impulses which form a fate.

Ronald Hayman: One of the things I like very much about it is that it doesn't take him to any extreme action as your early central characters have often had to be carried to in order to expose themselves.

Arthur Miller: Yeah well that's a limitation as well in my sense of the reality of this kind of a man. He couldn't have done what he did with the discipline with which he did it and then suddenly break with the whole character that he's got. This too is unacceptable today. You see it implies that people have limits. What we're presented with all the time is somebody suddenly doing something which is absolutely inexplicable by any standards for the theatrical effect. And it is easier to do that because, again, nobody on the stage has a past any more.

Ronald Hayman: In a sense *After the Fall* is the play in which you've come most directly to grips with this kind of battle against disintegration and it was a great pity that the reaction to it was obviously so utterly different from what you'd expected.

Arthur Miller: They never dealt with the play in any way, shape or fashion. There's a threatening idea in it. What it's saying in effect is that choice is still there, necessary and implicit and that the disaster is there and that you choose to hope because you are alive and don't commit suicide, which implies a certain illusionism and so forth but the only hope there is nevertheless.

Incident at Vichy was written as a companion piece. Even when one doesn't know what one has done, finally the responsibility for it can only rest with oneself. But the character who reacts with conscientiousness is the most unalienated on the stage. He's the only one who's approachable.

Ronald Hayman: But the style is so different from *After the Fall*.

Arthur Miller: It is the structure of the dilemma, the structure unabashed. I wanted to deal more objectively with experience. There's a certain amount of alienation in the way it's presented, in the way people stand up and say what they are. It's rather in a Molière tradition. A man gets up and tells you pretty much what he's about; the only question is what meaning the conflict will arrive at. There are types, there are kinds of people who act severely within the limits of their types and most of the people on stage are like that in this play.

Ronald Hayman: But the action isn't inside the head.

Arthur Miller: It's the play most related to *Death of a Salesman*. I have worked in two veins always and I guess they alternate. In one the event is inside the brain and in the other the brain is inside the event. In *Death of a Salesman* we are inside the head. That's why I've needed two kinds of stylistic attack.

Arthur Miller and the Meaning of Tragedy
Robert A Martin/1970

From *Modern Drama* 13 (1970): 34-39. Reprinted by permission.

R.M.: In earlier essays and statements you have said that tragedy reflects certain qualities, and I take it that when you wrote *All My Sons, Death of a Salesman, The Crucible,* and *A View from the Bridge,* tragedy was a definable quality to you. For example, "Tragedy makes us aware of what the character might have been"; "Tragedy is the consequence of man's total compulsion to evaluate himself justly"; and later, in the "Preface" to the *Collected Plays,* you said, "The less capable a man is of walking away from the central conflict of a play, the closer he approaches the tragic existence."

Since you wrote those lines, there have been three more plays, and I am wondering if you feel that tragedy is still basically the same, or, in the light of *After the Fall, Incident at Vichy,* and *The Price,* has it become something else?

A.M.: Well, those elements you just mentioned and which I have written about, are qualities which I see in the tragic character and tragic situation. But I have the feeling as time goes by that since what we're talking about really is maybe a function of man which goes back into the Bible and into the earliest Western literature, like the Greek drama, it is unlikely, to say the least, that since so many other kinds of human consciousness have changed that this would remain unchanged. But we are at the mercy of certain texts in discussing the whole thing, basically Aristotle, and we have taken, I think, those pronouncements out of context so that now one never knows whether someone is talking about a contemporary tragic possibility or the historical one. For example, I don't think a Greek could have discussed the whole problem without the idea in the back of his head of God. It would have been of the first order of importance because what it is, is the relation not of man to man, but of man to God. The relation of man to man is a psychological problem, or a social problem. But this is a religious problem, and it would undoubtedly have been a religious problem to the Greeks. And to us, you see, we never mention this at all, and it probably is like talking about religion in our times, in a way, as opposed to the way religion would have been talked about before Christianity became what it is today. "Before God died," as they say.

I think that what I'm dealing with most of the time is an attempt by myself probably, more than by what I call a character, to reach out beyond the real world toward some humanistic call which I wish or believe to be working on the history of man, working on human situations. I'll be more specific about it. I think that people, for example, we all, violate our natures in the course of life, and what we're trying to do all the time is to get back to the structure which is human. By one compromise or another, by one mistake or another, or by one ambition or another, we end up where we're no longer ourselves. We're empty, or we feel that we have no possibility of some kind of reconciliation with existence, and there are various intensities with which we pursue that reconciliation. Now some people, the majority probably, learn how to put off the problem. It's really basically one or another kind of procrastination.

R.M.: In this letter you said that you had "not ceased to arraign society, but that society had moved into the play."* Are you saying that you're writing equally about man's relationship to his Gods, whatever they might be, and that the Gods themselves have moved into society?

A.M.: Right. Now if we're going to talk about tragedy at all, it seems to me that we've got to find some equivalent to that superhuman schema that had its names in the past, whatever they were. Whether they went under the name of Zeus's laws, or, as in Shakespearean times, reflected a different ideology toward man, they also had lying in the background somewhere an order which was being violated and which the character was seeking to come to some arrangement with. Now we're in a worse situation because the conception today is that it's a totally real universe. There is nothing but society, and consequently we're left with a kind of sad comedy when we try to do tragedy. You reach out and you hit the void. I think that in *King Lear* Shakespeare came to the void too, but my attempt has been to find some—I wouldn't call it a definition of man—but a kind of articulated, suspenseful potential.

R.M.: In which of your plays do you think you have done that most closely?

A.M.: Well, I tried to do it more in *After the Fall* than in any other play.

R.M.: Is that why Quentin spreads his arms between the light fixtures in his room?

A.M.: Yes. Well, he's quite aware when he does that, that it is an archaic reconciliation. That is, it doesn't work. He doesn't believe in God. But he's going through what is at that moment the only available gesture which men could go through in order to climb above their suffering. But now it's simply two light fixtures on the wall; there's no cross there and he hasn't deserved it. In other words, he hasn't earned that kind of glory. I wouldn't call it glory, exactly, but a kind of peace. In short, the reason we can't, I don't think, any longer really get a grasp on tragedy is because of the absence of a religion, and that what we've got left is the human half of the old Greek and the old Elizabethan process. The psychology of man is basically unchanged. It has to be or we wouldn't be able to watch Shakespeare any more with any emotion; we would be simply like archeologists. But we don't look at it like archeologists. We're moved by it, we're suspended by it, we're shocked by it, and all the rest of it.

R.M.: What's replaced the death of the Old Gods? Eugene O'Neill once said something very similar, in that he was talking about the death of the Old Gods and said that there was nothing left to replace them but materialism.

A.M.: Right. What I'm trying to assert—or reaching toward—is a humanistic, but nevertheless universal, potential, I suppose, which has for me a mystical quality. Why is it that in all countries men in the most degraded situations respond to the call for justice when they haven't even been taught that there is such a thing? The Algerian who has been on his knees for generations suddenly overnight stands up and throws out a tremendous empire after ten years of fight. Now you can say this has all got to do with bread and butter, and it does. But bread and butter alone doesn't make a revolution. Bread and butter alone doesn't raise slogans to which people respond with all their energy and give their lives for. I relate that to the fact that whenever a child is born, that child—for a certain length of time before it's indoctrinated—insists on its share of food. It is offended when it is treated unfairly until it learns that it has no rights in certain societies. In other words, every child brings into the world a system of ethics. It's almost a biological thing as I see it. Society then goes about in various ways, depending upon the society, in bending that natural gift, so to speak, into its own purposes.

R.M.: A gift of innocence?

A.M.: I would almost call it—it sounds as though I'm saying man is born good, but it's really above that. He's born trying to preserve life. He's born on the side of life, and we gradually teach ourselves how to enjoy death and all its manifestations, and how to give ourselves to it.

R.M.: If you apply that view to Quentin, then he's betrayed time and time again, it seems to me. First he is betrayed by his parents when his mother doesn't tell him that she is going to Atlantic City, then he in turn betrays Maggie not out of hate, but out of love. If there are no more gods for Quentin, and there is only the law and justice and truth, how is he betrayed as a human being?

A.M.: He is betrayed by—it sounds contradictory given what I've just said, but it isn't—he is betrayed by his illusion that we are fated, that our real nature, the real nature of people, is to be consistent, to be unified one with the other. Implicit in that play is the idea of a primeval unity of people, a community, a family which is all for one and one for all. It's almost a family without personality. There is only a common bond, which he discovers was never the case, so he only betrays himself in that respect. But it goes further. He sees through the course of his life that unless by act of will he insists (on the level not of instinctual wishes, but on the level of awareness) that he creates good faith and behaves with good faith, it will never exist. He has got to will it into existence. And why? Because otherwise, we're doomed. Otherwise, we're serving death. And he knows this because it is in himself.

R.M.: Is that why he says, "I guess the main thing is not to be afraid?"

A.M.: Right.

R.M.: And that's what Quentin ultimately realizes?

A.M.: Yes.

R.M.: In spite of the betrayal, it's important not to be afraid.

A.M.: Yes. In a way, it's a play which is trying to recreate through one man an ethic on the basis of his observations of its violation. He says, in effect, "I see perfectly well that we all harbor in ourselves the destruction of each other. We all harbor in ourselves these murderous desires. We all harbor in ourselves this breach of faith." I can't accept that as his last word. Why? Because if I do accept it as his last word, life has no reason for me. It involves me, then, in simply making a game of it. There is the aspect of a game throughout the play that is best said by Mickey: You arrange yourself vis-à-vis somebody . . .

R.M.: For five minutes . . .

A.M.: Yes. He manages to pacify his wife, you see, and he could get along great that way. What Mickey is setting forth for Quentin is a life without conviction, without real feeling of any kind. It is simply a life surviving within this scheme of mutual destruction. What you do is, you don't involve yourself in it, really. You simply withdraw from it, but you make a game of involving yourself.

R.M.: Is that why Quentin—and I think this question has troubled critics—is that why Quentin feels partly responsible and partly guilty, but not entirely responsible and not entirely guilty?

A.M.: Right. Because he recognizes in himself some Mickey. In other words, if he could look at Mickey and say, "This is beneath all contempt even," you would have a big scene of arraignment. But he doesn't! He looks at it and it has resonances in his head (by the time this conversation is on) of all the other instances and of all the other experiences where people have acted just that way, except without Mickey's rationalizations and without anybody raising it to the level of a principle of some sort.

R.M.: Is this also true of Reverend Hale in *The Crucible?*

A.M.: In a way it is. You see, what Hale is saying—he's got the line something to the effect that life is holy and therefore anything that takes it . . . you see, when Elizabeth Proctor says, "It's the devil's argument," it is—it's devilish—becaue it leads one to indifference of a sort. That's the tragic dilemma in *The Crucible*, by the way. Hale is saying a very profound truth which . . .

R.M.: "Life, woman, life is God's most precious gift?"

A.M.: Yes. And the way to enhance life is under no circumstances to urge anybody to sacrifice himself. Well, the tragic time comes when in order to save his soul a man feels the necessity (and I think we don't want to do it ourselves, but we sense the value of him doing it) of sacrificing himself. And that to me is a tragic dilemma.

Now in *After the Fall* what I was trying to get at was an awareness. It really is a play about the awareness of a man who sees what human nature is and arrives very close to the conclusion that it isn't worth the candle because it's all a pretence at some kind of faith. He then says, "I've either got to do this—I do get up in the morning and I'm full of joy, and that's true too." By joy he means there's some ambience of faith, that there is something he could do in which he could utterly believe.

R.M.: I was just thinking, though, of faith. It is an act of faith when Quentin dares to get married again, so when Holga appears holding flowers she is symbolic of faith in the midst of the knowledge of betrayal.

A.M.: Right. I think the key line to me is that Quentin sees the potential of disaster in himself as one looks at "an idiot in the house." There it is, I can't close my eyes to it, because it's there and it came from me—that perversity. But that isn't the whole desideratum, so to speak. That isn't the whole thing at the bottom of that test tube after all the filters have filtered out the dross. There's something else in there. "It's my consciousness," he's saying in effect, "that I can live differently. If I didn't know it—if it weren't so alive in me, it couldn't be alive," you see? "And that, too, I choose." He makes a choice at the end: "I choose to go that way." And we're fully aware that this struggle will never end.

*In an unpublished letter Miller wrote to me previous to this interview. *RM*

Conversation: Arthur Miller and William Styron
Rust Hills/1971

From *Audience* 1(Nov.-Dec. 1971): 4-21. Reprinted by permission

Arthur Miller, the playwright, and his wife, the photographer Inge Morath, live in a large, comfortable house on a hillside overlooking the farms and woodlands of Roxbury, Connecticut. Not far away live William Styron, the novelist, and his wife, Rose, an associate editor of *The Paris Review*. The two couples are good friends and see one another often. One afternoon in June, 1971, I drove over from my own home in Stonington, sent by *Audience* to listen to the two men talk, and very kindly invited by Mrs. Miller to stay for dinner with the four of them. The conversation took place in a small study with a big desk which Miller uses "just to pay bills"; he has a separate studio to work in. Styron settled into Miller's desk chair and Miller straddled a chair in the middle of the room. We had two tape recorders going.
Participants:
AM: Arthur Miller
WE: William Styron
IM: Inge Morath
RS: Rose Styron
A: *Audience* (Rust Hills)

IM: I just wanted to take a couple of pictures. I'll take them quickly, then I'll be out. Okay? Just while you're starting?

WS: What kind of questions you going to ask, Rust?

A: Well, I think one of the things I want to ask you is advice. It was all Inge's idea originally—

IM: I said, "Writers should talk to each other."

AM: Yeah, and they do—

WS: I think it's a good idea.

A: Well, you know, interviews have kind of run their course. I mean, everybody's sick of interviews: the people who get interviewed, the readers, maybe even the interviewers. And, but— you guys must *talk*, and if we could—I know it's hard to simulate that, but, uh—One thing that surprised me when we cast about for people to do these *Audience* "Conversations" with one another, we kept coming up with names of writers. Maybe it's just that I don't know any musicians, or something like that, but it doesn't seem to me that painters or musicians or anyone *talk* as well as writers, which is kind of an irony.

WS: Musicians talk well, painters don't, I've found. Would you agree, Arthur?

AM: Painters are impossible.

WS: They really are, verbally, with a few exceptions, like Bob Motherwell. On the other hand, I've known some marvelously articulate musicians. People like Sam Barber and—well, Lenny Bernstein, and Aaron Copeland, are truly gifted conversationalists. But painters, generally speaking, are—(*breaks off, laughs, starts again*) I think I decided not to live out near East Hampton because I'd have to listen to all these painters.

A: Another thing I don't have an idea about is whether these conversations should have a central theme for each one, or a theme that continues from conversation to conversation, or just be the kind of interaction that occurs between the two people involved—have it shape its own form. ((*to Miller*) I should think it would be a little like putting two characters together on a stage, or is that presumptuous?

WS: No, I think that since you're trying this out and don't know what form it is going to take, you should just let it have its head and see what comes out of it.

A: What do you two normally talk about? You're neighbors here, and you get together—

WS: Well, I guess over the years we've talked about just about everything.

AM: Yeah, including, uh, well, sometimes local stuff.

WS: Connecticut politics, the arrival of the Connecticut state income tax—

AM: Taxes in general.

WS: God, taxes in general.

A: And real estate, surely real estate?

WS: Land, carpentry, construction, buildings.

AM: I don't know, I think that, uh, the issues of—if there are any—of *writing*, come up least of all.

WS: Just about, I think that—without being necessarily boorish—that writers conversing with one another tend to talk about *non-literary* matters probably more than . . .

AM: (*interrupts*) Unless it's the critics.

WS: Yes. (*both laugh*) The critics always come in for a rough time, especially if it's around the time a work is appearing, right?

AM: Yes. In fact I was just over in the bookstore this afternoon to pick up a book I had urgently ordered three months ago and completely forgot about. I thought I couldn't live without it, and I just remembered today that I'd ordered it. And there was Bob Anderson . . . In the bookstore. And in two minutes what we were talking about was who was going to succeed Richard Watts on the *Post*, and—who's the other guy?—somebody else who looks like he's going to be succeeded. And I've heard this disastrous conversation all my life.

WS: Well, it's especially true, I think, Arthur, in the theater. We fiction writers bitch as much about literary critics as you playwrights do about drama critics, but I think they don't have this overwhelming power in the world of books that they do in the theater, and that's why playwrights tend to carve them up—

AM: Well, they kill you. They can really destroy you. But that's a funny thing—I remember Chekhov writing somebody a letter saying that if he had listened to the critics he would have died drunk in the gutter.

WS: True.

AM: I guess it was a different situation in Moscow in the nineteenth century than it is here, but it doesn't matter.

WS: You mean (*pause*), it doesn't matter in what way?

AM: I mean that, uh, presumably they didn't kill off any other Chekhovs. (*pauses*) I guess. (*pauses again*) In the long run. Or Ibsens, or anything of the kind. Ibsen—I was just reading a biography of Ibsen, in which he was inveighing against critics in the same way. They exercise, they *import* trouble, I think. But in the final analysis maybe they're not as important as we make them out to be. I don't think twelve people in this country could name the Norwegian critics at the time of Ibsen (*Styron laughs*), and yet they were the real bane of his . . .

WS: Bane of his life. Well, my feeling about critics is very interior, and it has to do with maturity and growth and one's own self-confidence, because when I was a young beginning writer, the slightest slur could just cause me the most horrible despondency—

AM: Yeah, cringing.

WS: *Cringing,* that's what I wanted to say. And as I've gotten a bit mellower, I would still have to be frank to admit I still don't *like* harsh criticism or those attacks that writers always get, but I've found that I've developed a very thick skin over the years. If one is subjected to the kind of vituperation that, say, *Nat Turner* received, one's epidermis *has* to become callused. And I do tend to agree with you that perhaps the first thing a *young* writer should try to do is remember that critics really do not count for a whole lot.

AM: I think, though, they mean a tremendous amount to a young writer, because in effect they launch him.

WS: You mean in the positive sense?

AM: Yes. Without them it's pretty hard for a man who's never been heard of to make any impression, because the public doesn't know his name and has no reason to buy his book or see his play. You're so to speak born under a curse in these fields: you enter by virtue of their support, more or less, or at least their negligence.

WS: Well, certainly to be cast into total oblivion like so many young writers are by the book reviewers, as distinct from the critics, is an unfortunate thing to happen—especially when the young writer happens to have talent. Most full-fledged critics, of course, don't pay much attention to new writers per se anyway, unless . . .

AM: Right. They're busy with established people.

A: Has a critic, as against a reviewer, ever pointed out anything to you in your work that you didn't know was there?

WS: Never! (Audience *laughs*) I honestly don't think so.

AM: I never had that experience. In fact, I've talked to numerous writers in my life and I've never heard one say that, even the ones who were favorites of the critics. I think that what we call criticism is most of the time just a projecting of one man's—is just what the work reminds the critic of—in one way or another. I had one—I wish I'd saved it, it must exist—it was a review by George Jean Nathan, who was then finishing his career, when I came in, and he reviewed—I can't remember which play, I think it was *All My Sons*. And the *whole* review—it wasn't a condemnatory review and it was sort of, uh, interested in the work. But all he did for a double column in the

Hearst paper which he was then working for—the New York *American,* I think it was, or the *Journal,* or the *Journal-American,* whatever it was called, was: he listed *all* the plays—and there must've been one hundred—which in some way, shape, or fashion this play of mine evoked in his mind. Not saying it was copying them or anything—all it was was a display of his memory. And I would say, of the hundred, eighty-five I had never heard of, or of the authors. Many of them were Hungarian plays that had never reached Budapest (*laughs*). That was the archetype of that kind of criticism for me. He was quite open about it, though. He felt, I think, that his audience expected erudition and would sit there and marvel at how much he knew. I never *did* understand what his influence was. (*pause*) But I guess that twenty years earlier, when he was a great partisan of O'Neill's, and—on the whole, I guess his taste was to—he was a debunker of the ordinary theater.

WS: Yes. I think there is something to be said for the craft of criticism when it is addressed to the task of illuminating and elucidating work. I think this can be a very high-level sort of activity. And if done by the hand of a master—like an Edmund Wilson or a Leavis or a Rahv—it can really bring us into a new awareness of the work. And this is what the high function of the critic is. Almost all valuable criticism seems to me an attempt to do this. Negative and destructive criticism is of almost no value whatsoever, it seems to me.

AM: Well, they're interested, aren't they, in telling you what's in or out? What's to be admitted into the halls.

WS: Yes. This is what makes critics like that of very little value. They remain essentially hack reviewers with fancy prose styles to give them a kind of fake cachet. But basically, because as Arthur says, it's a matter of letting a writer in the hall or out, their function is that of a flunky, a doorman.

A: (*laughs*) But they'd say they were keeping up the standards.

WS: Well, they're not, because their personal esthetic is too degrading, too antipathetical to literature. There are undoubtedly certain critics who've become famous as practitioners of hatred and destruction. I could name a few—but won't. This is not to say that literature shouldn't always be under examination. One does not wish for shoddy goods to be accepted as fine material. But the distinction I'm trying to make is between the doorman—and the true critic, who is usually a man who has dedicated himself to the task of showing us what's of value in a work. Valueless works do not usually need to be torn down; they are already on the junk heap.

AM: Yeah, well, the whole thing is in a context, in this country anyway, of a dwindling audience. Perhaps this is true for fiction, it's certainly true of the theater. In other words, the importance of the critic to the survival of the work is in proportion to the social debilitation of the art. Where you have a thriving theater, which is inexpensive, easy to get into, and is a part of the lives of the people, then the make-or-break power of the critic is minimal. Those who are more fastidious in their tastes might consult them for their opinion or to buttress what they already think. But in times like that criticism doesn't have any effect on the art of the time. There is no gate-keeper because there is no gate. It's rather a flow of life that goes in and out of these playhouses. For example, in England until recently the critics were self-consciously aware that the American critic had a power that was inconceivable in England. There was no critic or group of critics in England that could literally close a show, and the reason was simple; the price of the thing was so minimal, even in an inflated economy, that people would go to see a play because they thought there was an interesting actor in it, or because there was a good scene in the play, or because the idea appealed to them—and even though they knew the play had been dismissed by many critics. But you'd spend the little ticket price there was, if you were interested in the theater, just to see what it was you wanted to see about it. Now when that price starts rising, as it has in England, people begin wanting some kind of guarantee that their six or eight bucks, as compared with two dollars or a-dollar-and-a-half, is not going to be thrown away. *Then* the critic becomes the gate-keeper.

A: In the same way the price of the average first novel has made the gate-keeper almost necessary there too.

AM: Yeah, sure. The publishers all tell you now that to publish a new and unknown work of maybe doubtful acceptability grows harder and harder by the day and in some places is impossible anymore, simply because the cost of production is what it is. *(to Styron)* We've got an example here, in the book you reviewed only two weeks ago, on the front page of the *Times Book Review.*

WS: Jim Blake.

A: Jim Blake's letters from prison, mostly to Nelson Algren?

WS: Right, it's a fascinating book.

AM: But there is apparently no advertising budget for it of any description.

WS: None at all. It's a felony.

AM: There just isn't any at all. Blake said he nearly got in a fist fight with the Doubleday advertising manager. Now here they've got a front-page positive review by William Styron, and I understand they simply have not got—in other words, that was not the horse that was going to run.

WS: It was dead before it started.

AM: It makes you wonder why they published the book at all.

WS: It's too bad. (*A pause*)

A: Do you ever, when you're talking, talk about what you're working on? I mean, do you know what Bill's working on? And do you, Bill, know what he's working on?

AM: I know Bill's working on a book.

WS: I know Arthur's doing something called a play. (*both laugh*) No, I think we wait until the moment of fruition before that. I can't say it exactly bores me to talk about work in progress, but after a while if you talk about it too much, it becomes a very tiresome subject to yourself. And therefore I think it's often advisable just to shut up about it and talk about other things and just wait for the moment. (*to Miller*) Because I think I've been to all your first nights in the last six or seven years, and this is where you learn what it's all about.

AM: Although, you know, I was going to say it doesn't do any good reading things to people, excepting I was just thinking that the Russians were always reading things to each other, and I suppose they still do.

WS: I remember you read a couple of short stories to us one night. I think short stories make the perfect readable commodity—a manageable length, and one does not drone on too long.

A: Willie Morris told us that you have a short story about your grandfather arriving in this country?

AM: Yeah, my father.

A: He says it is absolutely marvelous and that we must move heaven and hell to get you to let us have it.

AM: Well, it was part off something else, that's why I didn't let it go. I wanted to do more with it, and I haven't had time.

A: Is it related to the play? It seemed to me that Morris told Geoff Ward that it was related to the play, the one you're working on.

AM: Well, in a way it is. But only remotely. That wasn't the reason that I—I thought I would write a large kind of memoir, which I started to do, then stopped doing. I haven't decided quite what form to do it in. It's not quite ready. Willie read sort of the raw material, which is— it could be published.

. **A;** Lord knows, we'd love to do it. Is it true you sometimes write a short prose version of what later becomes a play?

AM: Well, that happens. But I generally don't publish them, because it gets broken off somewhere, and suddenly I realize I'm writing a precis of what I feel I can do better on the stage. It seems to me that there are a lot of words on the prose page (*laughs*) and sometimes with five exchanges of dialogue it seems to me I make it come to life, you know. Whereas on the printed page it doesn't quite do that.

A: (*to Styron*) You can't agree with that.

AM: No, no, I mean for me. I'm looking for an audience, I suppose.

A: You're imagining an audience.

AM: Yeah, yeah.

WS: Well, I've noticed just recently in writing this movie script I've been working on with John Marquand—it's my first attempt since college to do something in dramatic form—it's not for the stage, it's strictly for film. But I feel the enormous sense of immediacy and aliveness . . .

AM: *Isn't* it?

WS: It's such a sense of freedom to be unshackled from the restraints of those formal, stately, Latinate . . .

AM: It's vulgar! It's vulgar!

WS: (*laughs*) Yes, but . . .

AM: I mean vulgar in the *old* sense, it belongs to the people.

WS: Yeah, yeah, you're *talking* here. These lines are just rolling out from your characters, and they have such a sense of freshness, even when possibly they're not very good. Nevertheless, you're not sitting down with that ghastly moment, the famous moment Paul Valéry describes, when he says he *could not write that line.* That's why he never wrote a novel. The line being—what is it?—"the duchess went out at five in the afternoon—" I mean, that is the bane and horror of being a prose writer. The furniture. Moving people in and out of rooms.

AM: (*laughs*) To me, there's a screen—I love prose, I love to write it and read it—it is a different screen, though, between yourself and the reader or the audience. And I always feel the screen is down—in other words, that dialogue is evidence. It's a delusion, of course, because after all you're creating the dialogue too. I mean, if a man comes to the door, you can describe him, but suddenly he says something, and it all changes. *He is a witness to himself.* And you're standing aside and not there.

AM: Excepting you're in great control. You could argue that you're in as much control as you are on the printed page, because how many misinterpretations—*(to Styron)* as you can be the witness—can there be to a novel. I mean, the reader's left to his own devices. And he hasn't got the control you could exercise over his imagination by selecting the actor, and by inflecting the lines. The controls are there. The problem is that most playwrights vacate because they're overwhelmed by the professionalism of other collaborators, like the director and the actors, and they simply walk away from the whole business. But you don't have to necessarily.

WS: That's I think the strength and the weakness of drama, of the *task* of playwrighting, if I get it correctly. The weakness being, okay, you've written a masterpiece, but a masterpiece can be destroyed by a horrible performance. Whereas a work of prose—fiction, let us say—doesn't yield itself to that kind of destruction. You have a bad reader, but that's the reader's fault. The work itself—

AM: Stands there.

WS: —has its own integrity.

A: *(to Styron)* You had a lot of bad readers with *Nat Turner,* didn't you?

WS: Well—it's complicated. *(laughs)* Yes, I guess I had a lot of bad readers.

A: Did you ever do that piece called "Nobody Knows De Trouble I Seen" about it?

WS: Well, someday I'm either going to do it myself, or—a lot of people have said they wanted to do it and have asked if I have the information. I have a bushel basket full of stuff that I would love to give to somebody I trust someday to put together in a way that would put it all in perspective. There's probably been more controversy on *Nat Turner* than any American novel since Harriet Beecher Stowe's. In fact, there are now two books out on the controversy itself. But what they are, are merely collections of essays that have been written about the book.

A: Yes. (*to Miller*) Have you ever had a missed reaction? Did *The Crucible* have any of that kind of . . .

AM: Oh, sure. So did *Salesman* to a degree, but that's all been forgotten. But *The Crucible* was certainly completely dismissed by a large part of the people—and in anger, too. Because it was regarded as a specious defense of the Communists, namely that: there were no witches, but there *are* Communists.

WS: Uh huh, I remember that.

AM: A lot of angry stuff came out of that.

A: Did you answer at the time, the way Bill is considering an answer?

AM: Yeah, I did. I had some interviews and tried to answer it. But of course at that time the furies were riding high. In the McCarthy times the winds were blowing so fast you couldn't hear yourself think. And I don't recall any important person coming to the defense of even the principle involved, let alone the play itself.

WS: You mean, when you say that, there was for instance no long responsive essay in the Sunday *Times*, saying: let's put this matter straight.

AM: No, there wasn't. They would have just as soon forgot the whole thing. It took about four to five years before the play was done again, off-Broadway.

WS: Then it damaged the play at the time?

AM: Oh, definitely, definitely. You see, I'd just had *Death of a Salesman* on, which was an immense hit. And this play came in, and it wasn't all that long later. As soon as the sense of what it was about became apparent, you could feel a coating of ice over that audience. It was just thick enough to *skate* on. It was sheer *terror*. It was *real* terror. I had been in the theater a long time by that time and I'd never experienced such a sensation. In fact, people I knew quite well— newspaper people and so on—when I was standing in the back of the theater and they came out, didn't turn to nod to me.

A: (*whispers*) Wow!

AM: It was as though!—It was at the Martin Beck Theater, I'll never forget that evening—and you know, newspaper columnists and people I didn't know all that well, but I *knew* them, they'd interviewed me, and we'd shaken hands a few times. And they walked right past me as if I was another post holding up the ceiling. It was quite something.

WS: Yes. Well, that must have been at least as unsettling to you as it was to me when I had my reaction, because yours was coming not from a minority group as mine was, although—alas!—it was coming from the minority I had written about. Nonetheless, the hostility *you're* describing was coming from your peers, so to speak.

AM: It came from almost every quarter. And it was frightening to me because at that time no one could tell what the end result of the McCarthy movement would bring. There was no real resistance to it. The youth were inert. The trade unions were as much with it as anybody else. Where could you look for any ally? You know what I mean? Well, man alive. To tell you the truth I stood back there and I thought: well, if this is the way it is, then the jig is up. No one knew he was going to die . . .

WS: We were saved just in the nick of time.

AM: Right, right.

WS: This can be a very disheartening thing to have happen—to have a work of literature attacked on ad hominem and at the same time political grounds . . .

A: Well, you both chose to write—historically, admittedly—but about contemporary issues and you didn't conceal their relevance, and you both got a reaction . . .

AM: Oh, sure, sure we did. You know, the final pay-off to this was that I was in England, and Olivier did *The Crucible* about—oh, I can't remember now, it was in the middle sixties—and I happened to be there, so we went to see it. I sat behind two youngish people in their late twenties, and after the first act, as we were getting up, the girl turned to the fellow and said, "I heard this had something to do with McCarthyism." And he said, "What was that?"

WS: (*laughs*) That's beautiful.

AM: I thought to myself: no wonder it's impossible for scholarship ever to re-create the conditions under which a work is done.

A: But I think to feel disheartened is—You know, if you're going to write *engaged* art, you either have to not do it, or stay out of the kitchen. What I mean is: there's going to be some *heat*.

WS: Well, there's always going to be some heat. But I don't think I'm mistaken to say that the intensity of this kind of heat was such that other controversial works do not generate, not like *Nat Turner* and *The Crucible*. And when I say "disheartening," I mean it in a temporary sense, because as Arthur is clearly pointing out, these things are temporary, that works of literature, as distinct from polemical works or works of propaganda, have their own life. And this is what the hope of every writer is: to create such a work. But the disheartening part in my own case is that the hysteria of the attacks by blacks has tended to cause young black people either not to read the book at all, in the last couple of years, or to read it with such hostility that they get a warped version of it. And I think that this is unfortunate, because *unlike* Arthur in the case of *The Crucible,* I had eloquent and noble defenses by totally detached and dedicated people—historians, left-wing historians, too, like Genovese, and Duberman who maintained in strong and uncompromising terms that *Nat Turner* was historically sound. But it's hard to get such a message through to people who've been brainwashed.

A: So it appears the critics are maybe of some use sometimes, in a case like that?

WS: Yes, well, I guess so. (*laughs*)

A: Well, if you discount the professional critics as obviously having really no influence on either of your work, and if you don't swap manuscripts between yourselves, do you just work *entirely* alone, or is there any sort of influence before it comes—?

AM: Well, I work alone. But in the last years I've had a strong friendship with Bob Whitehead, Robert Whitehead, who is my producer. And I do read to him in the course of the work. I like to do that because I—Well, we both want the same thing, see? It comes to that.

WS: Sure, you have a vested interest. I have the same relation with Bob Loomis at Random House, almost exactly.

A: I see: the producer on the one hand for the playwright, the editor on the other for the novelist. Same function.

WS: In my mind, "editor" is just a catch-all word for a friend, and Bob Loomis happens also to be a friend, besides being an editor. I feel an empathy with him, and this allows him to be one of my best audiences. I'm sure it's the same way with Bob Whitehead and Arthur.

AM: Oh, yes.

WS: Bob never fails to call me on something he doesn't feel is working. I remember I read him a scene, which more or less *is* in *Nat Turner,* in the final version, and I knew it was somehow going wrong the way I was writing it—it was getting wordy and inflated and so on. So I read it to Bob, and he saw the trouble immediately. After I'd read it, you know, I waited for his reaction, and he said, "That's the only scene you've read so far that doesn't ring true to me." And we talked it over and we agreed it had to do with the fact I wasn't close enough in this scene to Nat's point of view to make it really ring with the verisimilitude that the other scenes had. It was a matter of merely shifting a few little stage directions, so to speak. I did it, and it's one of the scenes that has been quoted in critical articles as one of the better scenes in the book. I feel that shows the value of being able to bounce your work off a receptive person.

AM: I think it can be important, but I can see where somebody wouldn't need it at all. That's possible.

WS: An editor could be your wife, or any kind of interchangeable person that happens to be sympathetic to your work.

A: But in both your cases it happens to be the person who sees your work through production. That's good that you're hooked up that way. (*to Miller*) You would then change scenes or something, at the suggestion of Whitehead?

AM: Well, he wouldn't suggest a change. What I can do is look into his eyes, see? (*Styron laughs*) And see whether that arrow (*claps hands, smack!*) has hit anywhere. It comes to that. Or sometimes I'll be writing a scene for Reason A, and the real strong effect of that scene is a result of B, which I'm completely overlooking. This will happen rarely, but often enough to make reading it worthwhile. I think more than anything else it's a—(*pause*) It's a break in the loneliness of the whole business.

WS: Yeah, that's another thing, it's . . .

AM: It's a lonely job.

WS: Well, you eventually come to a point where all of this— especially, I think, if you're writing a novel, although certainly it must be the same with a play—where you have all this dammed-up stuff you have put down on paper, and something in you in a very human way simply yearns for it to be spilled out.

A: Well, that's what I would *think*: that you'd talk with one another about it, and talk with others . . .

AM: Well, you know, except that I've found, and I think Bill has got the same feeling, that—You know reading something is a lot of work, or even discussing some work in progress. It's not anything but labor; it's a creative thing. And I think that at least at this stage of the game you tend to conserve a lot of energy—you know what I mean?—*that* kind of energy, you tend to kind of hold onto it. And, you know, if I were to listen to something another person wrote, I would feel obliged, willy-nilly, to say: well, what can I say that could be of use? And not just sit there and say, you know, "I like that." I mean, what the hell is the point? (*Styron laughs*) You see? In this stage I don't read it to Bob to have him say, "Oh, I like that." Basically I read it to him to say, if anything, "Gee, I don't dig that at all. I don't see what the hell you're—? What's it all about?"

WS: Yes. This is a very professional working relationship. You read it to your wife, who says she likes it. (*laughs*) And you read parts of it to your editor or producer as you go along. But then you wait for the moment you have the thing pulled together and, okay, you print it or put it on the stage. And *then*, then is when all the yearned-for—and anyone who says he doesn't yearn for it is a liar—all the yearned-for appreciation hopefully comes.

A: You don't miss any of the interaction of a literary community? People reading one another's stuff in the coffee shops of London in the eighteenth century or whenever it was, that kind of writers-group sort of thing?

AM: I *used* to do that. When I first started out I knew a half-dozen playwrights, guys all roughly my age, all unproduced. And we used to read plays to one another.

A: It may be something you need more when you're beginning.

AM: I think that's true.

WS: I think so. There's a terrific community of interest among young writers. They all tend to huddle together. And I claim—very unfashionably—that no harm can come out of these classes in creative writing. Of course, much of it is ludicrous and silly: I mean, you can't really teach a person how to make a fine novel, in any direct sense. But I went to several of these classes when I was very young, and I can remember nothing but good things about them. If for no other reason: I, as a sort of lonely young fellow managed to get with a community of like-minded people. Had I not been with them I would have been even more intolerably lonesome.

AM: I was in a play-writing class at the University of Michigan. As Bill says, you don't learn how to write a play. But at the age of eighteen or nineteen, the idea of becoming a professional playwright was like becoming an astronaut or something. It required an assertion of will and identity then that was just unbelievable. I emphasize *then* because there was no off-Broadway then. You either went on Broadway or you didn't go anywhere. The universities by and large didn't produce any plays except those that *had* been on Broadway. So you had to in one fell swoop scale that impossible fence.

A: Gosh.

AM: There were no try-outs, no anything.

A: Off-Broadway sort of serves like the Little Magazines for a fiction writer.

AM: Right, right. But you know, I think there is a danger in these writing programs if you get a director or a teacher who is too—I don't know how to put it. I think that it would be a terribly destructive experience to be put in the hands of a playwright who in his own work is very good, but the very fact he is that good and is that much of a personality would make it difficult for him as a teacher to open his arms to work that aesthetically contradicts everything he stands for and has worked so hard to form. It's a dangerous business.

A: But that's like a strong director for you, or a strong editor for Bill, isn't it? When you were working with Kazan you were already established as a playwright?

AM: Luckily when I came to Kazan I'd written about sixteen plays. But if I'd come to a strong director very early it would have been a deforming experience. An artist, especially in his youth, is exposed, up there naked, and somebody can just give him a wrong look and he can *blush* himself into oblivion. Because you're most inpressionable then. When you've just written your first things, if someone coughs, you know (*laughs*), at the wrong moment, you sink through the floor. (*Styron laughs*) That's why the best writing teachers are probably those who are most bland about it all. They wouldn't necessarily even be good critics. But they'd be good receptors. They'd be terribly excited about anything that had some value. I remember I used to rail in my heart against one or two of the teachers I had because they weren't tough enough on the others—

WS: —On your fellow students? (*laughs*)

AM: Yes, I'd say, "Jeez, he hands out this praise too easily." But then, even then, I realized: well, that's really his job; his job is to support somebody, not destroy him.

WS: This is the great thing about William Blackburn, with whom I studied at North Carolina, and, I might add, about Hiram Haydn, later at The New School in New York. As teachers, both of them created a *broth,* an environment in which young people were allowed to get truly excited. And I think, in retrospect, that both Blackburn and Haydn lavished, in a sensible way, possibly too much praise. But *far* better that, because at this impressionable age you want a *festive* attitude towards life. I mean, with all the shit it is to be young, you want to have the attitude that literature is a feast, a thing to rejoice at. Far better to create this excitement—even if it's slightly promiscuous—than to get one of these goddamn awful sour, negative, academic . . .

AM: I once asked Professor Rowe—Kenneth T. Rowe, who was my teacher at Michigan—about all this, because it seemed to me that people were reading and submitting stuff that was of just no value. And he said, "Well, you know, these people aren't ever going to be playwrights"—by this time I was convinced that I would have to be a playwright—"but," he said, "they are going to learn to be better theatergoers."

A: A lot of people learn to read from creative writing classes.

AM: Sure. A lot of people came from all sorts of remote places to the University of Michigan, and these were little seeds he was sort of planting all over the United States. And in the long view he had confidence that if you had talent he couldn't hurt you—and if you didn't, he wouldn't hurt you either. It's a kind of mini-world, which a writer one way or another has to have early on, I think. Maybe he has to go and seek it himself, and if he's lucky he'll find it through another writer, or an editor, or a friend, or his wife, or a girl friend, or some damn thing.

A: Nevertheless, you are in Roxbury, Connecticut, both of you, and there is a fairly close concentration of talent around here. And it may be that when you get together all you talk about is carpenters and taxes, but you *are here* with one another, not living out in Montana or somewhere all alone.

WS: I think it is part of our Philistine heritage in this country that we adopt a pose of the non-community of literature, as if there were something somehow offensive about writers knowing each other. The idea of the sturdy individualist takes over when it comes to what a writer should be and do. The cliché runs like this: "I wouldn't like to live in New York City as a writer, because I myself prefer living here in Montana. Who wants to go to those literary salons?" As if there were something pernicious about salons in themselves. I myself, living in Connecticut, don't want to go to *many*, but occasionally I find it refreshing to be invited by a friend like George Plimpton to go down and come to a party at which I happen to see maybe ten other writers, many of whom I enjoy the company of enormously. This notion about avoiding other writers smacks of Philistinism, nothing else.

A: *(to Miller)* I don't mean to make it seem he's attacking you, but you never *do* go to parties in New York.

AM: Oh, I do occasionally, yeah. But you see my field is nomadic. People disappear into the wilds of Hollywood. The theater has never created much of a circle in this country. I often wish it had. But now it's a one-shot thing: you rent the hall, you put on the show, and then when the show is over everybody disperses, and that's the end of it.

WS: I noticed that, at some of the first-nights of your plays I've attended. As celebrant as many of them have been, there's always a sense of "Good-night, good-bye, that's all."

A: You don't all go off to Sardi's?

AM: Yeah, but it's for two hours, and then you've had it. There is nothing more.

A: Speaking about New York parties and the literary life makes me think of Thomas Wolfe's marvelous evocations of dreams of success, but then when he actually wrote about these salons and the parties, it would be bitterly, satirically.

AM: Well, going back to what we were talking about before, he had a profound relationship with Maxwell Perkins, who was his alter-ego almost.

A: Yeah, but who's to know what Perkins cut out of all those novels? They're still too long. Was the stuff cut any better or any worse or just the same?

AM: God knows.

A: The Perkins writers: Wolfe, Hemingway, Fitzgerald. How romantic and tragic the lives of the last generation of American writers were.

M: Well, this country kills writers, at a great rate. That's an old story. But I'm not sure it's all that different anywhere else, except maybe France.

WS: Well, they embalm them in France. The difference in being a writer in France as against being a writer here is just astounding. I never feel that I am "a writer" here, in terms of the public. I mean, I check in at a motel, and they don't—no one ever—

AM: No, no, never.

WS: On the other hand, if you get off at the airfield in Orly, you're surrounded by reporters and photographers.

A: I remember your once telling about the great reception you had in France for *Set This House on Fire* as against here.

WS: Oh, yeah, in France, in France they know who you are. It's the same way with Arthur. It's heady stuff after living in a country where you're always having to spell your name out.

AM: Let me tell you a funny story. It really is a funny story. When I first knew Inge. I guess we were just married. And she didn't know New England, so I said, "Well," I said, "let's go up to Boston, I'll show you all the Revolutionary Towns"—you know, Lexington, Concord—I thought she ought to know about these. And I said, "Gee, do you know we're near Salem? Why don't we go there?" Now when I was preparing *The Crucible* I went to Salem, which has the greatest witchcraft library in the world, which nobody goes into excepting a few scholars who are interested in that field, and I had spent about three weeks in that library. They've got stuff there that isn't even reprinted; there are manuscripts in there; it's a *marvelous* library. There are two old ladies running it. And I said to Inge, "Maybe those two old ladies'll still be there." Now at this time it had already been ten years since I'd been in there. So, as we're driving along, I notice she's fixing up her face. I said, "What're you doin'?" She says, "Well, there'll be a reception." I said, "A *what?*" She said, "Well, you're going back to this place I never would have heard of if you hadn't written about it." She'd seen *The Crucible* with Yves Montand and Simone Signoret in Paris, see? So I said, "No, no. You got it all wrong. They're not going to know who I am." Well, she wouldn't believe it. Well, we went in there—now mind you, there are probably three customers a month in this library, this is not a public library—so I walked in, and I said, "I want to show this lady some of the prints"—they had marvelous contemporary prints of the witchcraft, woodcuts and so forth—and we walked around, and she *would not believe (laughs)—*

WS: What happened? You mean?

AM: *Nothing* happened. I mean, we just went through like Sam Doakes of Lower Forks, Indiana. (*laughs*)

WS: (*laughs too*)

A: Surely neither of you, though, would prefer less anonymity. Surely you like to be able to live a regular life without crowds howling at you and like that?

WS: Oh, sure, there's a great advantage in—

AM: Oh, yeah, I was just going to add I'm not so sure that's all such a bad thing.

WS: No, it falls out in different ways. It *is* a good thing. Like the French respect to a great degree is a bit phony—not all of it, but some of it. Because most of those Frenchmen haven't read the work. But you acquire a kind of cachet . . .

AM: Yeah, it's a bit of a game there. They always have to know what's on, so they can carry on about it. I used to think it was terrible in America, but now I don't know. The only part of it—(*pauses*). If there could be a system whereby the writer remains anonymous— which I like—but that the public would know that some of the troubles they had, and some of the problems they've got, *are* being dealt with in works of art. Let them know some of their bewilderment is being worried about.

A: But in the case of *Death of a Salesman,* that's certainly a celebration of the bewilderment of the ordinary man.

AM: Well, that penetrated. I'll tell you a story about that, in the boon-docks. I went over to Waterbury. . .

WS: (*To Inge Morath, who has just looked into the room*) Inge, could I have another drink?

IM: Yes? I'm checking every so often, spacing myself rightly, I hope.

WS: You're very sweet.

A: I'm passing on this one.

WS: Did you get Rose?

IM: I got Rose, she said she'd been on the phone. So she's coming.

A: Would you begin again, Arthur?

AM: Well, you got it on the tape.

A: Yeah, I know, but I've forgotten. I've lost the trail.

WS: This is his story about going to Waterbury.

AM: Yeah, about Waterbury. Speaking about the penetration of a work. I went over to Waterbury because I'd bought a Studebaker and I went to the dealer—it was a new car, a new beautiful green convertible—to get it serviced. And there was a man sitting there waiting for his car to get serviced. So, we got talking a little bit, and I said, "What do you do?" And he said, "I'm a salesman." I said, "What do you sell?" And he said, "Church bells." And I said, "Really? Are there that many church bells? I wouldn't think there'd be a living there." He said, "Oh, you'd be amazed—the number of church bells crack, congregations want to get a new church bell, a bigger one, they get richer, new churches are built," he says, "I'm busy all the time. It's great—great field. What do you do?" (*Styron laughs*) So I said, "I'm a writer." He says, "Oh, what do you write?" I said, "I write plays." He says, "Well, what's the name—what kind of plays?" So I said, "Well, I wrote a play called *Death of a Salesman.*" (*Styron laughs*) Well, *he simply got up.* And he walked away and sat in a different part of the show room. He wouldn't even discuss the whole thing.

WS: Now when was this?

AM: This was forty—*fifty!* The play was just on. Isn't that marvelous?

A: But he must have thought you invented that, right?

AM: No, he knew about it. I could tell. It's forgotten now, but a lot of salesmen were very upset by that play.

WS: But it really got at him, huh?

AM: Oh, it frightened him.

A; That's more like Bill's reaction from the blacks, what you got from the salesmen.

AM: Yes, you *do* penetrate sometimes.

A: But it seems to me that when you *do* penetrate, really get at them, then you worry about it?

AM: No, no. Not me. I think the best thing that could happen is when ordinary people know something is there. It means something to them, even if they kick it around. I have a romantic faith in the truth. I feel something sticks somewhere in the mind, that it becomes some way of forming a symbolic conception of what happens to them. Because the problem most people have is the fragmentation of their experience: they can't make any sense at all out of anything that happens, excepting in a retrograde way—you know, they figure this is all because they've sinned, or some crap of this kind—instead of trying to make a conceptualization on some life-giving level. It would be marvelous if they could be more open to art—even medium art.

WS: Yes, but it would be great if they could discriminate between that medium art and real art, distinguished art. If they could realize, for instance, that a movie like *Easy Rider* has its place in the scheme of things, but it's not art, it's not even remotely art, even though it's fine and fun to go see.

AM: That'll never happen, though. That'll never happen.

WS: Well, it's the thing that bothers me most about kids today: that they don't distinguish . . .

AM: The best example I have of what it means to kids: we went to see—what was that movie about a photographer?—*Blow Up,* and we went into this delicatessen about a block away—Third Avenue there?—sat down at the counter to get a quick sandwich after the show, after the movie. And there were three young men dressed exactly like the hero of *Blow Up* with Leica cameras *hung from their necks.*

A: It happens that quickly.

AM: It was right there. And I said to Inge, "Baby, it's all an act—"

WS: You think they had consciously just donned this outfit?

AM: Oh, it was obvious! He had a certain kind of sunglasses. It was the *same* sunglasses. They were carrying the camera that way; they were wearing the jacket he was wearing. And the manner and everything. (*pauses*) I guess it's always that way, though. I guess a lot of people imitated the way they thought Hemingway was like.

WS: Well, I know this for a fact, because I used to go into The Dome in 1951, and there were several Hemingways who would drive up to The Dome on motorcycles, all Americans, all probably in their late twenties or early thirties, all with a mustache, at a time when mustaches were out of fashion. All of them would sit there silently, in The Dome on the terrace there, having their Pernod, and all of them thinking that they were Hemingway.

AM: Well, you know Tolstoy collected all these types who grew long beards and visited him.

WS: Oh, really?

AM: Sure! They'd sit on his porch, it drove his wife crazy, they'd all come and stay for months.

WS: (*suddenly*) *Hello there!*

RS: (*enters*) Hello! You're not finished?

AM: Finished? Well—

RS: I'll sit out there, and—(Everyone: No, no.)

WS: Don't you think we're sort of finished, Rust?

AM: We've got two tape-recorders going here.

A: Sit down and be recorded.

RS: Well, thank you. I thought you'd already be at the dinner table.

AM: You know what we should discuss though, if we can for a minute, a thing I think is very confusing to the young, is this whole question of this business of relevance, what various generations think is relevant.

WS: Is this thing still on?

A: You don't mind it still being on, do you, Bill?

WS: No, no, of course not, except— (*to Miller*) but *extend yourself,* Arthur.

AM: Well, I think we've gotten back to the crudest form of relevance. When Godard makes a movie he stops it in the middle and someone starts discussing the Chinese Revolution. You know? The theater's been full of it—relevance to Vietnam, and like that.

A: Isn't this kind of interruption part of the modern idea of fiction and drama deliberately setting out to destroy the illusion? Trying to introduce politics *unabsorbed* in a work of art.

AM: But this whole business of relevance to political and sociological fact is disastrous. In the theater, anyway, everything gets vulgarized, made more crude. They've taken from Brecht all his dross—that is to say, all the stuff he was stuck with, at the moment he was writing—and eliminated the poetry. And they call that a statement of some kind.

A: (*to Styron*) You've written perhaps the most celebrated political novel of our time—or anyway, you got the most reaction.

WS: But that's what Arthur's talking about. Because there's no recognition on the part of the attackers that the work has any literary merit whatever, which is almost a demonstration of how incredibly weird the whole situation is.

AM: That's right. Ultimately it comes to be an aesthetic question. I found in talking to some young people that they have no awareness of the articulation of a *central* concept. In other words, if you point out to them that something in a play or movie or book is utterly unmotivated, that it has no *textual* connection with what went before, what comes afterwards, their reaction is: "Well, why not?" You see? The idea of a *whole*, of any organic unity to a work of art, is not only rejected, but seems to some of them even strange. They don't see why *anything* can't be in a work *at any moment*. It sort of reflects the unexpected in society, perhaps, or the feeling that there is no unity in experience. It reflects the influence of surrealism too. The *surreal* quality was to break up relationships that "appear" to be logical or "appear" to be inevitable, so that that which is unrelated is exactly that which is related. You see? To put a wooden leg on an elephant, to put together that which is irreconcilable, is the essence of reality. And if it's done by somebody who has an organic sense of what is unified, so he can dis-unify it, that's one thing; but what has happened now is—and you see it in the young movies that are made—as soon as something gets contiguous and continuous, *smash it up,* lest it become linear, lest it become realistic. Which is a whole other convention. and yet the same people when you sit with them and they start talking about their lives, they tell continuous stories. In other words, they tell about how they were in love with this girl, and then *not,* and then it goes along, and you find out cause and effect. It's another art form, but they don't recognize that. They think it's a naked rendition of reality.

WS: You know, did you see *Easy Rider?*

AM: Yes.

A: No. I'm proud of myself for having gotten to see *Five Easy Pieces.*

WS: Well, no, that's almost a masterpiece. But *Easy Rider isn't,* in my mind. It exemplifies all the good things about our culture, namely our technological ability to do fantastic things easily. And yet it has an almost total lack of any moral or dramatic sense of what makes life what it is. And when you were just now talking, Arthur, I couldn't help but think again: *Easy Rider*—which was fascinating, but totally devoid of any moral tension, moral center.

AM: You know what I think it is?—I think it's the new Naturalism. That is, Naturalism in its worst sense: where you get the whole thing no matter how *boring* the damn thing was. *Nothing* was going to be left out. You never got into the people. And *Easy Rider* is that way. These are displacement figures—that is to say, they're up there having *scenic* adventures. Which is perfectly fine, but to attribute to it a deep artistic value is a sign of the moment—that is, that a lot of people who felt it was of the first importance do feel about life that it has surfaces but no depth, that it has consequences but not causes, that there is no center, it's simply that you do get on the motorcycle and go from one place to another.

IM: *(enters again and speaks to Miller)* Jim Proctor on the phone.

AM: *(leaves to talk with him, or uh—exits upstage left)*

WS: Jim Proctor?

IM: Arthur's publicity man, a marvelous incredible person. But you know what was interesting to me with all you were saying—I was just now down in Miami lecturing to students of photography, and it was just very interesting. Their whole approach is again different. You know? Finally one said to me, "How do I find my identity? I can do physics, I can do photography, I can do plastic styrofoam sculptures." I said to him, "You have too much money. It's very simple. You know, you wouldn't have so much money you'd have to stick with one thing and try to find yourself in it." He said, "You know, you are right." And it's *true*. It's like those modern painters who have so much money to buy those enormous canvases. If they would have smaller canvases they would do better work."

RS: You know, it's true. We know someone who does six paintings a day because he has these millions of canvases.

IM: You know, I knew a lot of painters including Picasso very well, and Braque, and they were really friends of mine. And often they would have just that much of a canvas, and it was *expensive*, so Picasso would do something marvelous on it.

A: It's a funny idea. Suppose you were to think that way about paper, Bill?

WS: (*long pause*) You mean? Well—(*laughs*) The analogy—I don't think it works. Paper's, we know, another medium.

IM: Even film, I hate to waste film, because—

AM: (*returns*) Jim Proctor's going to bring Katz's frankfurters.

IM: He's coming Saturday?

WS: He's going to do what?

AM: (*to Morath*) Yes. (*to Styron*) He loves to bring loads of delicious Jewish delicatessen frankfurters.

A: Oh, yeah, Kosher frankfurters.

WS: Well, they have some great ones in New York.

AM: Garlic in them. Oh, they're fantastic.

A: In our Finast there are nine different kinds of hot-dogs and not one of them is good.

WS: (*to Miller*) Save one of them for me.

A: Any of you read *The French Lieutenant's Woman?* (*Everyone: No.*)

IM: I must read that. Everybody says it. . .

A: Oh, no. I mean it's kind of a spellbinding thing the way Fowles does, but it . . .

IM: I think very soon we have to have the talking over dinner.

A: No, no. I'm not really *talking*.

AM: It's an historical novel, isn't it?

A: Yeah, it's a sort of an attempt to write a Victorian novel *now*, but the point is he *stops* every three chapters and destroys the illusion. Now it's quite true, I mean Fielding will stop and destroy the illusion, and so does Trollope, and so on. But the way he does it, it's just *total*, a total break. Just like putting in a lecture on China or something.

RS: But that breaking of the surface you were describing in the movies is exactly what occurs in most very young contemporary poetry, where they *cannot* allow an image or a thought to go through to three or four lines. They've got to break it and fill in with all these naturalistic details, throw it in and break the consciousness and move along to some paradoxical thing. You're not allowed to see anything whole.

AM: Yeah. Partly it's the whole surrealistic thing inherited from Europe. (*pauses*) It does reflect a reality among us. In other words, when you hear somebody's tale of woe or happiness or something, you end up saying, "I wonder what really happened?" (Everyone: Yes, yes)

The interpretation, which was formerly embedded in the way the story was told, as in Tolstoy—although he of course broke it up too, by suddenly launching out on a vast essay on Napoleon and the nature of war, let's not forget, it just seemed like a part of the tale because it's so long ago—the interpretation, the *stand* of the author is now of the first consequence. What his position is in relation to the material, so that he creates a kind of confrontation, *personally*, apart from his role as storyteller, with the reader.

WS: Pardon a personal reference, but this is what I've been trying to do in this thing I'm writing now. It's not all that original by any means, but it's the only one I know in recent American writing which simply starts out telling a story—(*breaks off*) I don't mention myself, by name. I do say, though, that this concerns the Korean War and my involvement in it and my training in North Carolina. I say I have written a novella about the Marine Corps, which some people will remember and I proceed to say: this is what happened to me. Okay, the alert reader, the one who has any acquaintance with my own work, will read this and say, "Well, this is old Bill Styron; it's a little bit of autobiography."

A: Here he comes again.

WS: Yeah, here he comes again. Trotting it out. (*laughs*) But the point is that what I'm writing is fiction. Except that everything that happens, that most of it, well, that a tiny bit of it, is true: I *did* go down to Camp LeJeune in 1951, I *was* called back in the Korean War. But I'm conning the reader into believing *all* this really happened to me and the events described really took place.

A: The author using his own known identity to establish realism.

WS: Exactly.

AM: Yeah, well I think there's a reason for that. You take what your audience reads, it's basically news magazines and newspapers and television—*factual* reporting, supposedly, of life. Now, inevitably you are trying to offer your bona-fides as a counter-authority on the basis that "I too have felt the whip of this experience on myself." I mean, if I write an article about My Lai, inevitably in the back of your head you're saying, "Well, what the hell does he know more than I do?—He wasn't there." This is a profound problem which is very contemporary. The author today is up against the necessity to establish his authority as he never was before.

RS: A perfect example is what John Corry was telling us night before last. He'd been asked to do two pieces on vanishing wildlife for *Cosmo*. He didn't know anything about these two particular pieces, but he was quite capable of researching them . . .

IM: (*who has been out of the room*) Will any of you forgive me if we go on talking at the table?

AM: We'll have to move all our apparatus.

A: Yeah, but let me just hear what John Corry said.

WS: Let's just finish this.

IM: Oh, I'm sorry, I didn't—

RS: He did not know from personal experience about either of these two wildlife situations he was writing about, but he sat in this friend's house in Virginia writing the two of them. And when he was finished, he went back and re-did them, saying, "Standing on a cliff in Colorado, *I heard* the vanishing wolf"—and he'd never been to Colorado, and as it turned out there weren't any wolves in Colorado. But he'd had to lend this whole thing an authority, and he did it quite successfully, although it was totally untrue. It worked.

WS: It's capturing your imagination. It's going to any trapeze length to—

AM: The author—he's the horse's mouth.

WS: Precisely. You know, it's just the *way* you do it, and this is very very important. It's been done before, but it takes new forms. What I want to do is make it look like autobiography, but then make it *fiction* on top of that in some curious way. Say, aren't we finished now, Rust?

A: Oh, yeah, yeah. And I think it has a focus about writing and *the* writer and that sort of thing. And in some wild way I think it's about *reality,* too. I'm going to try to edit it so it *sounds* real, to try to establish that authenticity and authority you spoke of. But when you two talk alone together, you probably avoid talking this way about literature and writing and all.

AM: No, we talk like *this.* But not about our own work.

WS: Except in a peripheral way.

IM: They tell each other whether they get on with it or not.

WS: "How'd it go today?" is what we say.

AM: There's two tape cassettes. I'll mark this one side "one" and the other side "two". The one that's in now will be "three".

A: That's a professional touch I'd never have thought of.

WS: Astounding that they could be this small.

AM: Well, you know that whole thing about literature in tape cassettes? This is the new book. The cassette rights to a book are going to be a big thing.

A: I don't know that I like that.

AM: Well, nobody's going to ask you. (*laughs*)

WS: But here, can you imagine all of that conversation in a couple of these?

Writing Plays Is Absolutely Senseless, Arthur Miller Says, 'But I Love It. I Just Love It'
Josh Greenfeld/1972

From *The New York Times Magazine*, 13 Feb. 1972, 16-17, 34-39. Reprinted by permission.

The voice on the phone traveled across years, tripped over geographies. The diction was cosmopolitan New York, but the accents, every bit as glottal and guttural as my own, were native Brooklyn. "We've just postponed the production of my new play till next fall," it was saying, "so my schedule has lots of openings these days. Like I'll be home tomorrow and Friday. And this is the best place for us to talk—no interruptions or distractions. Can you possibly make it tomorrow?"

"Hold on," I said "Let me ask my wife." Then: "O.K. Tomorrow's fine." "Now let me check with my wife." After a moment it came back on the line. "Tomorrow's O.K. She has a bewildered expression, but O.K. And why don't you have lunch here? It'll probably be right off the kitchen table because that's how we eat lunch around here."

"Fine," I replied, and hung up. In the living room, my wife asked, "Where are you going tomorrow?"

"To Connecticut," I said. "To see Arthur Miller."

"Oh," she said, and returned to her reading.

Arthur Miller is no longer the supercelebrity seen running around with Monroe, being harassed by the House Un-American Activities Committee or misfitting around Nevada. The media long ago went on their trendy way, and Miller has become one of those rare celebrity writers who has gracefully made the transition from the limelight back to the desk lamp. His recently completed play, *The Creation of the World and Other Business*, which he subtitled "a catastrophic comedy," is his fourth drama in the last eight years.

Such industry casts Miller, at the still-youthful age of 56, in the

unlikely role of a relic. He is an almost solitary survivor of that
nostalgic era when the theater, not the TV talk show or new
journalism, was the glamorous spot for the writer. The rest of the
playwrighting stars of the forties and fifties have all but vanished into
Hollywood, academia, publishing, death or some other dramatic
silence.

And Miller's past is as active as his present. He will be represented
in New York this season with a revival by the Lincoln Center
Repertory Company of *The Crucible* (1953). His 1950 adaptation of
Ibsen's *An Enemy of the People* has been the hit of the Madrid
season, and *Incident at Vichy* (1964) opened in Paris last autumn.
After the Fall (1963) and *A View From the Bridge* (1955) remain
theatrical fixtures on both sides of the Iron Curtain. *The Price* (1968),
his last Broadway play, and *Death of a Salesman* (1949), his most
enduring one, have received major treatment as TV-network specials
in recent years, and *A Memory of Two Mondays* (1955) was
produced last year on N.E.T.

Before driving out to Connecticut, I reviewed Miller's work and the
facts of his life that inform his plays. Born Jewish; Urban; Middle
class; Father a gruff entrepreneur. Mother more sensitive and
culturally attuned. Family physically dislocated and emotionally
traumatized by the Depression. As a young man in the thirties,
worked in an auto-parts warehouse. Then off to college, emerging
with a socialist fervor and a strong sense of moral rectitude. Joined—
or fellow traveled—with leftist political groups. Later virulently—and
then more compassionately—attacked former associates who
informed and gave names to Congressional investigating committees.
Married three times: a straight Midwestern woman, a neurotic show-
business beauty and finally a refugee from the Nazi holocaust.

A few details round out the real-life Miller. A younger sister and an
older brother. From his first marriage a daughter, 24, married to a
sculptor, living in Manhattan, and a son, 26, married and making film
commercials in Oregon. No grandchildren, but a young daughter,
aged 9, from his third marriage, to the Austrian-born photographer
Inge Morath.

But it is the ghost of Marilyn Monroe that still lingers, a hovering
distraction in one's considerations—biographical and otherwise—of
Miller. It is simply easier to recall that he was once a partner in an
attempt at the great American dream marriage with her than to

remember that he may actually have succeeded in writing the great American play, *Death of a Salesman*. So one must consciously try to keep the Monroe ghost in perspective to treat Miller with the proper respect. One must resolutely remind oneself that attention must be paid to him on his own terms for his own work.

Yet after turning off Route I-84 and heading north through cannon-ball-on-the-lawn and antique-shop country toward Miller's Roxbury farm I could not help but slow down as I recalled that a European correspondent, racing to cover a Miller-Monroe happening, was once killed in a crash on these roads.

Miller's farmhouse stands just a few feet from the road—less to plow out when it snows—but surveys acres of spectacular hills and a pond for swimming and ice skating. I parked my car and walked through an open garage containing a solitary Volkswagen onto a terrace behind the house, where a barking dog was announcing my arrival. Miller came toward me, wearing an open-collared shirt, slacks and high work shoes. Beneath his receding silver-gray hair, his face was still reminiscent of an unbearded Jewish Lincoln.

He greeted me, and as I paused to take in the view, which he seemed to see for the first time himself, he mused: "You look at all this and you wonder why people are so screwed up."

"Because they don't have it," I said, and he laughed. "How many acres do you have?"

"About 350," he said, and then added quickly and apologetically: "But don't forget I first began buying land up here almost two dozen years ago. I was just down the road then. I added on little by little. And then you could buy land for a song. Not like now."

Miller's wife appeared, slender and intense in blue jeans and a polo shirt, and Miller introduced us.

"When would you like to have lunch?" she asked.

I shrugged, and Miller replied, "Let me show him around the place first." As he guided me down a gentle slope I asked whether he worked any of the land.

"I have a neighbor, and I let him graze his dairy stock here in exchange for the use of some of his heavier equipment when I need it. And I have a nursery where I grow some trees that I sell. And we have a garden that keeps our cold cellar full of fruits and vegetables all winter long. But let me show you what I'm doing here."

He ushered me into the barn, which contained a studio-guest

room completed years earlier and a carpentry shop with every manner of woodworking tool. Now contractors were installing a darkroom and a studio shaped like a ship's prow for Mrs. Miller and an alternate studio-guest room for Miller.

"Now I'll show you where I work," he said, and we walked past the terrace up a small knoll to a frame cabin covered with natural shakes. It was furnished with a desk and typewriter, a few chairs, a simple cot and bookshelves. Snapshots of his wife and daughter were pinned to the wall. There was no clutter on the desk; it looked almost too neat to be a writer's work area. Miller slumped into a chair behind the desk. "See," he said, "I've got everything I need here and no telephone."

How does he heat the cabin?

"I've got that," he said, pointing to a fireplace, "and I can use electricity. But it costs a fortune. That's why I'm thinking of moving into the barn."

What does he use for a toilet? He pointed out the open door and laughed at the city boy's question.

We began to get reacquainted, bringing one another up to date on family blessings and mishaps. Having been a public man for so long, Miller is still guarded and wary. And, like so many theatrical people and politicians, he manages to combine extreme shyness with a bold sense of self, an almost excessive immodesty.

"You're putting on a little weight," I remarked.

"No," Miller replied, patting his thin-man's paunch and stretching his long legs, "I just don't stand straight. But if I started working around here"—with a wave he took in the whole farm—"it'd go away in a day. Which I'm going to do."

Does he write every day?

"Every day. Sometimes seven days a week. I get up every morning about 7 o'clock, and I'm here by 8:30, and I work until—it depends on the day. Some days I can barely get up here. Some days I'm out by 10:30, 11—just can't write much. And some days, once I get going, I can work eight hours—longer than that, around the clock. That's the beauty of this setup. I can set my own pace, go the way I want. If I get on a hot writing period there's nothing else I have to do."

How much of his writing does he ultimately use and how much does he discard?

"Depends on the play," Miller said, picking up his pipe and leaning forward to fill it. "This new play I've only thrown away about 75 pages. The playscript ends up maybe 140 pages. So it's nothing. But normally—sometimes—given all the revision I would make I'd write maybe 2,000 pages." He lit the pipe and exhaled. "I always work on a typewriter, plus three or four notebooks."

What does he use the notebooks for?

"Attempts at scenes. Organizing things. Developing them. I'll write a whole act sometimes and use only one scene, or a whole scene and use just one line. See, I'm discovering it, making up my own story. I think at the typewriter."

"But sometimes also there's another way of working: getting it all out in one burst. That's happened, too. This new one I did in about six weeks. *Salesman* was that way, too. Boom! One burst and it was done. But *After the Fall* took me over a year and still many months."

Once a play is finished what does he do?

"I write a play for myself, so if I like it we do it."

As simple as that?

"Yes, I go to Bob Whitehead (the producer) and say, "Let's do it." And we do it. There's an audience for my plays. They're there. They buy tickets and they come. For which I'm very grateful."

Even without a star, is a Miller play certain to attract theater parties?

"Oh sure," he said, and sucked on his pipe. "More than any show apart from maybe a musical."

What is the next step in the life of a play?

"Well, we decide on a director. Bob has his ideas, and I have my ideas, and we walk around and finally put them together and decide."

What about serving as his own director?

"I never want to. I did it on *The Price* because I had to. We came to a disagreement with the director, and there simply wasn't time for any alternative but for me to direct. But ordinarily I don't want to direct. I'm not interested in it that much. To be a director you've got to know all the actors available, ideally speaking; you've got to be a theater person in the sense that you like to go to the theater often, which I don't. Never have."

"And you can't think of directing as a chore, but rather as a means of creation. To me, directing is all after the fact. And I hate to put myself through it. Just the sheer proposition, for example, of going through month of listening to my own lines endlessly repeated is a prospect I just hate. And if you're directing you have to be there at rehearsals all the time. Oh, I come in part of every day and whenever something has been changed. But I don't want to be a director."

"Also, even though this rarely happens, I always hope the director will think of something marvelous that I haven't thought of, in terms of staging, in terms of decor or something. And a good director does have an approach to actors, especially American actors, which I basically don't have. He knows how to communicate with them on a less-than-verbal level. Which is what they respond to best."

Who is an ideal director for his work? What about Kazan, for example?

"Oh, Kazan's a marvelous director. He's also made his mistakes. Everybody does. But he's wonderful with actors, and he's superbly organized. I'm working with Harold Clurman now, and he has tremendous points. For one thing he's been in the theater for 45 years, and I think he's the best critic there is. Of me and everybody else."

Miller rose and stretched his long frame. "Come on," he said, "let's eat." He patted his stomach. "It's my lousy posture. I never could stand up straight. But pretty soon I'll work it off."

The Miller living room, separated from the terrace by sliding glass doors, exudes a comfortable feeling of Continental clutter. There are books and magazines piled atop a glass coffee table. End tables in a Spanish motif. Walls adorned with foreign theater posters proclaiming Miller productions. Inge Morath photographs of Russia. A mock marriage license by Saul Steinberg, the cartoonist. There are Eames chairs and an antique rocker, a modern rug, old figurines, Mexican candlesticks. Plant life is everywhere.

We lunched not in the kitchen but in a cheerful, traditional dining room. Mrs. Miller unobtrusively served excellent tacos with beer, pears and Brie for dessert and good coffee. Somehow a box of Mallomars materialized at Miller's elbow, and he nibbled on them while discussing what he termed "the crap-game aspect of playwrighting":

"Suppose you open the wrong night. When there's a big new event you're dead; it doesn't matter what kind of a play you had. If everybody has his head on Page 1, then it doesn't matter what's on Page 47.

"And nowadays, even before you open, there's the problem of casting. Used to be almost every good actor was in New York and available. But now the theater has become a fifth wheel for actors, too—something for them to consider when they're not doing a movie, or not in a television series or they're over the hill in movies, which is something I don't care about because that does not mean they're really over the hill as actors. But anyway, you make out a list of, say, 30 actors, and there're two you really care about. Well, the likelihood is you can't get those two actors for reasons that have nothing to do with the play—or anything. So you just have to wait, which is what I decided to do with my new play."

Given the theatrical realities, then, does it pay to go on writing plays?

"Absolutely not. It doesn't make any sense. You've got to be obsessed and stupefied with the glory of the medium. Because if you look at it objectively it's absolutely senseless."

Why does he do it?

"I love it. I just love it," said Miller, dipping into the Mallomar box. "I love the stage. And perforce I'm doing it for myself."

How does he manage financially?

"Well, my plays are done all over the world. I've made my living basically for many years now on domestic and foreign amateur and semiprofessional productions. And of course I've had plays on almost every two or three years in New York. And I'm assured of productions in Paris, London, Italy, all over Germany. That's what makes it possible for me to go on."

Is he fixed financially for the rest of his life?

"Yeah. Maybe not for the rest of my life, but for a long time. I wouldn't need too much more. I own this house and don't have to pay any rent—just the taxes and I have a roof over my head. And I could always do journalism if I had to."

When did he last face financial pressures?

"In the middle or late fifties, I guess."

Wasn't that the period in which critics consider him to have been essentially barren—those years with Marilyn Monroe?

"Barren?" said Miller, shaking his head. "That's when I did *The Misfits*. And I started to do a movie for the New York City Youth Board, but they knocked me out of the box with a big red-baiting campaign. Barren? That whole period I never had an empty day." He shook his head again.

"Anyway, that's all gone. Thank God. And I have more to do now than I have time to do it in. Besides the new play, I have another one almost finished and another one that I'm beginning to see in a form I can manage."

Mrs. Miller answered the telephone in the living room and we soon heard her speaking Russian. "She's terrific," her husband said. "After we came back from Russia a few years ago she decided to learn Russian. And she did it."

"What are your feelings," it suddenly occurred to me to ask, "about Women's Liberation?"

"I think a lot of it is terrific," Miller replied. "I think a lot of it should have been said a long time ago. But, like everything here, it gets said in hysteria. And I'm sure the media are the cause of that. You get tired of saying even a truth. It's as if there always has to be something new, so they create its perversion. I can't take seriously some of the idiocy that comes out of it. On the other hand, I'm sure if I talked to some people about it they could easily convince me to the contrary."

I mentioned that he had not prepared lunch, though he probably could have.

"I could have," Miller conceded, "but Inge loves to. She wouldn't let me prepare lunch. My wife can cook in about eight languages, and I can only make chops, chicken and steak." He resolutely pushed the Mallomar box away.

"I've tried, but it doesn't come out. I lived alone here once. I tried to cook and I had all the cookbooks and it was terrible. You have to have a certain talent."

Inge came in, a camera bag slung over her shoulder. "I'll be out photographing," she told Miller, "but I'll be back in time to take you to pick up your car. They called before to say it was ready."

I asked what kind of car he has.

"A Mercedes 280 S.E.L."

"It's a good car."

"Yeah, but I've been having troubles with it. But one thing I'll say, they take care of it. And when it's running it gets me into the city in two hours."

Does he get into the city often?

"Not as much as I used to. I can go a couple of weeks now without going in. And I don't miss it. I used to keep a place at the Hotel Chelsea, but I found that I was using it less and less. It was just a stop for me, and there were so many whores and pimps around, arguing all the time, I hated to bring my wife there. So I gave it up. Now when I stay over in town I stay with friends. I have enough friends with big houses and kids grown up and gone so there's room."

Does he go to the theater at all?

"Oh, I always go to see Pinter. And I go Off-Broadway to see some of the black playwrights like Gordone and that other fellow, Bullins, who I think are close to having some real vitality. Because they're writing about something. Their work isn't simply an exercise in some fashionable kind of pique. So I'm glad they're on."

Does he regret the absence of practicing playwrights of his own generation?

"Sure. It's always better when there are more plays that are interesting because then people assume there is something in theater, after all. But now I think there is a critical judgment—if you can call it that—that nothing good could possibly happen in the theater. And that *a priori* assumption is ridiculous. But I guess it makes it easier to be a critic under such circumstances."

Assumptions aside, isn't the theater dead anyway?

"No," said Miller, shaking his head emphatically. "There's been a displacement, but not a destruction. New York City fell apart. How can you expect a theater to exist in a jungle like that? There is no community, or even a facsimile of one. There isn't even enough community to safeguard a pedestrian, so how can you expect a theater to go on there?" He leaned forward across the table.

"Look. The middle class has always supported the theater. And the middle class has fled New York City. But when you say, 'Therefore the theater is dead,' it isn't so. Not true. Is Macy's dead? What's happened to Macy's? They went to the suburbs. Is the wholesale and retail clothing business dead? No. They simply registered the change in population."

"So what we've been living through, really, is a transformation in the population. It comes to New York to make its money, and it gets out as fast as it can. And New York is stuck with a theater district and purely extraneous crap, such as negotiations with unions and real-estate people, that were formed in an entirely different social era."

"But that doesn't mean the form of the theater is dead. Not at all. I showed my new play to my son. He read it, and it appealed to him very deeply. But that's not the point. His reaction was interesting. 'My

God,' he said, 'What a thing, and to do it all with just words.' You see, his attitude—and that of his friends—that the theater is dead simply masks the fact that they've never discovered it. They were born into TV and into a time when theater didn't amount to anything. It remains to be discovered, you know."

"And I think it's going to come back. Maybe not tomorrow or next year, but I have the feeling—not the feeling, the knowledge—that the day will come when theater again will surmount everything for the simple reason that it is an irreducible simplicity. It's a man up there facing other men. Somehow or other this always has to be possible. It takes less means than anything else we have, including painting. You don't need a machine. You don't need lenses. You don't need lights. You need a board and an actor. That's all you need; you don't need anything else. Except a certain amount of quiet, which is sometimes difficult to find."

Miller smiled and stood up. "Come on," he said, "let's go outside and get some fresh air. It's too beautiful a day to waste in here."

We sat on the terrace, looking out at the rolling hills, and began to talk away the afternoon. I asked which contemporary novelists he liked. Miller lit his pipe and considered, "I don't read many novels," he said. "I mean, I start to read a lot of novels, but I never finish them. I read Bellow's last book, *Mr. Sammler's Planet,* but I like everything he writes. He still has a joy in writing, which is the first thing necessary. I love Roth's work, too, for that same reason. He seems to have fun doing it."

Some critics, I pointed out, see a growing Jewishness or a more explicit Jewishness in Miller's work.

"I don't think that's so," he said, shaking his head. I'm not aware of it. That novel I wrote in '45, *Focus,* is about a Jew and anti-Semitism and so forth. So if I've had a preoccupation it goes way back. And I suppose my new play is Jewish in the sense that it is the Old Testament. But I don't see Jewishness really as something emerging."

What does he see emerging in his work?

"I can't see or predict the future. But I think my plays are getting more and more mythological; the people are becoming less and less psychological. Like, in the new play they're actually mythological. I mean, there's God and Lucifer and Adam and Eve and Cain and Abel. And perhaps it isn't as obvious to others as it is to me that the characters in all my other plays are also mythological. In *Incident at Vichy*, for example, I was not attempting to delineate psychological types. In fact, I did everything to strip the characters of any such thing. The characters were functions of the society, and I wasn't interested in whether they had any itches or not."

Was he saying that he was becoming less naturalistic and more symbolic?

"Yes," Miller answered, puffing on his pipe. "I think ultimately, if you live long enough, that's the way it ends up anyway. I think you see patterns finally. Earlier on in life the individual overwhelms your vision. But then when you see three, five, thirty variations of the individual there seems to be an archetype lurking in the background. Consciously, though, I'm still trying and I've always tried to put people up there on the stage. And it's quite obvious they're all projections of me, same as with any other writer. But I don't think I can write until I see some mythos. I don't think I could ever generate the energy to do a whole play just to tell a story about some psychologically interesting folks. I mean, the most psychological of my characters was probably Willy Loman. And I've become aware now that I was dealing with something much more there than Willy Loman, the tactile quality of the experience of that one particular character."

I commented on the irony that Miller is best known for realism while he sees abstraction as the thread that runs through his work.

"Yes," he said, "but you see, before *All My Sons* I had written 13 plays, none of which is realistic and none of which got me anywhere. So I decided at the age of 29 that I wasn't going to waste my life in this thing. I already had one child, and I couldn't see myself going on writing play after play and getting absolutely nowhere. I sat down and decided to write a play about which nobody could say to me, as they had with all the other plays, 'What does this mean?' or 'I don't understand that' or some such thing. And I spent two years writing that play, just to see if I could do it that way. Because I was working in a realistic theater, which didn't know anything else. But that doesn't mean I was ever at bottom simply a realistic playwright."

What would he have done if *All My Sons* hadn't been successful?

"I don't know." He took the pipe out of his mouth and stared at it. "I probably would have gone on anyway. But maybe not, because I'm capable of doing a lot of things."

Such as?

"Work of various kinds, like to be a carpenter. A good carpenter today makes more than 95 per cent of the members of the Authors Guild and gets a month's vacation, too—don't forget that. Eight dollars an hour—that's $64 a day. That's what they get here. God knows what they get down in the city."

Would he have considered being a novelist?

"Somehow, a book has always been sort of remote to me. It doesn't offer the same kick that comes from the direct experience of a confrontation with an audience. And when it comes to writing I think my talent has always been fundamentally and essentially for the drama. I've never been comfortable writing in any other way. You see, I know I can do in three pages of dialogue what would take me endless pages of words. I know I can do what would be like a 2,000-page novel in less than two-and-a-half hours on a stage.

"There's also a dramatic structure which I find endlessly fascinating. I love to vary and reform it. And I love acting when I write. I mean, I'm the whole cast, I play all the parts. And that's not in a book. And I love real actors, too. I love to sit there and change one line and see an explosion happen that wouldn't have happened if the line hadn't been changed.

"So maybe I never could have gotten out of this playwriting thing anyway. Perhaps it's always been just too embedded in my head. I mean, I had opportunities to go to Hollywood way back before *All My Sons* was produced. You've got to remember in those days Hollywood was making a picture every Monday morning, there were hundreds of pictures made every year. It was a going, glamorous, prestigious place with all kinds of high-paying jobs for writers compared to Broadway, which even in those times was regarded as dying and on its way out." Miller chuckled.

"You didn't even have to have written a play in those days. You just had to call yourself a playwright. And there was this Colonel Joy—that was his name, Colonel Joy—who came from 20th-Century Fox, and he'd carry playwrights out to the Coast in boxcars. Once everybody I knew, with practically no exceptions, vanished from the haunts of New York City overnight. I don't want to mention any names. But I know two guys I really thought were talented playwrights, and they never wrote anything else again. And I knew one fellow who had a remarkable play almost finished. He never got to finish it. In fact, whenever I would get out there in later years I would see him. And one day he said a frightful thing to me, quite seriously: 'What's your next assignment?' I said, 'I'm writing a play now.' He said, 'For whom?' I said, 'Well, I'm just writing a play, and then I'll see for whom.' 'Oh,' he said, 'you mean you're doing it on spec.'

"That's the story. He'd been living out there a long time. And I think after a certain length of time out there one loses one's independence, the feeling that one somehow has the right to invest one's time and life and talent the way one wants to."

I suggested that we turn to politics briefly, and Miller snapped: "I hate politics."

"O.K.," I said, "then we'll talk about your Puritanism." Miller raised his eyebrows and pursed his lips. "Clurman says that in your younger days you were much more Puritan, much more sure of yourself, than you are now. Do you feel there's any validity in that?"

"I was a Puritan and unsure of myself," Miller laughed. "What Puritan is ever sure of himself?"

"Do you feel more sure of yourself now?"

"Well, I know certain things that I feel more confidence about. As I've said it's purely an awareness of repetition. I know I can more or less rely on patterns, and to that degree I have more certainty than I did. But 'Puritanism' doesn't quite relate to what's happened to me and my work. I'd say, rather, that early on the emphasis was on writing as legislating, as though the world were to be ordered by the implications in my work. Later, in emphasis, 'what is' overtook 'what ought to be.' "

Which, I said, brought us back to politics.

"Look," replied Miller, leaning forward and putting his pipe on an end table, "when I said, 'I hate politics' that doesn't mean I turn my back on politics. You can't; politics is something like tying your shoes or making a living. And, God help us, I know our fate is political. Yet I also think politics now is becoming less and less connected to what's really going on. It's never been so true as it is now that it hardly matters which party is in."

Doesn't it matter that the Democrats lost and the Republican won in 1968?

"Nixon's irritating," Miller replied, "but, don't you see, in a way that's good. Because he strips it bare. You're under no

misapprehension as to what's going on. You don't get the illusion a
very nice man is making a mistake and wish he only knew better."

Who is Miller, a McCarthy delegate at the '68 Democratic
convention, going to support in '72?

"There isn't a candidate except McGovern who I think makes any
difference. And McGovern I don't think has a prayer—just because
he makes a difference. You see, what's happening—and it's been
happening for 30 years—is that we've become a corporate state. It
has become the function of the state to make it possible for immense
corporations to carry on their activities, and everything else is
incidental. There are always conflicts between the corporations and
between the Government and the corporations, but fundamentally
what we have is a socialism of the individual corporations of a
corporate socialism."

Then are the militants the only ones presenting alternatives?

"No," said Miller with a shudder, "because they haven't arrived at
any libertarian alternatives. The only alternative they've presented, if
you dig beneath the rhetoric and verbiage, is really another kind of
authoritarian socialism. I mean, even the rhetoric is intolerant and
authoritarian and tyrannical. The real argument with this system is
that it prevents a man from flowering freely. So why the hell should I
get excited about a rhetoric that wants to supplant an oppressive
ideology with a suppressive one? It doesn't make any sense. This is
not 1932, when there were still possibilities of having illusions about
the Soviet Union. I mean, then a man could say—as I did, and as I
believed, and I'm not ashamed I did because then you had to if you
had any brains in your head—that rationally the Socialist idea in the
Soviet Union made much more sense than anything that was
happening here; people were on breadlines and guys with degrees
were lucky if they could get jobs selling ties at Macy's or delivering the
mail. Really, it was tough stuff."

What is his political stance now?

"Well," said Miller, tapping his pipe against his hand, "everybody's
got some kind of a disembodied or confused anger, but I think
somebody—and I know this sounds corny—has got to take the part
of liberty and freedom. For example, when I became president of
International P.E.N. in 1965 I was amazed to discover the number of
writers in jail in the free world as well as the Socialist bloc. Whenever
I would start talking about this people would say, 'You've got to have

writers in jail, that goes with the territory,' or 'You can't have a revolution without scrambling the eggs.' But I think the human being has got to be the center of any ideologies going at the moment. I mean, people aren't thinking that way any more. They're all power dealers, redistributing powers, so it always winds up the same thing all over again."

Miller paused and let out a long sigh. "Maybe that's the fate," he said. "Maybe we're doomed. But my particular job as I see it is not to let myself get into that whole bit."

Hasn't he done that in the past?

"Oh sure. I believed the same thing years ago—that if you're going to have revolution in a country you've got to put the whole middle class in jail. It seemed very logical, intellectually sound. But that was before I started meeting some of the people who were in jails and some of the people who were putting them in jails."

How does he find his children politically?

"I think they're disengaged now. And how can you blame them? Under what banner are they going to get excited? I think one good thing about that generation is that they've been in and out of it quickly, and they didn't get burned up too badly. After all, they were disappointed in a Eugene McCarthy, say, but that's just a pimple on the nose. They weren't made to pay the price the way my generation did. Many of us were slaughtered as a result of this, both intellectually and worse—our hearts were torn out. Because it was a slower process. You had to go through the war in Spain, the Second World War, the Nazi time, the reconstruction of Europe and the rest of it. It was a question of 20 years; the disillusionment now is a question of 20 months."

Inge returned and warned Miller that he would have to be leaving soon. I said I had only one or two more questions to ask. The first was what he thinks his literary reputation is now.

"I have no idea," he replied.

Some people think his work has gone steadily downhill since *Salesman*.

"I don't see it that way. I've had the problem of coming out of Broadway, which was our only professional theater. And some critics could never accept the proposition that the product of a commercial establishment could have anything to do with art. It was simply not permissible. This was before a review was ever written. If there was any public attraction to your work that was conclusive proof it couldn't possibly have any worth.

"Now," he laughed, "a Mary McCarthy can get ruined by *The Group*. So, you see, this irony proceeds remorselessly to the bitter end. Consequently, you have to end up smiling at the whole thing. It's just a game, an illusion in a little room."

What about his reputation in the future?

"That's impossible to answer. I mean, when I was first coming up O'Neill was considered like old-fashioned jive talk—'Twenty-three skidoo.' And look at him now. Or the other way around—take Hemingway. Given the real impact that man had on letters 15, 20 years ago, it would have been hard to believe that nothing but a sneer would now greet the mention of his name."

Miller looked off at the hills for a moment. "Therefore," he concluded, "you can't hang any value on a current estimate. You can only pick up a thing and relate yourself to it and say, 'I believe in this. It meets some quality of reality that I recognize. It moves me this way. It moves me that way.' And to hell with everything else."

He rose, we said our goodby[e]s and he loped off toward the Volkswagen that would take him to retrieve his Mercedes.

Miller Takes His Comedy Seriously
Tom Buckley/1972

From *The New York Times*, 29 Aug. 1972, 22. Reprinted by permission.

For 25 years now theatrical audiences have hired, so to speak, Arthur Miller to do their brooding for them—about the millstones of commerce that grind a man to dust, about political hysteria, incipient fascism, anti-Semitism, the tug and pull of family strife.

Under the circumstances, what took place yesterday in the lounge of the ANTA Theater deserves at least a footnote in the annals of the American stage.

This event was the start of rehearsals of Mr. Miller's first comedy, *The Creation of the World and Other Business*. It will open in Washington on Oct. 17, which, coincidentally, is the playwright's 57th birthday.

To be sure, Mr. Miller, unable to change his ways entirely, has called his new work "a catastrophic comedy." But as he discussed it the other day in the offices of his producer, Robert Whitehead and Roger L. Stevens, in the fabled old Palace Theater Building, it became clear that the accent was on the noun rather than the adjective.

"I've always loved to watch really good comedy," Mr. Miller said, lounging on what might, in a less high-toned firm, have been the casting couch. "In fact, I like it better than the so-called serious drama when I go to the theater.

"The great moments of my life have come with great comedians. From Sid Caesar to . . . what's his name . . . Terry Hart, who was in *Room Service*, I could give you a scene-by-scene analysis of *Room Service*. There's a wonderful joy in that kind of laughter."

He paused, as he often does in conversation, to collect his thoughts, then went on: "When I was a boy the great ones were new—Buster Keaton, Charlie Chaplin, Fatty Arbuckle. I always

249

thought Arbuckle was funny, but not Keaton. The first time I saw
Chaplin I didn't realize that he was supposed to be comical. In every
one of his movies there was stealing going on, but I was brought up
in Harlem, where everybody was stealing everything, so I didn't get
the joke."

Unlike professional writers of comedy, who tend as a class to be
bilious, crapulous and full of psychic tremors as a dog is of fleas, Mr.
Miller, tanned, his weight down to 175 pounds on his springy 6 foot
2½ inch frame, relaxed and humorous, said that just thinking about
Creation put him in good spirits.

His visitor asked why it had been, then, considering the tonic
effects of comedy, that he had waited so long to write one.

"I tried," he replied, "but I never could line myself up with a
conception that didn't break apart into its more or less realistic
psychological elements, and things got less and less funny."

Like many playwrights, Mr. Miller is a pretty good deliverer of his
own lines. As he completed the preceding statement his voice
became slower and more doleful. Then he paused for two beats,
looked up and laughed again.

Whatever inexplicable change in outlook it was that allowed him to
finally move ahead took place about two years ago, he said.
"Basically it was for his wife, Inge Morath, the photographer; the
couple lives in the quiet and undramatic countryside of Roxbury,
Conn., about 15 miles north of Danbury.

"By some means which I'll never understand I began the way one
sits down at the piano, to improvise in various themes in the freest
possible way," he said. "Basically it was for my own enjoyment and
my friends. In fact, when I began doing these scenes I was working
on another, serious play. But when friends came over and I wanted to
read to them I found myself reaching for this one, or what was to
become this one."

"Gradually the play began to invent itself, and I finally decided that
I would see what happened if I seriously went about developing this
feeling that I had. It took about six weeks, and I never had a better
time writing anything."

Creation was ready for production last season, but Mr. Miller and
the producers were unable to cast it as they wished, and reluctantly
put it aside. Now they have their hearts' desire, with Bob Dishy as
Adam, Barbara Harris as Eve, Hal Holbrook as Lucifer, Steve Elliott
as God and Barry Primus as Cain.

When it came down to the point of explaining in just what ways the play went beyond the original script, Mr. Miller's language became vague. His listener sensed that, despite his offer to provide a script for perusal, which was vetoed by his director, Harold Clurman, that there may have been a certain interest in maintaining an air of mystery about it.

"Part of the process of the play is Adam's experience, waking up with God and how he learned the world," he said. "The wonderful thing is that the myth is true. It reflects exactly what happens to us in our earthly career."

"This God . . . "—he paused as though confronting indescribable mysteries— ". . . this God you will know forever. You'll identify with him and with all the other people, too, and if we do it right and I'm not incorrect about it you'll be very moved by the whole business and caught up in all the madness of it. I just think that God is a marvelous character, and a very moving one."

His questioner wondered aloud why he had gone to the Book of Genesis for inspiration.

"I have a tiny studio in the woods," Mr. Miller replied. "There are a handful of books there, and one of them has always been the Bible. I read it, the Old Testament, usually because the new one I can't understand too easily, so I've always had a rather intimate feeling about it."

"The thing that has always intrigued me is that I would start thinking about a Biblical character, think I understood him very well, look him up and find it was all wrong and that I'd invented a whole different role for him. So what happens is that one's fantasies get connected with this panoply of characters and stories until they are no longer what they are but what you make them."

Asked about his own religious beliefs, Mr. Miller said: "The play is the clearest expression of them that I've come to. What the play is probing is whether there is in the human condition a force which *makes* man's concepts of high, low, good and bad, right and wrong, inevitable.

"The answer is, I think my answer is, in the play, as to what it is that makes these things as important as bread . . . "—another pause—" . . . and sex."

His own religious upbringing began early, he said. "There was this old guy with a beard who came to the house and who I naturally mistook, at the age of 5 or 6, for God. He spoke in Hebrew, not one syllable of which I understood, so our relationship was very warm."

"But I got the basic idea of what he was trying to drive home and invented everything I thought he was trying to tell me." He laughed deeply. "You know, there is no religion that is closer to a man than the one he invents, so I guess you can say in that sense that I'm religious."

He slipped his heavy horn-rimmed glasses off his nose. "That is, I think there is a destiny beyond the bread and butter, but it consists, for me, in creativity. I think there is a spirit that can be killed in a society and in an individual that, for want of a better word, is the life spirit, the creative spirit."

"This is holy, and it takes great effort, a kind of prayer, to keep it alive and to nurture it. Without it, we might as well not be around. Life becomes simply a series of objects and chance relationships, and it gets pretty desiccated."

Although Mr. Miller has been quoted as saying that in good times and bad he believes there is an audience for his plays—and unkind critics have suggested that it is middle-class, middle-aged and stodgily earnest in its liberalism, he believes that *Creation* will have a special appeal to youth.

It is a question that has been much in his mind lately. His two children, both by the first of his three wives, are in their mid-20s, and only 10 days ago his son, who lives in Oregon, made him a grandfather for the first time.

"My experience with this play is that the younger you are the more it will move you," he said. "The world of this play is the world of the young. It isn't a world in which an old, creaky philosopher is making his peace. This is the world of creation, not of burial."

Arthur Miller: Interview
Robert W. Corrigan/1974

From *Michigan Quarterly Review* 13 (1974): 401-05. Reprinted
by permission.

(Excerpt from a longer interview, November 16, 1973)

Robert W. Corrigan: The first question that I have is that it seems
to me earlier in your career, Mr. Miller, you appeared to be quite
consciously attempting to write tragedy in the modern idiom.
However, beginning with *After the Fall*, you seem much more
concerned with making spiritual explorations into ideas like guilt and
responsibility and the problem of how to incorporate what one knows
to be the truth of his life, and how to make it come out in his actions
and so forth. You seem to be more interested in these kinds of ideas
than in dramatizing the tragic dimensions of these actions, and I
wonder if you could explain the reasons for what seemed to be a
shift in attitude and focus in your work.

    Arthur Miller: That's hard for me to answer because a lot of it is
subjective. I mean, it is not because of a theoretical consideration that
I changed the emphasis. I suppose when one is younger, at least for a
time, it is easier to contemplate death as a transcendency than it is a
little later on when the materials of existence seem to cry out for
some organizing principle with which to carry on life. It is also
probably that the society as I felt it has been death-bound, has been
in a state of such decay and longing for its own destruction that I
haven't felt the desire to celebrate destruction but on the contrary to
find some means in myself that would lay a hand on life and find a
principle in man to counter the destructive force. This has changed
the way the plays are written, I think. They have become an attempt
to discover a life-force in—you might call it—the biological structure

of human beings. In the earlier plays I believe what was being
examined was something like the imperative toward disaster,
something in the social situation and in the men and women who live
in it, whereby they are doomed. Later on I take the doom for
granted, I think, and look for some kind of life-line to hang onto. It
seems to me that society is already demonstrating what in earlier
plays I was trying to show.

Corrigan: You feel in the early plays then that society was in a
sense operating as a kind of force of fate?

Miller: Yes, I still think that. I think, we'll be jumping to another
idea if I say this, but you don't have to follow it up. It seems to me
that the only thing we've got in modern times that has any parallel to
the ancient divinities was a pleasure or displeasure that man had to
live with in the society, which is incomprehensible in its operations.
Nobody can predict its moods, whether it will turn to war or peace,
economic disaster or boom, over-employment or under-employment,
every condition of life is whimsical: which is very close to what the
Greeks thought about God. It is all we've got and what it lacks is
sublimity because at bottom, I think, most people, (I am not sure that
it is most people, but enough certainly) have no sense of divinity in
the government anymore but it has power. It has the power of the
divinity but not the sublimity of one and this is what cuts down the
tragic vision. It levels. So, all one can do is defend oneself against it
and resolve to find some means of living in the face of this insane
force. By society I don't mean, of course, merely the government. It
is the whole way we live, what we want from life and what we do to
get it.

Corrigan: So, ironically we are part of the very society which at
the same time is acting upon us?

Miller: I used some phrase years ago that the fish is in the water
and the water is in the fish. Man is in society but the society is in man
and every individual. To trace the lines of each as they wind around
together is one of my preoccupations. In order to arrive at some
leverage by the man on his own fate so that he can find a way to
swim or he can find a way to control that part of his psyche which is
already predetermined so to speak by his society. It happens in *Death
of a Salesman* when Biff opts out. He sees that his father is driven not
merely by psychological forces but by what he believes socially, by
what he strives for.

Corrigan: I wonder if the tragic form doesn't require that the playwright in some way express in dramatic, as opposed to visual terms, the protagonist coming to this awareness; in other words, Othello commits suicide too. Lear dies[,] Oedipus cuts out his eyes, but prior to these actions they come to see and accept the responsibility for their error, and we know they have accepted their destiny because Shakespeare and Sophocles have directly expressed this in the text of the play. And I wonder if the tragic form doesn't require this expression of acceptance.

Miller: It might. The problem is really that those figures, the authors of their fates, so to speak, were recognizable figures in the hierarchy of beliefs of their time. They were working with an audience and a culture that did in fact believe in the powers of heaven. They were trying to work out the relationship between man and God, so that they start with a consciousness which we don't have. Our idea is that that is completely self-contradictory: I am speaking of the United States, but it is pretty widespread in the West, this belief that man is free to pick out his own career. It is up to him to become what he is going to be so that society becomes an arena for his aggressions. He goes into the society to hack out what he can from it, and it reacts with him and against him, but by the time he arrives at his fate, excepting for a few people who we will mention in a minute, he can no longer disentangle where the outside world ends and he begins. A classical hero is working inside a religious cosmology where there is no mistaking a man for God; he is conscious to begin with that he is in the hands of God. Consequently, the only issue left is his responsibility. We are not quite ready to see that. We are in the middle of a scrambled egg and mucking about in it, and the difference between the points of contact with the man and his God, so to speak, are fused.

Corrigan: And yet it is interesting in your later work that you see people as being much more able to recognize their responsibilities.

Miller: Because in later work, the work itself is less subjective. In *The Crucible* there is no question but that it is the social organization which is conveying the tragic. John Proctor wouldn't be in that jam except for the actions of some politicians. Hence, the level of consciousness is far higher in John Proctor than in earlier protagonists. I mean, he does announce what the problem is and what the issues are because the real social situation makes that possible. He can verbalize what Willie—or most of us—cannot because the enemy is indistinct. It is all around us and inside of us.

Corrigan: Another question that I was going to ask you because it seems to me that your earlier work had a sense of structure that was in some ways related to the Ibsen-like structure, and then, beginning with *After the Fall*, my God, you have been exploring all sorts of different kinds of structures. And I was wondering whether the experience with *The Misfits*, the making of *The Misfits*, began to have any effect on your sense of what dramatic form could be.

Miller: I did a lot of work in radio. I don't remember how many plays I wrote, but it must have been 30 or 40 and they were just jobs of words, because you could move with the sound from two men on the moon to two guys in a submarine to wherever you wanted to go. The play you're really talking about is *All My Sons* which in my history is rather a sport. I wrote, I don't know how many plays before that, none of which had that form and I think I explained the other day, the reason that I wrote it that way was because first of all it happened that way. It was the kind of story that tells itself better that way but it was also trying to make myself absolutely clear which I hadn't been able to do before, clear to the theatre as it existed those days. But as soon as I had done that, I went back to what I had done before which was *Death of a Salesman* and all the rest of them. I have never really been happy with that kind of a continuous rendering of antecedent materials and so on. I mean in *Death of a Salesman*, the guy comes on and he says I'm pooped, I'm finished, there is no introduction of any kind. He says, I couldn't make it and you're right in the middle of it. And it just goes chop, chop, chop, chop, one cut to the next cut, right through the play. *The Crucible* is a mixture of the two but that is the way I, I am not a formalist in the sense that well, sometimes painters are. Painters can decide on a style and put everything in that style and make 40 pictures in 2 years in that style because he's playing really with a style more than a subject matter. I try to fit the form to what I am saying and to what, the way the nature of which that story seems to want to tell itself. I think that is what form is for, as an instrument, it isn't an object in itself, it isn't an entity to itself. There is no reason in the world why a perfectly conventional Ibsen-like play couldn't come out tomorrow and knock your head over. If it was done with sufficient excitement by the writer. After all most of the stuff written today which seems to satisfy most people is probably written in way-out forms but we're getting less and less charmed by all this because it doesn't work not because of the talent isn't there or the guy is simply using a popular form, with nothing much to say in it, or with insufficient talent. The emphasis that I would put on the forms are simply why it is that that form is used given the kind of material that is there. I think all this comes probably from the Elizabethan times when they did have a reigning sense of time, society, history—think of that iambic pentameter and the way they set up situations that were marvelously uniform, whether they were Shakespeare's, Beaumont-Fletcher's, or Marlowe's. You know that the plays were Elizabethan plays. There is no doubt about it. But I think today there is far too much niggling and worrying and harrying questions of form. We have *forms*, but we have no particular *form*. I ask, what are we trying to say? What is a man's real gut feeling about the life he is living? That is what I am interested in, you see, and that's the last thing anybody asks anymore.

Corrigan: You mean then, for example, that when you were writing *Death of a Salesman*, you weren't concerned about the tragic form.

Miller: No, that is after the fact. Just to lay that to rest: I read Aristotle years ago, and I read all the Greek plays, but I could not see that most of them conform to Aristotle's definitions. And furthermore, he was writing after the fact, he was confronted with drama which was trying to describe, don't forget. Aristotle was not the father of the drama, he was its stepson. I was interviewed by a psychologist, a couple of years ago, and he made it appear that the psychologists, Freud and Adler and the rest of them, and Jung, had made the fundamental discoveries about man, when in fact all the "discoveries" were old literature. That's primary, man is primary, and all this stuff is an attempt to analyze what exists. Now, I am interested in creating something that exists, rather than in an analysis of it. Do you see what I am driving at? And I think when the theatre gets too involved in analytical theory, then anyone who isn't a specialist in such theory, but is simply a sensible citizen looking for some insight into existence, is turned off. Why shouldn't he be? He can't get involved in the damn thing.

Miller Still a 'Salesman'
for a Changing Theater
Murray Schumach/1975

From *The New York Times*, 26 June 1975, 32. Reprinted
by permission.

"I'm 25 years older," said Arthur Miller, "and a year and a half wiser."

The 59-year-old playwright, still gaunt and loose-jointed, was
reflecting on changes in himself, the theater and the world the other
day because his Pulitzer Prize-winning *Death of a Salesman,* which
stunned Broadway in 1949, will reopen Thursday at the Circle in the
Square Theatre, with George C. Scott as director and star.

"The success of *Salesman*," said Mr. Miller, "gave me the feeling
that you could do anything with the stage provided your imagination
is intact; that there is no limit to the stage as far as ability to lead
people across heaven and earth with a few words. I still feel that
way."

As Mr. Miller reflected, in an East Side hotel room, he was much
more relaxed than in Philadelphia 25 years ago, where he worried
over last-minute changes and brooded over how Broadway would
take to a play that used new techniques to say that the crises of
ordinary people were subjects of high tragedy.

"Had *Salesman* been my first play," he said, "I'm not sure that I
could have gotten it on. When the title came out, it was a bit of a
shocker. Death of a king or an archbishop . . . but death of a
salesman . . . it caused some people to react as though this was an
absurdity. It's almost inconceivable now that this was the reaction."

With a wry grin that accentuated the natural gravity of his deep-
furrowed face, he told of a famous theater director who had invested
in the play, without reading it, because Mr. Miller had been successful
with *All My Sons,* and because Elia Kazan was directing.

"When he read the script," said Mr. Miller, "he withdrew half his
money. He said he couldn't follow it. There were others like him."

Since then, Mr. Miller said, the theater and audience have changed considerably, and they seem to be changing again. Both transitions, he said, were because theater and audience reflect changes in the nation.

In the 25 years he has written *The Crucible* (1953); *A View From the Bridge* (1955), which won the New York Drama Critics Circle Award; *The Misfits*, a novel, which became a movie; *After the Fall* (1963); *The Price* (1968); book and lyrics for his only musical, *The Creation of the World and Other Business* and short stories. He also received, in 1959, the gold medal for drama from the National Institute of Arts and Letters.

During that period, the published version of *Salesman*—in English alone—has exceeded 2.2 million copies in paperback, plus 74,000 copies in hardback, according to the Viking Press.

Mr. Miller has been reluctant to allow professional productions of the play in the New York area unless the cast was very professional because he assumes such productions would be reviewed.

In his personal life, his first marriage, to Mary Slattery, ended in divorce; and so did his second, to the late Marilyn Monroe. He is now married to Inge Morath, the photographer. They live in Roxbury, Conn. in a house that is set farther back from the road than the one he helped build at the time of *Death of a Salesman*.

In recent years, he has tried to shape into a play what he considers "the big issue today—Big Brother."

"My feeling, in a way," he says, "stems from disappointment with the Left. Any big organization has fantastic manipulative leverage. Big government, big business, and, in some cases, big labor.

"I worked for a year on a play on this subject. But it did not work out; the idea of economic power but not responsibility. Look at the C.I.A. You can have a trial of initials. Or the 'gas' shortage. Who is ever going to find anybody on whom this can be hung. I'm still fussing with this play. I put it aside a year ago."

He figures to get back to it. But meanwhile he is working on "two other projects," which he does not care to discuss, not even to say if they are plays. But he was quite willing to talk about the theater and audiences.

"The changes in the theater and the audience," said Mr. Miller, "reflected cultural strife. In the middle-fifties, from a more or less culturally coherent group of people, the theater-going audience became an atomized audience."

"Now there may be a new coherency forming in the theater audience, a kind of shared sense of values that is greater than in the last 20 years. I just smell it when I go to the theater. Why is it happening? Don't ask me. It may be that the reactions from Vietnam and race issues have been partly digested and incorporated into oldtime neuroses that society had. It is all seen now as just another form of disquiet, rather than the end of the world.

"There was a tendency for a time to insult tragedy, to annihilate the ego of the audience. That is a wonderful experience in expression. But it could have no long life in the theater. In the 1960s my play was being called old-fashioned by some people. This is not being said any more."

Mr. Miller became more fervent as he condemned the failure of self-styled scholars to look into the relationship between the theater and its audience.

"There is no reason to assume that the theater is any different from any other aspect of American life," he said. "Fundamentally, it was affected by the destruction of middle-class. I am surprised that no one has attempted a cultural history of the American theater in terms of its relation to the nature of the audiences. Either there is a relation or there isn't. I think there is. There are eight million Ph.D's running around doing some kind of nonsense. This should be done."

The theater went off "into various cliques," he said, because a "dead end had occurred as far as grasping a sense of reality is concerned. This was not primarily a theater problem. The theater was reflecting, rather than originating. There grew a sense of no longer being open to life, but of being scared of it."

Of his own thinking, Mr. Miller has found that he is not as much to the Left as he used to be. But he has no regrets for his strong position against McCarthyism at a time when this required courage.

"At that time," he said, "there was a definite threat from the Right. Since then there has been disappointment from the Left."

This brought him to the subject of politics, in terms of the two major parties in this country.

"The truth is," he said, "that I have always felt that politics as such is a form of athletics which most of the time has very little to do with any issues. This is probably truer now than ever. The differences between the two parties are almost impossible to tell."

"I've come to rely more and more—if I have any hope—on

individuals, who for one reason or another come down on the right foot out of a sense of duty, or of conscience. They are not limited to one party or economic group or philosophy."

Reverting to *Death of a Salesman*, he said, "it made me more well-known and that makes problems as well as opportunities."

How much money that play has made, Mr. Miller says he does not know. Nor can he guess how many millions have seen or read the only play to become a Book-of-the-Month Club selection.

"I think it's true," he said, "that wherever there is theater in the world, it has been played."

No country—either Communist or Fascist—has banned it. In the former it is hailed as anti-capitalist and in the latter it is put forward to show what happens to people who have no faith in God.

The only real trouble he had with the play, he said, was in this country, where after picketing by American Legionnaires, it was forced to close in Illinois. Partly, he said, the picketing was because of his strong position against McCarthyism. But partly, it was the play itself, which the pickets termed a "time bomb under American business."

And when Columbia Pictures made the play into a movie, the company became so worried before releasing it that it made a short documentary to be shown with the movie. Mr. Miller was invited to see the short.

"It was a travesty," he recalled. "The film showed that selling in the United States was one of the most secure and high class careers. It was a travesty. They were scared to death of distributing the movie because it might be construed as an attack on free employment. I raised enough hell so the short was never distributed."

Television, he said, has made an impact on theater by making American audiences even more restless than usual, shortening their attention span. But everything of importance affects the theater and audience.

"In this country," he said, "the theater is regarded as an isolated phenomenon, when, in truth, it is one of the most sensitive to economic and social surroundings. This applies even more to comedy than to tragedy.

"The theater is a leaf that changes with the passing season."

Arthur Miller on Plays and Playwriting

Robert A. Martin and Richard D. Meyer/1976

From *Modern Drama* 19 (1976): 375-384. Reprinted by permission.

The following conversation took place at The University of Michigan in the late spring of 1974 between rehearsals for the premiere production of Arthur Miller's latest work, *Up from Paradise*. As Guest-Artist-in-Residence with the University's Professional Theatre Program, Miller agreed to meet with a class in American Drama that was engaged in a study of the plays of Eugene O'Neill and Arthur Miller. The scene: a classroom: the cast: students and faculty members of The University of Michigan. In the classroom, Miller is relaxed and informal. When he says he prefers a question-answer format, twenty hands immediately shoot up. Miller points to a woman student in the front row.

Question: In *A View From the Bridge*, why did you start with a narrator? As I read it, he could just as well have been a minor character.

Miller: Well, it helps to put the play at a certain distance—like a tale. It struck me when I was writing the play that it was somehow reminiscent of something extremely ancient. It's a vendetta story, which is the basis of so much Greek drama. They are people who have a blood debt that they have to pay. That story came from a true story—I was partially a witness to it—and it struck me then that somehow something was being re-enacted: that I was telling a very old story as well as a contemporary one. I suppose it was like in painting sometimes, when a certain kind of painting will try to distance the center so that the eye has to search back for it. It's purely an aesthetic feeling. Alfieri—the narrator—is a minor character, except that he is very crucial to that play. He's a kind of chorus in that he represents common sense in the way that Greek choruses did. That is, common sense in relation to excess. Disaster comes from excess, and he is trying to keep Eddie Carbone in the middle of the road and not let his truth—that is to say, his real nature—come out. Because once the real nature comes out you're dead, and that's what his function is.

Question: In *The Crucible*, I'm interested in John Proctor's motivation for sacrificing himself. Is it something idealistic like honor or is it something more practical like his pride?

Miller: It's his pride, yes, and a mixed sense of unworthiness, which is, I suppose, a very Christian idea. Literally, life wouldn't be worth living if he walked out of there having been instrumental in condemning people who, by this time, he believes are much better than he is. However, this doesn't have to be a New England situation. It just happens that I'm presently reading a biography of Joseph Stalin. A lot of people were killed by him in the thirties. It wasn't infrequent that somebody cooperated with the Secret Police in condemning their friends whom they knew to be perfectly innocent of anything. As repayment for their services, they were given some extra favor. Then they shot themselves after they had gotten what they had bargained for.

Question: Shouldn't a person sacrifice his ideals if it will help humanity? What good does it do to die a martyr?

Miller: Well, it depends from whose point of view you're looking at it. The Salem witchcraft trials would have been stopped anyway; these things can't go on forever. But this one looked like it was going to go on a long time. It was a tiny population of whom about twenty people were hanged for no real reason. The thing that stopped it, finally, was when Rebecca Nurse, who was known in the community as a particularly devout woman, was about to be hanged. Instead of begging forgiveness for her sins, she was on the gallows with a crowd of people watching and she cried out to them, "I am as innocent as the day I was born." Because of her background and her reputation, suddenly they saw that it was probably the case. The troops had to break up the crowd, and they couldn't hang anybody anymore. It effectively was all over. The spell was broken by that one act of— whatever you want to call it—martyrdom. She could have gotten out of it. Now you can say, "Well, it would have ended six months later." I suppose, excepting that if you were the twenty-first person, you'd appreciate the act [*laughter*]. So, it depends on how you're looking at it.

Question: How involved do you get directly in the production of your play? How much of a final say do you have in how things are done?

Miller: Well, I would love it if they would take it and do it beautifully and I wouldn't even know about it until opening night. But that's not the way it is. I'm there all the time and I either cast it myself with the director and the producer, or else a lot of the time I don't know all the actors around so they bring them in. But I have to okay them.

Question: Do you have the final approval in the casting?

Miller: Oh yes, for everything. But every playwright does legally; we have a contract. A number of playwrights feel for one reason or another that they don't know enough—or are not certain enough—of their own opinion to do it. They can, however, veto anything—the set designer, composer, or whatever.

Question: This is in response to reading *After The Fall*. What is your view of the nature of God, or how do you view Him?

Miller: In relation to what?

Question: In relation to the characters in the play.

Miller: That would be hard for me to answer; they are all different people.

Question: Do you believe in God?

Miller: You're asking whether I believe in God?

Question: Yes.

Miller: I don't think that I could say I believe in a God in a conventional sense, no. I do believe that there is another level of human experience which we are only partially able to penetrate at exalted moments, and that, I think, is what religious people are referring to. But I don't connect it with any old guy with a beard [*laughter*] or a definable spirit of some sort. And certainly not with a theology.

Question: Which of your plays have you had the most difficulty in producing?

Miller: You mean in putting it on?

Question: Yes.

Miller: I think the last one [*The Creation of the World*]. It's usually the last one, but in this case it really is [*laughter*]. They never found the style of the play, and it's a difficult thing to do anyway. But we didn't have the luck or the perspicacity to create the style that the play needs. It's being done abroad now, and I'll see whether someone else is more successful.

Question: To what extent do you project an audience reaction in your plays? Do you ever alter the dialogue or the action in anticipation of how you think the audience might react to it?

Miller: There are times when there's some scene goes on, or a speech which isn't landing. I can see that it's not making its point, or that a scene is lingering too long, or has already made its point and we're going on and on after the point. I'll make changes that way, yes. I suppose my change would come under that heading because this is a species of communication, and if you're not communicating, you had better get started. There is another kind of change—a thematic change—where what's happening is perfectly available to the audience, but it's not saying what it should be saying. In other words, they're understanding what is there but what is there is not enough; so that is a harder kind of change to make. That requires a re-write which is more difficult and less technical.

Question: In *Death Of A Salesman*, how much would you say that Linda was responsible for the destruction of Willy and Happy and Biff?

Miller: I don't see her that way. If they had had another kind of mother and wife—well, it is already impossible because she is the kind of woman that Willy had to marry. It's rather inevitable that she be as she is. But I can't imagine that another woman would have made all that much difference to him.

Question: You don't think she contributed to Willy's destruction?

Miller: When somebody is destroyed, everybody finally contributes to it. She would have contributed, yes, but I would have to add that I don't see what she could have done about it finally. She could have done different things maybe, but I'm quite convinced that it would have come out substantially the same anyway.

Question: You don't think she could have done anything better with Biff and Happy?

Miller: Well, she is also sucked into the same mechanism; she's not apart from it. If she were apart from it, she couldn't very well have remained his wife for this long. That's what I mean by a self-reinforcing mechanism: once it starts to roll, whatever is excess is thrown off; whatever can cure it is thrown off. So it's simply a moot question—I don't believe it would have made any difference. There is a temptation to go up there and say, "Now look, Willy," but then you find that when you finish instructing him on how to live, he'll have some pretty damn good arguments, which will gradually weigh you down and you'll leave on the next train.

Question: Edward Albee has said that his purpose in writing plays is to teach people so that they will learn from it and hopefully correct their lives. Do you see this same purpose in your writing, or is your purpose in writing plays basically to express yourself as an artist?

Miller: I would agree with him. I didn't know he had said that and I'm rather surprised, but I am glad that he did [*laughter*]. No, I mean it. In any case, I haven't followed everything he has said or written about plays by any means, but I got the impression that he was claiming a kind of artistic virginity in relation to the theatre. I'm glad that I was wrong because I couldn't agree more with him. But you have to be careful about what is meant, and what *I* take it that he means.

People immediately jump to the idea that a play is some kind of therapy, or a prescription for good health; that it is a warning to sin no more and you'll be saved. It doesn't work that way—it can't, because the best that can happen is that the underlying forces that create the dilemmas are removed from their normal cover and confusion. Life is so chaotic that there isn't enough time and there isn't the requisite kind of serenity to see through the surfaces. Hopefully, a play can give a viewpoint, which will remove that cover of confusion and show what forces are going into the dilemma. If the dilemma is a recognizable one from the beginning, let us say, instead of remaining confused as to what is going into making it a dilemma, the play would dramatize the forces that have created it. Now that's saving the world in a way because you can't do anything about anything unless you understand it, or unless you have some vision of what the mechanics of disaster are. But the problem is, as I started to say, that people go in and feel that, "I saw that play but I didn't get any answer," and quite rightly. They won't get an answer because the answers are implicit in the definition of the problem.

If you see the *Doll's House*, to use an example of a play you all know, that play probably comes as close to giving an answer to a problem as you can hope for. But, fundamentally, what you're getting out of it is the idea that the woman is being treated as some kind of a less than dignified human being in a setting where one normally connected—at least in those days—a setting of bourgeois comfort in which everything was great. Her father and husband were in charge, she was handing him a cigar, and it couldn't be better. So what the play did was to open up the underlying life, as Ibsen saw it anyway, of what was really going on.

I have to add in speaking of that play that Strindberg thought it was a great disservice to mankind because it tended to make the woman the wronged party, when in fact he reconstructed the whole plot and showed that it was this poor man who was being strung up by the neck. So if you're going to talk about answers, you see, you can answer it anyway you like. Strindberg was not an idiot. He was very opinionated on the subject—he hated woman on the whole—but nevertheless there you are. He rejected Ibsen's answer, but I think it would be hard for him to reject his logic; it's the premise he rejected. Anyway, it opens up the issue and that is what saves.

Question: Before you begin to write, do you have a preconceived idea of how your characters are going to react in every situation, or do you find that they reveal themselves to you as you go along?

Miller: More or less, yes. Since I don't know what every situation is going to be, what happens is that certain forces are set in motion, and there is a kind of dialectic. It's like a lot of ping pong balls laid on a table on mousetraps. You let one go off and then it hits another one, which in turn bounces another way and they keep bouncing all over the table. So, it's not possible to project that far. However, I don't want to get too romantic about it; it is not as though one were completely blind. You know you're dealing with X and not Y and Z. You can't do everything, but there is an illusion in writing that you are really going to follow any reaction to where it leads.

Question: You've spoken in the past of the artist as a kind of fanatic who is concerned almost entirely with his own internal vision and tends to use things only if they conform to his image of the way things are. Do you think this subjectivity is something that an artist has to overcome, or is it something to use to his own best advantage?

Miller: At first it is something to achieve, and then you can try to overcome it. It's difficult to see things the way you see them and not the way you have been acculturated to see them. It's nearly impossible because the pressures are so great to agree with somebody, and furthermore your sources of information are pretty much the same as everybody else's. I think there is a life-long tension involved between that monomania and a concurrent second set of eyes, which never forgets that, after all, there is some kind of objective reality in the sense that the majority of people see things a certain way. If you lose that, I think you lose a necessary tension between your own vision and the common one. Therefore, you have no comparative line of evaluation between the two and you are liable to get completely out of sight as far as communicating anything. They're both necessary, in short.

Question: One of the latest moves to revive the motion picture industry is to film plays that were previously within the bounds of legitimate theatre. A case in point is *The Iceman Cometh*. I would like to know if you feel that this is beneficial to you as a playwright or to the legitimate theatre as a whole.

Miller: That's a rather special project you're talking about. It probably will not have any consequences later. In other words, people are not going to start doing it on a large scale. There is, admittedly, a limited audience for it in the first place, so the money won't be forthcoming, and that is why this happened. Landau—who produced the whole thing—got these plays for nothing practically and the actors for the minimum. The whole thing was first and foremost a terrific business idea. He got these big titles, and they were cast at a minimum cost so that the whole thing could be floated. On the whole, I think filming a play as a play doesn't make a good film, but it might be a good idea simply to label it as a play and then show it to millions of people who otherwise wouldn't be able to see it.

But if we are going to talk about it as a film, there are obvious reasons why plays done that way are not as good as films, *qua* film, because you're doing certain things redundantly. Take the language, for example. Plays usually move on the feet of language, and most films that are any good depend primarily upon a succession of images, which is quite a different thing and should be. After all, the image is about thirty-five times normal size; it's the most predominant element in the film, and will naturally dominate. Therefore, the primary object of a film is to control those images. Well, obviously, you can't do that if you're filming a play, which is depending upon words and the camera is in the service of the words. The images then become secondary, or are in competition with the words.

Nevertheless, I'm glad to see it's being done because we don't go to the theatre that much in this country, and it's great that people will be able to see *The Iceman Cometh* as a play in their home towns. I just saw a film of a play of mine, *Incident at Vichy*, which is filmed right out of the play. In other words, it wasn't reorganized for that purpose, and it is magnificently done. It happens in that particular play that it works very well as though it had been written for television. That would be possible too, but it is rather rare. It is also due in this case to what I think is the genius of the director who directed this particular production. It all depends on how the thing is done.

Question: In the introduction to Ken Kesey's *Garage Sale*, you comment on the fact that whatever social revolution may have existed during the sixties is over, but then you acknowledge that there is a potential in this country for a touch of revolution to recur or continue. You sort of ended nebulously without further comment. Do you have any observations on the possibility of that really happening?

Miller: Well, I can't end ahead of the situation. It's still a nebulous situation, so consequently it might be more comforting to be more concrete and definite, but I don't think you'd be reflecting reality. I do think that, just theoretically, if they continue to ignore the immense social problems in this country the way they are being ignored, something has to give. It's a question of time. How long? I don't think anybody can say. We are not solving the prooblems, not facing them, except through advertising. We advertise them out of existence. The government makes speeches speaking them out of existence; but they are there and you know it and I know it. How long it takes before the pressures become intolerable—a year, six months, tomorrow morning—I don't know. I walk around New York sometimes and I think it is coming in an hour [*laughter*], but it will probably go on for a couple years more.

Just consider the whole race problem alone. The unemployment among Blacks in some places is 25 per cent. How long does that go on before it catches fire? Nothing is being done about it, really. So, that's where it is right now. I don't know what to say; I don't think anybody does. But nobody ever knows what to say about these things because any great change always comes unexpectedly. It never arrives on time. It's always when it comes, that's when it is; and six months later everybody says, "See, it's obvious why it had to happen then," forgetting at the time that everybody said, "I don't see anything happening." We don't have the mechanism to say when, but I believe it is inevitable. There has got to be something happening only, as I say, because of the band-aid solutions that are being made. Maybe there are no others, I don't know. I think there might be. We can try anyway, but nobody is doing anything; not really.

Question: Why have you chosen drama as your medium of expression? Is it both for your own personal as well as, I suppose, the didactic values of teaching people?

Miller: It is fundamentally that I am a dramatist [*laughter*]. That answers the question, really, because that's my talent—to write dramatic scenes. Another man may want to say quite the same things as I do, but he thinks in terms of prose narrative or possibly even verse. There is a very special frame of mind—or deformation of mind—which sees things in terms of a stage play. I call it deformation because it's extremely rare, really, not only now but it has always been. In the so-called "great ages" of the drama, you end up naming three great dramatists when there were innumerable prose writers. There must be a reason for that. So I assume that I simply gravitated toward it because I was most comfortable doing it, and I felt most—it turned me on more than anything else—but that's purely subjective.

Question: Most of the people here today have studied your plays as well as those of Eugene O'Neill. I was interested in whether or not you thought that O'Neill established any sort of a tradition in playwriting in this country that has had any successors to it?

Miller: No, but he did something, I think, that was perhaps even more important. He gave us all the right to a certain kind of seriousness that this country had never accorded to the theatre or playwriting, which has been in recent years bled away to a great degree. But he gave anybody who followed it a right to lay out, to stake out, an important, high ground if he had the talent to occupy it. His devotion to his work and his discipline in pursuing the immense vision he had was a morale factor for anybody who followed him. That's a big contribution to make. As for the plays themselves—he used many different kinds of techniques and forms, but I don't really think he originated anything. But that's of no consequence. I don't think originality in that sense is of the essence at all. It was fundamentally his spirit and his immense capacity to tell a story on the stage. He was a terrific storyteller. This is looked down on now as being one of the lesser virtues of any writer, but I would prefer that it was looked down on by people who could do it [*laughter*].

Question: Most of your plays occur in a family situation, and I was wondering what is it about the family setting that appeals to you?

Miller: That reminds me of a lesson we had from a great President, Warren Harding. He never knew quite what to say (since he was probably stealing money most of the time) but he did say that, "Wherever I go in America, I look about and see people living together in families" [*laughter*]. This warmed the hearts of all the people, and it was one of the major discoveries in this century. I suppose I write about them because that's the way culture comes into us. It seems to me central to the human experience, it is home plate.

Question: Is there something that has to be resolved within the family first before one can look at himself and the society?

Miller: Well, yes. The family is, after all, the nursery of all of our neuroses, and it is the nursery of our hopes, our capacity to endure suffering, and so forth. So one goes back to the roots, I suppose, and that's why it is not just in my work, it is in a lot of other work also. But I would point out that I have written a lot of plays that have nothing to do with the family. I do believe, however, that as of now, it still is the relation of the mother to the children, and father to mother and mother to father, and the rest of it, so that the family constellation is the central matrix of the civilization. It seems to be in bad trouble right now, but I think it remains the fact nevertheless.

Question: Do you think that the family tends to be more of the "central matrix," as you put it, in American drama than it is in European and other drama?

Miller: Probably. I haven't counted them, but there haven't been a lot of European plays about families. I have a feeling that you are right, that maybe we deal with it more. I am not prepared to say why because I'm not really sure. There is probably a very interesting theory about it somewhere. One possibility might be that Europe has gone through periodic revolutions ever since the end of the 18th century. As a result, the idea of a man living in relation—not to his family so much—but in relation to a society which was unstable, which was being overturned all the time, with the money being changed and property relations being changed, would eventually have its effect. We live in the oldest continuous society in the world, even perhaps including Britain where there have been more revolutionary developments in a similar period vis-a-vis the class structure.

We relate, I would say, much less to the social and governmental system in our thinking and in our attempts to account for our fate, than a European does who is more likely to be always conscious that his fate is political. So that what happens to him is a consequence of political decisions. Therefore, maybe his attention goes out into social, political, and ideological sources of unease, of growth, and of life and death more than ours do (which are more private) because our government or society has remained, relatively speaking, until possibly the last decade, with few interruptions.

Another time was in the thirties, when it all seemed about to fall down, and some people think it did fall down. At that time, again, there was a lot of writing being done about the relation of the society to individuals. The social drama had a big spurt then. Of course, it is probably clear to every average human being that if there are twelve million unemployed or twenty million, whatever it was, out of a population of 120 million, you had to take it into account when you were about to set out into life. It wasn't just a question of how good you were, or how adequate you were in your studies or your job. You automatically understood that the state of the nation was intimately connected with your own survival. That attitude sort of passed once prosperity came back.

At the moment it's not so much a question of economic survival, I think, as it is social survival. The spread of crime and the alienation of whole groups of people from the society—that's the problem now. So once again we're face to face with social problems. Where did I start out answering this question? [*laughter*].

Question: Do you ever wish you could rewrite your plays after they've been produced? I've seen *All My Sons* described as an apprentice work for you. If you had the chance would you rewrite it?

Miller: No, I wouldn't know what to do with it [*laughter*]. I just wouldn't know—that's the way it is. It's a chapter of your life and there it is.

Interview with Arthur Miller
Christian-Albrecht Gollub/1977

From *Michigan Quarterly Review* 16 (1977): 121-141, Reprinted by permission

The following interview took place in August of 1975 at the playwright's home in Connecticut.

Gollub: In 1955, when you were asked about your favorite playwright, you answered, "Can't answer this for at least twenty years because we are all becoming. Besides I know a number of them personally. All playwrights are good." Twenty years later—in 1975—I'm going to ask you the same question: Who is your favorite playwright?

Miller: I find that I'm not related to any in my own work. I think everybody is running parallel.

Gollub: You don't have a favorite? If you had a choice, which other playwright would you like to go see—other than Arthur Miller?

Miller: I think the most interesting one to me has always been O'Neill in the last many years. Not originally, but as far as Americans are concerned. Pinter is very interesting.

Gollub: Why O'Neill?

Miller: I would say his intensity, the size of his work—it's marvelous.

Gollub: Which plays?

Miller: The best play he ever wrote was *A Long Day's Journey* and that's a masterpiece.

Gollub: Have you patterned any of your work after O'Neill?

Miller: No. That started and then went on and he didn't mean much back then. I don't take much from other playwrights, I think. At least I can't find it. I think you form very early and the influences will

273

more likely be much older work. I'm moved a lot by the Greeks and by Shakespeare.

Gollub: When did you first come into contact with literature?

Miller: When I was turning twenty.

Gollub: What did you read at that point?

Miller: A lot of Russians. And Shaw.

Gollub: What is it about Shaw that attracted you?

Miller: Laughs. The irony of his plays. Terrific style and stylishness. And his ability to handle ideas—which I think is unapproachable. Also O'Casey. *The Shadow of a Gunman* and the most important was *Juno.* That's a great piece of work.

Gollub: Most of the playwrights you've named have been foreigners . . .

Miller: Well, most of them have been dealing with what I was interested in, namely, the situation of man at any one time. It was far less profound and they were taking on problems which were not anywhere near as socially important.

Gollub: What about in the 20's and 30's—the workers' theater?

Miller: That had an effect at that time. That was important.

Gollub: A play like Odets' *Waiting For Lefty?*

Miller: Yeah, what was more important than anything was, he created one thing which had never existed before—a relation with the audience, with *an* audience. It was immediate. His theater was as important as—in the immediate sense—as the day's news. So the whole theater became, I found, a more politically important medium. It gave you the feeling that you could address your contemporaries— even that you could change the world. Not that he changed it, but no playwright has ever changed it. That was the assumption behind it.

Gollub: Did his work have any effect on the theater?

Miller: I think early on before I really started to write. The impact, the sense of being swept by a terribly relevant thing—that did. But he had a very special style. It's not appreciated as such, at least not widely. It was a lyricism which was very moving and challenging. Most theater was completely plotted. Plays were conventionally— even Shaw, or Ibsen, or O'Casey, or in a different way, even Chekhov—were fundamentally constructions. Which is what they are, of course, but Odets never succeeded in writing a well articulated structure. But he wrote absolutely fantastic scenes, marvelous scenes. he was one of the best, if not *the* best scene-writer we ever had. He wrote like an actor—which is what he was. And that immediacy, that shock of recognition was enviable. He had an immense effect on me.

Gollub: In 1962 Lillian Hellman, when asked about Arthur Miller the playwright, stated that, "Miller is good and I think will be even better as the years go on. He has force and spirit. Too much newspaper stuff and too much writing about writing. But it doesn't matter—he's good." Do you think tha statement is justified? Do you feel you've spread yourself too thin by not limiting yourself to one genre?

Miller: No. I didn't write all that much. I've written 42 pieces in 25 years exactly. The reason I know is I'm putting together a collection of my essays. I like it. I like to sound off on something. I fact, I rather regret I didn't do more or better pieces of various kinds.

Gollub: Do you have a favorite genre?

Miller: Theater.

Gollub: Why?

Miller: Just born to it. No sensible reason.

Gollub: What do you mean born to it?

Miller: I think a playwright is born, not made. Just like a musician.

Gollub: You don't think that it is an acquired craft?

Miller: No, what it is is not very good. I mean, it doesn't mean much. Anybody can learn how to write music, you know, but obviously that's not what you want to listen to. Similarly in a theater. You either know how to lead that elephant around inside of a living room or you don't. That's about the size of it.

Gollub: What about your novels, short stories?

Miller: I've always considered myself primarily a playwright and I think that's true. That may change because I'm working more with fiction now than I ever did. But in the past I felt unable to come as close to myself as I could on stage.

Gollub: How do you react to something once you've written it, once it's done?

Miller: I generally try to stay away from it. I don't like to look back. They're always full of things I wish I'd done differently.

Gollub: Do you always see something to change?

Miller: I wouldn't know how to change them. I just wish I knew how. I know that I'm not content with it most of the time. Somebody said a work is not finished, it's abandoned. I guess that's what you do finally. You do as much as you can do and know it's not enough. You feel, what the hell, I guess that's it.

Gollub: What about your plays? Aren't you called upon every so often—for instance now with the production of *Death of a Salesman*—to come and look and give your opinion?

Miller: That's involving the production. There can be many different approaches to a production. The script itself, once it's set, it's set; and that's what I mean.

Gollub: How do you feel when you see a play of yours performed?

Miller: Pained. There's always stuff I would like to jump up on the stage and show them how to do. You're dealing with an art that has to be interpreted. It is not like painting, it's not like prose. It requires othe artists, so you're always going to find a space between what they're doing and what should be done.

Gollub: You don't have any emotional distance from what you've done? You are always involved?

Miller: Oh, of course, it's far more distant than when you've first finished with it, but you're always anguished to see it. Especially if something is going wrong and I'm immensely pleased if something is going right, unless it's an amateur production, a college production. Then there's a different order of experience.

Gollub: Have you ever seen a play of yours performed so badly that you absolutely couldn't stand it and had to leave?

Miller: I stay away from them generally. I don't see many of them, hardly any, in fact. And I don't go unless I'm pretty sure that it's not going to be too painful. So I can't say that I have.

Gollub: The production of *Death of a Salesman* with George C. Scott now . . . did you see it?

Miller: Oh, yeah, I saw it before it opened and again now.

Gollub: And you were pleased?

Miller: On the whole, yeah. I think that it has an enormous effect, primarily because he has a heroic approach to it instead of a piddling little shoemaker's approach. There aren't many actors of that scope, so I appreciate that. The play is really one continuous poem. It has no scenes. It has no interstices. It's all one thing and it takes a gigantic wind to sustain it. You can't do that play with a petty, little strategy. It takes a man that's willing to fall on his sword to do it. He's eminently one of those actors. And I'm glad. I appreciate that. It moves me to watch him.

Gollub: Has the play changed any since it was first written?

Miller: Two years ago I would have been unable to answer that. I would have been open to the idea that probably it had. I find that it didn't. It may be because we're in the grip of another recession which many people just now write 'depression.' It isn't at all strange for people to see somebody desperately worried about money. Had this particular production come along ten years ago, maybe they would have felt it was exotic. They don't now, certainly. They sweat in there. The same way they always did in 1949, 1950.

Gollub: Because they see themselves?

Miller: I guess. And they know that this is not an invented and tendentious piece of work.

Gollub: Why does the public so often identify with characters in your plays?

Miller: That's a mystery. I don't understand it. I can't say I write for myself. I'm always trying to communicate to something out there. But I don't know this public. I never knew the public. I don't know what the hell they want. I mean, they appreciate other things that I don't. They seem caught up in all sorts of cultural rubbish. So I don't share with them what you would expect.

Gollub: What kind of cultural rubbish are you referring to?

Miller: Well, they go wild about all sorts of shows that I don't think are all that necessary. They don't vote the way I think they should.

Gollub: What does their voting have to do with their theater preferences?

Miller: Sometimes it betrays an attitude toward life, not always, but in certain cases. In other words, I'm not sure I share the superficial side of their lives very much. But apparently I'm worried about what they're worried about. As long as that remains true, I guess they'll listen to a certain degree. I'm not the most successful playwright in the United States by a long shot and so I shouldn't sound, and I don't mean to sound, as though I have my finger on the pulse—because I don't. I just try to believe that my reaction is somehow shared by enough others. And sometimes it is, sometimes it isn't. It doesn't always work. I don't think anybody out there is particularly looking to me as an authority.

Gollub: Who is the leading playwright in the United States?

Miller: I don't think we have one anymore. Certainly nobody—if you want to put it that way—who, no matter what he opened with, would automatically, because he wrote it, carry with him some big audience. And after all, that's the only test I know of for this. There's nobody that can do that. I failed. Williams fails. Anybody else. Albee failed. That is, fails to carry an audience. It's a pragmatic theater. It goes with a hit and stays away equally easily.

Gollub: What about the old standbys—you've mentioned some of them: Williams, Wilder, Lillian Hellman. Why are they, or why are you resting on your laurels and keeping away from the theater?

Miller: I don't count myself as resting on my laurels. I'm writing all the time. They should be doing our plays all the time and in any other country they would be. The American theater is particularly deficient in its capacity to keep alive its own repertory. It took 24 years for this play to come back. In another country it'd been done year in year out in some way or another. They are in Europe. My plays are done all the time—constantly. And they've been done since the beginning. And not just my plays. We generally in the past had supported revivals to a great degree. I don't think you can do either now. It's got to be something extraordinary to get them in—either an actor or some explosion of interest for some reason or another. But in the normal course people stay away quite happily from a play that has already established itself.

Gollub: Why do you feel you are more successful in Europe?

Miller: I don't know. For one thing they have repertory theaters there. They have ongoing theaters which constantly renew themselves with older work. I mean, Chekhov isn't done here either. And Ibsen very rarely. And for that matter, O'Neill. We just don't do these things.

Gollub: Why not?

Miller: Oh, it's commercial theater. These theaters there are not making money. They're all funded; publicly supported. So they're a cultural operation which is paid to keep alive the culture of that country or the international culture as it applies to that country. We don't have any such thing here—at least not on a professional level— going on all the time. There are attempts at it. The APA, I guess it's called. There are several others. The British had it, but they're losing it now because of one thing or another. It goes against something in the Anglo-Saxon mind, I think. It's a European, continental form of civilization.

Gollub: Do you object to commercial theater?

Miller: I do to one aspect of it. That is, with the course they're on now. A burden is placed on a play which it ought not have to bear and indeed doesn't, is not capable of bearing. That's bad. The good part of it is that paradoxically enough, it is also more adventurous than theaters which have to please a group of subscribers all the time. It's like symphony orchestras. The audience resists novelty, resists new composers. More so than theater, but the analogy isn't altogether inept. The emphasis of the commercial theater is new, something new—and that's good. But you pay for it with this make or break, hit or flop thing. A play can even now be well received by the critics and people don't come because it may be a little difficult. Years ago I was in Sweden. They were doing—what's his name? Their genius there . . .

Gollub: Strindberg?

Miller: Strindberg. I went in and there was hardly anybody in the theater. This was their national theater. Maybe a hundred people in a sizable theater. It turned out that they didn't expect any more, but they do him every year. They have a festival of Strindberg. At least they did in those days. That's 25 years ago. And I asked them why, how they justified this. And they said, well, he's a genius. He's the best playwright we ever had and we're gonna do him every year. Now for the few people, that came in, it was a marvelous experience and I thought the productions were fantastic. They were great. But the average Swedish audience wasn't interested. But none of them would probably argue against this procedure. It's a bit like a museum. They wanted it kept alive. They just didn't want to be bothered by it. So the new generation—students and so on—could come and see it. I've met students who are too young to have seen 99% of the American repertory and will never see a first-class production. They see mostly inept, amateur, semi-professional, college productions. And some plays you can do that way, but other plays require acting of a kind that you simply don't get. And they never really see what the size of the work is. You can't do most of O'Neill in college. You can't do a lot of mine in college either. You can't do a lot of Williams in college and so forth. I mean, you can do them, but you're doing a sketch, you're not doing a show. It's just the sheer question of the age of the actors, experience and so on. This is equivalent in music, let's say, to having no symphony orchestras, so that whoever hears Mozart is going to hear him in a high school band. That's where we're at.

Gollub: Do you feel you're suffering because of this?

Miller: Oh, I've long since stopped bemoaning it. I just accept it as

the way it is. Occasionally these plays are brought back. They're
done in Canada. There's a production of *The Crucible* now playing in
Toronto. At Stratford up there. They're always doing something of
mine somewhere.

Gollub: Are you part of the 'theater museum'?

Miller: Of course, some of my plays are a quarter of a century old,
so anything that's more than three years old in this country is a
museumpiece. So, I guess so. In a way they are. Except I don't think
people react to them quite that way, but when they do come, they're
moved as of now. The amount of audience in any country that is
interested in the theater academically is tiny. That's true of Germany,
Russia, anywhere. Theater should be speaking to its moment, but it
ought to keep alive the past or you won't have any future. Then
you're condemned to repeating unknowingly what's been done and
lose the artists of the theater as well as the audience. It ought to keep
aware of what has happened.

Gollub: What do you feel is your role in the theater in the 1970's?

Miller: I have no role. I don't see it that way. We don't have a
dense enough theater to speak of anybody having a role. I write my
plays, that's all. None of us has any function, I don't think, excepting
possibly a few producers who should have a role of keeping it all
going as well as they can under very difficult circumstances. When
you have to raise something like quarter of a million dollars to put a
play on, that's pretty tough.

Gollub: What was the last play that you wrote?

Miller: The last play on Broadway was—what was it?—*Creation
of the World*, which we're just doing into a musical now.

Gollub: Why did you write it?

Miller: I liked the idea. I thought it was beautiful. I wrote it to
create something beautiful.

Gollub: The title is *The Creation of the World and Other
Business*. What 'Other Business'?

Miller: Human business. The business of the people becoming
human.

Gollub: You show Adam as being somewhat more of a god than
God Himself. He's giving the names to the animals. He's telling God
what to do. Why is that?

Miller: That's out of the Bible of course. That's what he did in the
Bible.

Gollub: But God seems to be an oaf . . .

Miller: He's an oaf, but He's running it. If it were different we wouldn't be in this spot.

Gollub: What spot is that?

Miller: Out to kill each other off.

Gollub: Do you think that's what people are trying to do?

Miller: Yeah.

Gollub: Who?

Miller: All of us. Inside the society. Between the societies. Getting ready for another war. Somewhere. Sometime. We tried it in Viet Nam. Killed a couple of million there, I guess. Or whatever it was. And now building up these armaments to a point where there'll be no going back. It's a terribly dangerous thing we're sitting on.

Gollub: Is that what you tried to express in *The Creation of the World?*

Miller: Yeah. But there's only one decision that could be made and that's man's decision. He's got to make the choice—live or die and God is just there giving him the means.

Gollub: Might this message not get lost in a musical?

Miller: No, it's sharper in fact. Song is terrific for driving home whatever is there.

Gollub: Don't you think the audience might walk out just whistling the tune?

Miller: Not necessarily so. In fact, it's sharper than it was in the other version.

Gollub: Who is doing the music?

Miller: Stanley Silverman. He's a terrific young composer, but he's not through yet. So we're waiting on him. But I expect he will be in the next month or two.

Gollub: Is the entire play set to music?

Miller: Most of it. It's almost all music. There are scenes, but it's reset. It's got a different key, different diction, esthetically speaking, you won't be aware of when they're talking or they're singing. And it's a fundamentally musical experience, but it's got a wonderful story now. I'm not going to direct it though. Bob Dishy is going to direct. He played Adam in the original production. We haven't cast the other parts yet, because I'm waiting for this music. And we can't cast those things without seeing that people can sing the music. We're not in a position to cast it yet.

Gollub: Do you anticipate any big names being in it?

Miller: No. It wouldn't be important here anyway. They're all young. They will have to be. I wouldn't expect any stars, no.

Gollub: Any nudity?

Miller: No, we don't need any nudity, because the whole thing is metaphorical anyway. There's nothing more realistic than naked people. They'll be costumed. I think nudity would defeat the metaphor.

Gollub: Will they be costumed to look naked?

Miller: No, I doubt it. I haven't got the costumes yet. We haven't worked on that at all. The original ones were not bad. They were laughably suggesting nakedness, but it was obvious that they had body stockings on which were painted. And that's a good idea. It's saying naked, it isn't being naked. This conforms with the play which is, after all, not literally the creation of the world. Music is a highly emotional and visceral art and that's enough.

Gollub: Should a play suggest more than it actually states?

Miller: Sure. If they're any good, that's generally what happens.

Gollub: Is this what your plays do?

Miller: I would hope.

Gollub: When you write a play, do you have the entire concept in your mind beforehand?

Miller: No. I work it out as I go. It's all discovery. It's a long process.

Gollub: Which of your plays is your favorite?

Miller: I frankly don't have any. They're all different problems. I try different and varied ways of achieving. What one can do, the other one doesn't. Or what the other one can do, the first one doesn't. From one moment to the next, my preferences change, depending on the hour, what I feel that week about what the theater ought to be, what *I* ought to be and so on.

Gollub: What do you feel at this moment? Is the *Death of a Salesman* your favorite play?

Miller: In some ways, in some ways not. I love it, but it's a different proposition than some of the others.

Gollub: Is there any one of your plays that you are dissatisfied with?

Miller: All of them.

Gollub: In what way?

Miller: Oh, there are secret ways. Things I'd failed to do and wished I had. But that's between me and the plays.

Gollub: When you see a production of your plays, do you see things that you really didn't intend to put in?

Miller: Oh, sure. This always happens. Oh, yes, definitely. Actors are not just dumb animals. Good actors are creative people. And there is simply no substitute for really sensitive intelligence and a willing body. They all bring a different personality to the role which creates a different color than one ever dreamed. That happens. As it should. It's just like a violinist. One violinist playing the same music as another one—you can hear a difference—it sounds different. You know it's the same music, but it's simply got different depths. That's what's fascinating about it all and one of the chief attractions of writing for the theater because the prose work is there and that's it. Which has its virtues. Nobody can horse around with it. They can't make it much worse than it is. By the same token, they can't make it better either. It's alive. There's nothing as dynamic as a play in terms of its interrelations with people like that. But one pays a price for it.

Gollub: Are you willing to pay the price?

Miller: I think less and less so. I just don't think about it any more. I'm not interested in the theater as a spectacle any more. Or at least much less so. I do love to watch a good actor doing anything.

Gollub: Do you go to the theater often?

Miller: Rarely, but I go enough to keep some idea of what's happening.

Gollub: Why don't you go?

Miller: I never did much. Unless I'm tremendously interested, that's an awful long time to be sitting there.

Gollub: Two to three hours is a long time?

Miller: Oh, when you know what's happening behind it. And if it's not anything truly original, it is a long time.

Gollub: What's happening in the American theater today? Is it dying?

Miller: I don't think so. There's more playwrights trying work than there have been in many years. In a way there's more opportunity for them than there ever was, far more than when I came in. I think if its suffering at all, it's suffering from two things. One is that the audience is totally unintegrated, unorganized. The theater does have to have some rudimentary organization of the audience. Like certain of the existing funded theaters do have. You can't go on hoping to pick up an audience off the street. That's becoming less and less likely because the prices are high. That's one problem. The other problem is the whole general American problem, or you might call it the world problem. This disorientation, the absence of any ongoing confidence that anything is true. The play is making an assertion even when it doesn't intend to. It's organizing experience around some synthesis. When there is not the least underlying consensus, this becomes extraordinarily difficult. That's one reason why there are so few plays written or that the ones written are rather tentative. Of course the playwright can't invent a coherency for the world, at least, not out of his little head. Something has to be out there and respond to him. And what's out there is either degeneration or chaos. It makes life tough.

Gollub: Should a playwright withdraw into an ivory tower?

Miller: He does at his peril. It's all right if he takes into the tower with him some of life outside. But he, after all, is addressing his fellow citizens, you might say. He'd better know where they are. Somehow, if only by his instincts. Or he simply won't operate. Won't bring.

Gollub: Do you think the playwright should write for people that can pay $10, $15, $20 per ticket?

Miller: I'm sure that most of these playwrights are not thinking that way. They're probably writing for their peers. That is, people of their generation. Look, if the truth were faced, the theater would end in the morning. That's a fact. It's terribly narrow. I've made this kind of statement a hundred times before. It is socially narrowed down to a clique, in effect. I mean, I'm supposed to have a big success here in New York with the revival of *Salesman*. Well, the truth of the matter is, it's going to play a total of 12 weeks. There are about 650 seats in the theater. So it's about something on the order of 6500 people a week. So it'd be under 80,000 who'd see the whole thing.

Gollub: That's very limited.

Miller: To say the least. Now we could go on, but Scott has got other obligations. But even if it ran a year, if you're going to count numbers—it's senseless.

Gollub: It is not profitable?

Miller: Not under these circumstances, no. However, it hasn't been a mass art in my lifetime. It was never a mass art, not since probably the middle 20's before the sound movies came and wiped out all theaters. But this is a delusion. It's in fact remarkable that so much attention is paid to it.—If you consider the fractional part of the public that ever gets to see it. Of course plays—it has to be said—also have other lives, come movies, television shows. Few of them last long enough so that they are reproduced in colleges, amateur theaters and so on for some years later. Some are read in considerable numbers. Especially with the paperbacks in recent years. There is a sale—a respectable sale. This country is notoriously unable to create a large reading public compared to Holland or Denmark or some others. We read more than the French, but not as much as the Germans and Swedes and some others. But given our resources and the standard of living, our readership is tiny. So you can consign a whole cultural enterprise to the garbage pail if you look at it statistically. I suppose there's some other perspective that justifies it. People want it. Those who do want it, want it very badly. That few people do support a very expensive enterprise. It's worth going that way and you can only hope that one day society will be reorganized and there will be some kind of a mass theater.

Gollub: Is the general public uneducated?

Miller: They simply haven't had the opportunity to go. There's been no theaters. No theater in Toledo, Ashtabula, Champaign or elsewhere that can be called a high level provincial theater. So you can't blame them for what they haven't got. It's not their fault. We've just never conceived in this country yet the prospect of organizing the audience. It's not impossible. Symphony orchestras do it to a degree, have done it traditionally. They always have their troubles, but they assume that there's no money. There's no money in the theater either. The trouble is that once in a hundred a show makes a lot of money for somebody and this keeps this delusion alive.

Gollub: Are there any up-and-coming playwrights to watch for?

Miller: My problem is that I don't go enough to make judgments about people. The latest stuff I've seen is by Ed Bullins, who's a very talented writer and a maturing writer, I think. There are numerous others whose names I know, but I don't know their work well enough to say. There undoubtedly are. There's always people.

Gollub: Do they ever approach you for advice?

Miller: In some cases, yes.

Gollub: And what advice do you give a young playwright?

Miller: There's only one piece of advice: It's a thankless task and anybody who looks at it otherwise is kidding himself. It's a thankless task which occasionally could pay off very big. But most of the time it doesn't and one simply has to go on. If that's what you want to do, that's what you want to do. You can't look at it in terms of whether it makes any sense.

Gollub: Do you think that the theater makes any sense?

Miller: For me, yes. I love to write. I express my life that way.

Gollub: Is the film taking the place of the theater?

Miller: No. It'll never take the place of the theater. The theater is doing better business now than it's been doing for twenty years.

Gollub: But it is still not where it used to be.

Miller: Well, in some ways it's better than it used to be. There are more regional theaters, off-Broadway theaters—not off-Broadway, but non-Broadway theaters. It's more widespread. I'm not talking about the level of their work necessarily, but there they are. There's a lot of theater going on in this coontry. I think it's a cliche that it isn't. If everybody kept saying it so long you're going to believe it's true, but it isn't true. You know when I came into this, it was literally confined to five, six blocks on Broadway. And that was it. Beyond that you had nothing but second class, third class road companies of one kind or another. Certainly nothing originated outside of New York. A lot originates outside New York now, so that's improving.

Gollub: When you wrote your first play, did you write it with the intention of producing it on Broadway?

Miller: No, no. I was in college [The University of Michigan]. I wouldn't have expected it to be produced on Broadway.

Gollub: Why did you write it?

Miller: Well, we had the Hopwood Awards then, they still do. And I wanted to submit it for that. I got excited with the idea that I might be able to write one. It's like a mountain. It was just there. I thought I might be able to get up on top. I didn't get on Broadway for a decade.

Gollub: So you had some failures before you had the overwhelming success?

Miller: Plenty of them.

Gollub: Do you learn from your failures?

Miller: Yes. To think more sharply, more intensely about what I'm doing, what I want to do. Whether, in fact, what I thought is now on paper.

Gollub: Is a commercial failure also a personal failure for you?

Miller: Inevitably. To a degree. But then you've got to heal, to recover.

Gollub: How do you recover?

Miller: Go back to work.

Gollub: At one point you wrote, "The very impulse to write springs from an inner chaos, a crying for order, for meaning and that meaning must be discovered in the process of writing or the work lies dead as it is finished."

Miller: I would agree with that.

Gollub: You should, you wrote it.

Miller: Well, I don't always agree with what I wrote.

Gollub: Do your opinions change?

Miller: No. That's, I think, the case. It's just so.

Gollub: But you don't strike me as someone with inner chaos or turmoil.

Miller: You don't know me.

Gollub: You make a very calm and collected impression.

Miller: I'm just tired today. I've been working all morning. That's my temperament. I look calm and collected. That's so I don't waste energy, but that statement is true.

Gollub: Which people do you read now? Do you read for pleasure?

Miller: I read at random mostly if I hear of something that sounds interesting. I don't read in any pattern. I'm as likely to be reading a book on mythology as a novel or a collection of stories on whatever. It all goes down and mixes up with the soup. I don't have an orderly campaign of educating myself. I just finished Saul Bellow's latest book, *Humboldt's Gift*. He's a genius, I guess. He's collecting, he's a collector. He's a great magnet for all unrealized ambitions, thoughts in society and time and the psyche. He's kind of a psychic journalist—which is invaluable. He's just simply interesting which most writing isn't. His work seems necessary, which is high praise. It seems to mark the moment.

Gollub: Is a lot of writing trash?

Miller: Not trash, just for any writer to produce something. One can say this book is necessary. That's a rare gift. And it doesn't always happen. It doesn't happen regularly with every writer—even the ones who've done it. You've got to write a lot of unnecessary stuff to get something that's necessary. If something's trash, it's simply something that I don't think solved anything.

Gollub: Should all writing solve something?

Miller: Yeah. Solve some esthetic problem. Solve some problem of blindness, deafness.

Gollub: You don't believe in writing for entertaining?

Miller: Well, I can't read it. It's like listening to Musak. You do that when you go to the dentist, but I wouldn't take the effort to sit down and listen to it. I don't know of any entertaining writing anyway. Simenon I like to read and that's purely entertaining I guess. But he's such a craftsman. At least it reminds you of the structure of the world somehow. But just to display the ability to tell a story or spin out words is not to me more important than a lot of other things I could be doing. No writer worth anything, worth reading, hasn't got what he thinks of as a message. He's got a vision which is totally his own. That's all the message is if it's worth listening to. Otherwise you go to a newspaper.

Gollub: What about a very personal message that might not affect a lot of people?

Miller: That's what I'm talking about. When we speak of entertainment, I assume something that is written to capture an audience rather than to express something. If you're chasing an audience—even with deftness—I agree that it takes skill to accomplish that, but it's like inventing the lightbulb again. We did that already. So why do it again?

Gollub: What are you working on now?

Miller: I'm working on another play, I'm working on the musical.

Gollub: Do you have any title as yet?

Miller: No, I don't. That'll come. Later I hope. But I got a lot of work.

Gollub: How about an autobiography? Is that at all in the making?

Miller: I don't know. I keep being asked to do one, and I guess maybe one day I will. I've got a lot of material that I've written over the years—just memoirs which I've never published. I did publish— last December in *New York* magazine—an article about 1949 which was in the nature of a memoir.

Gollub: Do you object to people knowing about your personal life?

Miller: Well, no. I object to them inventing it when it isn't there.

Gollub: Do they do that?

Miller: Oh, frequently!

Gollub: Doesn't that make you more interesting, more glamorous and possibly more successful as a playwright?

Miller: I don't know. It's very irritating. I just assume it wouldn't happen. But I realize that if you're in the public eye, as any playwright is, there's an immense curiosity. I wouldn't intend to be writing an autobiography in that sense. All I would ever attempt, I guess, would be some—I don't know what to call it—some . . . appreciation of the time I was living. I don't think my life is of any interest as such. I don't think any likes his. It's where you can see something like the human situation in a man's observations about his time. Whether there's any light thrown, so that one comes away from it somehow a little heavier than he went into it. Because each of us only has a capacity to absorb so much. We're all prejudiced in one way or another and have been blinded to various kinds of experience that we actually went through. I think memoirs, autobiography, something like that, can help to translate chaos into something that is a usable past. Give an image where there was only a blur. Or resurrect part of the past that you didn't even know was there. That's the sort of thing I'd be interested in.

Gollub: Do you regret anything in your life?

Miller: Oh, sure, a lot of it. Why not?

Gollub: Everything doesn't transform into another experience you can put down on paper?

Miller: Not quite, no, that's optimistic.

Gollub: Are you not an optimist?

Miller: I'm a dispassionate observer of the ongoing disaster of the human race. I wouldn't be surprised if we had the worst possible conclusion to the whole adventure. On the other hand, I'm open to persuasion. I wish the hell, very passionately—that we make it. I try to do whatever I can to help it—which isn't much. But most of what we do is either senseless or hostile, and it's amazing that we lasted this long, it really is. I guess just that is enough to give you some faith.

Gollub: Do you have faith?

Miller: That kind, yeah. I have faith in the accident that not everybody is going to get killed. The germ will start sprouting again.

Gollub: Are you afraid for yourself also?

Miller: I'm too old for that now. I have children. And I fear for them sometimes in this slaughterhouse we live in. I don't know the human sympathy I suppose most people have. But its a touch-and-go proposition, I think. Very dangerous.

Gollub: Life?

Miller: Well, life and the way this world is now organized. There's too much power in too few hands. Just one example—there's no question that either now or in the future the atom bomb will be in the hands of—if it isn't already—in the hands of beleaguered fanatical regimes who have never shown any great—some of them—have never shown an enormous responsibility any more than we did when we bombed Hiroshima and Nagasaki. What are you going to make of that? One of those things can be brought in anywhere on a freighter, on a truck. Kill half a million people—that's that. Why not? Put it on an airplane. That's where we're at. This stuff is all over the place now. It doesn't bear thinking about.

Gollub: It doesn't bear thinking about, but yet you are because you have definite opinions.

Miller: Well, you've got to think about it. You've got to wonder: When does that madman decide that it's the best thing for the human race?

Gollub: What madman are you referring to?

Miller: I don't know where he is yet. He's somewhere in there.

Gollub: You think there's one individual?

Miller: This is the great thing about it: You don't need to mobilize any big forces. You need a chain of command that involves a few people. They all have to be persuaded that they're right or that it's necessary. That's it.

Gollub: Do you feel that you chose the wrong profession?

Miller: No. As it turns out, I've written things that have lasted longer in the public consciousness than most other things. So in that way it's better than a lot of other disciplines. Can't complain about that. But I wouldn't want to be anything else but what I was. I've had a wonderful time.

'All in a Boiling Soup': An Interview with Arthur Miller

James J. Martine/1979

From *Critical Essays on Arthur Miller,* James J. Martine, ed., (Boston: G. K. Hall, 1979): 177-188. Reprinted by permission.

The transcript of this interview, recorded in New York City on 13 February 1979, is presented here in the hope that it may be useful to critical scholars and the larger audience of Miller's works.

Miller was lean, tan, healthy, immaculately attired, and looked twenty years younger than his age. He was more than courteous and cooperative. He is unpretentious and instantly likeable. Our conversation was immediately informal, and he makes one feel very comfortable. We chatted as though we had spent our youth in the same neighborhood, which in a sense is true, although the neighborhoods were in separate cities.

Re-reading this transcript, I am not sure that Miller's inflection, his intonation, his wit and comic sense are done justice. There are places in which Miller and I were both enjoying things. I know I was. But, by and large, he spoke carefully and reflectively.

Question: You have said many times that Ibsen was important to you. Would you say something about your own reading as a young man at Michigan?

Miller: Ibsen's importance at Michigan when I was a student there was actually second to when I stumbled across the Greeks. I suppose they're both parts of one unified ideal which I didn't feel at the time, but which in later life I saw was unified. Both of these kinds of drama are densely formed. They are attempting to communicate, obviously, but at the same time they are *private,* to be sure. Ibsen was, like any writer of any value, a private man and was not simply a public speaker. But the purpose of the form was not self-indulgence but to express to his fellow citizens what his vision was. The same thing is true of the Greeks.

At Michigan, of course, we were in a moment of great social stress, when the virtues of being totally cut off from man and from society were nonexistent. One didn't consider that—at least I didn't. Art had a purpose, which was communicative. And I fell heir, so to speak, to the notion of the dramatist being a sort of prophet. He was the leading edge of the audience. This was implicit in the whole notion of literature in the 1930s.

But, of course, it was also part of the Ibsen and Greek notion too. Aeschylus, on his tombstone, after all, doesn't speak of himself particularly as a writer, but as a defender of the state and the democracy against the Persians. That's how he wanted to be remembered. I'm sure that infiltrated into all his work too. It certainly did into the *Oresteia* and many other works as well.

Anyhow, as a general statement, I think I drew from these two sources for my form—certainly for my ideas of the theatre's purposes. That was *very* important.

Question: What do you read now? What is worthwhile today generally in literature: novels, poems, essays?

Miller: Well, I read completely at random. I usually, unless I get caught up in something which will really sweep me along for periods, I read bits and pieces of a lot of books. I get books every day from publishers. So, I dip into them. Occasionally, I find one that's interesting for a couple of chapters. But I find, that the older I get the more I wish to cut. I get impatient with writing, whether it be prose or dialogue or verse, which is overwritten. So I get impatient with a lot of things that I read.

Now as for what I would be reading, let me think. I'm just reading now *The Coup* by Updike. I was reading a book by a philosopher named Kaufman on religion about two days before. I was reading Rilke this morning just before I came here. It's a hodgepodge. But I pick up, if not ideas, then stringencies. A good writer makes you feel how slack you are. I get more strict with my own thinking as a result of reading anything that's well done. I was reading Conrad the week before.

Then, I read a lot of newspapers, which is fundamentally a waste of time. It makes you feel that there was only one newspaper, and that all of these are reprints of that newspaper—for ever and ever and ever, in all countries, at all times. Still, you have to find out what the latest version of the old disaster is.

I should keep notes of what I'm reading. I can't think at the moment whether . . . oh, I just picked up from a book shelf Grace Paley's book of short stories which were really wonderful. I'm reading them again: *The Little Disturbances of Man.* Then, I was reading seed catalogues—a lot. What else? I read a pamphlet put out by the government on grafting apple trees. I have land up there, and I'm always resolving to be a farmer, and then it goes away after a little while. I do a lot of work on the land, but not professionally.

I read poetry I suppose more than a lot of people do—just for pleasure. I have a large number of books of poetry in my house, and I just keep going back to them. And they would be anything from Wordsworth to May Swenson to Muriel Rukeyser to . . . it wouldn't matter. It depends on my mood.

Question: Would you evaluate other American writers, particularly playwrights such as O'Neill, Williams, and Inge?

Miller: I can't evaluate writers. What I can do is say what, if I've gotten something from somebody, because we're all, I think, in a boiling soup. What one man or woman is doing is . . . we change the flavor by what we add, and it changes all of us.

Question: Your thoughts on Ibsen are well known. What of Pirandello (never mentioned by you in earlier interviews)?

Miller: I must say that I didn't appreciate Pirandello—I didn't know about Pirandello, I don't think, in college. In the last fifteen years, though, I've come to regard him as maybe one of the most important writers of the Twentieth Century. He really formulated for the stage at least, the temporal concept which is be-deviling everybody. That is, the question of what is real in terms of space and time, when the human subconscious is so powerful and recreates reality wherever it turns its attention. He started out, I suppose—I'm just imagining this—I imagine that early on in his career they must have regarded him as a trickster and as rather amusing and comical when, of course, he was a tragic writer. He was looking at the whole thing from a tragic viewpoint—which is, I think, possibly why it seems so lasting. His work is quite lasting. How popular it is, I don't really know, but I don't see that many productions—at least in New York. There should be. *Henry IV* is a really massive piece of work.

Question: Is there any common denominator—a consistent factor that great playwrights share?

Miller: I think the one thing which they share, which is difficult to evaluate after they're gone is, to use that awful word, their relevance for the moment—because the theatre is a very passing show. Most of the time, it is a matter of fads and fashion, as to what seems to be important. The most discouraging thing anybody can do is to look up the list of Pulitzer prize winning plays of the last decades and you see what I mean. I'm sure that however many there are, ninety-five percent or more you wouldn't even know the titles of anymore. It's quite amazing. So that, paradoxically enough, in order to last very long they have to be very temporal. They have to be applicable right then and there. Most plays don't get a second chance; I've said that frequently. If they fail the first time, they dispirit and discourage all imitators—that is, all the amateurs, the other producers. And it takes generations before somebody fresh with no preconceptions looks at the script and thinks that he understands what the author was about. And sometimes that's true. It even happened with Shakespeare for a long time. So I would think that the first thing that—I don't know about "great," but—*significant* playwrights need is a relevance to their time. Otherwise we probably just would never think about them, never hear of them, if you haven't heard of them when they're going, when they're alive. They just become part of the debris of history, and God knows how many plays we've lost because they didn't seem to pertain to anything at the moment. Who knows? But that's one thing they'd have to have.

I personally prefer to think that the ones that I know who have lasted—the ones I know about—have shared a kind of tragic vision of man. The ones that are too happy about it all seem to fade away. Now I'm thinking of, as a contradiction to that statement, Wilde— Oscar Wilde—who is a formidable writer of comedy. But, of course, his view of man is, underneath the laughs, a pretty tragic view. He's giving you the bright side of that disastrous vision he had. So, it's maybe not inapplicable even in his case.

Question: Have you been able to discern *your* influence on newer playwrights and the theatre?

Miller: I really haven't, excepting I've noticed from time to time—I used to, more than now; I don't think it's so fashionable now—that there was a tendency to misuse flashbacks. They thought I was using flashbacks in *Death of a Salesman.* And they're not flashbacks, in my opinion. There was a lot of imitation of that play. Beyond that, I can't say. I don't go to the theatre that much.

Question: You've said that the theatre can't die because "we must have, in order to live at all, some kind of symbolization of our lives," [*Theater Essays,* p. 308] and you speak of an art which expresses "the collective consciousness of people." As well, anyone who has seen your plays—almost every one treats this in one way or another—and read your essays recognizes the central fact and importance of the word "community" to you. Would you expand for a moment on your concept of "community" and "the collective consciousness of people"?

Miller: The concept of community, I think this is a vital notion, is a very slippery one and difficult to talk about. But, to be boringly obvious about it, the community, meaning the audience for all intents and purposes, in the theatre, and the atmosphere outside the theatre, *lean* on plays directly. If tomorrow morning we had suddenly an atomic strike on New Mexico, and the United States were confronting doomsday, it's perfectly clear, isn't it, that the theatre simply couldn't go on the way it's going on now. There's no way that it could do that.

Question: How might this concept of community be said to apply to your major protagonists, Willy Loman, Eddie Carbone, or John Proctor, all men, if we are to understand them, seen in the context of the community in which they live?

Miller: I suppose that I have assumed the collective or the community, not in any one member necessarily, but as a whole, contains the ethos that the character is working with and against. They contain the source of all the moral energy in the play. It may be a community that is perfectly visible as it is in *The Crucible,* after all, and it is in *A View from the Bridge.* Or it may be not visible as in *Death of a Salesman* where we don't have a crowd on the stage; we only have what they believe on the stage. The men are in the society, there is no question about it. They are working, whether openly or implicitly, in relation to the ethos of the time that they are in—and the class of people that they're in even. I don't figure this out. I mean, this is nothing I have to diagram. It is just the way I feel anyway. I think that man is a social animal; there's no getting away from it. He's in society the way a fish is in the water, and the water is in the fish. I can't possibly disentangle them, and I think those plays indicate that.

As a matter of fact, I've tried, I think, in the interest of truthfulness, to take as far as I can that awareness of my own in these dramas—because I'm under no illusions that people really invent themselves. They do to a degree, but they're working with a social matrix.

Question: If part of *your* matrix, then, is the Greeks, and part of the product of the Thirties, how important do you feel ethnic background is for an American writer? Has it influenced you at all? What of socio-economic background?

Miller: These are vital for a writer, in America especially. Obviously, they form his vocabulary—in a way. You can't conceive of Faulkner except as a part of that society, a part of that region, even though he transcends it. But any writer worth discussing, that's true of. That again forms one pole of the tensions that a writer works with. He's both trying to express it, at times he's trying to transcend it, in certain cases he might even try to disguise it. But it's there; it is part of his equipment, part of the given that he has to work with. There's no doubt about it. Of course, the final question, as always, is how good a work he has done. But that he has been openly expressing some ethnicity is beside the point really. We've got writers like Bernard Malamud who is essentially a Yiddish writer in America. But Bellow probably isn't. He's one step, or several steps, beyond that. I'm Jewish, but I have a different attitude toward these problems in my work—toward that situation. And there are as many Roths—there's still another—. Updike is sort of an ethnic. He has responded, I think, in subtle ways to the ethnicity of so many of the Jewish novelists around him and of the influence of Jewish critics, and has asserted himself as what he is. It makes for more richness to me. I think it just enriches the whole scene.

Question: You have said [in a 1958 interview with Philip Gelb published as "Morality and Modern Drama"] in response to John Beaufort's claim that Willy Loman is not the average American citizen, that Willy can't be the average American man, but that Willy Loman is a person "who embodies in himself some of the most terrible conflicts running through the streets of America today."

If we agree with "Tragedy and the Common Man" (1949) that "tragedy is the consequence of a man's total compulsion to evaluate himself justly, [and] his destruction in the attempt posits a wrong or an evil in his environment . . ." and, further, that the "under-lying struggle is that of the individual attempting to gain his 'rightful'

position in his society"—would Willy have been better off in the
1960s? Or today? Is the social environment better or worse today?
What would have happened to Willy Loman today? Are there more
Willys today than ever before? Have the conflicts deepened or
lessened?

Miller: This has to be a subjective answer, because I'm not a
pollster, and strictly off the cuff because I don't think in those terms
really. I mean that Willy is for me a dramatic character. He's not a
sociological entity. He's not a real citizen—put it that way. He doesn't
vote or have problems outside the ones that I deal with in the play.
He's fiction.

But I suppose I would have to say that I think that the society
around him now, as opposed to when I was writing, would be even
more amorphous than it was then. And part of the problem he had
was amorphousness. He not only couldn't climb the ladder, he
couldn't find it. And now I think it's possible life is even more abstract
than it was then. I have just the gut feeling now that maybe people
haven't even the security to believe that *they're* right and that
something is wrong. We've *dismissed* the whole society, which means
we've *accented* the whole society. I mean everything now is up for
grabs. But at the same time, the kind of alienation that exists now
seems to me to be quiescent, it isn't actively taking up psychological
arms against anything. People fundamentally feel defeated. You see,
Willy is not defeated. Everybody thought he was in those days, but
he isn't. If he were, then he would be sort of sitting on a rocking chair
and telling you some of his troubles. He would be quiescent. And I
get the sense now that there is a feeling abroad that the situation is
either so complicated that nobody can solve it or that there's simply
no use in making broad, generalized outcries—such as that play
makes. And, maybe, maybe Willy still had, and this I realize is
paradoxical, but he may still have carried forth a kind of beautifully
naive insistence on certain values—even some which never really
existed. He keeps talking about the old days when people acted
better toward each other, and I strictly doubt that that was true, but
nevertheless he feels they were. There was a comradeship among
people of the same *métier,* the same kind of work. Perhaps that's
true. I don't know. But the separation now of human, intimate
psychological need and the marketplace is cool, almost total. You
see, Willy is demanding of the market and of his job some real return

psychically. He simply can't settle for being this robot that apparently people now believe is inevitable. Many of them even seek it. They want to be a robot; they don't want to be forced to feel anything. He's revolting because he's being told not to feel anything. And I'm wondering whether it hasn't gone way over the edge, comparatively speaking, now; where the technocratic idea has won that the human being is there to serve the machine. Simply. And that this is now accepted as inevitable and probably even as a social good. And that the person who isn't able to be absorbed into the machine is a misfit, and has to be psycho-analyzed into accepting this proposal. So things have gone farther than they were then probably.

Question: You have said several times [as late as 1967 in "It Could Happen Here—And Did"] that the paranoid politics of McCarthyism could happen again. Is our society farther from such a possibility following the events of the past few years?

Miller: Well, of course, I'm of the belief that paranoia is just beneath the skin of almost all of us. We can be persuaded without too such difficulty that hidden, undefined dangers are imminent and can overwhelm us. And consequently the next step is to believe that there is a group in the society carrying explosives to blow us all up. As we all know, paranoia is based, in part, on reality. Let's face it, there are people walking around with bombs who really would like to blow us all up. The question is how many and when. One simply has to learn how to forget this fact. That's normality. The paranoid is simply somebody who can't forget it, who can't forget what we all know to be true. The rest of us lapse into some persuasion that we're living in a more or less reasonable situation and that if we step on the starter of our automobile it is not going to set off a time bomb. The paranoid knows goddamned well that it is going to set off a time bomb.

Question: Then the playwright as *vates,* as prophet, sees things getting worse?

Miller: Yeah, oh yeah, in that sense.

Question: Which is a significant sense.

Miller: Which is a hell of a significent sense. But, yes, it is.

Question: In 1972, you said [in "Arthur Miller vs. Lincoln Center" in *The New York Times]* that "our cultural life seems to be drying up, we're becoming a utilitarian society in the crudest sense, namely, that which is not bought cannot be art." In the half dozen years since then, has our cultural life improved, gotten worse, or remained the same?

Miller: This is a question I would rather not answer. I'd rather ask it because when I compare the present with what I knew of the past, I think there are probably more opportunities now than there used to be—and in more places—to see some kind of art, to hear some kind of music, and to participate, even, in some kind of art be it amateur or semiprofessional, a symphony orchestra or theatre company or something like that. I don't know the statistics; I have a feeling that there are more, and that the chances are better now.

Let's not forget that when I started in theatre there was no off-Broadway theatre, of any description. You arrived in New York, if you were stupid enough to come here, with a play which a commercial producer would put on Broadway or you didn't ever see your work done. Even in colleges when I was at school, the drama department only did the latest Broadway hits. My first play—nobody at Michigan would do it. Not because they didn't like it, but because nobody ever did a student's plays, and it was finally done by the Hillel Foundation which had no theatre. But they had a building with an auditorium which was for meetings, and they let me use the auditorium. And we got a gang of actors from the drama department who put the play on there. And this was not particularly reactionary. There were very few places in the United States—I think Carnegie Tech was one; there was a drama school there, but I suppose you could count them on one hand—where a new play by a student could be produced. Of course, this goes on all over the place all the time now. Not only in colleges but in New York. So it's better that way than it used to be.

Question: All My Sons does [as you say in the Introduction to the Collected Plays (1957)] "lay siege to . . . to the fortress of unrelatedness." Has this sense of social unrelatedness worsened or been ameliorated in the years since that play was first written?

Miller: Just as a remark, I would say that the whole notion of going into a theatre and sitting with a lot of other people and watching a spectacle, especially now when you can watch television or the movies with greater convenience, tells me that, apart from the fact that it's a little more exciting to see a live actor on the stage, it's also exciting to sit next to human beings. I think people need that; they have to feel that when they laugh together there is a relatedness. They learn what's funny.

It's an old story, for example, that if you've got a comedy, and you play that comedy to five or six people who are usually partisans of the play, I mean they'd be the producer and the staff, it's a totally different procedure than if you'd play it to a house full of people. Part of the reason is that we laugh because others are laughing. They form part of our judgment as to what is funny. We also react emotionally, in part, because of the way others are reacting. We are social beings; there is nothing degrading about that. It's rather an elevated thought, in fact. It's what will save us if anything does.

I think that the theatre does break down an unrelatedness in people—to a degree. It refreshes the spirit which now experiences the reactions of other people, if only through looking at a common spectacle.

Question: In 1966, [in the *Paris Review* interview] you didn't quite seem overdelighted at the movement in theatrical criticism away from reporters who had no references in aesthetic theories of drama to academic critics or "graduates of that school." Yet you have apparently an excellent relationship with "academics" and are considerate of them. Are, then, criticism and scholarship two separate entities in your mind as they might be said to apply to your work? Do you read criticism of your work?

Miller: The question of criticism is very important; maybe it's too important for me to speak off the cuff about. Important only in this respect: it can lead or mislead the young and burden people sometimes for years and years and years with misconceptions about the value of things so that they overvalue or dismiss out of hand plays, writers, actors, actresses because some critic who had their ear for the moment has taught them to do so. A critic, like any other professional who is not fundamentally a creative artist should try to make himself unnecessary. That is, he should try, if this is conceivable, to so educate the taste of his public that they don't need him anymore. This, of course, is the worst thing you can say to any living critic that I know of—and understandably. But I do believe that. I think that a critic is a teacher, should be a teacher. He shouldn't be a kind of clown who is trying to distract you from what you're supposed to be concentrating on. There's been a kind of undergrowth of performing critics—critics who one is supposed to observe as though they are doing a number. Those people, I think, get in the way of the act.

The first thing I would love to see in a critic is a certain modesty, because we now have far more critics than artists—because there's far more white space to fill. The arts almost exist in order for these people to write about them. And that's going a little far. I think that the whole question of why somebody likes something is not even discussed anymore. It's all a question of temperament. This critic has a temperament which prefers English to American whatever it may be, from tweed to tragedy. Another one really wants musicals. This is like having doctors who don't like measles, but they like tuberculosis—incompetent where it comes to measles but know everything there is about tuberculosis. There's something obscene sometimes about the showing-off, which is usually at the expense of some artist who may well be contributing something, for all one would know. Of course, one will never know because they close up shows too quickly.

I'm afraid that I have to agree with Chekhov who said that if he had listened to the critics he would have ended up drunk in the gutter. This goes on forever.

Question: How important were the critics to you?

Miller: They were very important to help me find an audience. This is what I'm talking about. I owe a great deal to Brooks Atkinson with whose work I often times disagreed deeply. His standards, his feeling about the theatre was oftentimes not mine; however, without him I would have had a much more difficult time at a crucial point in my life and that is when I wrote *All My Sons*. I was unknown, and so was the director, Elia Kazan; so were most of the actors in the play like Arthur Kennedy who was a young, upcoming actor but not very well known. And Karl Malden, whom nobody had heard of. The reviews in general were okay but not enough to really run that play for very long. Atkinson came back in a Sunday piece and he really did a tremendous reconsideration of the play, and that made it. From that day, the audience came and they listened, and it won all the prizes, and I won an audience. Without him, I probably wouldn't have, at least not then, and I'd have had to try all over again. Having won that audience, it made it easier for me to take off with *Death of a Salesman* and to try new approaches to the theatre, and to break up some of the reigning realism—I should say naturalism; it wasn't realism.

Question: Do you ever read academic scholarship on your own work?

Miller: I don't, unless somebody sends it, and I happen to be opening that mail right at the moment when I can read it. The only reason is—I have no disrespect for academic people at all—it's just that I think reading too much criticism of oneself makes you self-conscious—for a few hours. I'm not really all that interested in the past, in my own past. I have problems tomorrow morning. I've got a lyric I want to finish, or I've got a story I want to write, and that criticism can't help me do that at all.

Question: In 1967, you were prouder of *The Crucible* than anything else you had written. Does that remain so a decade later?

Miller: I'll tell you about *The Crucible;* first of all, it's the most produced of my plays, more than *Salesman* or anything else. I'm proud of it in the sense that it seems to reach the young very well. They do it all over the place. And I get very moving letters from them sometimes about where it has sent their minds in relation to liberty, in relation to the rights of people. It seems to affect their living as citizens. Which is terrific. And I kind of feel proud about that. They're stronger in their belief in the best things in America because of that.

Equally, it makes a statement abroad. *The Crucible,* I think I've said once, when it gets produced in some foreign country, especially in Latin America this has been true, it's either that a dictator is about to arise and take over, or has just been over-thrown. I'm glad something of mine is useful as a kind of a weapon like that. It speaks for people against tyranny, and that's nothing to be ashamed of.

Question: When Philip Gelb asked you about "the discipline whereby you sit down and write regularly," you responded that "I don't know how to write regularly. I wish I did. It's not possible to me." Yet, very few serious American playwrights have produced the quantity of your plays. How, then, do you work? To what do you attribute the magnitude of your canon?

Miller: About my work, working habits—frankly, I think like most writers who last at all I work all the time, that is, even when I'm not working. It's like Chekhov in *The Sea Gull:* Trigorin, when Nina says to him how marvelous it must be to be a writer, and he says something to the effect [that] Oh God, yes, it's marvelous, but you're never relieved of it; I look up at the sky right now, and there are some clouds going by and I think, well, I must make a note that that cloud looks like a grand piano. [Miller is paraphrasing Trigorin's long speech to Nina in Act II of *The Sea Gull.*].

I just never stop. But the amount I've written discourages me. I think I should have written far more. I destroy, I'm afraid, a large proportion of what I write. I can't satisfy myself—I can't find really what I'm trying to say, and there's an enormous amount of destruction of material that I go through, trunkfuls of stuff which I dread even thinking about. So, if it does seem that I've written a lot, I assure you I've written much more, but I'm afraid that I will never come to complete it.

Question: What do you do in addition to your writing? What are your hobbies? That is, what do you do to relax, to escape the pressures of the muse?

Miller: Well, I live in the country; I have really almost twenty years now, all the time. I've always had a place in the country, but I've lived there winter and summer for almost twenty years. I'm a pretty good cabinet maker, and I make furniture now and then. I also keep a good garden. I resolved to do some sculpting, but I haven't gotten to it yet. I play tennis. And, I guess I wander around wondering why I'm not writing—most of the time.

Question: You are the winner of the Hopwood Awards of 1936 and 1937 (University of Michigan), and Donaldson Award, two Antoinette Perry Awards, The New York Drama Critics Award, the Pulitzer Prize, and the Gold Medal from the National Institute of Arts and Letters. As well, you were the recipient of a doctorate (L. H. D.) from the University of Michigan (1956). What is your feeling about this kind of recognition? What is your attitude toward prizes generally? Do you think of the Nobel?

Miller: Prizes. Well, I just wish they would stop giving any at all. But, of course, I'm an old man now I guess. These prizes, most of the time most prizes are given so that we will recognize the prize-giver, and he will achieve some distinction by giving out the prize. The Nobel Prize, for example, the list of writers who never got it is certainly as grand in its achievement as the ones who did get it. I'm not even going to bother running down the names of the left-out in the last fifty years.

Question: What of television? TV has done nice productions of *Crucible, Price, Vichy,* and *Fall.* Do you like what television has done with your plays? What of the recent "Fame" production?

Miller: Television cuts plays, and I don't like that about it. Incidentally, *Vichy* had the best production I've ever seen of that play, apart maybe from the original that we did on Broadway—or off-

Broadway rather. That production directed by Stacy Keach was a marvel, I thought. On the whole, the others are not as good, I have to admit, even though I like the people who did them. I'm afraid that most of it is due to the fact that you can't cut plays without losing something, especially plays like mine which were cut already. You lose—you cut the sinews, and things dangle that were once muscularly connected and vigorous. You weaken them, and I'm afraid that this is true of both mine and other plays I've seen on television.

As for the "Fame," they missed the whole first twelve minutes of that, and I'm sorry that that happened. The rest of it was very good—was very well done. They did not know how to do a *crucial* scene in the beginning which set the whole play up. I'm sorry I wasn't there; it would have been very simple to do it.

Question: What of television's famous impact for good or ill—your opinion? Do you watch any television? What?

Miller: I watch television. Yes, I live in the country, and sometimes you want to see what's happening in the big world. I can't say I watch it at any length. It tires me out, and it's usually terribly superficial no matter what it's doing. It's being chased by the two arms of the clock. There's something hysterical about it always.

Unfortunately, I'm afraid, it is the only art probably most Americans ever get to see—if you want to call it an art. That's where they get the news, and that's where they get their opinions apparently. I personally would love to take it more seriously if the institutions would permit it, but they don't on the whole.

Now, I think, for example, the *Holocaust* program, which was done like a soap opera, I simply have to admit a fact, and that is that it brought to consciousness something which otherwise was not there. I've just talked to my brother-in-law who works in Germany, and he brought me some press comment on the *Holocaust,* which just happens to have gone on recently, and apparently it was a most devastating event in German history since World War II. Forty-seven percent of the German people watched that program. Now, forty-seven percent of the German people have not done one thing together—whatever it was. And he said that it had probably the most profound effect of any event in the public history of the German Republic. A whole generation knew nothing about this—the young generation. The older one, that knew, wasn't talking. The teachers had never been taught this. It was like you dropped out ten years of your life and lost them.

So, television is maybe the single most important artistic fact—God save the term—in the United States today. They say—I can't believe this—but I read somewhere the average American looks at it—I can't remember now whether it was—six hours [daily]. Well, what are we doing all the time? Don't they work or something? Apparently not. But I imagine in some homes it's on all the time with nobody watching it. But, anyway, it's a formidable fact. I mean, certainly the Bible at its most popular hour was not studied six hours a day.

Question: What remains to be done? What are you working on at the moment?

Miller: I'm just completing a rather shortish play—I don't know really how long it's going to take to perform, maybe an hour and a half—which I began in 1969, which to my astonishment is ten years ago. But these numbers are meaningless at this point.

I just did a film which is based on a memoir of a woman who was a member of the orchestra of the Auschwitz concentration camp called *Playing For Time.* That's in the process of being set up.

Question: Does the play have a working title?

Miller: Yes. It's called *Smoke.* I don't know whether it'll continue to be called *Smoke,* but I kind of like that title now.

They're doing a new production of *The Price* on 42nd Street in the Harold Clurman Theatre, which is just off-Broadway I suppose you'd call it. Which has a hell of a cast, and I have high hopes for that; Fritz Weaver is in it and Mitch Ryan and Joe Buloff and Scotty Bloch.

Question: Will you be involved in the production?

Miller: Well, I'll be involved in the sense that I'll go down after a couple of weeks of rehearsal and see what they've done, and give them my invaluable advice. But I'm not going to direct it or anything. I'm seriously considering directing my new play, though, which I may do in the same theatre.

Question: Do you have a projected date for it?

Miller: If I get done in the next couple of weeks, I may do it soon after that—if I can cast it properly, and I think I can.

Question: How about the musical?

Miller: The musical is called *Up From Paradise* and is supposed to go into production in the Fall.

Question: Hasn't it been produced before?

Miller: We did that in a sort of workshop performance in Washington last year. However, it wasn't completed; a lot of the music and lyrics hadn't been written yet, but now it's complete. It has a producer named Charles Hollerith, and I think we'll go ahead. So it seems anyway.

Question: You are doing the lyrics.

Miller: I do the lyrics and, of course, the book. It's based on *Creation of the World and Other Business*—vaguely. It's quite different.

And I've written and published two short stories this year in *Esquire* and in *Atlantic*. And I've written this book on China; well, it's really forty thousand words. It's a long essay or a short book, and, I don't know, other odds and ends. So that's where it is.

Question: How do you want to be remembered? What is your estimation of your legacy? How well do you think your intentions and reception jibe? How will literary history treat Arthur Miller? Are you satisfied with that?

Miller: I really don't know how to answer that, frankly. As for literary history, it just doesn't seem like anything I ought to think about even. I've seen so many writers, frankly, that had some effect on their time or even seemed permanent whose names would probably hardly be known now except to historians. There's always something new under the sun. There's always a change. Who can ever hope to predict any of this?

I've hoped that I've done my work honestly—and well. That's all I can really do.

Studs Terkel Talks with Arthur Miller
Studs Terkel/1980

From *Saturday Review* (September 1980): 24-27. Reprinted by permission.

Arthur Miller's new play, *The American Clock,* which begins its pre-Broadway tour in Baltimore next month, deals with the impact of the Great Depression of the Thirties on a middle-class American family. The play was, Miller says, inspired by Studs Terkel's *Hard Times,* a collection of interviews with veterans of the Depression. Recently, Terkel (whose new book, *American Dreams: Lost and Found,* is reviewed on page 64) also interviewed Miller about an era that still fascinates them both.

ST: Some time ago, you said the two most traumatic epochs in American history were the Civil War and the Great Depression. You, as a young man during the hard Thirties, were obviously affected.

AM: I probably had a distorted view because I was right at the bottom. I had the usual American upbringing: Everything was going to be better every year. An endless boom. I thought the system was foolproof because it was advertised as such. The bursting of the bubble was devastating because it had been blown up so big. What disintegrated with the Depression was any kind of faith in government. I'm speaking of 1929, '30, and '31. There was a scoffing at authority. It had in it the seeds of the Sixties. There was one basic difference: the question of guilt.

In the Thirties, people, in order to believe they were real Americans, believed they were responsible for their own fate. If a man found himself making $15,000 a year, he credited himself. When he lost it, he blamed himself. We've all heard about the psychic crippling, the suicides. I remember where I was living, in

Brooklyn, a stunned air all over the neighborhood. You'd see a lot of perfectly able-bodied men in the middle of the day. They had aged enormously. You'd sit in a room with these guys, many of them fathers of my friends, and you'd sense a premature senility. Thinking back on it, they were young men, in their forties. They blamed themselves.

ST: A Southern woman of my acquaintance remembered some of this. People saying: "If we hadn't bought that radio. . . ." "If we hadn't bought that old second-hand car. . . ." She was horrified by the preachers who'd tell the people they suffered because of their sins. The people believed it, God was punishing them. Their children were starving because of their sins.

AM: It was part of our theology. As ye sow, so shall ye reap. Remember, Americans had hardly participated in contemporary society. We had no Social Security at that time, no unemployment compensation, hardly any income tax. The average American could live and die without getting next to a government form, aside from a visit to the post office to sign a receipt for a letter. He had no personal connection with the government, so how could he deduce that "society" had the slightest effect on him?

Today, certainly since the New Deal, the relationship of the individual to society is altogether different. He expects certain things from society. He lives side by side with government measures from the time he's born. We've got a whole class of people who have never been off relief, have never had a job. Businessmen, really, have never been off relief, especially the big ones. There are many government measures that support industry. You can't conceive of business being really free of that any more.

ST: Chrysler, for one.

AM: That's an extreme case. Look at the interest rates, maneuvered and manipulated. They're no longer acts of God. It is decided how much people are going to pay for their money. They didn't do that in the old days, at least not in public. Now when something goes wrong, you'd have to be an idiot to really blame yourself altogether. When you lose your job now. . . .

ST: How was it with you in the Thirties? You had all sorts of jobs—though, I assume, with hardly any tenure.

AM: I sang on a radio station. If I may say so, I had a terrific tenor voice (laughs). I did that until I got tired of working without pay. It was a crap game. I wanted to become a professional crooner. It was a quick way up.

ST: You and Russ Columbo.

AM: I would have settled for that any time (laughs).

ST: The warehouse you once worked in was, I assume, the locale as well as the metaphor in your play *A Memory of Two Mondays.*

AM: Working anywhere was perfectly normal in those days. You got all the jobs you could get. People got fired at three o'clock in the afternoon. A guy would come through and say, "Well, it's all over, go home." There were few unions, no severance pay.

ST: The young protagonist, a reflection of yourself, is seeing the wasted lives of the others, the dreams all shot, as our system slipped on a banana peel.

AM: I have since come to believe we have a lot more to do with our fate than that play implies. But at the time, say, between 1932 and 1937, there seemed no conceivable way of escaping it. Nor did there seem to be the slightest hope any more by 1937. We were thinking every three months that something was going to work. The New Deal came up with one experiment after another, but nothing really happened. It would gasp for a few months and settle back to where it was. It was a despair that was matched only by the post-Civil War South. It lay there and seemed to have been mortally wounded.

ST: As though a dust had settled upon the land, a stillness beyond Appomattox.

AM: There are images that spring to mind in this play. When I was 16, I decided to go to sea. I walked into one shipping office after another till I found the U.S. Lines. They had these tremendous liners all tied up in the dock. I'll never forget the image: gigantic floating cities that were empty, stuck. In *The American Clock,* I have a guy who was the captain's steward on the SS *Manhattan.* He ended up in Brooklyn trying to stay out of the rain.

ST: You're not calling it *The American Clock* for capricious reasons, I'm sure. Time is obviously on your mind.

AM: It is a menacing image as well as a benign one. My interest in this play is formal as well as reflective. I was fascinated by the idea of having an objective view of society and running through it, as a counter-motif, the story of a family.

ST: Your juxtaposition of the specific as against the general reminds me of John Steinbeck's technique in *Grapes of Wrath.* The

Joad family's journey in the jalopy is seen in bold relief against the background of those thousands of others, all sharing the same dilemma. Well, the American clock is ticking away, the wind is rising, and we may be in for another big blow.

AM: It hit me the other day. Once again, we have an engineer as President. Hoover and Carter are not the same man, but their reaction process may be similar: minimalistic. Engineers are spiritually conservative: if you jiggle the machine too much, it may do an untoward thing. The tendency to do nothing as long as possible is regarded as the wise policy, the realistic one. The difference was in Hoover's successor. Roosevelt did everything with the machine. Nothing was the same from one month to the next. There may be debate as to how much was good and how much bad, but at least we got the sense of someone really swatting the ball.

ST: The "realistic" men fascinate me. In the Thirties, they wound up with custard pie on their faces, much in the manner of Mack Sennett comics. I'll never forget the Wall Street wise man, who had served as an advisor to Roosevelt, Truman, and Johnson. All I had asked him was: "How did it happen?" He looked heavenward. "October 29, 1929. It was like a thunderclap. Everybody was stunned. Nobody knew what it was all about. The Street had general confusion. They didn't understand it any more than anybody else. They thought something would be announced." Announced by whom?

AM: In the booming Fifties, Humphries, Eisenhower's Secretary of Treasury, was interviewed. Could it happen again? He said that, of course, it could, because they didn't know why it happened the first time.

ST: If it does come again, wow. During my travels, while working on *Hard Times,* I asked the question of scores of Depression survivors. Would the public's reaction be the same? Invariably, the response was: Hell, no! There is no longer the feeling of personal guilt. Sally Rand, the fan dancer, was astonishingly powerful. She spoke the thoughts of a great many. "I don't think there will be any more people queueing up in breadlines waiting to be fed by charity, God damn it. I think they will just go out and take what they need. The middle-class looks upon the deprived smugly: The poor we'll always have with us. Oh, yeah?"

AM: There is unquestionably a potential in the American people for extreme measures, if they are provoked enough. When a man loses his job, he loses his identity. This is not simply an economic question. He's sore. It's like he's gotten beat with a stick. Especially if he's in his middle age and he's put his inventiveness, his time, his hopes, everything into his job and suddenly he's nowhere.

ST: Status, feelings about his manhood, it's all there on the hook. I was told about some miners in Pennsylvania, during the Depression. While they idled on the benches, whittling away, they were considered such failures—they looked upon themselves as such, too—that their wives refused to go to bed with them.

A guy in Kansas City told me about his father, a good carpenter. One day he came home with the tool chest on his shoulder. Laid off. With his loss of job, his authority, his sense of self, was gone. Now began the tension, especially between the father and son. This theme has always atttracted you, hasn't it? The conflict with Biff and Willy Loman in *Death of a Salesman.* Joe Keller and his surviving son in *All My Sons. . . .*

AM: About 10 years ago, *Esquire* magazine sent out a questionnaire to 15 writers. What had they in common psychologically? You know what it was? A failed father. Either a suicide or a drunk, an economic disaster, a father who fled—the disillusionment of the boy at about the time of puberty. Hemingway, Faulkner, Steinbeck, go down the list. . . .

ST: And yourself?

AM: And myself. It's practically foolproof.

ST: In one of your theater essays, you spoke of your father. You implied there was hardly any communication between the two of you. You hardly spoke to the man in years.

AM: No, it wasn't that. It was like two searchlights on different islands. I had no animosity toward him. I simply had no great relationship with him. As I grew older, we became much closer. I began to understand what it was all about, too.

Combine a father's failure with the society in which he lives—after all, as the wage earner, he brings the social system into the house—you'll see what'll happen.

ST: In *The American Clock,* the father, a successful man, believes very much in the system.

AM: Oh yes, up to his neck.

ST: Suddenly, that which he believes in fails, collapses. So the guy

himself collapses. I'm thinking of a kid who recently drove me
through Kentucky. He talked of his father, a fantastic salesman, a
great con artist, a self-styled big shot. For one reason or another, he
goes down. Suddenly he's an old man, a dead failure. He sits at
home, plays solitaire, works crossword puzzles, watches TV, hardly
walks more than 10 feet out of his room. Know what the kid said to
me? "My father is Willy Loman. *Death of a Salesman* is about him."
The two older brothers and their wives don't want the old man
around. Shame and fear. His failure terrifies them.

AM: They might catch it (laughs). The question is whether
anybody can avoid identifying himself with his failure or his
prosperity. In *The American Clock,* the father *is* his business. Even
when he's not around his business, he's busy working at it. It's
probably one of the reasons why, as a class, businessmen have
created more than anybody else. In a way, they're like artists. They
really pour themselves into their work. There's no way of divorcing
themselves personally from what they're doing.

ST: Freud referred to *arbeit,* work, as one of the two prime drives
of man. The job is the extension of himself. If it's gone, he's gone.

AM: I wrote an essay once about the equivalents we have for
gods. The closest thing we've got is the economic system. Look at the
story of Job. Good man, did everything right. Suddenly, for no
acceptable reason, his faith and existence are being challenged. He
asks questions, but there's no answer. The Greeks had the Sphinx.

There's another element in this play that is in my other work, too.
The son moves in to assert the life force. It does not end in total
surrender which is remarkable, given the insanity and surrealism of
the social situation. The play ends on a very positive note. The teller
is still alive to tell it, and hopeful.

ST: And growing. As the old man is slipping, the son takes over.
It's reminiscent of Biff realizing the truth about himself at the time of
his father's death. He knows who he is. Willy never did. For that
matter, it's Joe Keller's boy, too, in *All My Sons.*

AM: The father in *The American Clock* is absolutely the opposite
of Willy Loman. He does not have illusions. He is a realistic man and
does not surrender to his own defeat.

ST: I found this fascinating. He accepts relief, without self-
flagellation. He goes to the welfare station. He is not encumbered by
false pride. I talked to quite a few businessmen who lost everything
during the Depression. A remarkable number went on relief. Though

they recalled the moments of humiliation, they realized, in retrospect, it was not their fault. Others erased the memory and the shame of it.

AM: This man, under duress, is able to separate himself from his condition. He is not a guilty man, by any means.

ST: It's a pretty large canvas you're painting. Calling it a mural is, I imagine, not accidental.

AM: I have experimented with formal problems since the time I started writing. There's an attempt here to do two things at the same time, which is the nature of a mural. Rivera's and Sequieros's in Mexico are prime examples. Large Renaissance paintings are in that order. When you look close at any face, it may turn out to be a real person's. When you step away, you see the whole pattern, the grand movement. It's fundamentally a picture of many people interacting with each other and with the heavens. I don't care for a theater that is absolutely personal and has no resonance beyond that. We've become so accustomed to that we've forgotten that for most of mankind's history, the theater was quite the other way. Theater was involved with the fate of the kingdom and the importance of power, of rank, of public policy. It's in Shakespeare. It's absolutely essential in Greek drama. Ours is almost excessively bourgeois in that it presumes the world really has no effect upon us.

ST: Challenging solipsism in the theater has always been your impulse. You've been racked up on more than one occasion for this.

AM: They call this political in a condemnatory way. In Greece's best times, people who were nonpolitical were regarded as idiots. It was the idiot who didn't understand that man was social, that our fate in the deepest sense of the word was bound up with all of mankind.

ST: The air we breathe is political, you might say.

AM: Let's be more literal about it. The fact that the air is poisoned now is a political fact. Had there been a different attitude on the part of society toward the abuse of the earth and of the air, you would not have people in Love Canal dying of unnatural causes, of poisons. Of course it's political. Does that take away people's character?

ST: Trouble with you is that you regard theater as serious business. Okay, let's pin this down. What is the anxiety, the preoccupation, that most possesses Americans today?

AM: At this moment in our country, there is this imminent sense of some deep dislocation about to take place. For many, it has already happened.

ST: And the American clock is ticking away.

AM: What is positive about it all is the impatience of the people with the empty reassurances that Carter tends to give. That's terrific. They took it far longer in the Thirties. Now they feel the mess is man-made. It is not an Act of God. They have secularized the economic system. They think: What the hell, we made it, we can unmake it. We can readjust, tinker with it. Don't tell us to sit around, waiting for three years before we eat again.

ST: You think that explains why the young people in the audience responded so enthusiastically to *The American Clock?*

AM: That's what I'm most interested in. A lot of people who lived through that time would just as soon not hear about it any more. It's bad-luck time. It's the younger people who are really thirsty for the news that this play brings. I suppose it's because they never got a straight story about what really went on at that time.

ST: You tellin' me? In my wanderings across the country, digging out hard-times memories, I came across scores of kids who had never heard of the Great Depression. The only reference to it by their parents came in the form of a bawling out: "You never had it so good." "The way you throw money away. . . ." "The food you leave on the table. . . ." "But they were never told what it was really like: the terror of losing a job, the humiliations suffered, the sense of shame.

Paradoxically, it was also a time of great excitement, of neighborhood rallies and demonstrations, of wildly creative federal arts projects. And there was a camaraderie: the passing of a cigarette butt to another, a street-car transfer changing hands, a morning newspaper handed over to the next guy.

AM: There was a cheerfulness I've tried to capture in the play. Some of the gayest songs in our popular repertoire came out of the Depression. I've called upon quite a few. And the humor, which was fundamentally positive. It had a bitter edge to it naturally, but it was not black humor. It was healthy.

ST: I think all this was recognized by the young playgoers who were cheering the night I saw the show. They were discovering a moment in our history they hadn't known before. At a time of fashionable despair, it makes for exciting theater.

AM: I hope so. I've attempted a play about more than just a family, about forces bigger than simply overheard voices in the dark. It's a story of the United States talking to itself. . . .

'The Absence of the Tension':
A Conversation with Arthur Miller
Leonard Moss/1980

From Leonard Moss, *Arthur Miller* (Boston: Twayne, rev. ed. 1980): 107-122. Reprinted by permission.

I wanted to see what Arthur Miller was thinking before I finished the second edition of my book on his life and work. On a hot summer afternoon, July 27, 1979, he greeted my sister Toby Gutwill and me at his home in the country near Roxbury, Connecticut. Tall with a bit of a paunch, dressed in shorts and sounding almost as gravel-voiced as George Burns, he showed us a simple graceful chair he had designed and put together from pre-Revolutionary wood salvaged from his barn.

His manner was as simple and graceful as his chair. He was comfortable, enthusiastic, sensible, anecdotal—a wholly satisfying conversationalist. At sixty-four, Arthur Miller is in a good place, and I do not refer only to the pleasant hills around Roxbury.

We left him, after three hours, heading for a chore with a shovel.

Arthur Miller: What do you want to talk about?

Leonard Moss: I want to say hello. I'm not going to conduct an interview. I don't have a list of questions to ask.

AM: Well, that's a relief! Have you been to New York to see *The Price?*

LM: I saw the original production but not this revival.

AM: It's properly done this time. It wasn't the other time because we had a lot of bad luck. One man got taken to the hospital a few days before we opened, and the other conked out after a week. We had to recast. But it wasn't that so much as my redirecting it in an atmosphere of emergency after the director and actors fell out.

LM: Do you remember my letter asking about the relationship between the two brothers and their father?

AM: Yes. But it's fundamentally a social or moral problem, it isn't simply a psychological problem. The play is examining what you might call the architecture of sacrifice. And of course society depends on sacrifice; everybody has got to do a social duty. We expect the police or the authorities to do that, certainly. There has to be the sort of a person who gets gratification from doing it or you're not going to have a society. And Victor, of course, is a policeman.

LM: Isn't it possible to get some kind of amalgamation of the two points of view, so that you don't have to get the super-egoistic type, and neither do you have to rely on the sacrificial type?

AM: Yeah, hopefully you could, but you ain't gonna get anything if the ironies don't get lifted into view. See, a guy like the older brother frequently is the one who invents new procedures because he is not bound by any reverence for what exists; he's perfectly selfish and temperamental and idiosyncratic. Whether it be in physics or automobile engineering or business, those types add something new to the way the world goes. But they're hell on their relatives—their wives and their children! And the other brother is a terrific husband and father.

LM: You were talking about one of the actors in the original cast who almost died before opening night. Does the idea of dying worry you?

AM: I've been dealing with that for years and years and years. I used to say that plays such as I write are written from the lip of the grave, as though the ultimate judgment was lying upon us all and the object was to find out what it was, if possible. It wasn't that I was attempting to deal with my own death. I thought about the world that way, perhaps simplistically, as though there was a judgment that could be made. I can't imagine trying to write tragedies or anything approaching them without that in mind. You can write comedies with everything left in abeyance, but if you think of any of the Greeks shrugging their shoulders and saying "I don't know what anything means," it's not possible with their structure; it is too pointed, it's too definite, it's too much like an arrow trying to reach a target, as

compared with let's say a Chekhovian play, which can end with one
foot in the air.

LM: Sometimes I think it's a *negative* judgment—getting back to
The Price as well as Greek tragedy—on the failure of some of our
institutions or values.

AM: It's getting clearer now why we're in such trouble—clearer
than maybe ten years ago. And it's that, first of all, history is taking
place at a velocity that is unbearable. Tremendous movements begin
and end in a year or two. Take something with tremendous meaning
for us, like Vietnam, which was maybe the most important event in
the history of this country in the twentieth century (apart from the
Depression), something that turned us around more violently than
anything else. In a space of a few years, Vietnam has become
another failed ideal. We had to create a kind of ideal out of it—those
of us who hated the war—at least a negative ideal.

A lot of people—this is almost impossible to digest—have a feeling
that there is no hope about anything. It's not that they particularly
hoped about Vietnam—it's an exemplary situation. I have gone
through this now maybe ten times, from the Spanish Civil War. It's
been one after another, where of necessity a younger generation
believes in an ideal which promptly collapsed or became something
else or degenerated.

Now it gets repeated at a quicker velocity—the Soviet Union went
from 1919 or '20 for about twenty-five years before a final judgment
could be laid upon it, though some people out there still refuse to
make any judgment. The Chinese went from '49 to at least '66
before any kind of real doubt could be leveled, and that's a long time.
Now it takes about a year or two—take the so-called revolutions in
the Third World, like Africa. The revolution takes place on Tuesday,
by the next Thursday they're lining people up and shooting them
down, and we're back where we started from as far as creating a just
society is concerned.

LM: But isn't there some handwriting on the wall? It could be just
a long transition to working out a new temperamental type—say,
between the two brothers in *The Price*.

AM: Well, my only question is this. When one side wins too
thoroughly there is a real question in my mind whether, given the
contemporary means for indoctrination and social control that exist—

secret police and radio and television and the rest—I wonder what chance remains. We take for granted that both sides are going to persist.

To a degree that's true—they will. Take Czechoslovakia. The Czechs are in an exemplary condition. There's a country that was democratic in our sense of the term—people got elected and they got thrown out. And in a real sense the power resided in the people. It was set up by Wilsonian democrats, and that's the way it was. It wasn't a case of people inured to thousands of years of tyranny and not knowing any different. And they knew they were advanced technologically—they made the best cars in Europe.

OK—they get invaded by the Russians, who very intelligently decided that what they had to do was destroy the cultural inventors, especially those who really were wedded to some other kind of vision, whatever it might be. It might be a Catholic vision—it needn't be West European capitalism—or it might be a Communist vision that was anti-Soviet. They have driven out an army of intellectuals, who now live in Western Europe and some in America.

I had one of them here who still lives in Czechoslovakia. In a moment of candor he wondered whether the spirit, which is skeptical and courageous—the counterforce—could really go on or be quite completely wiped off the face of the earth. This has happened. Many people there really don't understand what this kind of guy's doing by resisting the regime, and the reason is that physical conditions of life there are not all that horrible. They still have an underlying technology that they use—it's crippled, it could be far better utilized if it were not sat on by these oafs—but people still get their beer and live a lot better than people live in Moscow because they naturally do things more efficiently.

So you have to raise a question about time. You are saying "a long-term transition." OK, but I can see a transition too, to something else, to where that imagining of what you could call a voluntary kind of life is crushed.

And a lot of Americans don't have it anymore. When you talk to them about it, in between not wanting to hear about it, they're scared. See, it's a very fragile kind of plant that exists in history only a few years. In the United States, only since the Civil War up until maybe 1930 is when its heyday was; then it got knocked out of existence, apart from the Communists. There is an internal mechanism working in both systems—no question about it—to integrate everybody into the system.

I think that's why people instinctively make so much of writers, who really don't deserve all that much attention most of the time: they're not that smart and they're not that good. Most writing is not worth the paper it's written on, except it gives us amusement of some sort. But there's a sense that these anarchistic people are trying at least to create something new; there is an instinct that something in the procedure of art is our last gasp. We are the reminders of independent craftsmanship.

LM: Analogous to the procedure that has to be incorporated in our lives.

AM: Right. See, everybody wants to be an artist now. I get invitations, probably ten a week—a writer's workshop, a playwright's workshop, a lecture here, a talk there. "Tell us something."

It wasn't that way when I was growing up. Take my old neighborhood. All types—football players, saxophone players, dentists; I was the only one who ever came to be a writer. You read *Studs Lonigan* or any book about a neighborhood. You didn't find people walking around saying, "I'm going to be a writer or an artist." I'm sure that if you wrote the same sort of book about a later generation, I'm sure more people dream at least of escaping the system by being an artist. Don't you think there's more of that now?

LM: I can't see it. There's a lot of people who go for the money in writing, but I don't see the idea there that it's a creative thing to do.

AM: But all these courses! When I went to the University of Michigan it was the only school in the United States that gave a playwriting course. It was the only school that I was aware of where a student could enter a writing contest and win money. It was so rare—that they actually thought that much about writing. And of course Harvard would never have a course in creative writing because they felt that it wasn't serious.

LM: It's become more respectable—

AM: and more widespread.

LM: But as you once said, "many writers, few plays."

AM: Oh, I don't mean that they actually create anything—that's got nothing to do with it. It's this image of the Bohemian, of the free man who doesn't go to work every morning, and out of himself creates his *living*—that's what I'm talking about. It's really the reincarnation of the old shopkeeper who lived upstairs and went down, opened his store, and sent nine children through college and raised eleven dentists.

LM: Somehow I can't see a generation of writers or artists at the present time leading the way. It seems to me it's going to come from somewhere else, maybe even the politicians, unlikely as that seems. There aren't many on the horizon right now who—

AM: who will do what?

LM: Who will give us models for living differently, more creatively, more openly.

AM: My prejudice is that for a great many people the enviable model is the writer.

LM: Where are we going to get models for the kind of life that you keep talking about in your plays and getting your characters to approach—some kind of amalgamation of the two Franz brothers in *The Price?*

AM: That would be great! The only thing I worry about is not so much the amalgamation but the tension, the unhappiness of not having that model. The tension, for example, is terrific between the two brothers, that they give way completely.

LM: But that tension has gone on for thousands of years.

AM: We have lost a lot of it. I used to know a guy who lived around the corner; he's dead now. His name was Theodore K. Quinn. Nobody ever heard of him. He used to be the Vice President of General Electric Corporation, but he was an old Populist underneath all that. He helped buy out one business after another for General Electric, and he was the witness to what he thought was a disaster.

The guys who ran the little businesses were terrific spiritually. They were independent, they were tough, they were witty, ironical, and they talked back. The Company would buy out their businesses, pay them very well, and make them the managers. So they were doing absolutely everything they had done before, except one thing: they no longer worked independently, they were parts of this gigantic octopus.

And he told me that he realized he was witnessing the end of an era, and the end of a kind of person. 'Cause what happened was they grew more and more irresponsible. The idea was "don't make waves." They would see something's not going to work and say nothing: "Be quiet—it'll collapse, and when it collapses it'll change by itself." So what becomes of the virtues of science? He wrote several books. He tried to stop this monopolization, with very little success.

The point is the integration of everybody into one unit; we've simply lost the sense of real independence.

LM: It *could* happen that integration could work in a creative way.

AM: Yes, very often. But at a tremendous cost.

LM: We are still talking in traditional terms—the either/or. Either we'll become mindless robots or—

AM: Well, you have to be ready to concede something to make this compromise. It depends on what. I'll tell you one thing: in the East (for example, China), that particular tension is gone—or never really existed. You educate yourself with only one thought in mind: to find your niche in the hive. Which is of course largely true here. The artist is the only one who has any independence at all, such as he has. Since that philosophy and that system occupy most of the world, the question is how we proceed from here.

LM: What I heard you saying before was that we keep the tension between the two poles intact.

AM: If possible.

LM: That doesn't give you the final answer.

AM: Without the tension you'd have no question. My problem is that I can't see people asking these questions. Here's the irony: the Socialist idea is an integrationist one; they claim a rational society where your talents are used instead of wasted. The irony is that up to this point—the Soviet Union has been around for sixty-five years or so—the fundamental equipment has been taken from *us*, brought into being by these "half-mad liberals" whose existence the other system would suppress. And it's a real question in my mind whether the time will come when they will slowly bind themselves into a well-integrated *stop*. It's not just a question of Capitalism-Communism. It's hard to find a difference. The tension has gone.

LM: So what's going to happen?

AM: Now they have to turn themselves around. Chrysler Motor Company is practically out of business. They sold a big plant to Volkswagen. Symptomatic—they build a brand-new plant in Pennsylvania never occupied. They never manufactured a *bolt* in there. Volkswagen moved in with a small car and they can't build enough of them. Wait six months here for a Volkswagen. You ain't gonna wait two minutes for a Chrysler; they're paying you two dollars for gas money to come to a Chrysler showroom.

This is all that brick that forms in the head; the concrete slowly settles down. They seem to have lost the strength to bear the tension of conflict and growth. Their ingenuity left them. They got so well integrated that they weren't even capable of competing with another capitalist industry. It's a good example of the absence of the tension.

LM: How does the tension get renewed?

AM: This is a hard question.

LM: Do you have a personal model in the moral world—anybody or any work?

AM: There used to be. There isn't any longer because I've used up all my capacities to emulate. I used to think very often of Chekhov as a person, but I know that I'm not like him. In terms of works, I would have liked to live in Greece with the tragedies.

I attach myself to Ibsen because I saw him as a contemporary Greek, and I suppose it's because there was a terrific reliance in him as there was in the Greeks on the idea of the continuity between the distant past and the present. "The birds came home to roost"—they always did; your character was your fate. I like that immensely. Beyond that, there was something about Ibsen's character I didn't like; personally he would have been insufferable. Lots of writers are totally unreliable, selfish, consumed with their own psyches, vain.

LM: Sounds like Walter again, in *The Price*. Anyone else?

AM: Only bits and pieces. When I grew up I couldn't stand Eugene O'Neill's plays. It seemed to me the dialogue was so phony: you laughed at that kind of dialogue. It was fit for old melodramas, it wasn't serious, you couldn't read that stuff. Nobody I knew spoke that way; nobody I knew spoke good English—what kind of Americans spoke like *that*? Nobody. So I couldn't stand that.

And then it seemed to me the plays were so weighed down with the psychological task he had set himself, like being a modern Aeschylus, that I couldn't see the life in it. He wrote a couple of marvelous things; the best thing he wrote was *Long Day's Journey into Night*, his last play. But a lot of the rest is just plain academic stuff, and I have a feeling one reason his reputation grew was that it became available to academics.

But as time went on I felt more and more the weight of his seriousness, finally; despite all, he was pitting his life on his next discovery, which no other writer I knew was doing. Fitzgerald did it; Hemingway didn't do it (Hemingway goofed off); Dreiser did it. So I was moved by that.

But I could never identify myself with him as a person. He seemed to have to consume his own children. I can't identify myself with that.

I've never become involved in writing as an avocation. I don't enjoy, after ten minutes, too many theoretical discussions, or literary discussions. I will admit that when I was starting out I used to read a lot of criticism about anybody, especially Marxist criticism. It was a new idea at the time to locate the society in the novel; this I had never thought of. Especially during the Spanish Civil War.

I don't know, I've got tremendous notebooks full of stuff I can't finish. There must be 100,000 words.

LM: What's in your way?

AM: Can't see the end of it. A thing to be something has to not be something else. I sometimes read three novels in a week and then I make a note of what I felt about them. I do that because I will not remember a month hence anything about them. Anything. It'll get all fused with all the other things. In other words, it failed not to be everything else! It succeeded in being *everything*! It's terrible. You take the characters and you find you can put them in a different book. It's a rare work that is stamped with real creation, very rare. As perhaps it should be.

LM: Have you ever thought of using historical material further, bringing your ideas and experiences together with established facts? I think of Werfel's *Forty Days of Musa Dagh* or the book you reviewed for the *New York Times* on the Spanish Civil War [*The Life of Manuel Cortes* by Ronald Fraser].

AM: Yeah, I have. In a different age a lot of adaptation was done by playwrights. Shakespeare ransacked Sir Thomas North; I did it with *The Crucible*. I also wrote a play about Cortez and Montezuma 'way back (never produced). I tried that play again about five or six years ago. Yes, I have thought of it. And I'm sorry that I didn't do more with it, because the great thing about working out of stock material is that the story is there. See, stories can be a waste of time as far as the final work is concerned. Yet you can't proceed without them.

LM: And you're a lover of stories.

AM: Yes, finally it is one of the best ways of putting everything else, one of the most efficient means. Look at what Shakespeare did with Plutarch. It would have saved me a lot of wasted time, all those attempts to create a total story. I don't call it a story: it's a career, the play's career—its trajectory, its path. Find the entry. It's easy to shoot an arrow; it's hard to follow it once it gets far away, and it's almost impossible to see it land—you have to imagine that.

LM: So what about the possibility of trying historical ideas now?

AM: Well, I tried it again. I did it again with a book of Studs Terkel dealing with the Thirties. I worked for a whole year on it, and gave it up. I suppose what I'm demanding of myself now is an absolutely intimate connection between the event on stage and myself.

I wrote another play which we did in Washington, and I may do some revision on, called *The Archbishop's Ceiling*, which is about some Czech writers now. I would call it a historical work. I just got fed up with it; I got angry at the material and the production—all wrong.

LM: *Are you going to revise* The Archbishop's Ceiling?

AM: I was just this morning for the first time in a year looking through some notes about it. I move in tremendous spurts: I plan and plan, and then do something absolutely different. I've written the first act of another play I had no intention of writing, and now I'll see if I can put the rest of it together.

LM: I'm not going to ask about what's in the mill.

AM: That's what I'm working on, that play. I've written a book about China, a 40,000-word report and speculation, with photographs by Inge Morath, my wife.

LM: I read the essay in the *Atlantic*.

AM: That's about twenty percent of the text. What do you teach?

LM: A little of everything. I'm in comparative literature. I teach our classical literature course. I teach Shakespeare, I have a course called Arthur Miller and Eugene O'Neill.

AM: It's courses like that make people say to me, "Gee, I didn't know you were still alive!" A British director who was staying at my house said, "Eighty percent of the people who know you are living say, 'How old is he?' If they were students they studied this, and maybe their children did, so they figure, 'He must be ninety-four'!" I'm sixty-four.

LM: Have you read *The Forty Days of Musa Dagh*?

AM: 'Way back, when it first came out.

LM: For some reason, when I read that I thought, "Here is a great vehicle for Arthur Miller to do an adaptation, either as a screen-play—"

AM: Well, I'll tell you what I just did, which I hope you'll see: I wrote a film which Vanessa Redgrave is going to play, and they're starting to shoot. And I worked from a memoir written by a woman who had been in the Auschwitz women's orchestra. She's a half-Jewish Frenchwoman. She got picked up with the Communist resistance. She was a café singer. They nearly killed her there. It's a chaotic book, but I think it will make a marvelous movie. There's a piece of history; see, I know how to do that. I did that in two and one-half weeks (actually, four). Of course, the movie industry has lived on adaptations. It's just that you are at one remove from what you write—it's inevitable.

LM: I don't want to sound like a Jewish mother giving you advice, but you could probably knock off something about the Spanish Civil War in no time. Is it available to your imagination?

AM: Oh yeah, yeah. I used to know a lot of people who were there; friends of mine died there, in fact, that I went to Michigan with. I have an ongoing memoir that I've been working on, on and off, for years, and one chapter is about a guy named Ralph Neaphus. He came from New Mexico and was a volunteer in the Spanish Civil War. He was nineteen. I drove him from Ann Arbor; he'd never been east of Ann Arbor; his father was a rancher. I drove him to New York, and he stayed at our house waiting for his commission to go. He got killed. And twenty years later I went to Ann Arbor and was amazed at this Socialist club named for him. That was in the Fifties and they were persecuting the club members.

LM: I've always admired the great patience you have during public appearances and interviews, and the very good sense with which you answer the most idiotic questions.

AM: Well, you can't be too selective or there won't be any conversation. Academia harbors a lot of nonsense, but not only academia—the newspapers are worse. What's marvelous is that they interview you as if they are never going to leave, and it all ends up about eight paragraphs.

They made a pretty good movie of me, though; it will be shown in New York in October. Made by a Canadian—Harry Rasky. There is a real inner continuity in that film that surprised me. It was shot in Harlem, in Brooklyn, on the waterfront, and up here.

LM: Did they go to any of your former houses?

AM: Yes. In fact when I was in Brooklyn two old ladies came charging out of their houses, calling me. I said to one of these tottering old gals, "gee, this place looks better than it did when I lived here in the Depression." She said, "we're all like your mother used to be." She hadn't seen my mother for thirty years. "Your mother was strict." She wasn't strict at all. That was a dream that they had, that if you were strict your children would turn out OK.

LM: What was your mother like?

AM: She was very warm, very nice, musical. She was a good storyteller. And subject to fits of depression. A Jewish mother.

LM: What was bothering her?

AM: What bothers everybody in this country? Frustration. You are surrounded with what you think is opportunity. But you can't grab on to it. In other countries there's no opportunity, so there's just a general feeling of fatality. Here, no matter what happens to the economy, everybody can think of somebody who made it. Uncle Harry, look at him.

LM: And he didn't make it with any more intelligence—

AM: He's dumber than anybody!

LM: Did that bother her?

AM: Oh yes—we came through a very rough time. I suppose we're going to have it again, now.

LM: Can I ask, How do you feel? Where are you at these days?

AM: Quite frankly, all I really care about is what's going on in this room [Miller's studio]. I hear rumors of things outside. I don't look for a helluva lot, for too much change. I've seen too many repetitions of things I never thought I would see again. We don't change very much—a tiny bit—it's almost imperceptible. Fashions change. You can get very skeptical—I am—about people dying for anything except greed. And there's been a lot of that. We've expended a lot of people for no goddam good reason.

LM: That's been weighing on your mind through the years?

AM: Yeah, we get careless of human rights. The older I get the more I feel I'd be at home in Periclean Athens, and I could get along great in Dickens's London. I don't think a helluva lot has changed, with one exception. It's a big exception, and the one I hope we don't lose.

I think there's two ways of looking at life. One is that you hope to

fit in completely. It's a feudalistic way; they got it in China, they got it
in Russia. In my opinion, socialism in our time is a reversion to an
elitist organization of society. Power is at the top and it flows down.
The bottom supplies the troops, and the top supplies the direction,
the inspiration—and it tries to plan and to be praised. The world
awaits a democratic socialism.

This country may be alone in the world in having had no
feudalism. The longer I live the more important that becomes to me.
It may not ultimately be decisive, but up to this point it is. I think it's
the one thing we've got that no other society on the face of the earth
can say. And it may be the reason why we have added so much to
the world.

It's the whole idea that you can see in the Declaration of
Independence, the Constitution, and the Bill of Rights, that the power
is in the people—literally, not metaphysically. And that the laws come
out of them, and all the order of society. The people at the top are in
a literal sense appointed by them.

This sounds so corny and so obvious that it's not even worth
discussing except that it doesn't exist anywhere else, including in the
"democratic" countries. They had a long-term feudalism which was
based on a native aristocracy which swung the country around its
head. And we didn't have that. I've just come back from China, and
I've spent time in Russia, Poland, Hungary, Czechoslovakia, France,
Germany, Austria: this is where the difference begins.

Our cultural or race memory takes for granted that finally the
culture represents—and is *supposed* to represent, and *must*
represent—the sense of right, or the sense of the world felt by the
masses of people. Not in a metaphorical sense: you are supposed to
be able really to stand up and tell a Congressman he's full of shit,
which happens now and then. It even happens right here in
Connecticut. I think that this is the essential difference, and to me it's
the only hope there is.

Because if you get integrated into a system heart and soul, belly
and head, I despair. I really do, I despair. I don't think that the
invention comes out. It stultifies people; they find *every* good reason
not to do something. Because it's dangerous to do something. Then
you've got to have heroes; then you progress by somebody being
crucified. Then you know he was right.

We have done a remarkable amount of killing of fathers in this country—legally. And the invention comes out. Right now, we're suffering from a hardening of the arteries.

LM: Did you say "killing of fathers"?

AM: Yes, this is the essential thing: if you can kill the fathers without the government falling down, you've got a real civilization. There's hope, there's continuity.

A place like Russia, imagine, a leader falls like Stalin, it's like kicking over an anthill—chaos. They're still suffering from it, they still haven't come to terms with that. Now with Mao in China, they're just terrified that he could have been as wrong as he was. They don't even want to hear about it, even though objectively they know they've got to face this or they can't go on. They can't go on repeating errors endlessly in order to defer to the memory of some beloved saint.

See, we don't do that.

LM: So you still have a kind of weary hope.

AM: It's a weary hope in this country because of that history. We have something terrific going for us in the sense that people are ninety-nine percent their history, their cultural history. In their little one percent they have choices to make, but their conditioning by history is formidable. Well, our history is good in this; we're in great shape that way.

The Chinese are conscious now that their fundamental problem is invisible. They have concrete problems which are obvious, but the fundamental problem is inside: they revert to feudal relationships at the slightest stress. Both those who want more freedom and more progressive thinking and those who are innately bureaucratic and don't want anything to change, both sides. The enlightened ones recognize this, and Mao recognized it but was helpless to stop it in himself. We have nothing like that, and they envy us, our capacity to make changes when necessary even though they are root and branch changes. I mean getting rid of a leader like that is something that tears the gut out of these people, including the French. It's a heroic kind of thing which we ought to recognize as such.

LM: There has to be the other pull, opposite to General Electric taking things over.

AM: Exactly, exactly. And that is the saving spirit: the tension makes for civilization. If one takes over completely, it's all over. If you're going to knock off leaders every week, the game is over. If you're going to keep them there no matter what they do, the game is over. And that includes ideas and dominating notions of how life goes.

And no matter where you go, including Cuba, where they are supposed to hate us, they wish to God they had that thing. Because the door is always open. As soon as some monolith starts to form that tries to run the country, there is an innate disgust. *Free*—that's great!—it's a natural, built-in brake which transcends ideology.

Yeah, that's what *The Price* is about—the tension. I didn't name it, but if the idea gets into the people then the seed is planted.

LM: It's a little hard to see the openness, the change in *The Price* because both brothers are so fixed.

AM: I never resolved it. I didn't want to let the audience off the hook. They're very comfortable in the second act of that play. They say, "Ah, this poor nice policeman: how he was screwed by that rich neurotic jerk." Everybody hates surgeons anyway.

LM: So we're all going to love the policeman.

AM: Oh yes, it's terrific, he's our hero. Well, it turns out at a certain point he had something to do with his fate. It's marvelous once the audience can discover that, and then slowly they get to see—"Oh yes, this is a deeper pond than I've been swimming around in"—and they come at the end to appreciate it. They stand up and bravo at the end. They're happy to be treated like adults—it's quite wonderful! I haven't been to a play where people have done that in years: they're not supposed to care that much. They sure do care.

LM: Why do they applaud?

AM: They are grateful for having been forced to live through this thing. I could have let them off the hook; they sense that. I say, "You're grown-up people. This is the way it really is, isn't it? You need this search."

LM: But isn't there a lack of consummation, satisfaction?

AM: The satisfaction is the perception of the tension. 'Cause it is not solved, and life isn't. It can't be solved. It's a play without any candy.

LM: You don't feel that you've reached a dead end there?

AM: You reach a dead end only if all the energy goes out of the problem, but that surgeon's going to go on being a surgeon, and the cop is going to go on being a cop. But they are bigger for it; neither one will forget this evening. They become aware of what they have to see. The way they behave you know they are denying what they realize is true. Their denial is enormous, and when it gets that big you know it's saying the opposite.

LM: Could you ever write a play in which instead of a negative lesson, you just go out there and present a thorough-going, optimistic, here-it-is solution?

AM: The closest I ever came to that is probably in the last few minutes of *All My Sons*, where the surviving son does lay down the law as to what they should have done. And that happens in life. If the situation is that way then I'll do it, but to twist it around is impossible.

Dostoyevsky in *The Brothers Karamazov* tried to define at the end of that book in Alyosha the Christian way of life, and you believe it's possible, but it detaches itself from the rest of the book. The fundamental impulse of this book was tragic. There is some aesthetic violation that goes on here.

In *Death of a Salesman*, at the end Biff tries to say that this was unnecessary, that Willy never knew himself. But compared to the monstrousness of the whole action, he can't possibly counter that action with some opinion or connection as to what Willy should have been doing all this time. Emotionally, we cannot juggle the two things.

Furthermore, the emotions of people who have been through such events don't admit of it: the emotions occupy the whole space. I mean supposing that somebody you loved and knew well, by virtue of some failure to take precautions, died. Well, you could say, "Jesus, if he or she had only done this. . . ." That lasts only a minute or two, but compared to the grief—the sense of "my God, this can happen"—the other is sort of empty.

The Greeks tried to do that a lot. They made speeches about the right way to live, common sense—

LM: the tragic chorus, especially.

AM: Does anybody remember what the chorus says? You look at Oedipus: when that coal comes down the chute, that's what you hear, not some guy saying you got the wrong basement, deliver it up the street! It's going down the chute, and you can't stop it—that long drag of the past that becomes imperious at a certain moment, knows no bounds, and cannot be stopped.

LM: Can you ever funnel that coal in another direction?

AM: You try to. Look at Carter trying to generate the moral equivalent of a war for the conservation of energy. But who's going to get as excited about the conservation of energy as about the Battle of Stalingrad? Nobody I know. We would have to change our ways.

When you think of it, it's such a waste. It's such a waste—it's appalling!

After Commitment: An Interview with Arthur Miller

V. Rajakrishnan/1980

From *Theatre Journal* 32 (1980): 196-202. Reprinted by permission.

VR: In your later plays there seems to be a marked pull away from social purposes and ideological essences towards concerns which might be described as metaphysical, centering on the irrational levels of human experience. Do you agree?

Arthur Miller: Yes, I think that your question, or statement rather, is more or less correct. I would add one important thing, though, and it is that my idea of the metaphysical includes the social. I don't believe that man lives exclusively in either one or the other realm. I am firmly convinced that there is only one realm, not three or four or five, and this is all an articulated whole which the greatest drama, and even then only rarely, has been able to uncover.

There are lines of force—economic, political, mythic memories, genetic imprints—many more, and where they intersect in a human situation in which man must make choice—is drama. I have always felt this, even before I was conscious of any attempt to philosophize about it. If there is a question it is one of the degree of emphasis as to the primacy of social and other causation. My own feeling has been—in the last fifteen years anyway, perhaps even longer than that—that there are certain types and certain situations which are typical of man, and these get repeated endlessly in different societies and in different social arrangements. But there are, I believe, types of people who reproduce their own kind, apparently, through the millennia. This probably is one of the reasons why it is impossible for us to read a book or a play or a poem of an entirely different age, which may be hundreds and hundreds years gone by, and still feel at home with it, to some important degree. So when you say that there is a realm which is outside society, I don't think that is the way I would put it. I would simply say that it is one of the elements of the whole social situation.

VR: The silence in your dramatic career from 1955 to 1964 is generally linked with various circumstances in your private and public life. Taking a retrospective look, would you say today that these years were a period of gestation for the somber and interrogative mood which informed the plays that followed?

Arthur Miller: Yes, but it was also that the social presuppositions of the pre-World War II world—the Depression, liberalism, radicalism, Marxism etc.—began to dissolve in terms of their force for me. They became emptily repetitive, no longer instructive to me in the mid-50s. This was partly because I saw—what I just referred to—that there were indeed kinds of people who made of any moment in history what it was in them to make of it, and the power of these personalities to nullify even the logic of the social circumstance was so tremendous that I began to despair of ever coming to a useable pattern of understanding of what was happening in the world around me. I saw people who, as long as I had known them, were faithful to certain concepts, and suddenly overnight seemed not even to remember what it was they had spent a whole lifetime being faithful to. It was not simply a question of opportunism on their part, I think. The atmosphere changed; the air changed. The oxygen went out of the air for these ideas. And I, I certainly went into a period which was quite long, longer than I wished, in which it was not enough for me to see man as a social being, or even as a psychological being. . . . It simply didn't satisfy me. It was like being aware of an ache for the immemorial, not only in me but in the world.

VR: That in a way accounts for the air of puzzlement that pervades your later works.

Arthur Miller: Is it puzzlement, or a wish to rely upon action-in-itself, the what-happens—rather than on generalized historical conclusions?

VR: It seems to me that in your early plays evil is mainly seen as external, emanating either from the false dreams of a society or the nihilism of State ambition. But in *After the Fall, Incident at Vichy,* and *The Price,* evil emerges as an essential fact of human nature. Did this shift in focus have anything to do with the convictions born out of your emotional and intellectual encounters during the years of your absence from the theatre?

Arthur Miller: I did feel and I do feel now there is in people a tendency towards obliterating the murderousness of their own wishes. They simply go into a state of oblivion. They cannot see them and they cannot remember them, like great pain. As a consequence, these murderous episodes are endlessly repeated because the perpetrators continuously re-arrive at yet another state of innocence. It is a false innocence, of course. And still it is true in the sense that most of the time we genuinely cannot recall any other dimension of life. We simply feel that we are put upon, we are victimized, and that there is no corresponding aggression on our part to account for this at all. So we continually lapse into a state of innocence—which then brings on the next cycle of our murderousness, since the innocent are permitted to defend themselves. And so we rise up and kill whoever is handy, and the new murder seems to prove our innocence all over again, for how could we have killed except that we were driven to it from without?

VR: Despite some obvious points of contact between you and the hero of *After the Fall*, you have resisted the autobiographical interpretation of the play. Perhaps you may be able to tell whether, while writing the play, you shared Quentin's agonized feeling that he had lost a world consisting of easy indignations and doctrinaire certainties.

Arthur Miller: The reason why I have resisted the autobiographical interpretation of the play, as you have put it, is that *After the Fall* is not an autobiography in the sense that it was not my aim to personify myself on stage as such; it is a play about a theme if ever such a play existed. All my characters in all my works are autobiographical in the sense that, for me to write them, I have to have felt what these people feel.

The autobiographical element in any work is not a question of criticism, in any case, but of gossip. Is a work better or worse because we have managed to locate the originals of the characters? This is only another aspect of reductionism, the nothing-but nonsense, a sort of revenge upon the creative by the literal. For years Willy Loman was nothing-but my own father—who happened to have been a wholly different sort of man, and I myself was the fine student next door. In fact, I failed Algebra three times! Another aspect of this kind of "interpretation" and a less personal but equally foolish one, is in Simone Signoret's current autobiography where she states that John and Elizabeth Proctor were so named for their initials, J and E which conform to Julius and Ethel Rosenberg whose story *The Crucible* is alleged to tell. Of course the Rosenberg case did not even become public until the play was on the stage. And John and Elizabeth were the names of my characters in history.

It is perfectly true, though, that one of the essential parts of Quentin is the collapse of the symmetry of the world as he understood it before he became aware of his own culpability in it. In other words, before the fall he was struggling, as a man in society in any case, against forces outside of himself, and that gave life a certain symmetry and coherence. When he began to feel that he was in league with what he despised, to some perceptible degree, then action became intolerable. Action of any kind became very difficult. Again, it is hardly necessary to disclaim that this is merely me; I think this is the history of our times in terms of social reforms, in terms of social philosophy, in terms of the way Americans at least have viewed the world, if you, let us say, start a hundred years ago and work yourself up to this moment. They had gone through a stage in which they fundamentally believed in the perfectibility of man and society and everything else. And to believe that, you have to place yourself to one side of all evil. Everybody knows that he tried numerous times to correct his bad habits, and probably failed most of the time. It is other people's bad habits that he is sure he can correct. So the perfectibility of man is always referring to other people and other institutions. I think Quentin represents a kind of transformation of that situation into one in which he is trying to confront and define a world in which he is culpable, in whose evil he is really involved, not merely as a corrective philosopher but as a participant in whatever is wrong in what he is looking at.

This is what that speech means in which Quentin talks about how fine it was to face a world so wonderfully threatened by injustice. It means that he was absolved of any culpability for it.

VR: Leonard Moss has quoted you as saying that Albert Camus's novel, *The Fall* provided the point of departure for *After the Fall*. Would it be correct to interpret this influence as the sign—or result— of your exposure to existentialist thought?

Arthur Miller: I can be quite concrete about my contact with Camus's novel, *The Fall*. Actually I read the book for the first time in California in the early 60s when Walter Wanger, who was a producer, wanted me to make a motion picture out of it. It haunted me for one

very concrete reason. The springboard of the book is the failure of
the hero—or the anti-hero—to go to the rescue of a girl who he had
never even laid eyes on, really. It is just the idea of a woman, of a
living being who he has failed to connect with, and it symbolizes his
inability really to believe in his own feelings towards people, and
hence in his right to judge others' actions. This is on a psychological
level. This, of course, is a common . . . I wouldn't call it a dilemma, it
is like a hang-nail, a wound that never heals. And to anyone who
professes any humanist feeling at all, this should come as a
disquieting reminder. But, as Camus's protagonist passed from my
mind, I changed the question posed in *The Fall*, probably to a more
disastrous one: what if he had attempted to rescue her, and indeed
managed to, and then discovered that he had failed in his mission—
to overcome his own egoism which his action may even have
expressed; that there were innumerable complications about rescuing
somebody as a pure act of love? It was not simply a question of
whether or not he had the empathic power within himself to go to the
rescue of that girl. It was more difficult even than that. What it
required was the sacrifice of what he thought was true; maybe, his
intellectual humiliation was required. Maybe, even worse, he had
really to become a passive figure in horror of his or her geography in
order to save her. In other words, when one goes to save somebody,
one is seeking to recreate that person in a more positive fashion, and
one has also judged her. The girl in Camus's novel was suicidal; she
leaped in the river. She wanted to turn away from life. So he would
have had to give her back the will to live; but what if she disbelieved
in his good faith and claimed to perceive his selfishness in saving her?
Perhaps his blame surpasses his failure to go to her rescue. And
supposing he had tried to do this and then discovered that this was
not possible under any circumstances whatsoever—then, what is his
reaction? This is some of what *After the Fall* was about. Needless to
say, the play—rather than the gossip—remains to be reviewed.

VR: Perhaps one difference between *After the Fall* and Camus's
novel is that the latter shatters all consolations while your play ends
with the hero's decision, made in good faith, in favor of a positive
choice in life.

Arthur Miller: I would say that my play does end with the hero's
decision in favor of a positive choice in life. But there is always, I
think, the background of doubt to Quentin's final act of engagement
which never gets eradicated. Quentin acts within what he conceives

to be the possibilities given him at any moment. He decides in favor of life because he cannot deny that he finds hope rising in himself. As he says in the play, "With all this darkness, the truth is that every morning when I awake, I'm full of hope! With everything I know—I open my eyes, I'm like a boy!" It is idiotic, and yet there is something in him that is indeed a boy, that is young every day and insists he believe. "And this is as true for me," says Quentin, "as any of the despair that surrounds me." But I don't call this consolation; total despair is more consoling. Much more so since it does not challenge one to act anymore and justifies the far less troublesome stasis and resignation.

VR: In terms of technique, however, the name that comes to mind is Sartre in that your dramatic universe, like Sartre's, is nearer to realism or traditional naturalism. Perhaps you regard innovations in form as secondary to content?

Arthur Miller: Perhaps I am not the one to make comments on that. This is a question relating to literary forms. I have said so much on this subject in the past and I have written a lot about it also, some people think, too much. But I don't agree that my plays are naturalistic at all. You see, naturalism to me has a very concrete meaning. It is an attempt to bring on to the stage a picture of life uninterpreted, as far as possible, by the artist's visible hand; as though one should feel one were actually there. Well, I don't believe in that; in fact, I am thoroughly opposed to that. It is a lie in the first place. In the theatre one can't be "actually" anywhere but in the theatre. One is in the theatre facing actors. It is not the job of the theatre to reproduce life; it is to interpret life. And I have used a good number of interpretive forms, probably more than most practicing playwrights have. They are quite different. I made my first reputation with *All My Sons* which was a very traditional kind of a play, at least at times. But, I think there is more innovation, formally speaking, in *Death of a Salesman*, for example, than any other American play that I know of. This is a broad statement, but I believe it is a fact. I think there is more conscious use of the past two thousand years of formal experimentation in the theatre going into *Death of a Salesman* than any other American play that I could think of. In fact it has been so thoroughly imitated that it is often forgotten what an innovation it was. It's simply that for some people I made it all look perfectly "natural"—which is fine with me.

VR: Let me make myself clear. I regard you as a realist in the sense that you have created, for the most part, characters, and events with traceable roots in life. There are striking differences between your approach to the drama and that of playwrights of the Theatre of the Absurd, which is the most anti-realistic theatre I can think of.

Arthur Miller: Oh yes, that's true, yes. But if only the Absurd is . . . I can make a case like this. The Absurd is the modern day Naturalism. The Absurd is the most naturalistic dramatic form we have today. Why do I say that? If you stand on the corner of the street in which we are now, for an hour, you will see absurdities one after another in the formal sense of that term. You will see costumes that are absurd worn by ordinary people on their way to work or from work and hear more absurdities than you will easily bear. The streets are full of the absurd right now. The culture is absurd. What is more absurd than countries spending almost all their wealth on weapons with which to kill one another? What is more absurd than the fact of poverty in the United States? It is all absurd, and simply to report that faithfully, you end up—if you do it superficially and just show what you see—with an immature cult of meaninglessness.

VR: When I touched on the salient differences between your theatre and the Theatre of the Absurd, I also had in mind some of those devices used by Beckett and Ionesco like poetic fantasy, black humor and the devaluation of language . . .

Arthur Miller: Well, in *Death of a Salesman* we have the technique of fantasy and distortion of time which, again, are made to seem quite natural. But there is a violent compression in all of Willy Loman's memories, for example. I did it so that nobody is aware that it is done, you see. All those sectors of Willy's hallucinations are nearly hysterically compressed. Every time he remembers something there is not realistic continuity of speech, only of spiritual search and yearning. No one on God's earth ever spoke that way. But I made it sound as though they might have. For one thing, if I had done it realistically, the play would have been seven hours long, or seventy.

VR: *Incident at Vichy* seems to correspond to Sartre's description of the Theatre of Situation: "Dramas which are short and violent, sometimes reduced to the dimensions of a single long act, dramas entirely centered on an event, written in a sparse, extremely terse style." Did the "extreme situation" at the heart of *Incident at Vichy* call for a dramatic style of this kind?

Arthur Miller: I did not know about Sartre's description of the Theatre of Situations. The quotation you have given does seem to fit my play. See, I proceed from the inside out. I don't think, I will now write a play in the style of *Vichy*. Here in this play I was not trying to find the situation and characters which exemplify that or any other style. What happens is that I am obsessed, for one reason or another, with some situation or character or idea. And when I start to work at it, it cries out for a certain kind of formal treatment, it literally forms itself, and I help it along. In the situation of *Incident at Vichy*, the fact of the matter is that the victims are collected into a police room and they are not permitted to move. This happened before any playwright thought about them—even Sartre. The play is indeed one long act. It is basically a verbal play because, as much as any other reasons, the cops forbid people to physically move very much. But I wanted to write such a play. I enjoyed writing it, a verbal play that would have minimal movement.

VR: Many critics who have taken Leduc to be the dramatist's mouthpiece tend to view Von Berg's act of nobleness as arbitrary. Do you look upon Von Berg's act as an implied answer to the ethical nihilism that threatened to overtake Europe during the Nazi era, or as a beautiful private gesture valid within its own realm?

Arthur Miller: I regard Von Berg's act . . . yes, it is an implied answer to the transvaluation of values that took place under Hitler. But to me as a dramatist, its prime importance lies in the irony of the purely private action which manages to have tremendous public significance. I have always been fascinated by the transformations of human personality under the stress of certain extreme situations in life—the crazy changes that occurred in the course of a person's life at any one moment which made him look absolutely different not only from everybody else but from his former self. In *Incident at Vichy*, Von Berg defines himself through the act which in a way sets him apart from the rest of mankind. And that a saving act should come from what is normally regarded as a decadent personality (he represents a social class which, if not totally vanished, is certainly in decay) might sound strange. And, yet, there he is—for some ironical reasons, he is the one who can make this kind of a gesture. What it says, I feel, is that humanity can not be programmed finally. The unexpected could happen. Who knows but that the world will be saved by a most unlikely personality . . . at the last moment. And if this happens we shall see that the reasons for it were unpredictable and obvious.

VR: In writing *The Price* were you primarily concerned with the interrelationship of past and present? Or is *The Price* primarily about incommunicability and absence of love in human relations? The play seems to have two movements, one looking back to the Depression and the tragedy of middle class life, and the other pointing in the direction of the metaphysical despair characteristic of the post-War drama.

Arthur Miller: I am trying to recall what I felt when I was writing the play. Primarily, I suppose, it is a conflict which is unresolvable between dutifulness and self-sacrifice on the one hand, as against the more aggressive nature. Both contribute enormously to the world, ironically enough. The more selfish man may turn out to be contributing more than the self-effacing idealist. And that irony moved me very much because it leads in all directions. It upsets the ordinary symmetry that I spoke of earlier. But I have to say also that one of the delights in writing *The Price* was the character of Gregory Solomon. And to me he is the force of life with all its madness and its poetry.

I would add one more thing about *The Price*: there is an aspect of the cruelty of human existence in it, which is accepted by the play itself as well as by the character of Solomon. And, in effect, there is no solution to this problem which stands there finally like a fact of nature and not a problem at all. The play is a cul-de-sac for me; it simply lays out the forces that exist, and probably must exist. I don't know the solution excepting that Solomon takes joy in the dilemma, a joy that is not at all cynical, and there is life in him.

VR: Don't you think that Solomon embodies some kind of transcendence, though not a solution. . . .

Arthur Miller: Exactly, exactly.

VR: The chaos of old furniture which fills the Manhattan attic evokes the memory of the concrete stage images in the dramas of Ionesco and Beckett, like the chairs in Ionesco and the tape recorder and dust bins in Beckett. Did you, at this point in your dramatic career, feel drawn towards the devices of the Theatre of the Absurd?

Arthur Miller: I have always felt a kind of attraction for the so-called Theatre of the Absurd in the form of Ionesco's plays. But—I don't know why—I set myself in an entirely different task. I felt that, as far as I was concerned, it would not be sufficient for me or desirable even to draw parodies of life. For the plays of Ionesco and Beckett are parodistic in nature. They parody tragedy, they parody feelings, they parody plots. And I wanted to convey the emotions as I

felt them. I do feel the funny urge for parody or farce from time to
time; everybody does, I think. But I have always assumed that the
real job for me was not parody at all. It was to try to create empathy
in the theatre, and not the kind of distancing, achieved through comic
and grotesque means, which the anti-theatre of Ionesco and Beckett
creates in the audience. I felt that there was enough dissociation in
life, without my adding to it in the theatre. I wanted the spectators to
associate rather than dissociate. The measure of it all is death, and
that can't be parodied, at least not by the participant.

Now, coming to your question about the piled-up old furniture in
The Price, I am not at all sure that that isn't . . . you see, from my
point of view it is perfectly real to have an attic full of furniture which
is set there because, in effect, there is no decision yet as to where life
wants to put it. Of course I sense the condensation of meaning in this
content. But I prefer not to look at it theatrically when I am writing. I
don't invent this as another absurdist imagery. I deal with the piled up
junk in *The Price* as though it was real furniture in a real place and
people were really involved with this situation. That is partly the
difference between my approach and that of, say, Pinter or Ionesco.

VR: *The Price* seems to me the only play of yours in which a
pervasive stage metaphor is employed to define action and theme.

Arthur Miller: Well, that seems to be so . . . . *Death of a
Salesman* has it, in a way. It is not physical. You can play *Death of a
Salesman* the way I first wrote it, without any setting at all. On the
other hand I have used physical metaphor in *All My Sons*, which is
extremely important to the texture of the play. In fact, the set designer
for *All My Sons*, who was one of the most sophisticated theorists of
all set designers, Mordecai Gorelik, worried endlessly over the tree in
that play. He indeed designed the set, which served the play very
well, with the idea that the whole play was taking place in a
graveyard. And on the floor of the set there was a kind of hump
where the grave was. Now I had no such description in my text. This
was actually the backyard of a house, but I did certainly conceive of
the apple tree, the young apple tree which falls down in the storm. I
had never thought of it in the way we are discussing it now, you see. I
prefer not to think in those terms. I think that such symbols finally get
to be extremely arbitrary and dried out of any real human
connection. They don't move people. See, I believe people are not
all brains and need their instincts moved.

VR: During the 60s and the early 70s you actively championed various liberal or progressive causes, but I am unable to see that your radical politics affected the tone and temper of your plays written during this period, including *Creation of the World and Other Business*. Is it possible that the issues which agitated you as an intelligent citizen failed to stir your creative self?

Arthur Miller: The truth of the matter is that I was not as involved in political activism during this period as the generation just behind me, let us say, people who were involved with all sorts of protest. I was agitated by going to bed every night in a perfectly comfortable house when we were destroying a country overseas. It was as simple as that. I simply couldn't get it out of my mind. But it is true that I protested as a citizen rather than as a writer primarily.

VR: Have you been particularly impressed by any play, American or Continental, that you have seen in recent years?

Arthur Miller: Well, I will have to think a long time. First of all I should tell you that I don't go to the theatre very often. I don't know why that is . . . . I have read a lot of stuff.

VR: What do you think of some of those East European playwrights who very effectively communicate the nightmarish sense of living under a totalitarian system?

Arthur Miller: Do you mean Czechoslovakian? Well, I know several of them, Vaclav Havel is one, Pavel Kohout is another . . . . These playwrights have handled the absurd not in resignation and despair but in a spirit of social and moral resistance. To reach back to the earlier point of our interview, they both register the repetitiveness of evil and yet speak as though it can and must be cured; they maintain the essential living tension with the unattainable. Underneath their joke is what I regard as an amiable kind of viciousness, which arms a noble self-defense. Yes, I appreciate some of them very much.

VR: Thank you, Mr. Miller.

'The Will to Live': An Interview with Arthur Miller

Steven R. Centola/1984

From *Modern Drama* 27 (1984): 345-360. Reprinted by permission.

This interview, the transcript of a conversation I had with the playwright on June 25, 1982 at his Roxbury, Connecticut home, has been deliberately left in its colloquial form. I have tried to re-create as closely as possible the sound and spirit of our conversation in the hope of sharing with the reader the distinctive intonation, quick wit, and candor of Miller's responses.

S.R.C.: I've always been fascinated by your ability to maintain a singleness of vision in plays remarkably different from each other in form, style, mood, theme, characterization, plot, and even at times in language. Would you agree that this underlying continuity in your work derives from a vision of the human condition that can be described as a kind of existential humanism—a vision that emphasizes self-determinism and social responsibility and that is optimistic and affirms life by acknowledging man's possibilities in the face of his limitations and even sometimes in the dramatization of his failures?

Arthur Miller: That's very good. I would agree with that. That's a fair summary of what I feel about it—my own views about it.

S.R.C.: The one play that seems to provide the clearest revelation of your vision is *After the Fall*.

Arthur Miller: Just about, yes.

S.R.C.: Not many people see it that way.

Arthur Miller: Well, I think they were, to be quite frank—I've said this before; it's no news—but I think that they were blinded by the gossip and the easy way out. But it's not just in my work. I think people go for tags for any writer; you don't have to think about what he's doing any longer, especially if he's around a long time. But then simply you know what you think you want to expect. It may or may not have much to do with what he's doing. But, they find whatever in the work fits that expectation, and the other is simply not dealt with or is rejected. This is an old story here that we all know.

S.R.C.: Your vision, what I've called your existential humanism, seems to have a lot in common with Jean-Paul Sartre's existentialist philosophy.

Arthur Miller: You know that Sartre did the screenplay for *The Crucible*, and we were on the verge of meeting three or four times and never managed to because he was out of France when I was there. There was always a mix-up, and I always thought that there was more time than there actually turned out to be. But I think there was a relationship which was not programmatic in any way. It just means people leaning in the same kind of direction.

S.R.C.: So you wouldn't say it was a matter of influence?

Arthur Miller: No, no.

S.R.C.: Would you feel as though I were going for a tag if I pointed out some of the similarities between your vision and Sartre's existentialism?

Arthur Miller: Well, I don't think that's a danger because he certainly was always attractive to me in a vague way. But I'll tell you, I'm not a methodical, philosophical writer; I don't spring out of that kind of tradition. I work out of instinct. And so whatever similarities that there turn out to be, somebody's always related to something.

S.R.C.: Do you think an identification of these Sartrean correspondences in your plays could bring out the metaphysical issues in your work and help to put to rest the notion that you're merely a social realist, the tag which you seem to have been stuck with for some time now?

Arthur Miller: The social realist thing is what they were doing with Ibsen all his life. He was supposed to be interested in sewers because of *An Enemy of the People*, or in syphilis because of *Ghosts*, or in women's rights or something like that because of *A Doll's House*, and all the rest of it. Of course, what is inevitable is that these are all, in a certain sense, metaphors, and had the writer merely been interested in sewers, violence, women's rights, and the rest of it, we would have long since lost track of his name. These are metaphorical situations of the human race as it goes on forever.

S.R.C.: The great writer gets at the universal through the particular.

Arthur Miller: Sure. If you don't, you end up with a kind of blatantly philosophical dialogue of some sort that nobody really is interested in. It isn't the way these obtrude into experience. That's as simple as it can be.

S.R.C.: I read some of your unpublished works that I was able to get through the Humanities Research Center at the University of Texas. One of these was a letter you wrote called "Willy and the Helpless Giant," and in that letter you suggest that tragedy results when one tries to attain honor by putting on a mask and performing for the public instead of being what one really is and does best. In many ways, that idea parallels Sartre's distinction between being-for-itself and being-for-others. I'm wondering if that conflict isn't part of the tragedy of modern existence: individuals feel obligated to adopt poses or wear masks in order to make themselves feel significant or honorable?

Arthur Miller: That's true. But the question is how old a procedure that is, how old that process is. Because the more class-structured a society is (for example, a royal society like, let's say, the eighteenth-century or seventeenth-century French society), people had to fit into a mold that was given them by the class that they felt they belonged to. And all costume, dress, manners, habits, and the mores were predetermined, in effect, so that sincerity was hardly a value at all. It's just that it wasn't necessarily cynical. It was simply that the society and sincerity could not comfortably coexist. So that for the sake of good order, one had to adopt some kind of persona, which is not necessarily the one that one really has. Now, for us, I think this is an old thing in the United States. Alexis de Tocqueville mentions the fact that we don't want to be set aside from the mob. That means people will adopt a mask in order to be like everybody else. And maybe it's implicit in that statement that Americans don't want to be separated from the mask.

S.R.C.: That's an interesting way of establishing a connection with others.

Arthur Miller: But there's also a price to pay for that. And the price, obviously, is the loss of something. Society makes such a heavy demand upon the individual that he has to give up his individuality (and we do have a high percentage of mental breakdowns and neuroses and the rest of it). So, maybe it goes along with democracy, oddly enough.

S.R.C.: That's interesting.

Arthur Miller: I think that the British, for example, are far more able and willing to endure characters than we are. (What would you call characters? People who don't necessarily abide by the rules.) We're much less tolerant. We won't lend them money; we won't see them through school sometimes. We impose a discipline on them because they are different, and so on.

S.R.C.: So we place a greater emphasis on conformity?

Arthur Miller: Conformity is a terrific power here. To jump to another sector of this, I think it lay behind the power of the Un-American Activities Committee, because, after all, what they were threatening most people with was not jail, and it certainly wasn't shooting; it was being disgraced—social disgrace.

S.R.C.: What I was getting at in that question is whether tragedy could be considered as a fundamental condition of being. Take Hamlet as an example. Here's an individual who is obsessed with living up to the image expected of him by others. It's the same with Othello and Oedipus. It seems that all these characters find themselves torn between. . . .

Arthur Miller: Mask and reality. You ought to look into the whole question of the fact that the Greek plays were played in masks. I'm not sure where that fits here, but it just occurred to me. Well, of course, I have been very conscious of this as a writer, that is, of the conflict, the friction, the opposition between the individual and his social obligations, his social mask, his social self. And it always seemed to me that the perfect society would be one in which that gap, the friction, would be able to be minimized, but people don't seem to be driven crazy about it. It isn't that totally American kind of a thing, though, obviously. It's everywhere; it just takes different shapes. I suspect it's in tribal Africa. You see, there are social duties and social fears that can create a tragic event.

S.R.C.: That's why I mentioned Sartre; he's dealing with the fundamental condition of being human: being self-conscious.

Arthur Miller: It's certainly in the center of it.

S.R.C.: Well, it seems that the tragedy of displacement, which you have discussed in your essays, is really a type of existential crisis that results when one has to make a conscious choice between his public self and his private one. You say that displacement results from a character's violation of his nature through compromises or mistakes. And then his effort to regain his sense of identity against overwhelming obstacles makes the play take on a tragic dimension.

Arthur Miller: I think in the plays of mine that I felt were of tragic dimensions, the characters are obsessed with retrieving a lost identity, meaning that they were displaced by the social pressure, the social mask, and no longer could find themselves, or are on the verge of not being able to. There in the private man is the real one.

S.R.C.: In your Introduction to your *Collected Plays*, Volume I, you say that the one unseen goal toward which almost all of your plays strive is the "discovery and its proof—that we are made and yet are more than what made us." That statement seems to pinpoint the central tension underlying all of your plays, a tension created by the antagonistic forces of fate and free will acting upon each other.

Arthur Miller: Right. Did you ever read my first play on Broadway, which failed, called *The Man Who Had All the Luck*? In the line of this kind of discussion, that really was a very important play for me, because while the play failed, I learned in that play where I was positioned in the world, so to speak. And the play taught me something which I wasn't even aware of at the moment. But looking back—just this kind of a question is raised. He wants to know where he begins and the world begins; where he leaves off, the world begins. He's trying really to separate himself and to control his destiny.

S.R.C.: Or to make himself aware that he has been controlling it, and that he's not just a pawn of the forces around him.

Arthur Miller: Yes, right. So, it goes right back to the beginning in the most vague part of my career.

S.R.C.: That play didn't get the justice it deserved because the critics misunderstood it. If I'm not mistaken, a major complaint at the time was that the play displayed "jumbled philosophies" because you didn't choose to advocate either fate or free will. But why should you choose one and not see the interplay?

Arthur Miller: The interplay was the point! Well, you see, this was where they couldn't run with a tag. That's exactly what I started out by saying today. Had I been very clever and sophisticated about it, I would have thrown out a tag that they could run with and feel that they had it in their pocket. But I let the tension run on right through the end, instead of resolving it for them the way it never is in life.

S.R.C.: So you would say that dialectic exists also in your other plays?

Arthur Miller: Oh, yeah. No question about it. It goes right on now.

S.R.C.: Like Sartre, you often seem to concern yourself with the alienation of the individual in your plays. Frequently, alienation has something to do with the individual's recognition of (and reluctance to accept) his separateness. Such alienation is perhaps most apparent in *After the Fall*, but it is also evident in your other plays. Willy Loman and other characters also cannot accept the fact that they are separate beings.

Arthur Miller: That's right. You know, I have a line somewhere— oh, I think it's in an Introduction I wrote to *A View from the Bridge* or one of the editions of *A View from the Bridge*, but I could be wrong about this because it's now twenty years or more—to the effect that the underlying tension is that man is looking for a home. In other words, he's looking for an unalienated existence, and this can be terribly attractive and seductive and is the root of a lot of mystery. See, one of the greatest appeals of Christianity as well as of Communism is that it promises to end alienation. If I want to subjugate man, I can declare alienation a sin, and anybody who is alienated or causes anybody else to be alienated should be punished. See, this is what the Puritans did among themselves. This is what the Communist party does in Russia. And this is what the loyal extreme patriots in every country do. They're always against aliens, just as simple as that. It's the root of antiforeignism; it's the root of this philistinism that we're always confronting. And everybody does it! The function of a group is to define itself, and its definition is: "We are us, and you are you." You see?

S.R.C.: Isn't that a type of psychological projection? Couldn't people who create these groups of others, or outsiders, just as easily say: "We are good, and you are evil"?

Arthur Miller: Absolutely. "We are us."

S.R.C.: And they project everything they don't like about themselves onto others?

Arthur Miller: Absolutely. That's what it's all about. It's a form of psychological warfare. My view from the beginning has more or less been (it has shifted with each play to a certain degree) to find a form, in effect, for the condition of tension, rather than resolution of this particular dichotomy through consciousness, through being aware that indeed I am alienated. I'm not you, but that doesn't mean because I'm not you that I can't sympathize with you. Well, to maintain that kind of tension in all of the thing, especially in political and social existence, we're without and refuse to resolve it. You might be able to, but the solution is always false. That's the difficulty. And in a play, it's very aggravating for the audience.

S.R.C.: Not for the dramatist?

Arthur Miller: No. It's a condition of existence. In fact, you could almost say that the tragic view is that it is tragic because of the fact that it's unresolvable. We wish so for a pillow to lay our head upon, and it's a stone.

S.R.C.: So man is always alienated, and yet he is constantly striving to get beyond his condition.

Arthur Miller: Right.

S.R.C.: There's something dignified in his effort though.

Arthur Miller: I was just about to say that the whole point of it is that the aspiration is holy. See, the Biblical prophets are terrific because they refused to compromise. They maintained the tension through people like Ezekiel or Isaiah. Isaiah will project the plowshares and the peacemakers will be blessed and all the rest of it, but that's the aspiration. The implicit fact is that they're not around yet, these blessed people.

S.R.C.: So what makes the characters tragic is partially the fact that only a few people, perhaps, ever attain that kind of self-recognition, or get to the point where they try to transcend their condition?

Arthur Miller: Right.

S.R.C.: So the great mass of people aren't moved this way, or at least aren't aware of it?

Arthur Miller: The great mass of people are in the chorus. They perceive perfectly well what's happening, or very often. But, for whatever reason, they are bereft of the power or the lust for the power or the sacrificial nature that is required to go seeking. You know, the other day with that case, the Hinckley case, is a very good example of something like this. Now this was a jury, I think, of almost all black people, and they gave this perfectly horrible (to most people) verdict. And then people said, "Well, that's because they're so dumb, you know; they aren't educated people." Well, they interviewed them on television, and they were remarkably sophisticated. And they dug it very, very well. They were really on a knife-edge, and they reacted in a very sharp and profound way: they blamed the code. And they said: "That's the code, and that is all the choice we had by that code." Well, that's terrific. See, now there's an instance of people who perforce were put in a position of having to make moral decisions, which normally in ordinary life they wouldn't be required to do, not in a public way certainly. My point is that you don't have to be a "noble" creature. This is changing the subject slightly, but since you raised the question of most people, this is certainly most people. These were blacks in Washington, D.C. They dug it; they understood it perfectly.

S.R.C.: So, it's just that most people usually aren't placed in that position, or they prefer not to be?

Arthur Miller: Or they prefer not to be!

S.R.C.: But everyone could experience this same fate, this same tragic existence?

Arthur Miller: Sure. Absolutely everyone as far as social rank is concerned.

S.R.C.: In an interview a few years ago, you said that Americans seem to have a "primordial fear of falling." I was wondering if you thought Americans, more than anyone else, have that feeling because it goes with the territory?

Arthur Miller: I think that that is more American than any other country, yeah, in my observation. I think we are more afraid of losing caste, losing our hard-won place in the middle class. People will kill for that. I think that that causes more racial hatred and hostility and fear than anything else. Incidentally, I regard racism as a class phenomenon. I was born in Harlem, and I saw it happen in Harlem—I think I did, anyway. That's been my reason for it: that blacks are not acceptable more for the fact that they are working-class or poor than because they are black. If in a short period of time by some miracle there were hundreds and hundreds of thousands of black professionals, middle-class people, the thing would begin to fade. We're seeing it now with the Arabs, the sheiks, the wealthy Arab who was formerly a creature of ridicule. Well, now he can come in and buy up a whole city. With a new class identity he starts to take on a new kind of persona, a new kind of dignity. It isn't so jokey any more to see somebody walking around in those funny clothes which might conceal millions.

S.R.C.: So most people chase their American dreams because they know that success determines how much they are accepted by others.

Arthur Miller: No question about it.

S.R.C.: In *Incident at Vichy*, Leduc tells the others as they await examination that they have been trained to die, to be willing victims for their persecutors. I'm wondering if he implies in that statement that death is often preferable to life for those who would have to live without illusions. And, once again, isn't such self-deception a peculiarly American trait? Haven't we been trained to see the world through rose-tinted glasses? Aren't we essentially a nation of people incapable of coping with reality?

Arthur Miller: Yes. I think that tremendous power does that to people, incidentally. The British did it for two centuries as their power got tremendous. They were able to enforce their wishes upon the world. So they wished more than they observed. I think they were primarily that way, and I think the Germans were able to do this once where they had the power to do it. It goes with power; it goes with the territory.

S.R.C.: I'm going to take a different direction here. Some critics have complained about Charley's speech in the Requiem in *Death of a Salesman*, saying that it's out of character for a realist like Charley to be making sentimental speeches about dreams.

Arthur Miller: It's not even sentimental. You know that speech is almost a handbook of what you've got to think if you're going to be a salesman. Under the circumstances, of course, it is said over a grave, so naturally it is full of feeling and mourning. But it is objective information, so to speak; it is absolutely real. Those are the visionary qualities that make salesmen tick.

S.R.C.: Aren't you also doing in this play what Fitzgerald does with Nick in his portrayal of Gatsby? In other words, you have a character who is fairly objective throughout the work make that statement over the grave because it can carry more weight coming from him, a realist.

Arthur Miller: You're right! That speech is the obverse of the early speech that Charley makes in the play to Willy when he says: "Why must everybody like you? Who liked J.P. Morgan?" Which is an absolutely dead-on, existentialist kind of way of looking at salesmanship. This is the obverse of it. He knows damn well what Willy was feeling; that's why he can make that speech to him. This is now said as the obverse of the other, but it's complementary. These are two halves of the same thing.

S.R.C.: In an interview with Ronald Hayman some years ago, you defined fate as "high probability" and said that it is what happens "when a man starts out to do what he intends to do . . . [and] creates forces which he never bargained for, but whose contradictions nevertheless spring directly from the force of his thrust." Would you say that this is the kind of fate that's in the background of plays like *All My Sons, Death of a Salesman,* and *The Price*?

Arthur Miller: Yes.

S.R.C.: Many of the characters in these plays seem to believe that they have no free will. But don't they have free will and just fail to consider all the consequences when they commit themselves to certain courses of action?

Arthur Miller: Right. And I would add that it's all but impossible to take into consideration most of the time.

S.R.C.: We can't be that farsighted?

Arthur Miller: No, because the possibilities are too complex, too complicated, too infinite.

S.R.C.: But, eventually, we have to accept what we do; we can't say we are excused from responsibility because the consequence was beyond our realm of control.

Arthur Miller: Right. You started it. For me, the typical case of our time is the Oppenheimer thing. I use him as the symbol of the scientists who put together this ferocious world-ending trick hat. And what they were exercising was technical curiosity, a time-honored civilizing trait of mankind. And then it goes off, and as Oppenheimer says, he starts to quote Hindu scripture: "I've taken the shape of death. I started the dance and I end it by killing everyone."

S.R.C.: I'm going to shift directions again. In *The Price*, Solomon says he would not know what to say to his daughter if she were to return from the grave. Isn't Solomon essentially saying that no one can transcend the bounds of human subjectivity?

Arthur Miller: That's a good way to put it.

S.R.C.: Doesn't he imply that because each individual is totally and irremediably separated from the other, only each individual can take responsibility for what he is in life?

Arthur Miller: That's a very good way to put it. Yes. He accepts something there, doesn't he? He says, in effect: "I was the way I am; she is the way she was; and what happened was the inevitable result of that. So what could have changed it?"

S.R.C.: "And if she comes back, I still can't change it. So just accept it as it is."

Arthur Miller: Right. There's a kind of a cosmic acceptance of the situation.

S.R.C.: That kind of acceptance seems to occur in your plays where characters like Quentin, Leduc, Von Berg, or Solomon decide that they must accept what is and not try to mold reality to fit their perceptions of it.

Arthur Miller: Exactly. And from that comes not passivity but strength.

S.R.C.: That sounds again very much like Sartre. Like you, he was also accused of being a pessimist, and he responded to the charge by saying: "I'm not a pessimist; I merely believe in optimistic toughness." Isn't that also what you're saying?

Arthur Miller: Right.

S.R.C.: In *After the Fall*, both Rose and Elsie seem to betray the men they love because they want to deny their complicity in their husbands' problems in order to maintain their own innocence, a counterfeit innocence that helps them see themselves as victims.

Arthur Miller: Those particular women feel that they did not participate in the decision making (if you want to objectify the whole thing), so they are not going to submit to the victimization. And that separation takes place, in effect saying: "You made your bed, now lie in it; I'm not going to get in there with you." It's a reassertion of separateness, incidentally.

S.R.C.: With the kind of separateness, though, isn't there also some kind of betrayal?

Arthur Miller: Sure. It's inevitable because the implicit, although largely unannounced, larceny behind their relationship is that they were irrevocably joined. Right? And it turns out, they're not. It turns out that when the interests change, the arrangement has to change. This isn't cynicism, though, to me. It's just the way it is.

S.R.C.: I see Maggie in that play as a perfect illustration of the individual who counterfeits her innocence to appear as the helpless victim of others. I know you have spoken about this in some of your essays.

Arthur Miller: Yeah, right.

S.R.C.: Would you say that Maggie is guilty of bad faith, of lying to herself or of trying to see only the illusions, more or less?

Arthur Miller: Sure. In a way she's dying of the lie, as Quentin says to her. It's the only time in the play that he's absolutely right. She's a slave to the idea of being victimized. Oddly enough, it's a paradox that the awareness of being enslaved becomes the principle of the person. Instead of a key to freedom, it's a lock on the door. I guess it all comes down to a pact of nonrecognition with all human nature, which is what enslaves us all. And all these philosophical attempts are really, in one way or another, attempts toward a confrontation with the dialectic of how we operate.

S.R.C.: So what she does is self-destructive because she makes herself be what she really doesn't want to be?

Arthur Miller: It's conformity to a perverse image. In one way or another, we're all involved with that, but for some people it's terminal.

S.R.C.: In *After the Fall*, you seem to suggest that the original Fall, the Biblical Fall, is perpetually reenacted with each individual's fall into consciousness, his conflict with others, his struggle with his egotism, and his fundamental choice between good and evil, or as you have called it, his choice between Cain's and Abel's alternatives. Do you think that with the fall into consciousness comes the dilemma of choosing to live either for oneself or for others?

Arthur Miller: Well, people are threatened with freedom; it's the reaction to the threat of freedom. The fall is the fall from the arms of God, the right to live, to eat, to be conscious that there exists all the world. It's the fall from nonconscious existence and from the pleasant and unconscious slavery of childhood and so on. The fall is the threat of freedom, of having to make choices, instead of having them made for you.

S.R.C.: In a few different places, you say that man is in the society and society is in the man, just as the fish is in the water and the water is in the fish. That statement reminds me of Jung, and I was wondering if you believe his theory about the individual carrying around with him in the collective unconscious, deep within his psyche, the cargo of his ancestral past?

Arthur Miller: Yeah. I've often been tempted to believe that, although, of course, it's unprovable. And in my own case, I think, for example, I was never really a religious person in any conventional sense. I didn't even make sense out of the Bible until fairly recent years, if you can make sense out of the Bible. Yet, all of the ideas that we are talking about now are stemming from the Old Testament. The more I live, the more I think that somewhere down the line it poured into my ear, and I don't even know when or how. But I'm reading it again now, and I'm amazed at how embedded it is in me, even though, as I say, I never dealt with it objectively before.

S.R.C.: Do you think that we also contain racial instincts?

Arthur Miller: Yeah, I think so. I think that they're not racial instincts; that's kind of a gross way, a gross measure of it, calling it a racial instinct. There is a culture that is in gestures, in speech, in temperament, and in the reactions of one to another, which is certainly so basic that it is the first thing probably a kid, I think, is taught. And it goes right into the irrational of the unconscious before the child even gets asleep. We call this some kind of an ethnic or a racial inheritance. It doesn't matter, but I don't see how either one is saying that.

S.R.C.: That's interesting in light of recent studies which seem to prove that a very young child is extremely sensitive to his surroundings.

Arthur Miller: Oh, I have no doubt about that, no doubt about it. See, it's an ingenuous example of schizophrenic people, of mothers especially who tend to have those traits even though they might not break down. They look in the bloodstream for it, and maybe sometimes it is there. But there is a certain schizophrenic reaction to life which the child is subjected to or lives with. They're going to have a schizophrenic frame of reference. I don't see how you can avoid that. That's how that damn thing, I think, gets carried on from generation to generation. For a part of them there is a question about the blood and how the blood can be a problem suddenly. But there is a predisposition as soon as that—excuse the term—mother starts to infect each child or reality. How is it avoided? Well, we can't avoid that.

S.R.C.: Is that why Quentin says something to the effect that the sins of the father are handed down to the sons?

Arthur Miller: Yeah. There's a truth in it. It's true. The older one gets, the more of one's parents one recognizes in oneself. You'd think it would be the opposite; it isn't. The more purified it becomes, the more obvious it becomes.

S.R.C.: In a lot of your works, you deal with guilt and seem to suggest that guilt can become a type of bad faith if it provides an individual with an excuse for not acting or taking his life into his own hands.

Arthur Miller: Yeah, it's a cop-out—guilt—in one sense if it doesn't mean anything underneath to that person. Guilt is not guilt if it is conscious. It is then something even more sinister. But I suppose the way I perceive it is that guilt is a sense of unusable responsibility; it's a responsibility that can't be expressed, that can't be utilized for one reason or another. On the other hand, it is a way of self-paralysis. It's a many-faceted thing. It's self-love, but I don't want to go on with a list of what it is. But it may be the most complicated phenomenon that a society embeds in its citizens. It's the consent that one gives to superior power. It's the way that we police ourselves in the name of the greater power. I could go on and on and on about what it consists of.

S.R.C.: Would you say that at the end of *After the Fall*, Quentin transforms his guilt into responsibility?

Arthur Miller: He at least sees the need and feels the strength to attempt to do that, yeah.

S.R.C.: The fact that he accepts Holga's love and then their movement off the stage together certainly seem to symbolize that transformation.

Arthur Miller: Yeah, right. See, I think, too, what is resented in that play is that he refuses to settle with being guilty. This is where most people stop, because if you don't stop there then you've got to act. It would have been far more palatable if he shot himself or jumped into the river with her. I would add that *After the Fall*, the title, is probably—I didn't think of it then, but I was very moved years earlier by *The Fall* by Camus. In Camus's *The Fall*, the man is guilty for not having acted to save a woman he never even saw or knew. And that's his fall. He recognizes all kinds of culpability, a species of responsibility, you might say, that was unacknowledged by his actions. And he's given up judging people, etc. The question in my play is what happens if you do go to the rescue. Does this absolve? Does this prevent the fall? Supposing he had run over to the bridge where he thought he heard someone fall in, and had become involved with her and found out that she had an inexorable lust for destruction, at what point and when would he see wisdom?

S.R.C.: The point at which one says to himself: "Self-determinism—everyone has to be responsible for himself."

Arthur Miller: Exactly!

S.R.C.: I saw the connection between these two works, but I never saw it in these terms before.

Arthur Miller: That's why it's *After the Fall*.

S.R.C.: In *Incident at Vichy*, do you choose to have the prisoners face their interrogations alone to underscore, through their physical separation from each other, the fact that man must ultimately confront absurdity alone?

Arthur Miller: I hadn't thought of it in those terms. Actually, it was—what you say is true—but it is constructed that way because that's the way it was done in France.

S.R.C.: The play has a symbolic movement.

Arthur Miller: Well, a lot of these things turn out to be symbolic—these symbolic bureaucratic processes that they invent. They do it instinctively; they're the great instinctive behavioral psychologists.

S.R.C.: Do the white feathers that escape from the Old Jew's bag in *Incident at Vichy* symbolize ineffectual religions and value systems that make one take a passive or resigned posture in the face of his persecution?

Arthur Miller: I'll tell you that I didn't know myself what was in the bag, and that when I suddenly saw that they were feathers, it was totally out of some subconscious pocket in my mind. Then sometime later I saw a film, *The Shop on Main Street*, which is a Czech film, about a little town in Bohemia where all the Jews are rounded up. And they're told to bring a few things; they don't know where they're going, but they're going to their deaths, of course. They're loaded on the trucks, and the whole town is devastated; that is, it is emptied out of all the Jews that live in this town. And there's a shot of the town square where a little while ago we saw this crowd of people assembled and thrown into the vehicles. And what's blowing around on the square is the feathers. And this was a kind of a race memory of mine, quite frankly, because nothing like that ever happened in my family. My mother was born in this country; my father was brought over here at the age of six. But feathers—you see, you carry your bedding. It's the refugees' only possible property. It's light, it's warm, it's something he might sell if he had to, it's a touch of home, x, x, x; it has all kinds of uses. And also it's the plumage of birds that are . blown about. They're weak things—it does have an aspect of weakness, but also of domesticity, an uprooted domesticity. Then once they're released, you can't capture them any more. And there's a pathetic quality to that: the fact that the old guy's clutching what to our minds would be a practically valueless bag of nothing, of air. It's his identity, though. There's a lot of feed into that symbol.

S.R.C.: I identified it with religious systems because he just sits there praying instead of doing anything actively to try to change his situation.

Arthur Miller: He's transcended it; he's got one foot in heaven. He knows that this is the ancient persecutor, the face of hell, that comes in every generation, and this is his turn with him. And it's been happening forever, and probably will go on happening forever. And he's praying against it. With one eye or the other, he's got his eye on God, who's reaching out His hands to him.

S.R.C.: But is that an effective way of dealing with that type of crisis?

Arthur Miller: It's not effective; it's the last gasp of his limited range of possibilities.

S.R.C.: You present a lot of different characters in that play who have their own ways of coping with that crisis.

Arthur Miller: That's right.

S.R.C.: But only Von Berg, after being enlightened by Leduc, takes the action that turns things around and gives him a momentary triumph over his oppressors.

Arthur Miller: Yeah, right.

S.R.C.: Doesn't a similar triumph occur in *Playing for Time*, when Fania Fenelon refuses to play in the orchestra unless her friend is allowed to join her?

Arthur Miller: Right. Well, she's pressing it to the limit there.

S.R.C.: Isn't her survival itself another expression of her resistance to her persecutors?

Arthur Miller: Yeah, well I guess that story is the story of the survival of one who has a picked identity of herself. This is the survival of an alienated woman who knows she is alienated and has a vision of an unalienated world.

S.R.C.: How about one last question? Would you agree that affirmation in your plays stems from the fact that the individual has the potential for the kind of self-determinism that is found in Proctor's resistance in *The Crucible* and Von Berg's actions in *Incident at Vichy?*

Arthur Miller: Absolutely! Yes. I think, incidentally, that what you choose to call optimism is interesting. See, it's interesting, isn't it, that I'm generally thought of as a pessimist, and I've always denied it, even though most of the time I feel pessimistic, personally. But I find that the more I investigate my own feelings, the less capable I am of conceding that in truth there is no hope to the extent that one logically should lie down and let evil triumph, because there is too much evidence that I see of the will to live. It's everywhere. Maybe it's because I've lived for twenty-five years out here where if you look around, life is just overwhelming. It is simply overwhelming. It's also in my relationship with children; one sees that struggle in the child, his wish to be taught. If the lesson of life was that we are hopeless, we should have to teach children to breathe, and to struggle for hunger, to teach them to be hungry, to teach them to multiply; in other words, to awaken them to that tropism until death. But it's on the contrary. So you can see from that why I still have hope.

S.R.C.: Thank you, Mr. Miller.

An Interview with Arthur Miller
Matthew C. Roudané/1985

From *Michigan Quarterly Review* 24 (1985): 373-389. Reprinted by permission.

The interview took place on 7 November 1983 in the playwright's New York City apartment near Central Park. Throughout our conversation, Miller spoke patiently and frankly about his work and modern drama in general. Eager to speak, Miller never stopped the conversation, not even while in the bathroom washing up, dressing for the evening, or walking the crowded streets later that evening.

MR: Reflecting back upon five decades of playwriting, which plays hold the fondest memories for you?

AM: Each play comes out of a quite different situation. Sometimes I feel proudest of *The Crucible*, because I made something lasting out of a violent but brief turmoil, and I think it will go on for a while yet, throwing some light. It also happens to be my most produced play, incidentally. I also get a big kick out of *The Price*, especially the old man in that play. I still enjoy him, and that I created him.

MR: Few American plays have exerted as much influence as *Death of A Salesman*. In terms of characterization, language, story, plot, and dramatic action, why do you think this play continues to engage audiences on a national as well as international level?

AM: Maybe because it's a well-told, paradoxical story. It seems to catch the paradoxes of being alive in a technological civilization. In one way or another, different kinds of people, different classes of people apparently feel that they're in the play. Why that is I don't really know. But it seems to have more or less the same effect everywhere there is a dominating technology. Although it's also popular in places where life is far more pretechnological. Maybe it involves some of the most rudimentary elements in the civilizing process: family cohesion, death and dying, parricide, rebirth, and so on. The elements, I guess, are rather fundamental. People *feel* these themes no matter where they are.

MR: So you think that the plight of Willy and his family is as valid today as it was immediately after production?

AM: Who knows? People tell me that *Death of A Salesman* is more pertinent now than then. The suppression of the individual by placing him below the imperious needs of the society or technology seems to have manufactured more Willys in the world. But again, it is also far more primitive than that. Like many myths and classical dramas, it is a story about violence within a family.

MR: If *Death of A Salesman* is primitive in a Sophoclean sense, would you call it a tragedy?

AM: I think it does engender tragic feelings, at least in a lot of people. Let's say it's one kind of tragedy. I'm not particularly eager to call it a tragedy or anything else; the label doesn't matter to me. But when Aristotle was writing, there were various kinds of tragedy. He was trying to make definitions that would include most of them. There are tremendous differences between an *Ajax, Oedipus,* the *Theban Women,* they're all different and don't meet Aristotle's definition of tragedy in the same way. I suppose he was defining what he felt should be the ideal case.

MR: Throughout much of your theater, you seem concerned with the notion of the American Dream, with its successes and failures. Could you discuss the influence of this Dream on your artistry?

AM: The American Dream is the largely unacknowledged screen in front of which all American writing plays itself out—the screen of the perfectibility of man. Whoever is writing in the United States is using the American Dream as an ironical pole of his story. Early on we all drink up certain claims to self-perfection that are absent in a large part of the world. People elsewhere tend to accept, to a far greater degree anyway, that the conditions of life are hostile to man's pretensions. The American idea is different in the sense that we think that if we could only touch it, and live by it, there's a natural order in favor of us; and that the object of a good life is to get connected with that live and abundant order. And this forms a context of irony for the kind of stories we generally tell each other. After all, the stories of most significant literary works are of one or another kind of failure.

And it's a failure *in relation to* that screen, that backdrop. I think it pervades American writing, including my own. It's there in *The Crucible*, in *All My Sons*, in *After the Fall*—an aspiration to an innocence that when defeated or frustrated can turn quite murderous, and we don't know what to do with this perversity; it never seems to "fit" us.

MR: What is the relationship of form to content, and how have you arrived at the forms you've used in several of your plays which have a very inventive form—*Death of A Salesman, After the Fall*, which is almost cinematic, and the use of the narrator in *A View From the Bridge*. Did the form of these works come from the material or substance, or did the form come first? How does the creative process work for you?

AM: I think there is a dialectic at work. There are forces working in two directions. The central reality in my plays is the lead character. In one or two of them it would be the leading characters, like *Incident at Vichy* where, while there is one most important character, many others are on almost an equal rank. But basically the story is carried forward by one individual wrestling with his dilemma. I'm not sure I understand what element it is in the dilemma that moves me toward one form or another. *All My Sons* was actually an exception to a dozen or so plays that I had written in previous years which most people don't know about. Those were poetic plays; one or two were in verse; expressionist plays. Starting out I was never interested in being a "realistic" writer. I discovered the engine of the story at a certain point and *All My Sons* seemed a form that would best express it; and even though it was an unusual form for me to use, it best expressed what I was after, which was an ordinariness of the environment from which this extraordinary disaster was going to spring. The amoral nature of that environment; that is, people involved in cutting the lawn and painting the house and keeping the oil burner running; the petty business of life in the suburbs. So once I had that feeling about it, the form began to create itself. No, I am not really interested in "realism." I never was. What I'm very much interested in is *reality*. This is something that can be quite different. Realism can conceal reality, perhaps a little easier than any other form, in fact. But what I am interested in is the poetic, the confluence of various forces in a surprising way; the reversals of man's plans for himself; the role of fate, of myth, in his life; his beliefs in false things;

his determination to tell the truth until it hurts, but not afterwards, and so on.

In an early play like *All My Sons* it was realism as we know realism; but I hope all my plays are realistic in the sense that the view of life is on the whole a useful not a trivial one. The form of *Death of A Salesman* was an attempt, as much as anything else, to convey the bending of time. There are two or three sorts of time in that play. One is social time; one is psychic time, the way we remember things; and the third one is the sense of time created by the play and shared by the audience. When I directed *Salesman* in China, which was the first time I had attempted to direct it from scratch, I became aware all over again that that play is taking place in the Greek unity of twenty-four hours; and yet, it is dealing with material that goes back probably twenty-five years. And it almost goes forward through Ben, who is dead. So *time* was an obsession for me at the moment, and I wanted a way of presenting it so that it became the *fiber* of the play, rather than being something that somebody comments about. In fact, there is very little comment verbally in *Salesman* about time. I also wanted a form that could sustain in itself the way we deal with crises, which is not to deal with them. After all, there is a lot of comedy in *Salesman*; people forget it because it is so dark by the end of the play. But if you stand behind the audience you hear a lot of laughter. It's a deadly ironical laughter most of the time, but it *is* a species of comedy. The comedy is really a way for Willy and others to put off the evil day, which is the thing we all do. I wanted that to *happen* and not be something talked *about*. I wanted the feeling to come across rather than a set of speeches about how we delay dealing with issues. I wanted a play, that is, that had almost a biological life of its own. It would be as incontrovertible as the musculature of the human body. Everything connecting with everything else, all of it working according to plan. No excesses. Nothing explaining itself; all of it simply inevitable, as one structure, as one corpus. All those feelings of a society falling to pieces which I had, still have, of being unable to deal with it, which we all know now. All of this, however, presented not with speeches in *Salesman*, but by putting together pieces of Willy's life, so that what we were deducing about it was the speech; what we were making of it was the moral of it; what it was doing to us rather than a romantic speech about facing death and living a fruitless life. All of these elements and many more went into the form of

Death of A Salesman. All this could never have been contained in the form of *All My Sons.* For the story of *Salesman* is absurdly simple! It's about a salesman and it's his last day on the earth. There's very little ongoing narrative. It's all relationships. I wanted plenty of space in the play for people to confront each other with their feelings, rather than for people to advance the plot. So it became a very open form, and I believe a real invention. I initially titled it "The Inside of His Head" and had a set in mind, which I abandoned, of the inside of Willy's skull in which he would be crawling around, playing these scenes inside of himself. Maybe that throws some light on the kind of play I wanted it to be.

In *The Crucible,* we see the fate of the society from a religious, moral point of view; its merged sublime and political powers forcing the transmission of a man's conscience to others, and then of the man's final immortal need to take it back. In the area of morals and society it had to be a more explicit and "hard" play, hence its form. You know we adopt styles when we speak. When you're speaking to your mother you speak in a different tone of voice from when you're speaking to your class; you use different gestures when you speak to a friend and to the public; or to a policeman, or judge, or possibly a professor. So it's the kind of address that the play is going to make that also creates its form. The address in *The Crucible* was an insistence, hardly concealed in the play, that if the events we see in that play are not understood it can mean the end of social life—which is based primarily on a certain amount of shared trust. And when the government goes into the business of destroying trust, it goes into the business of destroying itself. So, saying this in *The Crucible,* what I believed at the time—the story of the Salem witch-hunt in 1692— was indeed saying it wanted that form. An aseptic form; it's less sensuous than *Salesman. The Crucible* is more pitiless, probably because power is at the bottom of it and because so much of the witch-hunt took place in a theocratic court. The witch-hunt was fundamentally a business of prosecutors and lawyers, witnesses, testimony. Literally the town of Salem did nothing anymore but attend court sessions in the church. It just about destroyed the town within the lifetime of those people.

In each of my plays the central creating force is the character, be it John Proctor or Willy Loman or Mr. Kelly or whoever. If I haven't got that, I haven't got anything. And the form comes as a result of the texture of what I feel about that person. I felt about Willy Loman that he talked endlessly, and in the play he talks endlessly. He had to seem to ramble, and yet be accumulating an explosive force, which is what happens when someone's talking a lot to himself and suddenly shoots himself. In *After the Fall* I wanted to confront somebody with his history, and rather than talk about it in a room in the third person, I wanted him to re-enact it. Maybe I can throw some light on *After the Fall* by saying this; it was done in India and the director came to see me and said that it had required no adaptation for the Indian theater. Now that was kind of a shock to me. He said, "In the old Indian plays the god comes forth and re-enacts his incarnations." And that's, formally speaking, what happens in *After the Fall*: the various paths circle around the issues, which evolve into the person we finally see on the stage, striving toward a purer awareness of himself and the people in his life. To arrive at that it was necessary to break down some more walls of realistic theater.

I've paid probably an inordinate amount of attention to form because if it's not right, nothing works, no matter what. Form is literally the body that holds the soul of the play. And if that body doesn't maneuver and operate, you have an effusion of dialogue, a tickling of the piano keys, improvisation, perhaps, but you don't have music.

MR: How much revision do you go through when composing a play?

AM: Before I am finished with a play I have normally written about a thousand to three-thousand pages. I suspect that in the case of *After the Fall* it may have been more. So obviously I'm searching around all over the place for what the play wants to be. I have a feeling that a play, if it truly exists, makes an *a priori* demand that it be born with certain shapes and certain features. Sculptors know that feeling: that within the rock is the sculpture, and what they're doing is knocking off the excess stone to find the ordained shape. What I do is go up one dead-end after another, picking up a little bit here and a little bit there until I discover where I ought to be and what it ought to look like. But, of course, the form depends a great deal upon how the play's going to end. If it's going to end in death, that has a tremendous effect on the way the play's going to be structured. It tends to draw it up tight because it limits time automatically. Form is a way of expressing the tempo on the stage. If we could sit for twenty-five hours, which some of our playwrights would like us to do, we would hardly need any form at all. You would just go on and on and on, letting the audience pick what they wished out of the scrambled eggs. I've often said that the best naturalism you could achieve would be to put a tape recorder on the corner of 42nd Street and Broadway and just leave it open! You would get a perfect absurd play, which would be interesting. I would contest that it isn't a play, but that's an academic point. It's not to my taste. Form is a choice, a selection of incident and feeling dictated by thematic considerations. That sounds like a definition! Maybe I better write that down!

MR: *A View From the Bridge* was first written as a one-act play, then a two-act play, but in the process the role of the narrator/chorus shifted. That's an unusual shift for you. Could you comment on this form-shift?

AM: This shift had to do with the circumstances of the play. That was a one-act play, in a time, incidentally, when you couldn't get a one-act play produced in New York. There wasn't an audience for one-act plays, so one wrote very few of them. But a friend of mine was in a Clifford Odets play—*The Flowering Peach*—which was failing on Broadway. He is Martin Ritt who later became a fine movie director. He called me one day and asked if I had any one-act plays because he had a cast of very good actors, and the producer was willing to let them use the theater on Sunday evenings to put on one-act plays. I didn't have any, but I wasn't doing anything and I thought, well, there *was* a story I'd known and loved for years but I could never figure out how to do a full-length play of it. So I said I'd try to do something, and I wrote *A View From the Bridge* in a week or two. That's how it started out; it had always seemed to me to be a one-act play. The form was also influenced by my own curiosity as to whether we could in a contemporary theater deal with life in some way like the Greeks did. Meaning: that, unlike *Salesman*, it would not suck tons of water like a whale; everything that is said in the Greek classic play is going to advance the order, the theme, in manifest ways. There is no time for the character to reveal himself apart from thematic considerations. The Greeks never thought that art could be a crap-shoot. They thought art is form; a conscious but at the same time an inspired act. But anybody could be inspired; it was only the artist who had a conscious awareness of form, and this set him apart as the cultic, social voice. When I heard this story the first time—I never knew the man—it struck me even then how Greek it was. You knew from the first minute that it would be a disaster. Everybody around him of any intelligence would have told Eddie that it would be a disaster if he didn't give up his obsession. But it's the nature of the obsession that it can't be given up. The obsession becomes more powerful than the individual that it inhabits, like a force from another world. That to me was interesting. So I began *A View From the Bridge* in its first version with the feeling that I would make one single constantly rising trajectory, until its fall, rather like an arrow shot from a bow; and this form would declare rather than conceal itself. I wanted to reveal the method nakedly to everybody so that from the beginning of the play we are to know that this man can't make it, and yet might reveal himself somehow in his struggle. I must say the play was not cast in the best way; it had very good actors who didn't belong; some actors couldn't really handle the localized language, didn't have the timbre or feeling for it. It failed. Peter Brook saw it and thought that I might have been too relentless in the sense that some of the life of the family, the neighborhood, had been squeezed out. So as soon as I started to let that life back in, especially the dilemma as seen by the wife, it began to expand itself and become a two-act play. It was done in England as such for the first time. That change, however, came from internal considerations. It came because I could see on the stage that I could give those actors more meat, and let the structure take care of itself a little bit. I relaxed the play in the sense of allowing it to have its colors.

MR: Do you consider yourself a dramatic innovator?

AM: I can only confess that the most completely achieved form that I know about is that of *Death of A Salesman*. This is to accommodate the full flow of inner and outer forces that are sucking this man. I daresay I made it all seem so natural that people have accepted it as real. But it's the actors who understand the crush of condensation; they are, sometimes, at three places at the same time. The melting together of social time, personal time, and psychic time in *Death of A Salesman* is, for me, its unique power. I just directed it in China and it struck me all over again. I've always paid a great deal of attention to forms. I've never really written in the same form twice. The only mode that I haven't done much with, although a little of that too, is the absurd. But I did two one-act plays last year—*Elegy For a Lady* and *Some Kind of Love Story*—which are of a different form than I've ever tried before. *Elegy For A Lady* takes place in the space between the mind and what it imagines, and sort of turns itself inside out. *Some Kind of Love Story* concerns the question of how we believe truth, how one is forced by circumstance to believe what you are only sure is not too easily demonstrated as false. They were great fun to do, and were destroyed by the critics, but that doesn't matter—they'll be back one day.

MR: Several of your plays have been done at one time and received one way, and done at a later period and received quite differently; I'm thinking especially of *The Crucible, The Price, After the Fall.* How do you account for the changes in the audience's perception of the spectacle?

AM: We have to remember that, maybe more than any other art, the play lacks independence as an artifact. It is a set of relationships. There really are no characters in plays; there are *relationships.* Where there are only characters and no relationships, we have an unsatisfactory play. A work has to be supported by its time. It's an old story. A work can appear and the audience might not quite know what to make of it. They don't get the clues the work is sending them. It's a sociological and anthropological manifestation. The plays are not accessible to the audience. They haven't tuned into it yet by virtue of their own experiences. Time goes by, and a thousand social developments, and they see differently; they see the same thing now, but with different eyes. When *The Crucible* opened, we were at the height of the McCarthy period. There was simply a lot of fear and suspicion in the audience. This has been said a thousand times; you know the story I'm sure. It was in many ways a disembodied theater. There was a fear of fear. Once they caught on to what *The Crucible* was about, a coat of ice formed over the audience because they felt they were being called upon to believe something which the reigning powers at the time told them they were not to believe. They would have to disobey very important social commands in order to believe in this play. Consequently the critics, who are merely registering their moment and, with few honorable exceptions, have no real independence from it, thought of *The Crucible* as a cold play. Now anyone who's seen *The Crucible* can level criticism, but that surely isn't a legitimate one anymore. It's that *they* felt cold; they were refrigerated by the social climate of that moment. I stood in the back of that theater after opening night and I saw people come by me whom I'd known for years—and wouldn't say hello to me. They were in dread that they would be identified with *me*. Because what I was saying in the play was that a species of hysteria had overtaken the United States and would end up killing people if it weren't recognized. Two years passed. Senator McCarthy died, the pendulum swung, and people began to recognize that he had been a malevolent influence. Some felt a little bit of shame, some felt angry that they had been taken, and others felt he was right—even though he was wrong. In any case, the heat was off. And the play was done again off-Broadway in a production that in many ways really wasn't as good as the original: the original had really fine, accomplished actors, and in the later one there was a much younger and more inexperienced cast. But the critics were overwhelmed with the play. That's because they allowed the play into themselves, whereas before they were afraid to. They suspected it of being propaganda that they had to defend their virgin minds against.

That was the most frightening change I have ever seen in the reception of a play, but of course there have been many other authors with similar fates. A play has to make an instantaneous connection with an audience made up of all sorts of people—some of them a little dumber than others. Some are smarter but less astute about the feelings they have. It's a mixed audience. That they should all be brought to the same feeling by looking at one play is really remarkable. It's almost too much to ask, but it happens all the time. A play's an arrangement by which the author speaks for himself and for his audience at the same moment. And for that to happen obviously takes a *lot* of luck—and a certain small amount of skill and talent.

MR: Reflecting upon Kate Keller in *All My Sons*, Elizabeth Procter in *The Crucible*, and say, Linda Loman in *Death of A Salesman*, could you discuss the roles the women play in your drama?

AM: A production of *All My Sons* was on in England two years ago and was directed by Michael Blakemore, a very fine director, who had never seen it here. He saw Kate (Rosemary Harris) as a woman using the truth as a weapon against the man who had harmed their son. Kate Keller is pretty damn sure when the play begins that, in the widest sense of the word, Joe was "responsible" for the deaths of the Air Force men. She's both warning him not to go down the road that his older son is beckoning him to go, and rather ambiguously destroying him with her knowledge of his crime. She

sees the horror most clearly because she was a partner to it without
having committed it. There's a sinister side to her, in short. This
actress caught it beautifully. The production was "dark" because of
her performance of the mother who is usually regarded as ancillary,
which she is not.

MR: Perhaps, then, there's more complexity to your female
characters than critics have generally recognized.

AM: Critics generally see them as far more passive than they are.
When I directed *Salesman* in China I had Linda "in action." She's
not just sitting around. She's the one who knows from the beginning
of the play that Willy's trying to kill himself. She's got the vital
information all the time. Linda sustains the illusion because that's the
only way Willy can be sustained. At the same time any cure or
change is impossible in Willy. Ironically she's helping to guarantee
that Willy will never recover from his illusion. She has to support it;
she has no alternative, given his nature and hers.

MR: So, in this context, Linda is supporting what Ibsen would call
a "vital lie."

AM: That's right. The women characters in my plays are very
complex. They've been played somewhat sentimentally, but that isn't
the way they were intended. There is a more sinister side to the
women characters in my plays. These women are of necessity
auxiliaries to the action, which is carried by the male characters. But
they both receive the benefits of the male's mistakes and protect his
mistakes in crazy ways. They are forced to do that. So the females
are victims as well.

MR: Do you try to get members of the audience to confront
themselves and others about key issues?

AM: I am not a teacher in the theater, despite what you may have
read. In the sense that a lesson is arranged on the stage that will give
us a certain moral. The play is really an attempt to order life. Now I'm
more than happy when people do arrange themselves on one side or
the other of the argument of the play. And I think it may do their
brain some good to move away from the anguish of daily chaos. But
the theater is not an educational institution, certainly not primarily. If
a play makes them feel more alive, it is more than enough.

MR: Regarding your adaptation of Ibsen's *An Enemy of the
People*. In the Preface you discuss some of the reasons for producing
another version of Ibsen's work in terms of style, language, and so

on. In light of the politics as well as the aesthetics of that play, can you discuss the different nature of "your" play—especially, since it's so different a production for you personally.

AM: Let me tell you how it started. Early in 1951 Frederic March and Robert Lewis came to me—they wanted me to do *An Enemy of the People.* The versions that existed in English were very stiff, ungainly, and they didn't think they could do them. This might throw a little light on our theater history: at this time there was no off-Broadway theater. You had to do this on Broadway, complete with the usual Broadway merchandise. What they were interested in was some response to the crucifying of left-wingers. March and his wife were in the midst of a lawsuit against someone who had accused them of being pro-communist. He was looking for some play which would clarify the principle behind his stand, and he found it in *An Enemy of the People.* I had never seen the play acted. Reading it again I thought it would be a hell of a thing to do; the backer was a very wealthy young Norwegian who had a lot of love for the United States and was worried that it was turning fascist. He offered to supply me with a careful, word-for-word translation of Ibsen's original manuscript, done by him. It would simply set each word next to each word; there would be no attempt to write English, and, as you know, any foreign language translated that way is really not a language but a set of disconnected wooden blocks. So with that I wrote a version of the play, trying to generate some contemporary feeling. It was not to be a museum piece. It was to threaten us! The play was a very threatening play in its time. I had to reproduce that feeling of threat. You couldn't do it with the other language. It was basically a question of language. Also, the play is monstrously repetitive. Ibsen, in his later years, couldn't remember having written it! He had done it very quickly—in a few months—in response to violent criticism of him for *Ghosts.* He was portrayed as a pornographer, a dreadful anti-social mechanic. He wrote this as a self-defense, based on the idea fundamental to the play, as I saw it: that before many people can know something one man has to know it. The majority in that sense is always wrong, always trailing behind that one man.

So do I feel the play's "mine"? Not really. Perhaps some of its humor, and a certain quickened throb not in the original. In any case before I did it, it was hardly ever produced here except by academic circles. Afterwards, it was put on fairly often, and still is because I made the play more accessible, I believe, to a contemporary audience. The original, for example, had long and arid debates about Darwinian questions which have been settled and nobody's particularly interested in anymore. Some of Ibsen's ideas seemed crackpot even then, however. He had in fact to go around explaining, especially to trade union meetings where he made speeches, that he hadn't intended to say that he believed in the superiority of an aristocracy. The play could lend itself to supporting the idea that an elite should be running the world because the average guy is rather an idiot—as he often is. But he was talking about the aristocracy of the intellect and the spirit. Meaning those people who are prepared to disinterestedly venture into the future. They have to sacrifice for it, and they should be somehow protected so that they're not lost to society. But *An Enemy of the People* doesn't quite say that. In the original version, it often sounds merely contemptuous of the ordinary citizen. But, on the other hand, maybe Ibsen really was.

MR: Earlier you commented that the central character often helps give shape or form to your play; but have you ever written a piece that was generated from a compelling thematic issue?

AM: *Incident at Vichy* is the closest I've ever come to that. The action originated from an actual event involving a group of men in Vichy, France. Incidentally, there's a man who's recently been arrested, Klaus Barbie, who ran the Gestapo in France; it was he who was running the program that I depicted in *Incident at Vichy:* the Germans hunting down Jewish people in the Vichy zone who were masquerading as French in order to escape the concentration camps. Barbie invented a lot of procedures. I'm very happy to say that in the play, written sometime in the '60s, one of the characters says, "These aren't the Germans, these are the French Police." And that's exactly where things are now. That is, yes, a thematic play. There's another element in *Incident in Vichy,* without which I wouldn't have written the play: that is, the time comes when somebody has to decide to sacrifice himself, and the act of sacrifice was interesting to me. And really the play comes down to that, the step from guilt to responsibility and action.

MR: When working with a director on a play, do you make many changes in the rehearsal procedure?

AM: I have, and most of the time to the detriment to the play. I'll tell you what happens. I've worked on Broadway where there's a very limited amount of time: three-and-a-half weeks and you're on. And we're dealing with a lot of overdone commercialization. And it costs a lot of money per day, so naturally you limit the day. The result? The power that now moves from the playwright to the director is inevitable because he's got to bring that curtain up. Sometimes, if I have a particularly sensitive and able director, this doesn't happen. But when you have a less than capable man, you have to make it possible for him to put that play on. So the playwright starts making up for his weaknesses. The playwright also has to consider what to do about actors who can't really sing on the pitch in which you wrote the music. The alternative is to let it stand there and know that they don't have a prayer: they can't hit certain notes and you've got to change the register. We have a very poor theater now, I'm afraid. It's poor in time: our theater doesn't have sufficient time to really stop and work on a difficult passage. Instead, the playwright is thrown the job of making the actor's or director's job pleasant, while at the same time protecting and defending his own work, as much as he can. Sometimes these things are contradictory and you don't always succeed. I've had that happen; there's hardly a playwright who hasn't from the beginning of time.

MR: Given all the economic, social, thematic, political, and aesthetic considerations that go into our theater today, and given all the problems our theater is facing today, what should or could or can theater be, and what in an ideal world should our theater try to accomplish?

AM: Well, that's a pretty big order. I think that a theater with the most vitality is a theater that confronts an audience made up of the whole people. We don't have anything like that. This is not merely a sentimentally democratic statement. When you break up society, as our theater audience largely does, into a very tiny fragment of the most well-to-do, it can only react in a certain way. I know when I go to Minneapolis or Dayton, there's a different atmosphere between the play and the people, because it costs next to nothing to get in—at least when compared to New York prices. A much wider group of people is in the theater, and I find this very stimulating. You see, Shakespeare had to address nobility, along with people who couldn't read and write; the whole gamut of society was in the theater, and that supported and invited the tremendous variety in his plays. As social and political revolutions took place in England after his passing, the audience got a more and more narrowly bourgeois ideological slant; it couldn't open itself to contradictions of its ideology. So the more you narrow your audience the more you narrow the plays that serve it. The mechanics of it are quite obvious; if you hand a producer a piece that offends a significant portion of the Broadway audience, not to speak of the critics, he'll think two or three times before putting it on. You are in that way bound to one level of consciousness. It's not a new thing; my argument with our theater on that level is that it's constricted to a degree greater than I have ever known in my lifetime. It is very important that people not have to pay $40 to get into the theater, because if they pay $40, they're probably not going to want what I am writing.

Another element in a great theater is that it tried to place aesthetics at the service of its civic function. See how the plays that we call great have made us somehow more civilized. The great Greek plays taught the western mind the law. They taught the western mind how to settle tribal conflicts without murdering each other. The great Shakespearean plays set up structures of order which became parts of our mental equipment. In the immense love stories, the wonderful comedies, there's all sorts of color. But back of these great plays is a civic function. The author was really a poet-philosopher. A forty dollar ticket brooks no philosophies, tends toward triviality. I believe that if we had some means of expanding our audience it would take awhile but playwrights would respond to that challenge. They'd smell *blood* out there!

The biggest reason playwriting is in such dire straits is because the audience is gone; it's not there anymore. We've been talking about this for thirty years. Back in the early fifties I even got the Dramatists Guild to convene a meeting of playwrights, unions, and producers to try to reduce our take and lower our costs. That was over thirty years ago, when it was $10 or $8, something like that, for a ticket. But I saw it happening. I saw friends of mine who could no longer go to the theater. People who loved the theater. They didn't have the money. There are places in the world where this problem, if not solved, has been dealt with, steps have been taken. One of them is England. The National Theatre; the Arts-Council in England. That's one of the reasons there have been so many English plays around. There's an English audience for those plays. A writer might not be able to make a good living at it, but he could feed himself on a play that was written, not for the West End, not for Broadway, but for those three or four weeks of performances that he might get with very good actors. This is not amateur theater. Some of the best people in England are involved in this. So my great theater would be a poetic theater. It would have to be because once you're confronted with the Great Unwashed, well, the only image I have is when you go to a prize fight, a ball game, or a political rally. I was a delegate to the 1968 Democratic convention, and *there* was the American people. That's the audience I wish I had. You know: real ugly toughs from Chicago, professors from Massachusetts; southern crackers from Georgia, Alabama. I could talk to those people. But I can't get 'em! They're not in my theater. And if they *ever* got into the theater, you would have something! You would have fever!

An Afternoon with Arthur Miller
Mark Lamos/1986

From *American Theatre* 3 (1986): 18-23, 44. Reprinted by permission.

I'm standing on the porch of Arthur Miller's house in Roxbury, Connecticut, and two German shepherds are barking like crazy but looking pretty harmless. A bustling, friendly old German woman lets me in, asking if I'm there to see Arthur. "Yes," I tell her, and then I see him. He's silhouetted tall and lean against a bright autumn sky, smiling broadly. We shake hands.

"You look great."

He asks, "You want a pear or an apple?"

"An apple," I decide.

"Oh." He looks at the woman, who is briskly polishing pears on a picnic table. "Here," he says, and leads me off the porch and into the late afternoon light.

We step out onto a hill of grass and walk toward a large, gnarled apple tree. The grass around it is dotted with mottled fruit. He picks up an apple and turns to me. His rag-knit beige sweater has holes in the elbows, the jeans on his stork-like long legs are worn. Despite (or perhaps because of) his glasses, his eyes are the same as I remember them—like bird's eyes, hawk's eyes: skillful, watchful, aware.

Time stops. My mind flashes back to 1972, when I was acting in his play *The Creation of the World and Other Business*. It lasted some 20 performances on Broadway, and its birthing was the beginning of my theatrical loss of innocence. Harold Clurman had been the director, but he was fired during previews at Boston's Colonial Theatre. Hal Holbrook and Barbara Harris were the original

stars, but we opened in New York with George Grizzard and Zoe
Caldwell. Miller rewrote the third act 14 times. I played Abel. I spent
the first two acts in the dressing room at the Shubert Theatre and
then got bonked on the head by Cain in Act Three. At that time in
my life, it was just about the most glorious opportunity a fledgling
New York actor could hope for. I was in a play by Arthur Miller.
Ironically, by the time it opened in New York, I had worked with
more stars and directors than if I'd done *three* Arthur Miller plays in a
row.

Looking at Miller now, 14 years later, I find myself remembering
the way he used to stand in the auditorium at the edge of the stage,
slapping the floor of Boris Aronson's fiberglass set with a rolled-up
script, barking up at the actors with a smile. "This is the best
goddamned play I've ever written. It's better than *Salesman!*" I
believed it.

I still believe in Arthur. He hands me an apple covered with
yellowish lumps and splattered with as many colors as an oak leaf in
October. "You can eat all that," he assured me. "It looks that way
because I don't spray."

He picks up an apple from the grass and bites into it. We begin
walking up the hill towards a weathered cabin chomping on our
apples.

"How much land you got here?" I ask.

"Two hundred acres. That apple tree was here before I came."

Idly discussing Connecticut real estate, we arrive on the cabin's
rickety deck, he pulls aside the sliding glass doors and we enter what
seems to be an abandoned study. Cobwebs tie the typewriter to a
mug full of pencils. Card tables sag with the weight of notebooks and
piles of dusty papers. The room is very spare, even haphazard. There
are old chairs, a fireplace, a few shelves of books with water-warped
covers. A perfect place, it strikes me, to get some writing done when
the time is right.

We settle into chairs and I set up a tape recorder. Since I'm hoping
to direct a revival of *The Crucible* at Hartford Stage Company in the
coming season, we decide to start the interview on that subject.*

Lamos: I read somewhere that you enjoyed the writing of *The
Crucible* more than any other play because you didn't have to worry
about the plot.

Miller: Yeah. You could write all day and when you got to a

*Mark Lamos (artistic director) has been with the Hartford Stage Company since 1980.

standstill, you'd think, oh shit, what do I do now? But then all you really had to do was open the history books.

Lamos: Is everyone in *The Crucible* a real person?

Miller: Oh, yeah. They all really lived. Most of that really happened. I made Abigail a little older. You know, in those days, a girl could get married very young.

Lamos: You wrote *The Crucible* in response to McCarthyism, a movement many people said couldn't happen here. Could what happened in Puritan Salem happen again in the 20th or 21st century? Did Americans learn anything from Salem?

Miller: There was a lesson learned, both by intellectuals and people in general, and I don't see the possibility of a hysterical reaction on that level. On the other hand, look what we did in World War II with the Japanese on the West Coast. This internment of people was done not by some arch-revolutionary racists, but by Franklin Roosevelt with the consent of a lot of us who got stampeded into it. It was born, as such things always are, of some concrete circumstances.

You see, in Salem a new governor had come in—the king's representative passed an edict that all land titles were up for grabs. There was a disputation about who owned what. If you're dealing with thousands of acres in a community that couldn't rely on a proper survey, and then suddenly the government says, "Well, you may not own what you think you own," a roiling uneasiness begins to develop, and a lot of people begin to talk about some kind of spirit abroad—of the Antichrist moving in to disturb the good sheep.

This had been going on for years in Salem before the outbreak of witchcraft. And Salem was a very isolated community—there wasn't any traffic going through Salem to Boston, a town that was, relatively speaking, far more sophisticated. Nevertheless, all the great preachers in Boston at the time were preaching witchcraft—they thought it was a great idea to "go hunting." So I guess they weren't *that* sophisticated! (*Miller laughs heartily.*)

I'll tell you a quick story about the son of the governor. He and his buddies from Harvard thought that all these local yokels in Salem who were carrying on about witches were touchingly stupid. These boys had read about it, and they thought it might be fun to horseback down to Salem early one morning and watch a witchcraft trial in one of the churches . . . which they did. At one point something so absurd was said by one of the witnesses or the preacher or somebody that the Harvard boys burst out laughing. They were promptly put in jail, and they were going to be condemned to hang. But by passing some money to the guards, they got out of there—and they didn't come back to Salem very soon! (*More laughter.*)

Lamos: Can you talk a little bit about the Wooster Group's production of *L.S.D.*, which used parts of *The Crucible* and reorganized it, deconstructed it? Your lawyers used an injunction, right? You closed the production.

Miller: There was no permission asked to do anything, although the Wooster Group later asserted that they had asked. The other thing was, I didn't agree aesthetically with it—it was a simplified cartoon of a much more interesting and complicated phenomenon. Had I thought it was wonderful, I wouldn't have objected—they owed me the right to agree with their production concept. I resented the arrogance in relation to me, which I didn't think the play deserved.

Lamos: My impression of *L.S.D.* was that they used *The Crucible* as a theme for a set of variations. Did you see it?

Miller: Yeah, I saw it. What they did was abstract a whole play into one brief act. The rationale was that since everybody knew the play, the actors could verbally maul it. It was a demonstration of their boredom rather than their getting to the center of everything in it. Well . . . it's a boring time in the arts. I told them when I'm dead and gone they could do what they liked with it. But for now I'm still around. See, they were treating the play like a "found object." And I said, "But it's a found object that nobody lost." (*Much laughter.*)

Lamos: You mentioned the Japanese situation on the West Coast during World War II. That reminds me that you once said, in response to some criticism of *After the Fall*, that concentration camps seemed to you to be the logical conclusion of 20th-century life. Do you still feel that?

Miller: Oh, yeah. Such camps occurred not just in Germany, you know, but also in Russia as a tremendous reaction to what you could call the Liberal Idea. They were the statement of people who were against the idea of a mixed society, where people have the opportunity to do anything they choose to do. The idea of a mixed society disturbs a lot of people, and the 20th century has by now so demoralized people as far as their individual existence is concerned that people are tempted—in every direction, from the point of view of dishonesty in business, even sexually—to be essentially *out for themselves*. I think the purging of the Jews was a logical consequence of the desire to make all people part of a single larger organism.

Lamos: A phrase you have used to describe your work as a playwright is "unearthing an inner coherency." Often in my own work I find people saying to me, "Gee it's amazing what you evoke by creating this or that stage picture." It seems to mean something to them outside of the theatrical moment itself. Now, of course, sometimes you strive for an effect; but at other times, people see things in your work that you didn't even know were there. A subconscious coherency. Do you feel that most of your work comes from a desire to make something knowable out of our chaotic responses. . . .

Miller: Yes. That's why I write, I think. I've often wondered why I went through all this, and I suppose it's the need to *make form*—and form is simply consistency. You find relationships between otherwise disparate things. Suddenly you see that there's a common thread running through everything, and when you locate that thread, you've got an organism. Incidentally, the actor and the director finally have to do the same thing: they have to find it for themselves—and that may be a different thread from the writer's, but it's a thread, nonetheless. Otherwise, there's no forward motion—you're not discovering anything.

Lamos: The horrible thing is, though, when the thread that you're discovering isn't the thread that the author is discovering—which is maybe what happened with *After the Fall* when audiences first saw it and perceived it as simply a play about Marilyn Monroe.

Miller: Yeah. But maybe we shouldn't think of that as a defeat in any way. After all, look at Shakespeare, at how *many* ways you can do a Shakespearean play, because each one is so rich. You can endlessly interpret them, just as you can, say, the Bible. And why *should* there be one meaning? When six people look at the same inkblot in a Rorschach test, they come up with six different images. And I'm afraid that's the way it's gonna be with art as well. However, if there is some rudimentary consistency, some form, some thread in the first place. . . .

I see a play now and then in New York that seems to have no

reason for existing at all. It just seems to be an effusion of some kind, under the license of I don't know what—free association or something. Which is very boring: it's too much like life. You don't want life in the theatre, you want art.

Lamos: Do you find that the way your plays are directed, designed or acted may give them differing focuses?

Miller: Oh, yes. For example, this last production of *Salesman* [on Broadway and for television], I realized at a certain point, was far more the story of Biff, the son, than it was of Willy Loman, the salesman of the title.

Lamos: Hmmm . . . because of John [Malkovich]?

Miller: Because of John. But I also think it was because of what's happened in the last 30 years—that is, the coming into consciousness of a youth culture, and the demands of youth. When I wrote *Salesman* there was no such thing—I didn't regard Biff as the leader of some movement.

Incidentally, when I directed *Salesman* in China, the guy playing Biff asked me, "Now is he speaking for the movement?" And I said, "Well, the movement was as yet 20 years off in the future; that rebellion of youth against the parent and society." That baffled the Chinese actor, because the idea of our man making a decision like Biff makes—to disregard his father's tradition and go off on his own—seemed very strange to him, unless it was couched in a political rebellion. The Chinese found it very crazy that Biff might be doing that just for himself.

And many Chinese people also regarded the play as very much a story of the mother. In China it would often be the woman, the mother, who would be worrying that way about the careers of her children. China is a hidden matriarchy. As in a lot of these macho-suppressed societies, it's the women who make the important decisions.

Lamos: You've just had your 70th birthday, and I wonder what you want to accomplish next?

Miller: Well, I've got a big play that is lying right over there in those notebooks, and I'd like to do that. I get very discouraged about *how* to do it, how I'm going to finish it. I need one scene, the last scene. I've been mulling that over for a couple of years. But when that's done, it'll be my big play. And I'm writing a book here about my life—I'm about half finished on it.

Lamos: Is it more difficult to get things on stage now than it was when you started writing?

Miller: Oh, yeah. As bad as it was back in the '40s and even the '50s, it's harder to do now because of today's costs—it's as simple as that. I've just recently written two one-act plays involving four actors, but I'm sure that if you tried to do them in the conventional way on Broadway today, it would cost you a quarter of a million dollars.

Lamos: The cost is ridiculously prohibitive today, even in the so-called nonprofit theatre. And with ticket prices so high, it no longer seems to be a theatre for the people.

Miller: What are your prices now?

Lamos: Twenty-one bucks is our top at Hartford Stage.

Miller: You see, this is a bitch, this is a terrible problem.

Lamos: I see a different audience in our theatre during the previews when they can come for eight bucks, and at the matinees which combine student groups with senior citizens. But the rest of the time, the level of excitement and of interaction between audience and actor often seems less variegated, certainly less vigorous, less . . . invested.

Miller: I kept saying this for years; I gave up saying it: There's a deal going on between a play and an audience, an unspoken social arrangement in which they're agreed to come and you've agreed to talk with them. Now if, for one reason or another, certain people are strained out of the audience, the nature of the event changes, it's weakened. You see, I go by two theatres of the past—Elizabethan and the classical Greek. In both cases you had more or less the whole society in those theatres. In America this happened during a short period in the '20s, when there were touring companies going around the country to places without a big middle class. These touring companies were drawing people out of the factories and the lower income groups in order to survive. They were competing with vaudeville, which certainly had a universal, working-class appeal.

But I think we have a theatre now which loses its political quality. By "political" I don't mean Republican, Democrat, Socialist or Communist—I mean it was theatre addressed to the *polis*, the Greek idea of community. And even though they don't realize it the playwrights themselves are sensitive to that little segment of the community, and they begin writing plays for this narrow audience. When I began writing, when Tennessee Williams began writing, we shared the illusion that we were talking to *everybody*. Both of us wrote for the man on the street. So consequently the architecture of our plays, the embrace of our plays, their breadth, was in accordance with that conception. It was the very opposite of an elitist theatre, the very opposite of an intellectual theatre.

And by the way, *Hamlet* is that kind of a play. . . .

Lamos: Exactly! *Hamlet* was written for beggars as well as kings.

Miller: You see, if you had the whole society in the theatre, it would temper the elitism—because those people of narrow mentality would hear laughter at moments in which they couldn't see the humor, or they would hear people gasping with feeling at something which they may have resolved to remain remote from. So a new aspect of social behavior and human interaction would begin to open up—the members of each part of society would become affected by their fellows in the audience. The less culturally hip would benefit as well and pick up some cues from those who were more hip.

Lamos: So our earlier playwrights assumed everyone would share the theatre experience and benefit from that sharing?

Miller: Absolutely. In America during the '20s and '30s, the person who went to see the Ziegfeld Follies would also be interested in seeing O'Neill. Nobody thought that was particularly amazing or even contradictory. What we've gotten in the last 15 years, as the theatre became more constricted, is a critical apparatus that reinforced the division. We got fewer and fewer plain, educated reporters writing reviews, and more "trained critics" who were bringing academic standards to bear on the theatre and looked down on stuff that had more feeling in it. I think there is a failure of many critics to allow themselves to react to feeling. It's an awful situation. In New York it's catastrophic because there's only one newspaper—and even if you had the greatest critic in the world on that newspaper, it would only make it *worse*, because it would reinforce a single authority.

Lamos: I want to ask you about TV and film acting. Somebody said that it's not really a performance controlled by the actor, it's just behavior that the camera picks up. Do you agree with that?

Miller: Yeah, maybe it is true. In the theatre, "as if" is very important. It's got to be "as if" you're doing it, because you can't literally be doing it. But the "as if" is *gone* in film. That element has been eliminated. When we started shooting *Salesman* for TV, we had to throw out the first two days of film because all the actors were doing it the way they'd done it onstage. And the director said, "This is intolerable. You can't watch this for two-and-a-half hours. It's too big, it's too loud. It's too demonstrated." Well, Dustin [Hoffman], being a film actor, understood that. But everybody starting talking (*softly*) like that, and I said, "There goes the whole play, there's nothing gonna happen!" But finally it did happen. We found a completely different level.

Lamos: Somewhere you talk about how listening to Beethoven and reading Dostoevsky had an effect on climax and structure in your work. You said, for example, that listening to Beethoven you realized how the climax was withheld and withheld, and this musical idea influenced your work.

Miller: When I started thinking about writing for the theatre, I thought of the play as a symphonic organization. The whole convention, the way of thinking about life in drama, was that stage action was a culmination of the past—through development, characterization, complication and so on—and through the whole first act you would tell about matters of the past that led to a specific dilemma. And the dilemma in the second act came to a crisis, and that crisis came to a climax in the third act. Well, this meant that you drew strands of meaning from all over the place to gradually show the wonder, the wondrousness of the event—how seeming accident, seemingly disconnected events, were really connected by one fatal element—be it the fatal flaw in the character who drew it all together, or in society itself. *Everything* was drawn *together*. Well, that's very symphonic. It's also very Greek.

And, with variations, that was the basic method of playwriting I employed. What happened was that sometime in the '50s, all that really broke loose. The new dramatic writing that came from the sense of disconnection in that time seemed to contradict the idea of the well-made play. Impressionistic writing emerged, the kind of thing Beckett was doing. His characters lived not in a specific place . . . but rather "on the earth." Ionesco's characters were . . . angles of irony. Characters like that had no personalities beyond the most blatant qualities—one was a rhinoceros and the other was a firebug or whatever—so that the whole idea of bringing the past to bear on the present, as such, was gone.

We don't have any past anymore. And we've got little plays as a result. They're little in the sense that they're about one small segment of an event. They don't need a past. Movies, incidentally, don't really have any past either.

Lamos: In the case of the Greek plays, how much did the audience's knowledge of the plot help to create theatrical excitement? How much do you think the excitement and power of Greek plays depended on the audience in Athens knowing the plot, those old stories—as we know Bible stories or, say, *A Christmas Carol?*

Miller: I think a lot; it gave the writers and presumably the actors as well the license to create their variations. The audience could relax. The story was familiar. It's a little bit, I suppose, like going to church and hearing a sermon on a Bible story. There's no question about how it's going to come out. But there's the atmosphere and the beauty of the actual telling, the minister's voice and his wearing of various sacred garments. . . . After all, what is a minister doing with most of these sermons? He's taking a well-known theme and making variations.

Lamos: Like a Greek *stasimon*. An ode. But then Ibsen really changed all that because he deliberately didn't want you to know the story.

Miller: That's right. *That* is melodrama. The evolution of the tale then becomes at once extremely important. You know, when we revived *Salesman* last year, 90 percent of that New York audience knew the play or at least they knew the story. But they wanted to see how we did it this time. We could have run it five years.

Lamos: Do you think a playwright has a moral obligation as a writer?

Miller: I don't like to call it a moral obligation. It's really . . . well, take Chekhov. When we read Chekhov now, we see his time through his plays. They get more journalistic to me as I read them—I notice the speeches where people are saying, "Why don't we do something?" You get the sense of a whole society that's stalled, mired, doesn't know how to work anymore. Chekhov proved to be politically prophetic. And I'm sure he was eager to say, "This is what's happening NOW." Otherwise, why would he have written those speeches? It's a long and honorable tradition, this business of telling the news. That's all the obligation I'm interested in. Certainly Ibsen was up to his neck in the news of the day.

But I think it's harder to do now as brilliantly as it once was, because this society is so *various*. Everything is disconnected somehow, and nothing coheres. Look at President Reagan—his supporters chucklingly acknowledge that you can't quite believe anything he's telling you. He's a nice guy—he just says things that have no basis in fact. And he says them very often and about very important things, like Star Wars. Even his advisors admit that it's a fantasy, not to mention the whole scientific community! But Reagan's gonna appropriate some trillions of dollars to this thing, and there's no *connection* made. The wires are being pulled out. That has to be said, you see? What I just said is a *statement*. It's a critical stance.

Lamos: What other writers have been influences on you?

Miller: I think probably the single greatest discovery I made was the structure of the Greek plays. That really blinded me. It seemed to fit everything that I felt. And then there was Ibsen, who was dealing with the same kind of structural pattern—that is, the past meeting the present dilemma. I loved the spirit of Chekhov more than anybody, but I could never think of writing that way—when you sit down to write, it's hard to be that wise and tolerant and loving.

Lamos: What about Clifford Odets?

Miller: He had a remarkably short career—less than five years. After he went out to Hollywood he ceased wanting to be a playwright. He wrote two more plays, one of which I thought was half a terrific play—*The Flowering Peach*—together with *The Big Knife*, which has some wonderful stuff, too. But even at that time he was disintegrating.

You see, to be alive in those days was to feel certain communal passions which everybody on the Left and all the artists felt—namely that the country had come to a moral halt, so to speak. The powers-that-be were morally bankrupt. The only alternative was the explosion of authority in the outside classes, the lower middle class and the working class. They were going to restore honor to the human race. Odets's career starts fundamentally in 1935 and it's over by 1940—the years of the Depression outcry. As soon as life got more ambiguous, which soon happened, his style seemed to be inappropriate. But while it was going, it was powerful—not just what he had accomplished but the idea of a playwright being a spokesman for something. After all, there *was* no politics in the American theatre until Odets. It was pure entertainment.

Lamos: Watching Larry Kramer's play about AIDS, *The Normal Heart*, at the New York Shakespeare Festival, I got so riled up, so

disturbed. I felt I had to walk out of the theatre and do something—
begin organizing and demonstrating and raising money. I wondered if
I was feeling something akin to what audiences felt in the '30s when
they saw Odets's *Waiting for Lefty*. Didn't they used to leave the
theatre yelling, "Strike! Strike! Strike!"?

Miller: When I saw *Waiting for Lefty*, I really believed that some of
those people onstage were taxi drivers. What was happening onstage
was part of what was happening on the *street*. Mostly you got the
sense that Odets was reporting some inner life about which you knew
very little. You felt too that he was making a statement: "IT'S ALL
WRONG!" The statement was all the stronger because everything
else that was going on in the theatre at the time was just
entertainment, pure entertainment.

Lamos: It's interesting to look at writers as part of their times.
Odets happened at a particular moment in American time; if he had
come along a decade later, perhaps he wouldn't have written plays.
Looking at Shakespeare, you think he could only have let that
extraordinary mind loose in the Elizabethan Age, that age that had
just discovered that the world was round, not flat, that there were
stars, planets. . . .

Miller: Everything was possible.

Lamos: Shakespeare is really the playwright of the possible.

Miller: I think that's true. But Shakespeare also had a mythology
to draw on. I learned how important that is in writing *The Crucible*,
where I had the history there, the myth to go back to. It's funny—
Shakespeare didn't really invent his stories . . . well, maybe *The
Tempest*.

Lamos: What I love about *The Tempest* is that it's based on a
news event.

Miller: A shipwreck.

Lamos: Absolutely. You know, Shakespeare was a member of the
Virginia Company. He may even have been an investor in that ship.
The play couldn't have been written if America hadn't been
discovered. The storm that begins the play was talked about all over
England. So *The Tempest* really was "news of the day."

Miller: No kidding.

The afternoon sun is setting. We continue talking as I pack up the
tape deck and we make our way back to the house at the bottom of
the hill. There we meet Miller's wife, photographer Inge Morath.

She's as handsome and energetic as I remember her being 14 years ago.

As we pass into the kitchen, Miller points to a framed poster of the French premiere of *The Crucible*, which starred the late Simone Signoret. Looking at that, I think of all the questions I didn't ask. But then the dogs begin to bark again, the old German lady (who turns out to be Inge's mother) shakes my hand, and Miller and I go out to the car. He remarks on its newness, we trade quips about foreign cars, and in a moment I'm wheeling down the drive under the rain of yellow leaves and onto a winding country road past leaning mailboxes, stone walls, barns.

Index